XXXIX

4 of 5

D1436661

The Accidental Guerrilla

The
Accidental
Guerrilla

Fighting Small Wars in the Midst of a Big One

DAVID KILCULLEN

HURST & COMPANY, LONDON

First published in the United Kingdom in 2009 by
C. Hurst & Co (Publishers) Ltd.,
41 Great Russell Street, London, WC1B 3PL

© David Kilcullen 2009

Printed in India
The right of David Kilcullen to be identified
as the author of this volume has been asserted
by him in accordance with the Copyright,
Designs and Patents Act, 1988.

A Catalogue data record for this volume
is available from the British Library.

ISBN 978-1-85065-955-6

www.hurstpub.co.uk

CRITICAL WAR STUDIES SERIES

Series Editors

Tarak Barkawi (Centre of International Studies, Cambridge University) and
Shane Brighton (Birkbeck College, University of London)

War transforms the social and political orders in which we live, just as it obliterates our precious certainties. Nowhere is this more obvious than in the fate of truths offered about war itself. War regularly undermines expectations, strategies and theories, and along with them the credibility of those in public life and the academy presumed to speak with authority about it. A fundamental reason for this is the frequently narrow and impoverished intellectual resources that dominate the study of war. Critical War Studies begins with the recognition that the unsettling character of war is a profound opportunity for scholarship. Accordingly, the series welcomes submissions from across the academy as well as from reflective practitioners. It provides an open forum for critical scholarship concerned with war and armed forces and seeks to foster and develop the nascent encounter between war and contemporary approaches to society, history, politics and philosophy. It is a vehicle to reconceive the field of war studies, expand the sites where war is studied, and open the field to new voices.

Contents

List of Abbreviations

ADZ	Afghan Development Zones (ISAF development and security project)
AFF	Ameriya Freedom Fighters (Iraqi tribal fighters opposed to AQI)
ANA	Afghan National Army
ANAP	Afghan National Auxiliary Police
ANCOP	Afghan National Civil Order Police
ANDS	Afghan National Development Strategy
ANP	Afghan National Police
ANSF	Afghan National Security Forces
AQ	al Qa'ida
AQI	al Qa'ida in Iraq (Iraqi AQ affiliate)
ASEAN	Association of South East Asian Nations
AUSAID	Australian Agency for International Development
BCT	brigade combat team (United States Army)
BRN	Barisan Revolusi Nasional (Patani Malay Muslim guerrilla movement)
BRN-C	Barisan Revolusi Nasional Coordinasi (successor movement to BRN)
CERP	Commander's Emergency Response Program (rapid aid/development funds for counterinsurgency)
CFC–A	Combined Forces Command–Afghanistan
CIA	Central Intelligence Agency
CIDA	Canadian International Development Agency
CLC	concerned local citizens
CN	counternarcotics
CNRT	Conselho Nacional de Resistência Timorense (Timorese National Resistance Council)
CPA	Coalition Provisional Authority
DAC	District Advisory Council (Iraq)
DEA	Drug Enforcement Administration (United States)
DFAT	Department of Foreign Affairs and Trade (Australia)
DFID	Department for International Development (United Kingdom)
DI	Dar'ul Islam (Indonesian separatist Muslim guerrilla movement)
DOD	Department of Defense (United States)
DOS	Department of State (United States)

EFP	Explosively-formed Projectile (especially lethal form of IED)
EPRT	Embedded Provincial Reconstruction Team
FALINTIL	Forças Armadas da Libertação Nacional de Timor-Leste
FATA	Federally Administered Tribal Areas (central region of the Afghanistan-Pakistan frontier)
FCO	Foreign and Commonwealth Office (United Kingdom)
FID	foreign internal defense (military technique of indirect support to at-risk government)
FRETILIN	Frente Revolucionaria de Timor Leste Independente (Timorese guerrilla movement)
FSP	Força Sigurança Popular (People's Security Force; CNRT security organization)
GAM	Gerakan Aceh Merdeka
GIA	Groupe Islamique Armée (Algerian terrorist group)
GOA	Government of Afganistan
GSPC	Groupe Salafiste pour La Prédication et le Combat (North African al Qa'ida affiliate)
HiG	Hizb-i Islami Gulbuddin
HUT	Hizb-ut Tahrir
IED	improvised explosive device
INL	International Narcotics and Law Enforcement Bureau (U.S. State Department)
INP	Iraqi National Police
INTERFET	International Force East Timor
IO	information operations
IRD	Information Research Department (of the FCO)
ISAF	International Security Assistance Force (Afghanistan)
ISI	Inter-Services Intelligence Directorate (Pakistani intelligence service)
ISR	intelligence, surveillance, and reconnaissance
JAM	Jaysh al-Mahdi
JI	Jema'ah Islamiyah (Southeast Asian AQ Affiliate)
JI	Jemaat e-Islami (Pakistani political party)
JIATF	Joint Interagency Task Force
KMTC	Kabul Military Training Center
KOPASSUS	Komando Pasukan Khusus (Indonesian special forces)
LeT	Lasykar e-Tayyiba (Pakistani terrorist group)
LZ	Landing Zone
MANPADS	man-portable air defense system

MNC-I	Multi-National Corps—Iraq
MNF-I	Multinational Force—Iraq
MSF	Medecins Sans Frontieres
NAC	Neighborhood Advisory Council (Iraq)
NATO	North Atlantic Treaty Organization
NDS	National Directorate of Security (Afghan intelligence service)
NGO	Nongovernmental organization
NII	Negara Islam Indonesia
NSS 2002	National Security Strategy of the United States 2002
NWFP	North-West Frontier Province
PRT	provincial reconstruction team
PULO	Patani United Liberation Organization
PUPJI	Pedoman Umum Perjuangan Jema'ah Islamiyah (General Guide to the Jemaah Islamiyah Struggle—JI strategy document)
QDR	Quadrennial Defense Review
QJBR	Tanzim Qaidat al-Jihad fil Bilad ar-Rafidayn (former name of AQI)
R	Bureau for Public Diplomacy (U.S. State Department)
RCT	regimental combat team (United States Marines)
RPG	rocket propelled grenade
RPKAD	Resimen Para-Kommando Angkatan Darat (Indonesian Army Airborne Forces)
RTF	reconstruction task force
SAI	Sahawa al-'Iraq (the Iraqi Awakening: tribal revolt against AQI)
SAM	surface-to-air missile
SASR	Special Air Service Regiment (Australia)
SOA	Sons of Anbar
SOF	special operations forces
SOFA	Status of Forces Agreement
TNI	Tentara Nasional Indonesia (Indonesian military)
TNSM	Tehreek-e-Nafaz-e-Shariat-e-Mohammadi
UNAMA	United Nations Assistance Mission for Afghanistan
UNAMI	United Nations Assistance Mission for Iraq
UNTAET	United Nations Transitional Authority in East Timor
USAID	United States Agency for International Development
USIA	United States Information Agency (abolished 1999)
USM–I	United States Mission–Iraq
UW	unconventional warfare

Acknowledgments

This book, like its wars, is a hybrid: part field study, part personal recollection; perhaps too academic to be popular and too populist to be purely academic. I wrote it between combat operations, research trips, diplomatic meetings, scholarly conferences, and policy planning sessions; on long-haul flights in commercial airliners, corporate jets, and military transports; in hotels, apartments, and cafes, library reading rooms, earthen bunkers, and armored trailers, on the couches and at the kitchen tables of friends and relatives. I amassed a desk full of research notes in battered, dusty, gridded Moleskine notebooks, and went through three laptop computers, none designed to suffer the abuse I inflicted on them.

Though its errors are mine, the book could never have happened without the support, advice, and review of many. I can acknowledge only a few, but I hope the others—especially those who would be at risk if named in a book like this, by someone like me—will recognize their influence and accept my thanks.

My family was there for me, during a time of incredible turmoil, when no one would have expected them to be. My mentors, whose insights are everywhere reflected in this book, included Eliot Cohen, Hank Crumpton, and David Petraeus. Hank, particularly, was far more than a boss to me. My oft-neglected Ph.D. supervisor, Carl Thayer, nurtured me—not always wittingly—throughout the decade-long process of putting my thoughts in order. My tolerant superiors—Eliot, Hank, Justin Kelly, Peter Leahy, and Condoleezza Rice continually amazed me with their understanding of my eccentricities. Meghan Bradley was a wonderful friend and insightful traveling companion in some of the worst, and best, places in the world. Virginia Palmer was a true friend when I needed one. Akbar Ahmed, Alexis Albion, Dean Bowley, Mike Brennan, J. B. Burton, Sarah Chayes, Chris Cavoli, Alexa Courtney, Audrey Kurth Cronin, Patrick Cronin, Terry Daly, Dave Dilegge, Toby Dodge, Karl Eikenberry, Andrew Exum, Ben Fitzgerald, Michele Flournoy, Robert Ford, Tom Friedman, Randy Gangle, Russell Glenn, Dan Green, T. X. Hammes, Bruce Hoffman, Frank Hoffman, Michael Howard, Harold Ingram, Karl Jackson, Tom Johnson, Colin Kahl, Justin Kelly, Terry Kelly, Bob Killebrew, Dale Kuehl, Elisabeth Kvitashvili, Larry Lamborn, Clare Lockhart, Larry Legree, Joe L'Etoile, Tom Mahnken,

Sloan Mann, Carter Malkasian, Pete Mansoor, Jim Mattis, Kathleen McInnis, HR McMaster, Eric Meissner, John Nagl, Bill Nagle, Mick Nicholson, George Packer, Michelle Parker, Tom Ricks, Barney Rubin, Marc Sageman, Philip Carl Salzman, Nadia Schadlow, Tammy Schultz, Kalev Sepp, Sarah Sewall, Erin Simpson, Vikram Singh, Emma Sky, Mark Smith, Rob Smith, Hew Strachan, Jim Thomas, Patrick Walters, Mike Vlahos, Fareed Zakaria, and many others contributed extremely valuable insights, some of which I hope they will still recognize. Janine Davidson—best friend, inspiration, confidante—was my rock. She is and always will be in a class of her own.

Several readers and reviewers provided detailed and extremely helpful input to earlier versions of this work. My publishers Michael Dwyer at Hurst UK, and David McBride at Oxford University Press, were endlessly understanding and helpful, and Jessica Ryan's determination kept me up to the mark as the book approached completion. And, for now anyway, it is done.

Washington D.C.
December 2008

Preface

Oddly enough, I had to leave the army to get into the war. I had served twenty years as an infantry officer in the Royal Australian Regiment, commanded military advisory teams in Indonesia, and taught small-unit tactics with the British army as the Australian exchange instructor on the Platoon Commander's Battle Course. I had deployed on peace operations on the islands of Cyprus and Bougainville, advised an Arabian Gulf state on counter-terrorism, and commanded a company on counterinsurgency operations in East Timor. By 2004, I was a lieutenant colonel on the Australian Army Headquarters staff, responsible for analyzing current and future conflicts and seconded to the Department of Foreign Affairs and Trade (DFAT) to help write Australia's counter-terrorism policy.

For one reason and another, I had been traveling for many years in greater Asia, learning the manners and beliefs of villagers, tribes, and townspeople in the Islamic world; by accident almost, I had become a student of guerrilla warfare in its Muslim variant. My interest was in the nature of conflict within and between nonstate social groups—tribes, clans, and families; districts and villages; religious sects—that build shared identity through common cultural, economic, and belief systems. Before serving as an advisor in Indonesia, I spent a year in intensive language and cultural training at the Australian Defence Force School of Languages, including a period of field research and academic study in Indonesia.

After language school, I did further specialized training, then commanded military advisory teams with the Indonesian army in 1994 and 1995, and later spent evenings and weekends for several years writing my doctoral dissertation on the political effects of insurgency, counterinsurgency, and terrorism in traditional societies, focusing on the Islamic separatist insurgency in West Java and the ethnic-separatist insurgency in East Timor as primary case studies. I took no time off work for study but, through judicious use of my generous annual leave and the allowance that language-qualified officers receive for independent travel within their "target country" each year, I was able to undertake several periods of residential fieldwork in Indonesia. I spent this time studying insurgents, militias, and activists, often working alone in remote areas with tribal and community leaders and local people. They taught me far more about guerrillas and the complex human terrain they inhabit than I could ever have learned from a book.

And then came September 11, 2001.

In mid-2004 I wrote a research paper (later published in the *Journal of Strategic Studies*)[1] that sought to understand the big war (the so-called War on Terrorism) in its relation to the associated "small wars" in Iraq, Afghanistan, the Philippines, the Horn of Africa, Thailand, Chechnya, Pakistan, and North Africa. These local wars are primarily guerrilla conflicts in traditional societies but are often partially sponsored or inspired by transnational extremist groups whose approach is essentially postmodern. I began to think that the War on Terrorism might actually be best understood as a form of globalized insurgency, with a vanguard of hypermodern, internationally oriented terrorists (al Qa'ida and its affiliates), making use of all the tools of globalization and applying a strategy of transnational guerrilla warfare, while seeking to organize, aggregate, and exploit the local, particular, long-standing grievances of diverse—but usually tribal or traditional—Muslim social groups.

It struck me that while neo-Salafi "jihadists"—a small, elusive minority in any society—are often implacable fanatics, the local guerrillas they exploit frequently fight because they perceive Western presence and the globalized culture Westerners carry with us, as a deadly corrosive to local identity. More often, they fight Westerners primarily because we are intruding into their space. Ironically, it is partly our pursuit of terrorists that has brought us into sustained contact with traditional nonstate societal hierarchies—Wazirs, Mahsuds, Kuchi, Albu Mahal, Janabi, Tuareg[2]—whose geographical and demographic terrain interests Western governments mainly because terrorists hide (or are believed to hide) in it.

The local fighter is therefore often an accidental guerrilla—fighting us because we are in his[3] space, not because he wishes to invade ours. He follows folk-ways of tribal warfare that are mediated by traditional cultural norms, values, and perceptual lenses; he is engaged (from his point of view) in "resistance" rather than "insurgency" and fights principally to be left alone. Whether or not he is manipulated by propaganda, advised or equipped by outside experts, or armed by an external sponsor, when he fights in his hometown or local hills in defense of traditional identity, he is a formidable opponent. The dynamic interaction between the modern international system of nation-states (especially its self-appointed defender, the United States) and these two discrete but often interconnected and loosely cooperating classes of nonstate opponent—terrorist and guerrilla, postmodern and premodern, nihilist and traditionalist, deliberate and accidental—may be part of what gives today's "hybrid wars" much of their savagery and complexity.

If this is true, then both traditional counter-terrorism and classical counter-insurgency are inadequate models for the conflict in which we find ourselves. Counter-terrorism, a discipline dating from the early 1970s, focuses on the enemy: the individual terrorist and the network of terrorist operatives. It seeks to destroy this network, proceeding from the assumption that removing the network removes the problem. In this sense, like most conventional warfare, it is "enemy-centric." On the other hand, classical counter-insurgency, a discipline that emerged in the 1950s but has much older roots in imperial policing and colonial small wars, is "population-centric." It focuses on the population, seeking to protect it from harm by—or interaction with—the insurgent, competing with the insurgent for influence and control at the grassroots level. Its basic assumption is that insurgency is a mass social phenomenon, that the enemy rides and manipulates a social wave consisting of genuine popular grievances, and that dealing with this broader social and political dynamic, while gaining time for targeted reforms to work by applying a series of tailored, full-spectrum security measures, is the most promising path to ultimately resolve the problem. Counterinsurgents typically expect intractable and prolonged conflicts to last years or even decades. Clearly, in a confrontation with violent extremism over many countries against diverse local guerrillas and globally oriented terrorists with regional allies, neither approach quite works, though counterinsurgency is much closer to the mark than traditional counterterrorism.

The world community of specialists in these issues is small and tightly knit. In August 2004, an American colleague invited me to speak at a conference at the Marine Corps Warfighting Laboratory at Quantico, Virginia, outside Washington, D.C. The session was chaired by James P. Thomas, a senior Pentagon official, head of the writing team for the Quadrennial Defense Review (QDR)—a comprehensive assessment of U.S. strategy, capability, and force structure. A highly intelligent man full of energy and creative ideas, Jim Thomas had written much of the previous QDR in the still-smoking Pentagon building just after 9/11, and was now putting together a team to analyze irregular warfare for the 2005 QDR. He asked me to join the team, and within a few weeks deputy secretary of defense

Paul Wolfowitz had written to the Australian defence minister, Senator Robert Hill, asking if the United States could "borrow" me for a while.

I spent much of 2005 in a series of windowless offices deep inside the Pentagon, part of a small team writing the irregular warfare and counterterrorism components of the QDR and working to gain acceptance for a new approach to the War on Terrorism, which we (with many others) had begun to call the Long War.[4] We had mixed success: Secretary Rumsfeld approved several of our ideas, though others were vetoed or not funded, and our strategic approach (which emphasized an indirect approach that applied local solutions to local problems wherever possible) did not translate into force structure and equipment acquisition priorities. But, importantly, ideas that were too subversive even to write down when we first began talking about them in late 2004 had become accepted wisdom (or at least, the object of institutional lip-service) by the end of 2005. And that year I made many friends and contacts in the huge American defense and intelligence bureaucracy, and found numerous like-minded people working intelligently and diligently toward the same end, often in ignorance of each other or even unwittingly pitting their efforts against each other's programs.

One of these friends, John Nagl (author of *Learning to Eat Soup with a Knife* and a veteran of both Desert Storm and the Iraq War) put me in touch with the strategist Eliot Cohen, who became a valued friend and mentor.[5] In mid-2005, Eliot invited me to a private conference, held at a beautiful resort on the leafy shore of a lake in the far northern United States. There I met Hank Crumpton, a legendary figure in the Central Intelligence Agency, an old Africa hand who had many years' experience in counterterrorism and had led the Agency's intervention in Afghanistan after 9/11. We discovered that we saw the conflict in very similar terms, and diagnosed the key challenge—the complexity of fighting local "small wars" in the midst of a globalized conflict, while better integrating the military and nonmilitary aspects of national power—very similarly.

A few months later, Hank Crumpton was appointed as United States coordinator for counterterrorism. The Australian government received a request from the office of secretary of state Condoleezza Rice, asking if I could be seconded to the U.S. State Department as Hank's chief strategist. Australia again very generously agreed (not without considerable cost and difficulty for my parent organization in Australia, which displayed an amazing level of flexibility and understanding for which I will always be grateful), and I spent the next two years developing counterterrorism and counterinsurgency policy in Washington, and implementing that policy in the field in places as varied as Indonesia, Thailand, Afghanistan, Iraq, Pakistan's Northwest Frontier, the Horn of Africa, Paris, Geneva, and London. This experience—which included field work in counterinsurgency and counterterrorism in all theatres of the War on Terrorism, diplomatic work with governments and international institutions, working alongside tribal irregular forces cooperating with us against al Qa'ida in Iraq, and tribal diplomacy with local leaders—convinced me there was sufficient evidence supporting my analysis of the conflict environment to make the argument worth setting out in detail as I tried to do in this book. My experience of the wars in Iraq and Afghanistan also led me to conclude that while many classical counterinsurgency techniques apply to modern conflicts, in overall terms we face a transfigured form of hybrid warfare that renders many of our traditional ideas irrelevant.[6] During 2006, I published research papers on both issues, and on the relationship between subversion and terrorism in Europe.[7]

In Baghdad during the Surge in 2007, I served as senior counterinsurgency advisor to General David Petraeus, commanding general of Multi-National Force–Iraq. I was officially a diplomat, but this was not diplomacy as traditionally understood, and the environment was nonstandard to say the least. Several embassy colleagues were killed by mortar or rocket fire within a hundred feet of my desk. Others, working "outside the wire" (i.e., out in the community) with the embedded provincial reconstruction teams, applied all the skills of diplomacy and development but at the tribal or village level. Some carried weapons periodically; all were immersed in an environment where negotiation and violence, persuasion and coercion, intermeshed at every level. I spent about two-thirds of my time in the field operating with Iraqi and coalition military units, military and police advisers, civilian reconstruction teams, aid personnel, intelligence staff, and local community leaders at the village and district level. The other third of my time was spent planning national counterinsurgency approaches, dealing with senior Iraqi and U.S. government officials, training civil and military staff in whole-of-government methods for dealing with the conflict, and shaping the international debate. The complex interaction between local and global factors, tribal and postmodern groups, preindustrial and globalized cultures, could not have been plainer.

This book, then, is the result of my wanderings, physical and intellectual, over the past several years. It is divided into three parts, and has three objectives. Chapter 1 seeks to establish a conceptual framework for the current pattern of conflict; its objective is to disentangle the complicated discussion, current in both government and academic circles but often somewhat opaque to the public, about the nature of contemporary and future warfare. It tries to help the nonspecialist reader better understand the strategic logic that underpins current conflicts, and make greater sense of the underlying trends that drive complex, often confusing events. In doing so, it lays out the accidental guerrilla syndrome, which I theorize explains some of these trends. Chapters 2 and 3, dealing with Afghanistan and Iraq, respectively, add detail and context to the broader concepts established in chapter 1. The aim of these chapters is to describe the nature of conflict, as lived by those who experience it, on the ground today in Afghanistan and Iraq, and in so doing to illustrate the strength of the evidence that we face a cluster of accidental guerrillas, exploited by a transnational vanguard and fought out through dozens of localized conflicts. I hope to give the reader a feel for the environment, and to demonstrate how today's wars are prosecuted. Chapter 4 looks briefly at a series of other conflicts—East Timor, Southern Thailand, and Pakistan—to show how widespread the phenomenon is and to identify key variants in it. It also examines radicalization and subversion in Europe, to show that the same dynamics we can identify in full-blown conflicts in the Middle East also exist much closer to home. The final chapter briefly begins the larger task of exploring the practical questions arising from the accidental guerrilla phenomenon. Its objective is to examine whether and how nation-states, particularly Western democracies, can adapt to this environment, develop long-term strategies that deal with global threats, mitigate the damage caused by hybrid warfare, end such conflicts, avoid them where possible, and win them where necessary.

A Note on Terminology

Throughout this book, I use the term *takfiri* to describe the enemy's ideology, and the phrase "*takfiri* terrorist" to describe those who use terrorism to further that ideology. The doctrine of *takfir* disobeys the Qur'anic injunction against compulsion in religion (Sûrah al-Baqarah: 256) and instead holds that Muslims whose beliefs differ from the *takfiri*'s are infidels who must be killed. Takfirism is a heresy within Islam: it was outlawed in the 2005 *Amman Message*, an initiative of King Abdullah II of Jordan, which brought together more than 500 'ulema (Islamic scholars) and Muslim political leaders from the Organization of the Islamic Conference and the Arab League in an unprecedented consensus agreement, a "unanimous agreement by all Muslims everywhere as represented by their acknowledged most senior religious authorities and political leaders." Al Qa'ida is takfiri, and its members are universally so described by other Muslims, whom they routinely terrorize. In my view, and (compellingly for me) in the daily vocabulary of most ordinary local people, religious leaders, and tribal leaders with whom I have worked in the field, "takfirism" best describes the ideology currently threatening the Islamic world. I prefer it to the terms jihad, jihadist, jihadi, or mujahidin (literally "holy war" or "holy warrior"), which cede to the enemy the sacred status they crave, and to irhabi (terrorist) or hiraba (terrorism), which address AQ's violence but not its ideology. Takfiri is also preferable to the terms salafi or salafist, which refer to the belief that true Muslims should live like the first four generations of Muslims, the "pious ancestors" (as-salaf as-salih). Most extremists are salafi, but few salafi believers are takfiri, and even fewer are terrorists: most, although fundamentalist conservatives, have no direct association with terrorism.

Prologue

West Java, December 1996

War is not a chess game, but a vast social phenomenon with an infinitely greater and ever-expanding number of variables, some of which elude analysis.

David Galula, *Counterinsurgency Warfare* (1964)

I

They chose a rainy night. Mount Guntur—a jungle-covered volcano whose name means "thunder"—was skirted with ragged mist, the damp air cooling after a hot day and a crescent moon rising. Lightning played over the mountains as on most wet season nights in Java; Guntur and the other volcanoes encircling the Garut valley reddened the clouds from beneath. The hands on my watch, just visible in the darkness, glowed close together on the dial: four minutes to midnight. I was sitting outside—I never sleep well in the field—gazing up at the jungle hills, watching a rain-bearing storm front roll into the valley, mulling over the previous week's fieldwork results, and trying to get myself sleepy enough to face my damp, stifling mosquito net.

I saw them as the moon came out from behind a cloud. They were about ninety yards off, picking their way in single file along a bund between two *sawah* rice fields. Four young men: one carrying a case, the others with long knives. I slipped inside the house. Two minutes later, they knocked softly on the door and one asked politely in the local language, *bahasa* Sunda, whether they could come in.

The case held a guitar, it turned out, and the knives were nowhere in sight as they came in and we sat down to talk. Two of them were local boys from the valley, but the other two were silent, and one of them seemed to have difficulty following our conversation in mixed Sundanese and Indonesian. They had heard of me, the eldest-looking boy said. They understood I was asking a lot of questions about Dar'ul Islam (DI)—the guerrilla movement

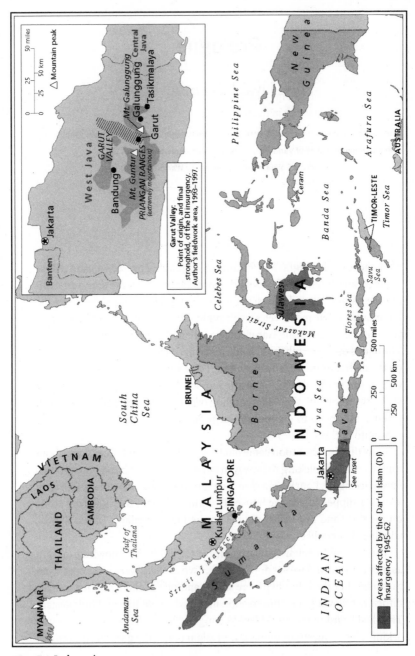

Map P.1 Indonesia

born in 1947 in this valley, which swept across three provinces and two other islands, and whose last stand had been in these hills in 1962. What was the nature of my interest? I had been seen with the *kepala desa* and *babinsa* (local civil and military officials): was I a police officer, or perhaps a spy? This was, what—my fourth trip here? People knew me from previous visits. I had been living in the hills, hanging out in the villages, talking with the people. Why did I not simply look up the movement in a library? It was all in the history books.

I thought for a moment. Rain began to spatter on the corrugated iron roof. Of course I knew it was all history now, I said. But everyone knew that victors wrote the history, and the secular Republic had defeated Dar'ul Islam, after all. I was interested in local people's perceptions and memories, the folk stories and legends of the uprising, the residue of folk memory about the rebellion, not the official version I could find in books: I had already been through the archives in Amsterdam and Jakarta. What I wanted was to see the movement as local people saw it, then and now, in their terms. I was not a police officer, let alone a spy; I was a professional soldier. I had been a language student in the provincial capital and worked in the hills, years before, as an adviser with Kopassus (they shifted a little as I mentioned the Special Forces, a name to conjure with during those last days of the Soeharto regime, one that offered talismanic protection in some circles, not least in the criminal underworld). Local villagers and friends had told me of the movement. Now I was writing my doctoral dissertation on the political effects of insurgency in traditional societies, and wanted both sides of the story.

One of the silent pair joined the conversation. That was all very well, he said in broken, accented Indonesian. But what did I think about Israel and the Palestinians? What about America's attempts to impose its debauched culture on the world? Blue jeans, Nike runners, CNN, the Internet, alcohol, pornography, and drugs: weren't the Americans and Jews undermining the faith, encouraging unbelief, and creating *fitna* between Muslims? What gave the West any right to interfere with Muslim countries? Why was America failing to defend Muslims in the Balkans against atrocities by Christian Serbs? Why did America support apostate regimes that oppressed Muslims around the world and trampled on religious freedom? Why did the West allow Jews to repress the Palestinians? What did Christians think about this—I was a Christian, wasn't I?

This line of questioning seemed rather a non sequitur.

"If you don't mind my asking," I said, "your accent is unfamiliar to me: where are you from?" The two had a short conversation. I spoke virtually no Arabic in those days, but knew enough to recognize the cadences. "Exchange students from Yemen," they answered, "studying in local schools." "Well then," I said, "you're like me—we're all learning from our Indonesian brothers. I'd be happy to listen to your thoughts and learn from you too."

The rain was heavier now. The mood had softened a little, the local boys were beginning to smile, and things were somewhat friendlier. They seemed to be putting me through some kind of test and, by sheer good fortune, my answers so far seemed adequate. The youngest—he was about 20—got out the guitar, and we sang local folk songs, interspersed with discussion of Indonesia, the Middle East, Western fashions and technology, Sundanese *dangdhut* pop music, and Hollywood movies. We drank Pepsi, swapped stories, and parted at around four in the morning. By now, we were quite relaxed, even the Arabs were laughing with me, and we farewelled each other with every assurance of friendship.

As they left, I took a deep breath and went to my battered canvas rucksack, propped against the inside wall of the house and still damp from the preceding week's work in the hill-jungle. I felt inside the pack until my hand brushed the carefully waterproofed packet of Cohiba cigars nestled inside my bivouac bag, and I pulled a cigar from its tattered cardboard tube and lit up. I sat outside until first light, smoking slowly and contemplating this new development, until the *adhdhan* began to reverberate from the loudspeakers of nearby mosques, the thin blue wood-smoke of breakfast fires started drifting across the valley floor, villagers appeared in the fields, and I stumbled sleepily inside to make a cup of tea.

II

Within a few days, new informants started coming out of the woodwork— "You should talk to old Mrs. N, her husband was an *imam* who worked with the movement"; "Go see Mr. P in Cibugel village, he can tell you how the village was attacked"; "Talk to Mr. K about the train ambushes and how the movement completely closed the rail system"; "Mr. M knows the cave complex on Mount Galunggul where the fighters used to hide, and is willing to take you up into the jungle to see the caves." I began to know another whole network of locals who, it turned out, had been watching me for some time and trying to decide whether to trust me. My midnight visitors seemed to have influenced the decision for them: no matter what you do or when, in Java someone is always watching. Over time, my understanding of the environment and the insurgency shifted in subtle but important ways. Eventually, I was invited to meet the son of the movement's founder, still living under house arrest in a local village. He was courtly and delphic; even the man from the regime's security services—a small, neat fellow with a trim moustache who was always hanging around chain-smoking in the background—deferred to his prestige. He gave little away, but his quiet, charismatic manner and ascetic mode of life spoke volumes.

Of course, my interest in DI was far from solely historical. The movement was clearly still very much alive in 1996, but at that time its leaders and organizers were working through special political action, religious activism, and local and regional propaganda to revive its fortunes. The guerrilla conflict had been merely suspended in the 1960s: the movement persisted, and though the armed struggle was not on the table at present, people acknowledged that there were many forms of jihad and when the time was right, this could change.

But something else was nagging me: the Arabs in the hills. They were clearly lying—they were much too old to be school exchange students; university students, maybe? Perhaps they were children of Yemeni immigrants, of whom there are many in Java, though most live in Central Java province, not in West Java. And what was I to make of their practiced dialectic and global perspective? It was alien to the outlook of local people I knew. The locals welcomed interest from an outsider who could tell their story and perhaps help end what they saw as the suppression of their political and religious freedom. But these Arabs seemed to have a different agenda, even looking bored and irritated by my detailed discussion with their friends about local issues, personalities, and events. What was going on?

We now know that the remnants of DI went underground after losing the guerrilla struggle in the early 1960s. The movement revived in the 1980s, was suppressed by the Soeharto government and revived again in the 1990s. World events played a part. The Iranian revolution inspired radicals across the Muslim world during the 1980s. The mujahidin of the Soviet-Afghan war returned to their home countries bringing militant new ideas in the early 1990s. And the Gulf War, its aftermath, the sanctions regime

against Iraq, the wars in Chechnya, and the two Palestinian intifadas contributed to a rise in Islamic political activism toward the turn of the twenty-
first century. We spoke of the "greening" of Indonesia—*penghijauan* is the
Indonesian word, and green, of course, is the traditional color of Islam.
After Soeharto's regime fell in May 1998, the DI movement reemerged
transfigured. Many, though not all, factions within the old DI community
now supported groups like Negara Islam Indonesia (the Islamic State of
Indonesia), Abu Bakar Ba'asyir and his Jema'ah Islamiyah (JI) movement,
or other groups that were Salafist and global in orientation.

After 9/11, some Western analysts and political leaders saw JI as simply
a local clone and ally of al Qa'ida (AQ) and as the successor movement to
DI. But after what I had seen in the hills, this did not ring entirely true for
me. For one thing, the ideology of the old DI was strikingly different from
that of Usama bin Laden's AQ. The DI movement was nativist, orthodox,
highly traditionalist, xenophobic, opposed to modernization, and mysti-
cal in approach, with strong *sufi* overtones in its theology. It was organized
as an imamate with military regional commands, alongside a robust parallel civil administration that sought to govern territory and population.
It sought an Islamic state in Indonesia, not a global *jihad*, and it had few
overseas links. Its methods were rural guerrilla warfare and mass action,
not terrorism per se—though like all insurgents, DI fighters (many of
them what researchers today would call "child soldiers," fighters in their
very early teens) committed gruesome atrocities in the service of insurgent
ends.

By contrast, Jema'ah Islamiyah is globally oriented, originally based on
a cell structure with regional *mantiqi* commands (though this is now much
eroded through effective police and intelligence work by Indonesia's new
democratic government and its international partners). Jema'ah Islamiyah
is willing to employ, and adept in the use of, all the tools of globalization. It is pan-Islamic, anti-*sufi*, and neo-Salafist in a way that would have
seemed puritanical to the old DI fighters with their amulets and charms,
and adopts an Arab-centric worldview that would probably have offended
the staunchly local DI leaders of the old generation. Jema'ah Islamiyah
seeks a region-wide caliphate across South-East Asia, not a separatist state
within Indonesia. The two movements are therefore very different in outlook—yet many people from the same families, even a few of the same
individuals, are involved in both. Meanwhile, some of the old DI tradition
endures in groups like the Islamic Defenders Front and Lasykar Jihad, and

the Acehnese separatist movement Gerakan Aceh Merdeka (GAM; the Free Aceh Movement) continues to pursue a long-standing independence struggle with strong links to the old DI, but quite separate from JI.

There were two distinct types of groups here, it seemed. Both were anti-Western and motivated by religion; both were using terror, subversion, and insurgency. But one had a worldwide, subtly Arabized, global outlook, while the other was more local, with a strong dose of traditional anticolonialism and opposed to the impact of modernity in its westernized, American-dominated form. One group wanted to impose its Salafist vision of society across the Muslim world or large parts of it, to radically change the relationship between the *ummah*, the world's Muslim population, and the rest of humanity. The other sought mainly to defend its cultural territory against encroachment; it had no universalist offensive ambition. Clearly, what we faced here was not one class of enemy but two. Furthermore, it seemed that the second type, the local guerrilla, was a defensive fighter of primary concern to local governments, while the first type, the transnational terrorist, had offensive intent and was coming after Westerners, wherever we were. This became all too apparent of JI in the Bali bombings of 2002 and 2005, and in other JI attacks and plots across Indonesia, the Philippines, Singapore, Malaysia, and Australia. By contrast, a local-focus group like Lasykar Jihad disbanded itself as the communal conflict in Maluku, which gave rise to it, dissipated, and GAM remained resolutely local and separatist, refusing to cooperate with either AQ or JI.

And clearly, while religion was subjectively very important to members of both movements, the theological content of their ideology did not seem to be the primary driver. If the same individuals and families could belong to two such theologically different movements within a generation, then theology alone was not a sufficient explanation for their behavior. Similarly, if radical Islam was the key, why did so few Indonesians, out of the many millions who shared the theology, join the movement? Local factors must also be at play. And why did these movements erupt at specific moments of societal flux and political instability in Indonesian history, even though their theological basis in Islam had been present in a relatively constant form for centuries? The motivational basis for DI and JI behavior seemed to lie somewhere else—in the notion of religion as rebellion, belief in the redemptive power of violence and sacrifice, in family traditions of belonging to a subversive or insurgent movement, in the deep structures of mass movements, or in the nature of the social networks and local institutions themselves.

I never discovered who the two Arabs were, or where they came from. Perhaps they *were* just students—students who traveled by night, with long knives, dropping in uninvited on foreign researchers to quiz them on Arab-Israeli politics and the global role of America. Whoever they were, we now know that in the second half of the 1990s DI was undergoing an internal transformation, separating into factions that would later compete for leadership, some supporting the global AQ agenda and joining JI, others remaining true to the old Muslim-separatist vision of DI. And my encounter with them started me on an extended train of thought and action that has led me to see today's conflict as a complex interaction between two interdependent trends: small wars and global confrontations, local social networks and worldwide movements, traditional and postmodern cultures, separatist and imperialist ambitions, nativist and pan-Islamic traditions. Our actions in what western governments have called the "war on terrorism" to date have conflated these trends, blurring the distinctions between them and masking the very real disputes and differences of interest among their members. This has enormously complicated the West's challenges and multiplied our enemies. So the first task in understanding the conflict in which we find ourselves is to disentangle these strands and look carefully at them, as they exist in their natural environment.

Looking back, more than a decade later—sitting in my tiny map-lined office in the North Wing of Saddam Hussein's old presidential palace in Baghdad, between field operations in a tough, nasty counterinsurgency fight—I realized that this wet-season night in 1996 had been a turning point for me, a first glimpse beneath the placid surface of the world as it appeared during those last, optimistic, sunlit years before September 11, 2001.

The Accidental Guerrilla

Chapter 1

The Accidental Guerrilla

America...goes not abroad in search of monsters to destroy....She well knows that by once enlisting under other banners than her own, were they even the banners of foreign independence, she would involve herself, beyond the power of extrication, in all the wars of interest and intrigue, of individual avarice, envy, and ambition, which assume the colors and usurp the standard of freedom. The fundamental maxims of her policy would insensibly change from liberty to force. The frontlet upon her brows would no longer beam with the ineffable splendor of freedom and independence; but in its stead would soon be substituted an imperial diadem, flashing in false and tarnished lustre the murky radiance of dominion and power. She might become the dictatress of the world: she would be no longer the ruler of her own spirit.

John Quincy Adams, U.S. secretary of state,
Address on the Anniversary of Independence (July 4, 1821)

In April 2001, five months before 9/11, I was studying at the Australian Defence College, attending a year-long course in strategy and national security policy for military officers and civilian officials. One morning, we received a distinguished American visitor, a retired general who spent much of his two-hour lecture talking about how ground warfare was disappearing.

The future threat environment, he said, would involve high-tech air and maritime campaigns, peace operations like Kosovo or Bosnia, humanitarian missions like Somalia, or stabilization missions like Sierra Leone or East Timor. Maritime conflict might arise with China over Taiwan, or with North Korea over its nuclear program,[1] and there was a slight possibility of the occasional brief, lopsided land conflict against a technologically and tactically unequal adversary, like the 1991 Gulf War. But serious ground combat was increasingly unlikely, he said.

The second half of the twentieth century had seen the United States achieve unprecedented dominance in conventional warfare through precision air and maritime strike, satellite- and sensor-based intelligence, and high-speed communications: a high-tech, network-based "system of systems." Any rational adversary would see the writing on the wall, eschew warfare as an instrument of policy, and instead choose to compete with the West in ideological or economic terms, since confronting us directly on the field of battle would be suicidal, as any potential enemy would know. Even if, through miscalculation or sheer stupidity, our enemies did fight us, U.S. military prowess was such that their defeat would be swift and decisive. The key challenge for Western militaries was therefore to keep up with the extremely fast pace of technological development being set by the United States, the so-called revolution in military affairs. This would allow allies to contribute ground forces for relatively frequent but low-intensity peacekeeping interventions, while contributing "niche" air and maritime assets to round out U.S. forces in the highly unlikely event of a major conflict. Large-scale, long-term ground combat operations? Not so much.

One of my Air Force classmates had the temerity to point out that in fact, many wars were currently going on around the world—95 at the turn of the twenty-first century, according to one count—and almost all of these were land wars. It seemed that, in fact, ground combat was not becoming a thing of the past at all; around the world millions of people were engaged in it. True, technologically advanced democracies did not seem to be directly involved, except in conflict resolution or mitigation roles, but could we count on this always being so? Warfare seemed to be a phenomenon of the developing world, occurring within states or between ethnic or religious groups in parts of Asia and Africa. Nevertheless, didn't the large number of ongoing internal and ethnic conflicts invalidate our distinguished guest's view that war was disappearing?

Well, said the general, internal or ethno-religious conflicts weren't really wars, and civil wars didn't count under the classical definition of war either. War, formally declared, as a means for furthering policy objectives, was *organized violence between states*, in which the outcome was decided through the clash of armed forces on the battlefield, and this type of war *was* disappearing. The other conflicts we were seeing around the world arose from internal unrest, ethno-sectarian violence, narco-terrorism, or state fragility. Though we might choose to be involved in stabilizing or ending them, these would be interventions of choice, not wars of necessity, and our activities could not really be classed as "warfighting" but would be "military operations other than war."

Another classmate asked about the book *Chao Xian Zhan* (*Unrestricted Warfare*), published two years earlier by senior colonels Qiao Liang and

Wang Xiangsui of the Chinese People's Liberation Army.² She pointed out that this book's key argument was that Western countries, particularly the United States, had created a trap for themselves by their very dominance of conventional warfare. Confronting the United States in direct conventional combat would indeed be folly, but rather than eschewing conflict, other countries or even nonstate actors could defeat the superpower through ignoring Western-defined rules of "conventional" war, instead applying what the authors called the "principle of addition": combining direct combat with electronic, diplomatic, cyber, terrorist, proxy, economic, political, and propaganda tools to overload, deceive, and exhaust the U.S. "system of systems." She emphasized that the authors advocated computer network attack, "lawfare" that exploited legal loopholes, economic warfare, attacking the viability of major corporations and financial institutions, media manipulation and deception, and urban guerrilla warfare.

Indeed, in an interview with *Zhongguo Qingnian Bao* (the official newspaper of the Chinese Communist Party Youth League), subsequently translated by the CIA's Foreign Broadcast Information Service, one of the authors, Colonel Qiao, said that "the first rule of unrestricted warfare is that there are no rules, with nothing forbidden."³ Qiao said strong countries would not use "unrestricted warfare" against weak countries because "strong countries make the rules while rising ones break them and exploit loopholes....The United States breaks [UN rules] and makes new ones when these rules don't suit [its purposes], but it has to observe its own rules or the whole world will not trust it."⁴ Didn't this perhaps suggest, my colleague asked the general, that land warfare would continue into the new century? Rather than disappearing, might it change its character in response to the Western dominance of one particular high-technology *über-blitzkrieg* style of fighting that had become conventional orthodoxy but was not the only conceivable approach? Might our very dominance of this style of warfare have created an entirely new, but perhaps equally dangerous class of threats?

"Hmmm...no, I wouldn't really worry about that, if I were you," said the general, with a breezy, dismissive wave of the hand. United States dominance of conventional combat and precision strike would be enough to negate such new threats, reducing them to nuisance value only.

Listening to these exchanges, thinking back to my experience on operations during the preceding five years in Cyprus, Lebanon, Bougainville, Papua New Guinea, and East Timor—and remembering the Arabs, that night in the hills of West Java in 1996—I remember scratching my head and wondering what I was missing. Whether they admit it or not, most field officers think generals and politicians are wildly out of touch with reality, so I was prepared to cut this particular general some slack just on principle. But still, it felt as if there was more to this little difference of opinion than the normal generation gap.

Odd though it now seems, there was nothing particularly unusual before 9/11 about this "end of history" view of warfare. Some people saw as faintly ridiculous the notion that Western democracies would ever again deliberately initiate a war or that, even if one did break out, the West would be anything other than rapidly and sweetly victorious. Some took the same view as the general. Some emphasized the need to preserve technological superiority and a conventional war-fighting "capability edge" for deterrent purposes. Others focused on a crop of new security threats—people smuggling, narcotics trafficking, epidemic disease, natural disaster, climate change, poverty, state failure, terrorism, and civil unrest—many of which were internal and non-state-based, and related to *human* security (the welfare of individuals and groups in society) rather than *national* security (which, classically defined, focuses on the survival and political interests of states).[5]

At the same time, some thinkers were arguing that hybrid warfare, "a mixture of phenomena" involving a shifting combination of armed and unarmed, military and nonmilitary, state and nonstate, internal and international, and violent and nonviolent means would be the most common form of twenty-first-century conflict.[6] Like the authors of *Chao Xian Zhan*, these theorists saw the "principle of addition" and the complexity and many-sidedness of modern conflict (what Qiao and Wang called its "omni-directionality") as conceptual keys. In the "viscous medium" of ground combat, with its fear, hatred, chaos, and friction, the difficult but essential task of integrating military and civilian actions into a viable political strategy, under the arc-light scrutiny of the international media, would be critical: tactical virtuosity or operational art alone would count for little. Western countries would seek to master, control, and prevent violence, would uphold international norms (which, of course, they had themselves established in their own interests), and would tend to focus on preventing and ending conflicts started by others, preserving the status quo, rather than initiating wars themselves as an instrument of policy.

One of the best-considered expositions of this argument, known as counterwar theory, came from Brigadier-General Loup Francart of the French army, a highly innovative strategist whose 1999 book *Maîtriser* la violence: Une option stratégique argued that in the twenty-first century, ground forces would mainly be required to intervene in extremely complex conditions of state failure and in humanitarian or peacekeeping environments, where law and order were compromised and state institutional frameworks were lacking.[7] Such forces would have to uphold the law of armed conflict (such as the Geneva Conventions) in the face of adversaries who ignored it, and Western countries would be seeking to control or end violence rather than, as in traditional warfare, to achieve policy ends through violence. This approach could be considered a "counterwar strategy," where the key threat to be mastered would be the conflict environment itself, rather than a particular armed enemy.[8]

It turns out, of course, that ground warfare is far from a thing of the past for Western democracies. Eight years after 9/11, with wars in Iraq and Afghanistan and many other conflicts going on worldwide, the persistence of warfare on land into the twenty-first century is hardly a matter of dispute. And while human security, hybrid warfare, and counterwar strategy have certainly proven extremely important in today's complex operations, the notion that Western political leaders would never again initiate conflict preemptively or for policy reasons has proven spectacularly ill founded, while ground combat ("conventional"—that is, bound by the set of conventions favored by the current establishment, i.e., the West—or outside it and therefore "unconventional") has proven all too common, intense, and protracted. It would require another entire and rather different book to fully explore these issues, which remain hotly contentious: even analysts who follow them for a living are conceptually divided, and thinkers like Rupert Smith have done a better job in examining these questions than I could.[9] Instead, this chapter merely seeks to provide a context for the true core of this book: the case studies of Afghanistan, Iraq, and other conflicts that follow. To do so, it lays out four ways to think about the threat, examines the risk of terrorism and approaches to managing it, and explores the implications for international security.

The Twenty-first-century Security Environment

HYBRID WARFARE

What, then, are the key features of the threat environment? In general terms, we can begin by affirming the empirical validity of the hybrid warfare construct: today's conflicts clearly combine new actors with new technology and new or transfigured ways of war, but the old threats also remain and have to be dealt with at the same time and in the same space, stressing the resources and overloading the systems of western militaries. The "principle of addition" described almost a decade ago by Qiao and Wang clearly applies.

New actors include insurgent groups operating across international boundaries like Jema'ah Islamiyah (JI), Lashkar e-Tayyiba (LeT), and the Afghan Taliban; global terrorist networks with unprecedented demographic depth like Hizballah and al Qa'ida; and tribal and regional groups with postmodern capabilities but premodern structures and ideologies like some Iraqi insurgents. The new actors include gangs in Latin America and elsewhere whose levels of lethal capability and social organization are fast approaching those traditionally seen in insurgencies.[10] They also include "micro-actors with massive impact"[11]—like the eight terrorists who killed 191 commuters from 17 countries in the Madrid train bombings of March 11, 2004, spectacularly swaying Spain's general elections three days later and prompting its pull-out from Iraq. There are also armed commercial entities like security contractors and private military companies, and local and communitarian militias of various kinds.[12] In the maritime domain, the resurgence of piracy threats in the South China Sea and off the Horn of Africa suggests the existence of new and extremely well-armed and capable threat groups.

New technology includes new communications and media tools, high-lethality individual weapons, nanoengineering, robotics, and new kinds of explosives and munitions. New ways of war include Internet-enabled terrorism, transnational guerrilla warfare, and the emergence of an insurgent media marketplace. These have overlapped in the proliferation of weapons of mass destruction via networks like that of A. Q. Khan, which was ostensibly non-state-based (though Khan subsequently claimed that his relationship with the government of Pakistan was in fact very close).[13] And all of this exists alongside robust conventional and nuclear threats from traditional state-based adversaries. States still invade states, as Russia showed in its invasion of Georgia in August 2008, Israel in its invasion of Lebanon in 2006, Ethiopia in Somalia in 2007, and, of course, the West in Iraq and Afghanistan after 9/11.

Post-1945 institutions like the World Bank, the International Monetary Fund, the nuclear nonproliferation treaty regime, and the United Nations have proven ill suited to the current environment, leading to widespread calls for reform. Some thinkers have questioned whether the "1945 rules-based order" still applies.[14] The United States, with national security institutions developed mainly under the Truman administration,[15] has struggled to adapt these institutions to post-9/11 threats. As the distinguished Singaporean diplomat and scholar Kishore Mahbubani has argued, policies like the invasion of Iraq, diplomatic unilateralism, comparative neglect of the Israel-Palestine peace process, extraordinary renditions, detention facilities like Guantanamo Bay, "water-boarding," and domestic surveillance have created the impression that the United States has walked away from the global rule-set that Washington and its key allies created after 1945. As noted earlier, Qiao Liang predicted in 1999 that America "has to observe its own rules or the whole world won't trust it." This perceived breach of trust has indeed proven very harmful to America's reputation and wider interests, as well as to the functioning of the broader international system. In particular, events since 9/11 have exposed the limits of the utility of force as an international security tool, while as the eminent strategist Sir Michael Howard points out, framing the problem as a "war on terror" has tended to militarize key aspects of foreign policy.[16] I will discuss this issue in detail below, but first I will lay out a mental framework for thinking about the environment.

FOUR WAYS TO THINK ABOUT THE ENVIRONMENT

As this discussion highlights, today's threat environment is nothing if not complex, ambiguous, dynamic, and multifaceted, making it impossible to describe through a single model. So this section examines the environment via four frameworks which, taken together, give a fuller picture of the threat, its characteristics, and its implications than could one framework alone. The four models are the *Globalization Backlash* thesis, the *Globalized Insurgency* model, the *Islamic Civil War* theory, and the *Asymmetric Warfare* model. These are neither exhaustive nor mutually exclusive, but together they form a basis for the case studies that follow.

Model 1: A Backlash against Globalization

The dozens of colonial insurgencies and guerrilla wars of the 1940s, 1950s, and 1960s—the conflicts Khrushchev called "wars of national liberation" in January 1961—seem in retrospect part of a pattern of "wars of decolonization." Between 1944 and about 1982,[17] almost all the old European empires crumbled, subject peoples gained their independence through armed or unarmed struggle, and the newly independent countries faced forbidding development and security challenges. Though each colonial conflict had some unique characteristics, all followed roughly similar pathways and contributed to a larger metapattern of conflict, fully visible only in retrospect. The threat environment within which the former colonial powers, the new postcolonial states, their internal constituents, and the broader security system operated was colored by this larger pattern, and by the proxy rivalry—global in scope and extremely intense at times—between the Soviet Union and the Western world.

The globalization backlash thesis suggests that, likewise, we may look back on today's conflicts as a series of "wars of globalization," in which each conflict differs but all follow similar pathways in response to one key driver, globalization, and in which a backlash against globalization provides the organizing principle for many conflicts. Globalization (a technology-enabled process of improved communications and transportation that enables the freer movement of goods, people, money, technology, ideas, and cultures across and within international borders) has prompted the emergence of a Western-dominated world culture, an interdependent world economy, and a global community of business, political, and intellectual elites. This is the world so insightfully described in economic terms in Thomas Friedman's 2005 book *The World Is Flat*, as a combination of "levelers" like personal computers, the Internet, open-sourcing, outsourcing, off-shoring, and streamlining of supply chains, along with a mutually reinforcing convergence between them.[18] Even the most avid apostles of globalization hesitate to suggest that its effects have been uniformly positive: indeed, most acknowledge that it has created a class of global haves and have-nots, and simultaneously (through globalized news media) has made the have-nots very aware of what they are missing, of how the other half lives, thus creating tension and anger through perceived "relative deprivation." Even beyond its uneven economic effects, the globalization process has thus also prompted a political and cultural backlash, often violent, against the extension of Western political and cultural influence, the disruptive effects of modernization and global integration, and the failure of markets to self-regulate in a way that protects the interests of people outside "core" countries. Such diverse figures as John Ralston Saul,[19] Paul Collier,[20] Thomas P. M. Barnett,[21] and Usama bin Laden,[22] among others, have commented on this. This globalization backlash has six principal implications for the international security environment.

First, traditional societies across the world have experienced the corrosive effects of globalization on deeply held social, cultural, and religious identities—sparking violent antagonism to Western-led modernization and its preeminent symbol: perceived U.S. cultural and economic imperialism. This antagonism takes many forms; at the nation-state level it includes reflexive anti-Americanism, economic and cultural protectionism, and a tendency to "balance" against U.S. policy initiatives or (conversely) to free ride on America's coattails. At the nonstate level, antagonism ranges from politicized but relatively benign cultural phenomena: one example, at the most benign end of the spectrum, is the slow food movement, which originally emerged as the Arcigola organization, a protest against globalized food culture prompted by the opening of a McDonalds franchise in Rome in 1986.[23] More violent examples include antiglobalization attacks by activists like those who sabotaged the Seattle meeting of the World Trade Organization in November 2001 or disrupted the Davos forum in 2007.[24] It also involves violent internal conflict between communities divided by their response to globalization (as in parts of Indonesia and Africa); the persecution of minorities associated with globalization processes (such as Filipino immigrant workers in parts of the Middle East); and ultimately full-scale civil war and international terrorism.

Second, globalization, by its very openness, affords its opponents unprecedented access to its tools: the Internet, cellphones, and satellite communications, electronic funds transfer, ease of international movement and trade. Globalization has also prompted the proliferation of low-cost, high-lethality individual weapons systems like assault rifles, portable antiaircraft missiles, rocket launchers, mines, and extremely powerful blast munitions such as thermobarics.[25] Consequently, the opponents of globalization—from environmental activists to G8 protestors to AQ operatives—are paradoxically among the most globalized and networked groups on the planet, and the most adept at using globalization's instruments against it. Unlike traditional societies, which embody a xenophobic "antiglobalization" focus, some of these actors serve a vision of "counterglobalization"—a world that is just as globalized as today but (as in the AQ model of a global caliphate, discussed below) is organized along radically different lines. This is an extremely important distinction to which I shall return later, since the first group opposes globalization and seeks to insulate or defend itself from globalization's effects (and thus has a fundamentally defensive focus), whereas the second seeks to hijack and exploit globalization to attack and ultimately control the West (a basically offensive outlook). These groups have different interests, and one of them (the "counterglobalizers" like AQ) tends to exploit and manipulate the other (the "antiglobalizers," of which there are hundreds of local examples worldwide). This pattern was highlighted by Akbar S. Ahmed, whose 2007 book *Journey into Islam: The Crisis of Globalization* presented a compelling and detailed account of interactions with Islamic scholars and students across the Muslim world during field research in 2006–2007, demonstrating the destabilizing effects of globalized communications and extremist ideology.[26]

Third, globalization has connected geographically distant groups who previously could not coordinate their actions (for example, connecting insurgent and terrorist groups in different countries or connecting radicals in remote areas, such as Pakistan's Federally Administered Tribal Areas [FATA], with people originally from there who now live in immigrant communities in the West). This unprecedented connectivity means that widely spaced and disparate microactors can aggregate their effects, to achieve outcomes disproportionate to the size and sophistication of their networks. It also means that ungoverned, undergoverned, or poorly controlled areas (such as the FATA, the Sulu and Sulawesi seas between Indonesia, Malaysia, and the Philippines, the Sahara desert in North Africa, or the triborder area in Latin America), which used to be significant for local governments but less relevant to regional security, now hold international importance as potential safe havens and points of origin for terrorist and insurgent attacks on many points of vulnerability in the international system.

Fourth, the diversity and diffusion of globalized media makes what public relations specialists call "message unity"—a single consistent message across multiple audiences—impossible for democratic governments and open societies. Concepts such as "the international media" are less relevant now than even a decade ago, since they treat media organizations as actors or interest groups to be influenced, whereas in fact under globalized conditions the media space is a domain, an ecosystem, or even a battlespace, filled with dozens of independent, uncoordinated, competing, and conflicting entities rather than a single actor or audience. This is because the modern media space is very different from a traditional broadcast media system (such as a traditional newspaper or television network) in which a few media producers develop, own, and deliver content to many consumers, and yet also different from a web-based system (like early internet forms of "new media" such as blogs and Online journals) where many content producers interact with relatively few consumers. Rather, the new social network–based media (such as content-sharing applications like Facebook, MySpace, or YouTube) allow enormous numbers of people to become both consumers and producers of media content, shifting rapidly and seamlessly between these roles, sharing and producing information, and thus developing multiple sources of information, almost all of them outside the control of governments and media corporations.[27]

This carries consequences for Western governments—pursuing unpopular policies in the teeth of negative media coverage is harder, and state-based information agencies such as the State Department's R Bureau (the much-reduced successor to the United States Information Agency, which the Clinton administration abolished in 1999) have less leverage in this atomized and privatized media marketplace. But the atomization of the media also creates a profoundly new and different space in which individuals can communicate and form social/information networks that are innately free, democratic, non-state-based, and founded on personal choice. Even repressive societies like China, Iran, Burma, and parts of the Middle East now have enormous difficulty in suppressing information and preventing communication between their citizens and the wider world. Globalized information systems therefore, on balance, favor freedom but also carry new and sometimes poorly understood risks.

Fifth, as noted, the uneven pace and spread of globalization has created haves and have-nots; the so-called gap countries[28] in Africa, the Middle East, Latin America, and parts of Southeast and Northeast Asia have benefited far less from globalization than core regions of western Europe and North America, while Paul Collier's "bottom billion" has suffered far more than people in those regions.[29] Some gap countries (Burma, North Korea, Syria, Iran, Somalia, or Pakistan) are actually or potentially what successive U.S. administrations have described as "rogue states," or else are safe havens for terrorist activity. But the United States has neither the mandate nor the resources to police or directly administer the world's undergoverned areas, nor would the American people be likely to support such a strategy. Indeed, trying to control and integrate every area of undergoverned or ungoverned space in the world could be seen as an aggressive attempt to bring about further globalization (thus increasing the backlash against it), as a coyly veiled bid for world domination, or as a means of formalizing an American role as a surrogate world government: a role that neither Americans nor others would be likely to accept. Hence a policy of international cooperation and low-profile support for legitimate and effective governance through local authorities, building effective and legitimate local allies, is likely to be a more viable response.

The final, obvious implication is that globalization is inherently a phenomenon over which governments have little control. As the financial crisis of 2008 demonstrated, large shifts in the global economy, and the well-being of millions of people, are set by market forces and individual choices exercised through the connectivity that globalization enables. This means that even though globalization has obvious negative security effects, governments have great difficulty in attempting to channel or stop it. Thus the antimodernization backlash within traditional societies, and the existence of networked counterglobalizers like AQ who exploit it, will probably be a long-standing trend regardless of Western policies.

This last observation relates to the second model for the environment: global insurgency.

Model 2: A Globalized Insurgency

The global insurgency thesis suggests that the "War on Terrorism" is best understood as an extremely large-scale, transnational globalized insurgency, rather than as a traditional terrorism problem. This model argues that by definition, AQ and the broader *takfiri* extremist movement it seeks to lead are insurgents (members of "an organized movement that aims at overthrowing the political order within a given territory, using a combination of subversion, terrorism, guerrilla warfare and propaganda").[30] According to this way of thinking, defining such groups via their use of a certain tactic—terrorism (which they share with every other insurgent movement in history)—is less analytically useful than defining them in terms of their strategic approach. Like other insurgents but unlike a classical terrorist organization (which draws its effectiveness from the motivation and cohesion of a small number of people in clandestine cells), AQ draws its potency from the depth of its demographic base (the world's 1.2 billion Sunni Muslims) and its ability to intimidate, co-opt, or mobilize that base for support. And as I shall show, AQ applies the same standard four tactics (provocation, intimidation, protraction, and exhaustion) used by all insurgents in history, though with far greater scope and ambition.

This implies that the best-fit conceptual framework to deal with AQ is counter-insurgency rather than conventional warfare or traditional counter-terrorism. Like other counterinsurgencies, the civilized world's confrontation with *takfiri* extremism is therefore population-centric—that is, its key activities relate to protecting the world's Muslim population from AQ intimidation and manipulation, countering extremist propaganda, marginalizing insurgent movements, and meeting the Muslim population's legitimate grievances through a tailored, situation- and location-specific mix of initiatives that are mostly nonmilitary. Killing or capturing terrorists is a strictly secondary activity, because it is ultimately defensive (keeping today's terrorists at bay) rather than decisive (preventing future terrorism). Conversely, programs that address the underlying conditions that terrorists exploit (thus preventing another crop of terrorists from simply replacing those we kill or capture today) are ultimately decisive. Clearly, like any military or law enforcement strategy, countering AQ requires both the kill/capture of current terrorists and programs to counter their ideology and address the underlying conditions they exploit. These efforts are complementary (addressing both the supply and demand sides of the equation) rather than opposite choices. Still, and perhaps counterintuitively for some, activities to kill and capture terrorists seem (and are) offensive at the tactical level but are in fact strategically defensive, because they contain the problem rather than resolving it. This approach would differ very substantially from traditional counterterrorism, which is enemy-centric, focusing on disrupting and eliminating terrorist cells themselves rather than on controlling the broader environment in which they operate.

But although it is an insurgency, the *takfiri* extremist movement differs in key ways from a traditional insurgency because of its scale. Unlike other insurgents, the "given territory" in which AQ seeks to operate is the entire globe, and the "political order" it seeks to overthrow is the political order within the entire Muslim world and the relationship between the world's Muslim population (the *ummah*) and the rest of world society. This, again, has major implications for international security.

First, the unprecedented scale and ambition of this insurgent movement, and the unparalleled connectivity and aggregation effect it has achieved through access to the tools of globalization, renders many traditional counterinsurgency approaches ineffective. For example, traditional "hearts and minds" approaches are directed at winning the support of the population in a territory where insurgents operate. But under conditions of globalized insurgency, the world's entire Muslim population, and the populations of most Western countries, are a target of enemy propaganda and hence a potential focus for information operations. But such a large and diverse target set is, by definition, not susceptible to traditional locally tailored hearts-and-minds activities, and the difficulty in achieving message unity (noted earlier) undercuts such attempts anyway. Likewise, traditional counterinsurgency uses improved governance and legitimacy to build alliances with local communities and marginalize insurgents; in a globalized insurgency, this approach may work at a local level with people in a given insurgent operating area, but may still have little impact on remote sources of insurgent support (such as Internet-based financial support or propaganda support from distant countries).

This implies the need for unprecedented international cooperation in managing the terrorism threat. Since 9/11, such cooperation has in fact been excellent (especially in areas such as transportation security and terrorist financing). United States leadership has been central to this effort, but international support for U.S. initiatives has waned substantially since the immediate post-9/11 period, largely as a result of international partners' dissatisfaction with U.S. unilateralism, perceived human rights abuses, and the Iraq War. This implies that America's international reputation, moral authority, diplomatic weight, persuasive ability, cultural attractiveness, and strategic credibility—its "soft power"—is not some optional adjunct to military strength. Rather, it is a critical enabler for a permissive operating environment—that is, it substantially reduces the friction and difficulty involved in international leadership against threats like AQ—and it is also the prime political component in countering a globalized insurgency. This in turn implies the need for greater balance between the key elements (diplomatic, informational, military, and economic) of national power.

In this context, it is important to clearly understand the role AQ plays. I describe its "military" strategy in the next section, but its organizational strategy is worth examining here. Al Qa'ida acts as "inciter-in-chief,"[31] or as Ayman al-Zawahiri describes it, *al talia al ummah*, the "vanguard of the *ummah*," a revolutionary party that seeks to build mass consciousness through provocation and spectacular acts of "resistance" to the existing world order. It works through regional affiliates (AQ in Iraq, AQ in the Arabian Peninsula, AQ-Maghreb, Groupe salafiste pour la prédication et le combat, Jema'ah Islamiyah, Abu Sayyaf Group, etc.) to co-opt and aggregate the effects of multiple, diverse local actors in more than 60 countries. It is this ability to aggregate and point all the players in one direction (via propaganda, technical assistance, broad strategic direction, and occasional direct guidance) that gives AQ its strength. This implies that a strategy which I described in 2004 as one of "disaggregation," cutting the links between AQ central leadership and among its local and regional allies and supporters, may be more successful than policies that lump all threats into the single undifferentiated category of "terrorists."

Fundamental to counterinsurgency is an ability to undercut the insurgents' appeal by discrediting their propaganda, exposing their motives, and convincing at-risk populations to voluntarily reject insurgent co-option and intimidation. In the context of a globalized insurgency this translates into diplomatic initiatives that undercut AQ credibility on issues like Israel/Palestine, Kashmir, Chechnya, Afghanistan, and Iraq. This cannot simply be "spin": it demands genuine attempts to address legitimate grievances. This in turn implies political initiatives to construct credible and legitimate alternatives for the world's Muslim population, instead of the current limited choice between support for AQ or "collaboration" with the West. In this context, the Amman Message initiative of King Abdullah II of Jordan is an extremely important first step, bringing together religious and political leaders from across the Islamic world to condemn AQ's heretical *takfiri* ideology.[32] Muslim initiatives of this kind exist, though they often receive little attention in the West. Being local and indigenous, they are much more powerful and credible than Western initiatives: the role of counterpropaganda efforts, wherever feasible, should be to support and amplify such Muslim initiatives rather than to generate competing Western messages. This also implies the need for counterpropaganda capabilities (discussed below) to discredit AQ and inoculate at-risk populations—including immigrant populations in the West—against AQ's appeal.

The final major implication is that an indirect, highly localized approach—working by, with, or through genuine alliances and local partnerships wherever possible—would probably be much more successful than a policy of direct U.S. intervention. This is because many governments in the world rightly resent U.S. interference in their internal affairs or cannot, because of domestic public opinion, accept direct U.S. counterterrorism assistance, making overtly U.S.-controlled or -funded approaches unacceptable. On the other hand, virtually every government in the world has an interest in protecting itself against domestic terrorism and extremist subversion. This implies that wherever possible, Western countries should seek to build genuine partnerships with local governments and civil society networks, operate behind the scenes, avoid large-scale commitment of U.S. combat forces, support locally devised initiatives, and apply diplomatic suasion (rather than force) to modify local government behavior. There is thus a trade-off between effectiveness and control: local initiatives afford less control but carry greater likelihood of success. In military terms, countering globalized insurgency therefore looks less like traditional single-country counterinsurgency and much more like a very robust aid, information, and foreign assistance program, supported by diplomatic initiatives, stabilization operations, and foreign internal defense (FID), with troops deployed only where absolutely needed.

Local governments are likewise fundamental to the third way of thinking about the threat: as a civil war within Islam.

Model 3: A Civil War within Islam

The Islamic civil war thesis suggests that the current turmoil within the Islamic world, along with the spill-over of violence from Muslim countries into the international community via globalized insurgency and terrorism, arises from a civil war within Islam. There are several variants of this model, but all see AQ and its associated *takfiri* terrorist movements primarily as a response to a series of internal dynamics within the Muslim world: a youth bulge, corrupt and oppressive governments, a dysfunctional relationship between the sexes that limits the human capacity of societies by denying productive roles to half the population, a deficit of democracy and freedom of expression, economies dependent on oil but unable to provide fulfilling employment to an increasingly educated but alienated young male population, and a generalized *anomie* and sense of being victimized by a vaguely-defined "West." As a group of prominent Arab and Muslim scholars have shown in successive editions of the United Nations *Arab Human Development Report*, these dynamics have created enormous potential for unrest, and a well of grievances into which movements like AQ can tap.[33] This suggests that although it uses the West as a target of convenience, the real threat from AQ and the broader *takfiri* movement is to the status quo in Muslim countries, through activities directed initially at overthrowing existing political and religious structures in the Islamic world, and only then turning to remake the relationship between the *ummah* and the rest of global society. Again perhaps counterintuitively, this theory would imply that AQ terrorist violence is not fundamentally directed at the West, but rather *uses* attacks on Western countries and exploits their responses in order to further its real objective: gaining ascendancy over the Islamic world. What we are witnessing, this model suggests, is a battle for the soul of Islam, a violent competition for control over one-eighth of the world's population.

Both Faisal Devji, in *Landscapes of the Jihad*, and Akbar Ahmed, in *Islam under Siege*, advanced variations on this approach.[34] Ayman al-Zawahiri, identified as the principal AQ planner and ideologue,[35] also expressed this thinking in a statement shortly after 9/11. He outlined a two-phase strategy: in the first phase, AQ would focus on the greater Middle East: "this spirit of *jihad* would...turn things upside down in the region and force the U.S. out of it. This would be followed by the earth-shattering event, which the West trembles at: the establishment of an Islamic caliphate in Egypt."[36] Only after the success of this first stage, that is, the destruction of the current political order in the Muslim world, would the second stage begin, using the caliphate as a launching pad against the West, to remake the world order with the Muslim world in a dominant position. "If God wills it, such a state...could lead the Islamic world in a *jihad* against the West. It could also rally the world Muslims around it. Then history would make a new turn, God willing, in the opposite direction against the empire of the United States and the world's Jewish government."[37] A related document, the "General Guide to the Struggle of Jema'ah Islamiyah" (Pedoman Umum Perjuangan Jema'ah Islamiyah; PUPJI), issued by AQ's Southeast Asian ally Jema'ah Islamiyah (JI) in 2001, suggests similar strategic thinking. This document declares JI's objectives to be the establishment of an Islamic state in Indonesia, only then to be followed by the creation of a pan-Islamic state in Southeast Asia (*daula Islamiya nusantara*) covering Malaysia, Indonesia, the Philippines, southern Thailand, and Singapore. Only once this superstate was created would JI's aim become the establishment of a global pan-Islamic caliphate.[38]

Some analysts have focused on the threat to the West implied by what some extremists call the "caliphate concept." But, as advocates of the Islamic civil war thesis would argue, it is clear that the *takfiri* aim is first to overthrow and control power structures in the Muslim world, and only then to turn against the West. They might argue that if ever an extremist coalition should succeed in gaining control of the Middle East, it would have its hands full simply governing and controlling that area, though (like the Iranian Revolution, discussed below) such a revolution would also export violence and radicalism and thus destabilize the rest of the world. They might also argue, with strong justification in my view, that these statements—Zawahiri's after 9/11 and PUPJI—represent a snapshot of terrorist thinking that has been well and truly overtaken by events (as I shall show). In any case, the Islamic civil war thesis suggests that the primary threat of takfirism is against stability in the Arab world and the broader Muslim community worldwide, and only secondarily against Western governments and populations. By intervening directly against AQ, this theory suggests, we have not only waded into someone else's domestic dispute but have also treated AQ as a peer competitor worthy of our top priority and full attention, thus immensely increasing AQ's credibility and clout in its struggle for ascendancy over the *ummah*.

A second variant of the Islamic civil war thesis focuses on the Shi'a revival, a process cogently described by Vali Nasr, which involves, first, the rise of Shi'a theocracy under the banner of the Iranian Islamic Revolution and Ayatollah Khomeini's ideology of *vilayet-e faqih*, and second, the empowerment of the Iraqi Shi'a majority as a side-effect of the fall of Saddam Hussein.[39] This revival, resulting in the emergence of a so-called Shi'a Crescent from Iran to Lebanon, is deeply disruptive of established power structures in the Muslim world, especially in countries (such as Kuwait, Saudi Arabia, Lebanon, several Gulf states, and Pakistan) that have substantial but politically disenfranchised Shi'a minorities, some of whom (as in Saudi Arabia's Eastern Province) happen to live atop extremely large oil and gas reserves, making political instability in these areas a global concern. As Patrick Cockburn has shown, the importance of Iraqi Shi'a political and insurgent leaders like Muqtada al-Sadr cannot be fully grasped without reference to this pattern of Shi'a empowerment and its disruptive effect both on the established, Sunni-dominated order in Ba'athist Iraq and on the existing Shi'a religious and political establishment that has emerged since the fall of Saddam Hussein.[40] In a real sense, in Shi'a Iraq since 2003 we have been witnessing a violent internal social revolution as well as an insurgency against occupation. Likewise, Hizballah, as a Shi'a organization that embodies elements of terrorist, insurgent, propaganda, charity, and social work, with a global reach, profound political influence in the Levant, and a client-proxy relationship with the Iranian regime, is a non-state instance of expanding Shi'a influence. Hizballah's good military showing in the 2006 war with Israel led the Israeli government's Winograd Commission to conclude that Hizballah had significantly strengthened since 2000, and that the Israeli Defense Force was simply not prepared to deal with its increased threat and capabilities.[41] Leading Hizballah scholar

Andrew Exum, writing just after the war, suggested that its performance was such that "enemies of the United States will likely seek to emulate Hizballah's perceived successes in southern Lebanon."[42]

A third element of the Islamic civil war thesis is the geopolitical rise of Iran in its own right, as a powerful nation-state, nuclear threshold power, and potential regional hegemon, sitting in a geostrategically unassailable position astride the Gulf, the Caucasus, Central Asia, and Afghanistan, with a large population, long coastline, and enormous, rugged territory; an economy benefiting from increased world oil prices; increasing regional influence; a blossoming alliance of convenience with the Taliban in Afghanistan; and the potential to have a satellite buffer-state in southern Iraq. Again, this increase in Iranian influence is threatening and destabilizing to regional players like the Gulf Cooperation Council countries and particularly Saudi Arabia, though some Saudi analysts have concluded that the threat is overdrawn. For example, the Riyadh-based Saudi National Security Assessment Project concluded in September 2006 that

> the Shi'a will attain more rights, but a full "revival" is not possible due to demographic, economic, and military challenges. Globally, Shi'a are outnumbered by more than five to one, and in the Middle East they are a clear minority. Economically, Iran lacks the strength to further its self-proclaimed ambitions or Shi'a movements elsewhere. While a major power, Iran's oil might doesn't match its rhetoric. Any military confrontation between Iran and its neighbors will bring in the U.S., and the acquisition of nuclear weapons will prompt other regional powers to do the same. There will be no hegemon in the Middle East, but instead a balance of power among the two or three leading countries in the region.[43]

This process of turmoil and internal conflict within the Islamic world has four major implications.

The first relates to American strategic choices. Immediately after 9/11, U.S. leaders opted for an activist policy of direct intervention in the Muslim world, recognizing that instability and conflict within Islam could spill over to harm the West in general and the United States in particular. The invasion of Afghanistan, the active promotion of democracy, women's rights, and governance reform in the Muslim world, and the subsequent invasion and occupation of Iraq can all be seen as enacting this approach. Likewise, the establishment of several Joint Interagency Task Forces

(JIATFs) to project military power and civilian development assistance into unstable regions (all Muslim, like the Horn of Africa, the trans-Sahel, and the southern Philippines) and, more recently, a focus on Israel/Palestine via the Annapolis Conference are further instances of a policy that could be characterized as one of "direct intervention." This policy sought to fundamentally restructure the Islamic world, to remove the perceived causes of extremism. The direct intervention approach was very understandable, given the need to be seen to do something after the immense provocation of the 9/11 attacks, but its results (the strategic, moral, and material costs of the Iraq War, the failure of the Middle East democratization agenda, widespread American unpopularity, loss of credibility, a crisis of confidence among Western allies in the Muslim world, and a boost to AQ recruitment and support) have proven contrary to U.S. interests, at least in the short term.

One possible alternative would have been a containment policy, seeking to prevent the bleed-out of violence and instability from the Islamic world into the rest of global society, while encouraging and supporting Muslim leaders to resolve the internal turmoil within Islam on their own terms. This, too, would have carried severe risks, not least the possibility that authoritarian regimes in the Middle East would have seen the West as weak and continued oppressing their populations anyway. Moreover, given the integration of Muslim populations in almost every Western country and the globalization-enabled connectivity noted earlier, one could argue that the "Islamic world" simply cannot be quarantined from the rest of global society and left to stew in its own juice, as some "separationists" have suggested.[44] Indeed, we could regard direct intervention and separationism as opposite extremes along a spectrum of engagement, and as I argue later, there is a strong case for adopting a policy of balanced response that makes limited use of intervention within a context of continuous engagement and a broader containment approach.

A second obvious implication is that, under current conditions, the United States is fighting against all parties to this civil war at once. Iran and AQ are natural opponents, as are Shi'a communitarian militias and Sunni rejectionist insurgents in Iraq, and Iran and the Taliban were enemies before 9/11. But Western powers are currently fighting all sides, partly (according to this theory) because the West has stepped into the middle of an internal conflict, prompting all players to turn against our intervention as if we were outsiders interfering in a violent domestic dispute. Partly, however, the fact that Western countries find ourselves fighting all sides arises because we have been insufficiently agile in distinguishing different and contradictory forms of Islamic extremism from each other, and have failed to listen to Muslim allies—like King Abdullah II of Jordan, or former president Abdurrahman Wahid of Indonesia—who understand the problem and its potential solutions in much greater and more nuanced detail than Westerners ever could. In some cases, we have fought enemies we had no need to fight, and have chosen to fight simultaneously enemies we could have fought in sequence. We have, in other words, signally failed to follow Frederick Hartmann's strategic principle of "conservation of enemies," which states that although enmity is a permanent feature in international relations, successful powers must avoid making, or simultaneously engaging, more enemies than absolutely necessary.[45]

A further implication is that we are failing to fully exploit the ideological and interest-based differences between our opponents (cleavages akin to the Cold War Sino-Soviet split). These differences exist not only between Shi'a and Sunni groups, but within takfiri movements, which, because of their extreme intolerance of even slightly differing points of view, have a strong tendency to fragment along ideological fault-lines into ever smaller and more fanatical groups.[46] As I have argued elsewhere, the takfiri extremist enemy is naturally vulnerable to a disaggregation approach that seeks to turn factions against each other and disrupt the overall effects of extremism.[47] But our tendency to lump all threats together under the banner of a "global war on terrorism" tends to have the opposite effect, unifying these disparate groups in the face of a common external foe, through a fusion mechanism that sociologists call "primary group cohesion" (which I discuss in detail in the Afghanistan and Iraq case studies).

A final observation: there is a certain amount of irrationality in our Iran policy, arising in part from the experiences of the U.S. Embassy hostage crisis in Teheran in 1979–1980, so vividly described in Mark Bowden's 2007 book *Guests of the Ayatollah*.[48] There is baggage on both sides, of course: some Iranians remember the U.S.-led overthrow of the Mossadeq government in 1953 with equally vivid bitterness,[49] while others, opposed to the current regime, blame America for the revolution of 1979. This baggage sometimes makes American policy-makers reluctant to accept the historical and geopolitical fact of Iran's importance in its region, and hence the underlying legitimacy of Iran's long-term aspirations to play a regional role, including in Afghanistan and Iraq. Of course, the United

States and the rest of the international community have a clear interest in ensuring that Iran plays a constructive role in these countries, rather than its current highly destructive and destabilizing one. Still, it seems clear that distinguishing Iran, as a country, from the clericalist regime in Tehran and from the Iranian people it oppresses is fundamental to developing an effective Iran policy. The youthfulness of Iran's population, and Iranians' widespread dissatisfaction with the only regime many of them have ever known, are key advantages for the United States. But lack of diplomatic representation in Tehran, along with limited willingness to engage in discussion with Iran's leadership group—engagement that would of course have to be backed by force and international consensus, and addressing the broadest possible range of issues in partnership with other Muslim allies—severely limits U.S. options and restricts situational awareness. This makes it harder to clearly discern the Iranian role in an Islamic civil war, or to formulate viable policy responses to it.

Model 4: Asymmetric Warfare

This model examines the security environment functionally rather than politically, from the standpoint of military capability. This theory argues that the underlying strategic logic of terrorism, insurgency, internal conflict, and unconventional warfare arises from a fundamental mismatch (or asymmetry) between U.S. military capabilities and those of the rest of the world. As noted, the United States currently possesses a degree of military superiority in conventional capability that is unprecedented in world history. No other country, or combination of countries, could expect to take on the United States in a conventional force-on-force engagement with any prospect of victory. This is underlined by the enormous scale of American defense spending: according to recent unclassified estimates, the U.S. defense budget accounted for 54.5 percent of total global defense spending in 2007, with the other 45.5 percent representing every other country on Earth combined.[50] In mid-2008, counting supplemental budget allocations for the Iraq War, the U.S. defense budget is approaching 70 percent of total global defense spending. This unparalleled investment in conventional military capability has created an asymmetry between U.S. capabilities and those of virtually all other actors (friendly or otherwise) in the international security environment, with five major implications, as follows.

First, under these conditions, regardless of ideology, any rational adversary is likely to fight the United States using nonconventional means.

These may include propaganda and subversion, terrorist attacks, guerrilla warfare, weapons of mass destruction, or attempts to drag conventional forces into protracted engagements for little strategic gain, so as to exhaust the American people's political support for a conflict. Given overwhelming U.S. conventional superiority, and contrary to the pre-9/11 conventional wisdom embodied in the insouciant attitude of the general who visited my class in 2001, it turns out that adversaries do not give up the armed struggle under these conditions: rather, any smart enemy goes unconventional; and most enemies are likely to continue doing so, until we demonstrate the ability to prevail in irregular conflicts such as those we are currently engaged in. This may mean that, like Bill Murray's character in the movie *Groundhog Day*, we are doomed to live this day over and over again until we get it right: we may have to keep on fighting these types of wars until we win one.

The second implication of this massive asymmetry is that because its military superiority gives the United States the capability to destroy any other nation-state on the face of the earth, belief in the fundamentally benign intent of the United States becomes a critical factor in other countries' strategic calculus. Intelligence threat assessments typically examine the twin factors of *capability* and *intent*, focusing on capability because intent is subject to much more rapid and unpredictable change. But the destructive capability of the United States is so asymmetrically huge vis-à-vis every other nation on Earth that it poses what international relations theorists call a "security dilemma." Unless other countries can be assured of America's benign intent, they must rationally treat the United States as a potential threat and take steps to balance and contain American power or defend themselves against it. And efforts to improve U.S. military capacity, which American leaders may see as defensive, may therefore have a negative overall effect on U.S. national security because of the responses they generate. Again, this reflects Qiao Liang's insight that unless other countries trust the United States (that is, unless they believe it will follow its own self-imposed rule-set), the whole basis of international cooperation tends to be compromised. Thus the widely observed phenomenon of countries "bandwagoning" or engaging in balancing behavior against the United States, along with countries seeking nonconventional means of attack and defense, may not necessarily indicate hostile intent on these countries' part but rather it may simply be a rational response to overwhelming U.S. conventional military capability. Nor is such anti-American behavior necessarily a sign that the United States is doing something wrong: rather, it may simply be an inherent structural aspect of a unipolar global system, a security dilemma representing an inbuilt pattern that would have occurred whichever nation found itself in this position. Such thinking might suggest that American primacy, like the primacy of any other nation beyond certain limits that other nations find acceptable, could be inherently destabilizing of the global system and thus harmful to America's own interests. It also suggests that assuring other nations that the United States will exercise its power responsibly, sparingly, virtuously, and in accordance with international norms is therefore not an optional luxury or a sign of moral flaccidity. Rather, it is a key strategic requirement to prevent this previously noted adversarial "balance-of-power" response to the unprecedented scale of American military might. American power must be matched by American virtue,[51] or it will ultimately harm both the United States and the global system.

Third, however, the efforts of insurgents and terrorists since 9/11 may in fact have already put an end, through unconventional and asymmetric means, to the much-bruited military superiority of the United States, showing the way to all future adversaries and leaving Western powers with fabulously capable and appallingly expensive militaries that are precisely adapted to exactly the wrong kind of war. The post–Cold War era of unparalleled U.S. military power may have been a passing phase: AQ might indeed turn out to be, as Zawahiri called it, the vanguard of a new era of conflict. This is the analytical line taken by the historian Andrew Bacevich. In September 2006, the performance of Islamic militias and insurgents in the Palestinian Territories and Iraq, along with Hizballah's achievement in fighting Israel to a standstill (noted earlier) led Bacevich to describe a new "Islamic Way of War" that incorporates a "panoply of techniques employed to undercut the apparent advantages of high-tech conventional forces. The methods employed do include terrorism—violence targeting civilians for purposes of intimidation—but they also incorporate propaganda, subversion, popular agitation, economic warfare, and hit-and-run attacks on regular forces, either to induce an overreaction or to wear them down."[52] He concluded that

> in Iraq, the world's only superpower finds itself mired in a conflict that it cannot win. History's mightiest military has been unable to defeat an enemy force of perhaps 20,000 to 30,000 insurgents equipped with

post–World War II vintage assault rifles and anti-tank weapons. In Gaza and southern Lebanon, the Middle East's mightiest military also finds itself locked in combat with adversaries that it cannot defeat. Despite weeks of bitter fighting, the IDF's Merkava tanks, F-16 fighter-bombers, and missile-launching unmanned aerial vehicles failed to suppress, much less eliminate, the armed resistance of Hamas and Hezbollah. What are we to make of this? How is it that the seemingly weak and primitive are able to frustrate modern armies only recently viewed as all but invincible? What do the parallel tribulations—and embarrassments—of the United States and Israel have to tell us about war and politics in the twenty-first century? In short, what's going on here? The answer to that question is dismayingly simple: *the sun has set on the age of unquestioned Western military dominance. Bluntly, the East has solved the riddle of the Western Way of War.* In Baghdad and in Anbar Province as at various points on Israel's troubled perimeter, the message is clear: methods that once could be counted on to deliver swift decision no longer work.[53]

I would go somewhat further than Bacevich, to suggest that the tendency toward hybrid forms of warfare combining terrorism, insurgency, propaganda, and economic warfare to sidestep Western conventional capability is not solely an Arab or Muslim phenomenon. It may be that groups like AQ, Hamas, and Hizballah have been pioneers in applying this method. But as we have seen, Chinese analysts published a study into unrestricted warfare over a decade ago, several far-left and extreme environmentalist groups are believed to have studied AQ methods,[54] and at least two other countries (in Latin America and Southeast Asia) have adopted tactical concepts that seek to exploit asymmetric advantages against the United States and turn our very superiority in conventional war-fighting against us.

A key adversary advantage in confronting U.S. conventional superiority is asymmetry of cost. Currently, the United States is spending in excess of $400 million *per day* in Iraq, a level of spending (drawn entirely from supplemental allocations and therefore representing unforecast and borrowed funds) that is clearly unsustainable over the long-duration commitment demanded by effective counterinsurgency campaigns, which often take decades.[55] By contrast, adversaries deliberately adopt low-cost methods in order to sustain their operations over a longer time period than America can, for an acceptable cost. For example, the 9/11 Commission estimated that the 9/11 attacks cost AQ between $400,000 and $500,000, plus the cost of training the 19 hijackers in the United States prior to the attack.[56] This would make the 9/11 attacks the most expensive terrorist attack in history. But when one considers that the attacks inflicted a direct cost of $27.2 billion on the United States,[57] and that subsequent operations in the "War on Terrorism" have cost about $700 billion to mid-2008,[58] it is clear that the cost of the attack to America has vastly outweighed its costs to AQ, and that the cost of America's subsequent response has even further dwarfed, by several orders of magnitude, what AQ spent on the attacks. This should give us pause, especially against the background of the 2008 financial crisis which many analysts have described as the worst since the Great Depression.

Another key aspect of asymmetry is the mismatch between military and nonmilitary elements of U.S. national power. United States military capability not only overshadows the capabilities of all other world militaries combined, it also dwarfs U.S. civilian capabilities. As an example, there are 1.68 million uniformed personnel in the U.S. armed forces.[59] By comparison, taking diplomatic capacity as a surrogate metric for other forms of civilian capability, the State Department employs about 6,000 foreign service officers, while the U.S. Agency for International Development (USAID) has about 2,000.[60] In other words, the Department of Defense is about 210 times larger than USAID and State combined, in personnel terms. (In budgetary terms, the mismatch is far greater, on the order of 350:1.) This represents a substantial asymmetry, particularly when it is realized that the typical size ratio between armed forces and diplomatic/ aid agencies for other Western democracies is between 8 and 10:1 (compared to 210:1 in the case of the United States). The overwhelming size and capacity of the U.S. armed forces therefore has a distorting effect on U.S. national power and on America's ability to execute international security programs that balance military with nonmilitary elements of national power.

Even within the armed forces, there is a substantial mismatch between the capabilities needed for the current international security environment and those actually present in the U.S. military inventory. This is starkest in terms of the lack of capacity for stabilization and reconstruction operations, and for counterinsurgency or FID. The vast majority of defense capability is oriented to conventional war-fighting, while even within Special Operations Forces the primary focus is on direct action (killing or capturing key enemy personnel) rather than on capabilities that support an indirect, military assistance approach. At a higher level of abstraction, the resources available for land operations (including both army and marine ground forces and the air and maritime assets from all services that support them) are substantially overstretched by comparison to resources for conventional air and maritime war-fighting, which are far more expensive but much less likely to be called on. Thus the U.S. military exhibits both a capability mismatch and an asymmetry of capacity.

Despite all this, the U.S. government has enduring requirements to meet alliance obligations, deal with the potential for conventional adversaries, and hedge against the threat of major theater conflict. And because capabilities for irregular or unconventional conflict are much cheaper to acquire than those for conventional conflict, and require less hardware and industrial capacity, they are paradoxically less likely to be developed. This is because, through the "military-industrial complex," a substantial portion of the American economy, and numerous jobs in almost every congressional district, are linked to the production of conventional war-fighting capacity. It takes factories, jobs, and industrial facilities to build battleships and bombers, but aid workers, linguists, and Special Forces operators are vastly cheaper and do not demand the same industrial base. So shifting spending priorities onto currently unconventional forms of warfare would cost jobs and votes in the congressional districts of the very people who control that spending. This makes it structurally difficult for the United States fundamentally to reorient its military capabilities away from conventional war-fighting or to divert a significant proportion of defense spending into civilian capacity. Hence, absent a concerted effort by the nation's leadership in both the executive and legislative branches, the pattern of asymmetric warfare, with the United States adopting a basically conventional approach but being opposed by enemies who seek to sidestep American conventional power, is likely to be a long-standing trend.

INTEGRATING THE FOUR PERSPECTIVES

Which is it then? Is the security environment best understood as a backlash against globalization (a technological-economic model of the environment), a global insurgency (a political-strategic model), a civil war within Islam (a geopolitical model), or an asymmetric response to Western conventional superiority (a military-functional model)? Or does some other paradigm—the clash of civilizations, Islamo-fascism, fourth-generation warfare, or something else again—explain the environment better than these four models? The answer, from my point of view, is that all four models explain some aspects of the environment but not others: they are all partial explanations:we have yet to stumble on some kind of unified field theory that fully explains current conflicts. It is also, perhaps, simply too early to tell. These four conceptual frameworks should therefore be seen neither as exhaustive (there are other convincing explanations) nor as mutually exclusive (there is no need to posit one as "correct" and the others as false). Rather, they offer a set of conceptual lenses that can be applied, with judgment and care, to make sense of events and to inform our understanding of field data like the case studies I discuss in subsequent chapters. But first there is more to say about terrorism.

The Accidental Guerrilla

Because of al Qa'ida's role in several ongoing conflicts and the influence of terrorism threats in current American security thinking it is essential, before considering specific case studies, that we rightly understand AQ's strategy and tactics. As will become obvious, a realistic appraisal of the AQ threat, and a rational policy response to it, depends on a sound understanding of AQ methods and objectives—including, particularly, a solid grasp of what I call the *accidental guerrilla syndrome* of AQ interaction with local allies—an understanding that has been somewhat scantly expressed in Western public pronouncements to date.

AQ MILITARY STRATEGY

I have already explored what one might call AQ's "organizational strategy": its desire to become the leading player in a loose coalition of *takfiri* extremist movements, to become the vanguard of the world's Muslim population, the *ummah*, and to act as a propaganda hub and center of excellence from which other movements can draw expertise, while exploiting their actions and aggregating their effects into a unified propaganda offensive against the United States and the broader international community. As noted, the leading counterterrorism analyst Michael Scheuer has emphasized that AQ sees itself as the "inciter-in-chief," not the "commander-in-chief": it seeks to provoke a global uprising against the world order and sustain that uprising over decades, in order to ultimately transform the relationship between the ummah and the rest of global society;[61] but it does not seek to directly control or systematically command the other movements within this coalition. Also as noted, AQ seeks to use the tools of globalization to aggregate the effects of diverse actors separated in time and space—to create a powerful movement whose efforts can be seen as akin to those of an extremely widespread globalized insurgency rather than a traditional terrorist movement.[62] So AQ's organizational strategy essentially boils down to creating a global takfiri coalition with AQ at its head.

Al Qa'ida's military strategy on the other hand, appears to be aimed at bleeding the United States to exhaustion and bankruptcy, forcing America to withdraw in disarray from the Muslim world so that its local allies collapse, and simultaneously to use the provoking and alienating effects of U.S. intervention as a form of provocation to incite a mass uprising within the Islamic world, or at least to generate and sustain popular support for AQ. In a statement released in late 2004, Usama bin Laden outlined this strategic approach as follows:

> All that we have mentioned has made it easy to provoke and bait this [U.S.] Administration. All we have to do is to send two mujahidin to the furthest point East to raise a cloth on which is written al-Qaeda, in order to make the [U.S.] generals race there to cause America to suffer human, economic and political losses without achieving for it anything of note…so we are continuing this policy of bleeding America to the point of bankruptcy. Allah willing and nothing is too great for Allah.[63]

Other AQ statements have indicated a strategic intent to provoke America into actions across the Muslim world that will destroy its credibility and that of the "apostate" regimes it supports, inciting the ummah to rise up and reject these regimes, create a neo-Salafist caliphate, restore Islam to its rightful place within the Islamic world, and then launch an offensive jihad to subjugate all non-Muslim peoples, in accordance with Muhammad's command to "fight them until they say 'There is no God but Allah'" (ahadith al-Bukhari [25] and Muslim [21]). From this it can be seen that AQ's strategy is fundamentally one of bleeding the United States to exhaustion, while simultaneously using U.S. reaction to incite a mass uprising within the Islamic world. Al Qa'ida itself sees its own function primarily as a propaganda hub and incitement mechanism, mobilizing the ummah and provoking Western actions that alienate the Muslim world, in order to further this strategy.

AQ TACTICS

In support of this strategy, AQ applies four basic tactics that are standard for any insurgent movement, as follows.

Provocation

Insurgents throughout history have committed atrocities, carrying out extremely provocative events to prompt their opponents to react (or over-react) in ways that harm their interests. This may involve provoking government forces into repressive actions that alienate the population or provoking one tribal, religious, ethnic, or community group into attacking another in order to create and exploit instability. Al Qa'ida or groups allied to it have carried out numerous provocation attacks. For example, on September 1, 2004, Chechen and Arab Islamist terrorists loyal to Shamil Basayev seized School Number One in Beslan, a town in North Ossetia in Russia's North Caucasus region, taking 1100 primary school children and adults hostage and holding them under lethally abusive conditions for several days before a rescue attempt by Russian security services. Ultimately, 334 people, including 161 children, were killed, and hundreds more were injured in this horrendous atrocity, which appears to have been partly designed to provoke conflict between North Ossetia and the neighboring North Caucasus republic of Ingushetia.[64] Similarly, AQ in Iraq bombed the al-Askariya shrine in Samarra on February 22, 2006, an attack on one of the two holiest shrines in Shi'a Islam, and one that was designed to provoke a major backlash by Shi'a Iraqis against the Iraqi Sunni community. As I discuss in chapter 3, this attempt at provocation was highly successful.[65] Perhaps the most obvious example of a provocation attack is 9/11 itself, which was designed to provoke a massive U.S. retaliation and prompt a spontaneous uprising of the *ummah*. While the worldwide uprising failed to occur, subsequent U.S. actions could be seen as playing into the hands of this AQ provocation agenda.

Intimidation

Insurgents seek to prevent local populations from cooperating with governments or coalition forces by publicly killing those who collaborate, intimidating others who might seek to work with the government, and co-opting others. This dynamic was highlighted by the classical insurgency theorist Bernard B. Fall, who served in the French Resistance in the World War II; he wrote in 1965 that any sound revolutionary warfare operator (the French underground, the Norwegian underground, or any other anti-Nazi European underground) most of the time used small-war tactics—not to destroy the German army, of which they were thoroughly incapable, but to establish a competitive system of control over the population. Of course, in order to do this, here and there they had to kill some of the occupying forces and attack some of the military targets. But above all they had to kill their own people who collaborated with the enemy.[66]

As Fall notes, insurgents also intimidate government forces (especially police and local government officials) in order to force them into defensive actions that alienate the population or to deter them from taking active measures against the insurgents. Likewise, AQ and its allies have mounted terrorist attacks with the intention of intimidating Western countries and forcing them to cease their support of U.S.-led interventions in Iraq (such as the Madrid bombings of 2004, already noted, and the kidnapping of Filipino contractors in the same year, which successfully knocked Spain and the Philippines out of the coalition).[67] More recently, on July 7, 2008, Pakistan-based militants associated with the Taliban and the Haqqani network (both AQ allies at different times) mounted a car bombing aimed at the Indian Embassy in Kabul that killed 41 people and injured more than 100, probably in order to intimidate Indian diplomatic and development personnel working on construction projects in Afghanistan, including the Kunar road program (discussed in detail in the Afghan case study). Another classic example was the attack by AQ in Iraq on the United Nations compound in Baghdad on August 19, 2003, which killed the UN secretary general's special representative, Sergio Vieira de Mello, along with 21 members of his staff, and forced the UN to withdraw its 600 personnel from Iraq less than a month later.[68]

Protraction

Insurgents seek to prolong the conflict in order to exhaust their opponents' resources, erode the government's political will, sap public support for the conflict, and avoid losses. Typically, insurgents react to government countermeasures by going quiet (reducing activity and hiding in inaccessible terrain or within sympathetic or intimidated population groups) when pressure becomes too severe. They then emerge later to fight on. This is one reason why an enemy-centric approach to counterinsurgency is often counterproductive: it tends to alienate and harm the innocent population, who become caught up in the fighting or suffer "collateral" damage, but does little harm to the enemy, who simply melt away when pressure becomes too great. Likewise, AQ and its affiliates have repeatedly gone quiet and drawn out the conflict when threatened, only to reemerge later. The classic example of this was Usama bin Laden's escape from Afghanistan, with key leadership cadres and a small number of core supporters, after the failure of U.S. and Northern Alliance forces to cut off his withdrawal after the battle of Tora Bora in December 2001.[69] He then established a new sanctuary in Pakistan but remained quiet for a lengthy period of regrouping before emerging with new operations in 2003.[70]

Exhaustion

Finally, exhaustion is an insurgent tactic that seeks to impose costs on the opponent government, overstress its support system, tire its troops, and impose costs in terms of lives, resources, and political capital, in order to convince that government that continuing the war is not worth the cost. For example, during the Soviet-Afghan war, working with the Afghan insurgents, U.S. officials analyzed the Soviet war-fighting system looking for weak links and vulnerabilities and then sought to overstress and overburden that system to cause it to collapse. In Iraq, the insurgents ambush and attack convoys and aircraft, so that each vehicle has to be fitted with expensive protective equipment—armor that alienates our forces from the population—and electronic countermeasures, and so that every activity takes much longer and costs much more effort, while carrying greater risk of death or injury. This imposes what Clausewitz called "friction" on a counterinsurgent force, and ultimately causes the government and the domestic population to cease supporting the war. As noted, an exhaustion strategy of this type is precisely the approach AQ adopted and bin Laden outlined in 2004.

AL QA'IDA: FROM EXPEDITIONARY TO GUERRILLA TERRORISM

The 9/11 attacks are an example of what we might call "expeditionary terrorism." Al Qa'ida formed the team for the attacks in one country, assembled them in another, ran the logistics and financial support for the operation out of a third, and then clandestinely inserted the team across international borders to attack its target. They infiltrated 19 people into the United States: essentially, an expeditionary raiding approach.[71]

Contrast this with the Madrid bombing in 2004 or the London 7/7 bombing in 2005. In the latter case, rather than smuggling 19 people in, AQ openly brought one person out: Mohammed Sidique Khan, who traveled by ordinary commercial airliner on his own passport to Pakistan for briefing and training prior to the attack. He then returned to the UK and formed the attack team inside that country, using British nationals.[72] Unlike 9/11, where AQ formed a team remotely and inserted it covertly to the target, in the 7/7 bombings the organization grew the team close to its target: not a true "home-grown" terrorism event, but rather a guerrilla approach that allowed AQ to sidestep the improved transportation security measures and international border controls put in place after 9/11 to defeat expeditionary-style terrorism.

Contrary to popular belief, most terrorist incidents since 9/11 have not been purely homegrown but have drawn on sponsorship, support, or guidance from AQ.[73] And as the 7/7 example shows, the expeditionary model now coexists alongside a guerrilla model in which local clandestine cells are recruited and trained in the target country.[74] Some cells are directly linked to AQ, while others receive training from AQ affiliates, or are inspired by AQ propaganda. There is a trend toward smaller, looser networks that are less capable, but also less predictable and harder to detect, than the more sophisticated networks of the pre-9/11 period.[75]

This suggests that AQ is agile in its operational approach, and willing to change and adapt as the situation develops. Before 9/11, as shown during the Harmony project[76] (an effort by the Combating Terrorism Center at West Point to translate and analyze a cache of AQ documents captured in Afghanistan in 2001), there was intense debate within the AQ leadership about the wisdom of the 9/11 attacks and the likelihood of a mass uprising as a result. In the immediate aftermath of 9/11, the mass uprising failed to occur, and expeditionary-style terrorism became more difficult, so the new guerrilla model emerged. Both now coexist, along with a reinvigorated AQ central leadership that is increasingly capable of planning and controlling attacks, and a population across large parts of the Muslim world (including Muslim populations in the West) that has been alienated by Western actions in Iraq, Afghanistan, and elsewhere and thus provides a recruiting base for guerrilla-style terrorism and a receptive audience for AQ propaganda.

This new model is extremely important in considering the accidental guerrilla syndrome, and this is an appropriate place to examine it in more detail.

THE ACCIDENTAL GUERRILLA SYNDROME

As I recounted in the prologue, I first began to notice the accidental guerrilla syndrome in the mid-1990s in West Java. But I did not come up with a name for it until 10 years later, after a conversation one afternoon on the Afghan-Pakistan frontier. With my State Department colleague Virginia Palmer, a former Africa hand with a wealth of field experience across Africa and Asia, I had been visiting Pakistan's FATA, which run for 1,200 kilometers along the Afghan-Pakistan frontier.

Virginia and I were working in the FATA with the Pakistan government, doing a detailed review of civil administration, economic development, and military policy on the frontier (discussed in more detail in chapter 4). Our job was to assess the situation and report on how effectively Pakistan was employing the $100 million per month (at the time—the amount is greater now) the United States was providing in aid to the Pakistani government. We were traveling with a small escort from the Khyber Rifles, a regiment of the paramilitary Frontier Corps. The escort commander was a young Punjabi major, a city boy from Lahore who now found himself up in the mountains commanding a unit of people whose language he didn't speak and whose culture, history, and outlook were distinctly different from his own. One afternoon, when we were eating together, after a long hot day in the hills, and discussing the latest developments with al Qa'ida, I used the term "foreign fighters." He said, "You know, we Punjabis are the foreigners here on the frontier. Al Qa'ida has been here 25 years, their leaders have married into the tribes, they have children and businesses here, they've become part of local society. It's almost impossible for outsiders, including the Pakistan army, to tell the terrorists apart from anybody else in the tribal areas, except by accident." By *accident*. His word resonated in my mind, and I realized I now had a name for the phenomenon I had long recognized.

This Pakistani officer described a syndrome that is easily summed up, though extremely hard to counter: AQ moves into remote areas, creates alliances with local traditional communities, exports violence that prompts a Western intervention, and then exploits the backlash against that intervention in order to generate support for its *takfiri* agenda. Al Qa'ida's ideology tends to lack intrinsic appeal for traditional societies, and so it draws the majority of its strength from this backlash rather than from genuine popular support. Subsequent chapters describe this phenomenon in the field, in Iraq, Afghanistan, Pakistan, and elsewhere, but it is worth laying out the theory—the mechanism by which, I hypothesize, the accidental guerrilla emerges—as a starting point for the analysis.

Based on field observation in several theaters of the "War on Terrorism" since 2001, I theorize that the accidental guerrilla emerges from a cyclical process that takes place in four stages: infection, contagion, intervention, and rejection.

In detail, the four phases can be described as follows.

During the *infection* phase, AQ or an associated movement establishes a presence within a remote, ungoverned, or conflict-affected area. I use a medical analogy advisedly here, because just as a virus or bacterium is more easily able to affect a host whose immune system is compromised or to superinfect an existing wound, so *takfiri* groups opportunistically exploit existing breakdowns in the rule of law, poor governance, or preexisting conflict. Terrorist infection is thus part of the social pathology of broader societal breakdown, state weakness, and humanitarian crisis.

In this initial phase, the *takfiri* group establishes local cells, support systems, intelligence and information-gathering networks, and local alliances. It often seeks some form of tacit agreement or loose pact with the regime in the country at large (as did AQ in the 1980s in Pakistan, in the 1990s in the Sudan, and in Afghanistan before 9/11) and also seeks to build relationships with local tribes and community leaders, often through processes of intermarriage and shared business interests. The group may

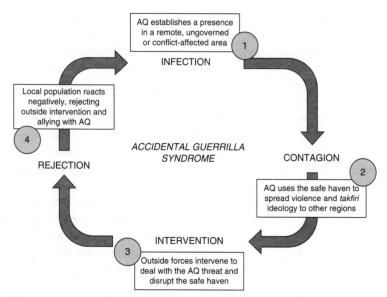

Figure 1.1 The accidental guerrilla syndrome.

establish its own businesses, run front companies, or operate in partnership (or competition) with local criminal or business syndicates. It may establish training camps, education or ideological indoctrination centers, recruiting and logistics bases, transportation systems, centers for the production of counterfeit documentation, headquarters camps, media production facilities, and caches of equipment and supplies.

Importantly, the establishment of this type of safe haven is often met with resistance from the local people, who rightly regard AQ and similar externally motivated *takfiri* groups as alien outsiders who do not have local people's interests at heart. Al Qa'ida typically responds with a mixture of co-optation and intimidation: killing local community leaders (especially tribal elders and moderate religious leaders) who oppose their domination; establishing alliances by marriage, sometimes forced, with local women; bribing or killing government representatives who interfere; arbitrating local disputes; funneling money into the local economy; and establishing an uneasy ascendancy over the area. Although AQ may appear secure in the safe haven, in fact it lacks intrinsic appeal to the local community, and there is always a dispossessed section of the local elite that is eager to regain its lost authority, and a disgruntled segment of the population who have had loved ones killed or harmed by the *takfiri* terrorists but feel too intimidated to act against the interlopers on their own.

In the second phase, *contagion*, the extremist group's influence spreads, and it begins to affect the country at large, other countries in the same region, and in some cases (enabled by the tools of globalization discussed earlier) other regions in the world, either directly through terrorist activity or "virtually" through propaganda and media influence. This is a critical stage in the process, since without it the terrorist presence in a given area would be unlikely to attract international attention or to present a threat to the world community at large, hence the next stage (intervention) would not occur. If not for his ability to spread contagion via globalization pathways, Usama bin Laden, for example, would be simply one in a long line of charismatic extremist fugitive leaders who have hidden out in remote mountain areas and waged guerrilla warfare against local authorities. Hassan i-Sabah, the Old Man of the Mountains, is perhaps the archetype,[77] while others since the mid–nineteenth century include Imam Shamil in the Caucasus,[78] Mullah Powindah, Mirza Ali Khan (the Fakir of Ipi), Ajab Khan Afridi in the Hindu Kush, and Mohammed Abdullah Hassan (the Mad Mullah) in Somalia.[79] What makes the modern phenomenon different, andjustifies a global response, is the potential for contagion: the bleed-out of violence to interconnected areas, the intersection between extremist ideology and weapons of mass destruction, and the global propaganda and destabilization effect of terrorist presence. Yet, as I shall show, the "cure" may be worse than the disease in this case, especially if it involves large-scale, overt, unilateral or heavy-handed Western military intervention.

In the third phase, *intervention*, external authorities begin to take action against the extremist presence, prompted by the ideological contagion or spread of subversion and violence emerging from the area. This phase may take several forms: intervention may be undertaken by the local (national or provincial) government only, by regional powers, or by the wider international community. Likewise, intervention may initially be nonviolent, applying aid and development measures and health, education, or governance extension programs. (This nonviolent approach usually does not last, because extremists react violently to the presence of external aid or governance workers, who then need to be protected by police or the military, so that violent clashes begin to occur.) Intervention may be episodic and short-term in nature, applying a "repetitive raiding" approach in the manner of a classical or colonial punitive expedition, or may adopt a long-term "persistent presence" approach.[80] It may be low-profile or highly public and overt. Finally and most important, it may involve only local indigenous personnel or may be based on foreign presence (noting that, as our Khyber Rifles escort commander pointed out in 2006, the definition of "foreigner" is elastic, derives from local perceptions, and can include someone from a different provincial or cultural area as well as someone from another country). In other words, there are many forms of intervention, and choosing how to intervene—ideally in such a way as to minimize local backlash—is just as critical as deciding whether to intervene in the first place.

I have noted that during the initial stage of development of an extremist presence, there is usually a local opposition to the terrorist group (albeit often cowed, impotent, or intimidated). But during the intervention phase, the entire local dynamic shifts. The presence of the intervening outsiders causes local groups to coalesce in a fusion response, closing ranks against the external threat. This reaction is lessened if the intervention is slower, less violent, more locally based, or lower in profile. But a high-profile, violent, or foreign-based intervention tends to increase support for the *takfiri* terrorists, who can paint themselves as defenders of local people against external influence. Such an intervention also creates grievances, alienation, and a desire for revenge when local people are killed or are dishonored by the intervening outsiders' presence. Due to the dynamic of "balanced opposition" (discussed in detail later), local people in tribal societies will always tend to side with closer against more distant relatives, with local against external actors, and with coreligionists against people of other faiths. In this sense, although the terrorists may have been seen as outsiders until this point, their identity as such has been not fixed but "contingent": as soon as foreigners or infidels appear in the area, by comparison the terrorists are able to paint themselves as relative locals and opportunistically draw on local loyalties for support. The completely understandable (and necessary) imperative for the international community to intervene and prevent extremist contagion can thus act as a provocation, causing the next stage in the process: rejection.

Again, I use a medical analogy advisedly here. The *rejection* phase looks a lot like a social version of an immune response in which the body rejects the intrusion of a foreign object, even one (such as a pin in a broken bone or a stent in a blocked blood vessel) that serves an ultimately beneficial purpose. Societal antibodies recognize the intrusion as a foreign body, emerge to attack the intervening presence, and attempt to drive it out. This is the phase in which local people begin to become accidental guerrillas, fighting alongside extremist forces not because they support the *takfiri* ideology but because they oppose outside interference in their affairs, because they are rallied to support local tribal or community interests, or because they are alienated by heavy-handed actions of the intervening force. The more the *takfiri* group can paint itself as similar to the local people and the more it can appear as their defender against outsiders, the stronger this phenomenon becomes. A loose coalition of local groups emerges to defend local interests against outside attack and, unless local communities are carefully co-opted and won over by the government, the intervening force can end up fighting the whole of local society, when its original intent was to rescue local people from the exploitative presence of the extremist group.

The implications of the accidental guerrilla syndrome are far-reaching, and dealing effectively with it is likely to require a radical rethinking of some key Western policies, strategies, and attitudes. But before turning to possible implications and remedies, I need to examine some real-world cases in detail, and to present the evidence for the emergence of hybrid warfare and the accidental guerrilla. The case studies that follow will do this through a series of local examples from Afghanistan, Iraq, and other conflicts from Indonesia to Europe.

Chapter 2

"The Crazies Will Kill Them": Afghanistan, 2006–2008

Ninety percent of the people you call "Taliban" are actually tribals. They're fighting for loyalty or Pashtun honor, and to profit their tribe. They're not extremists. But they're terrorized by the other 10 percent: religious fanatics, terrorists, people allied to [the Taliban leadership *shura* in] Quetta. They're afraid that if they try to reconcile, the crazies will kill them. To win them over, first you have to protect their people, prove that the extremists can't hurt them if they come to your side.

Afghan provincial governor, March 15, 2008

On May 19, 2006, a patrol was moving through a mountain valley in Uruzgan, Afghanistan.[1] It was the middle of a dusty Friday afternoon early in the Afghan summer, during the annual lull that happens when local guerrillas go home to harvest the opium poppy. The patrol—an A Team from Third Battalion, Seventh Special Forces Group out of Fort Bragg, North Carolina—didn't know it yet, but the lull was about to end: they were driving into the biggest firefight of their tour.

Afghan valleys typically have only one route in or out, usually a dirt track on the valley floor. This means that once you are inside a valley, the local population and, by extension, the enemy knows precisely how you plan to get out. The patrol was moving slowly, well spread out in light vehicles, when it was struck by a storm of fire from a Taliban column of 150–200 fighters among the hills overlooking the road. The ambush was remarkably professional: the Taliban had laid themselves out in an L-shape to block any breakout, and their heavy machine guns (ex-Soviet 12.7-millimeter guns: people call them "dooshkas" from their Russian abbreviation, DSHK)[2] methodically hosed down the stalled convoy. Several groups of Taliban cooperated closely, first halting the patrol, then forming a horseshoe-shaped blocking position to pin it down. Soon the Americans in the patrol realized with a sinking feeling that they were surrounded, as fire started to come down on them from every point on the skyline. The flat "crump" of mortars began to echo off the hills, and dusty smoke-bursts spouted among the vehicles: Taliban mortar teams behind the next crest shelled the 24 Americans and 12 Afghans, pinned in the roadside dust, as they pressed themselves into scraps of cover and tried to spot their tormentors and hit back. As the shadows lengthened, the ambushers were almost impossible to see: hidden observers with binoculars and radios directed their fire from grey stone sangars in the grey stone hills. The Taliban marksmanship and fire discipline were excellent: at five o'clock, as the sun began to dip, one American operator observed a Taliban fighter place five shots in a 50-millimeter group at 200 yards' range. Taliban snipers were achieving first-round hits, focusing on communications specialists, heavy weapons operators, and commanders. Staff Sergeant Christian Longsworth was hit, critically injured, and soon died—the sole American death in the firefight, though seven more Americans were wounded. Troops clearing the heights after the firefight found prepared sniper positions with 10-power optics, specialized sniper rifles, and camouflage "ghillie suits." The patrol fought a desperate battle, unable to extricate itself until it could organize a fighting withdrawal. Even then, night coming on, the weather closing in, miles away from their patrol base and with one dead and several wounded, the patrol faced a difficult return journey to the patrol base. All in all, it was a tough day out: Chief Warrant Officer Angel DeJesus and Staff Sergeant Erasmo Espino Jr. were later awarded the Silver Star for their heroic efforts in extracting the patrol from their position, heavily outnumbered and outgunned by the Taliban.[3]

The most intriguing thing about this battle was not the Taliban, though; it was the behavior of the local people. One reason the patrol was so heavily pinned down was that its retreat, back down the only road along the valley floor, was cut off by a group of farmers who had been working in the fields and, seeing the ambush begin, rushed home to fetch their weapons and join in. Three nearby villages participated, with people coming from as far as 5 kilometers away, spontaneously marching to the sound of the guns. There is no evidence that the locals cooperated directly with the Taliban; indeed, it seems they had no directly political reason to get involved in the fight (several, questioned afterward, said they had no love for the Taliban and were generally well-disposed toward the Americans in the area). But, they said, when the battle was right there in front of them, how could they not join in? Did we understand just how boring it was to be a teenager in a valley in central Afghanistan? This was the most exciting thing that had happened in their valley in years. It would have shamed them to stand by and wait it out, they said.[4]

It is this interplay between terrain, population, Taliban, and terrorists that makes Afghanistan such a difficult, dangerous, and complicated environment. It also means that Afghanistan, like Pakistan and Iraq, is a fertile source of insight into the patterns—global terrorists exploiting accidental guerrillas, societal antibodies emerging in response to Western intervention, the risk of playing into the hands of an AQ exhaustion strategy—which I have already described in general terms. This chapter extends the analysis by examining the insurgency in Afghanistan, and deepens it through a case study of Kunar Province, in the east of the country, where a road-building program integrating civilian and military effort into a single political maneuver has proved surprisingly effective since 2006, against the background of a sharp deterioriation in the overall situation in Afghanistan. As I shall show, the reason for this program's success appears to have relatively little to do with the road itself, and much more to do with insightful American and Afghan leaders who have used the process of the road's construction as a vehicle for political maneuver designed to drive a wedge between the local people, the local guerrillas, and the hard-core Taliban leadership in this area.

But before considering Kunar, it's necessary to survey the broader context and character of the conflict.

Afghanistan: A Campaign at a Crossroads

THE STRATEGIC CONTEXT

People often speak of "the Iraq War" and "the war in Afghanistan" as if they were separate conflicts. But as we have seen, Afghanistan is one theater in a larger confrontation with transnational takfiri terrorism, not a discrete war in itself. Because of commitments elsewhere—principally Iraq—the United States and its allies have chosen to run this campaign as an "economy of force" operation, with a fraction of the effort applied elsewhere. Most of what has happened in Afghanistan results from this, as much as from local factors. Compared to other theaters where I have worked, the war in Afghanistan is being run on a shoestring. The country is about one and a half times the size of Iraq and has a somewhat larger population (32 million, of whom about 6 million are Pashtun males

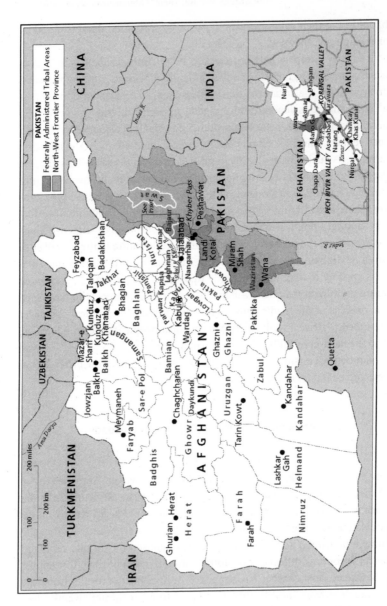

Map 2.1 Afghanistan

of military age), but to date the United States has resourced it at about 27 percent of the funding given to Iraq, and allocated about 20 percent of the troops deployed in Iraq (29 percent counting allies).[5] In funding terms, counting fiscal year 2008 supplemental budget requests, by 2008 operations in Iraq had cost the United States approximately $608.3 billion over five years, whereas the war in Afghanistan had cost about $162.6 billion over seven years: in terms of overall spending, about 26.7 percent of the cost of Iraq, or a monthly spending rate of about 19.03 percent that of Iraq.[6] In addition to lack of troops and money, certain key resources, including battlefield helicopters, construction and engineering resources, and intelligence, surveillance, and reconnaissance (ISR) assets, have been critically short.

Resource allocation in itself is not a sign of success—arguably in Iraq we have spent more than we can afford for limited results—but expenditure is a good indicator of government attention. Thus the international community's failure to allocate adequate resources for Afghanistan bespeaks an episodic strategic inattention, a tendency to focus on Iraq and think about Afghanistan only when it impinges on public opinion in Western countries, NATO alliance politics, global terrorism, or the situation in Pakistan or Iran, while taking ultimate victory in Afghanistan for granted. Two examples spring to mind: the first was when Admiral Michael G. Mullen, chairman of the U.S. Joint Chiefs of Staff, remarked in congressional testimony in December 2007 that "in Afghanistan, we do what we can. In Iraq, we do what we must," implying that Afghan issues by definition play second fiddle to Iraq, receiving resources and attention only as spare capacity allows.[7] The reason for Admiral Mullen's remark emerges from the second, larger illustration of this syndrome: by invading Iraq in 2003, the United States and its allies opened a second front before finishing the first, and without sufficient resources to prosecute both campaigns effectively. Western leaders committed this strategic error primarily because of overconfidence and a tendency to underestimate the enemy: they appear to have taken for granted that the demise of the Taliban, scattered and displaced but not defeated in 2001, was only a matter of time.

These leaders would have done well to remember the words of Sir Olaf Caroe, a famous old hand of the North-West Frontier of British India, ethnographer of the Pashtuns, and last administrator of the frontier province before independence, who wrote in 1958 that "unlike other wars, Afghan wars become serious only when they are over; in British times at least they were apt to produce an after-crop of tribal unrest [and] ... constant intrigue among the border tribes."[8] Entering Afghanistan and capturing its cities is relatively easy; holding the country and securing the population is much, much harder: as the Soviets (with "assistance," and a degree of post-Vietnam *schadenfreude*, from Washington) discovered to their cost, like the British, Sikhs, Mughals, Persians, Mongols, and Macedonians before them. In Afghanistan in 2001, as in Iraq in 2003, the invading Western powers confused entry with victory, a point the Russian General Staff lost no time in pointing out.[9] The Taliban movement's phenomenal resurgence from its nadir of early 2002 underlines this point: the insurgents' successes seem due as much to inattention and inadequate resourcing on our part as to talent on theirs.

Afghanistan is also a very different campaign from Iraq, though the two conflicts are linked through shared Western political objectives and cooperation between enemy forces. The Iraq campaign is urban, sectarian, primarily internal, and heavily centered on Baghdad. The Afghan campaign is overwhelmingly rural, centered on the Pashtun South and East, with a major external sanctuary in Pakistan and, as of 2008, increasing external involvement by Iran. There is somewhat greater international support for the effort in Afghanistan than for Iraq (though rhetoric often does not translate into action).[10] Afghanistan is seen as a war of necessity, "the good war," the "real war on terrorism." This gives the international community greater freedom of action than in Iraq.

Perhaps counterintuitively, events in Afghanistan also have greater proportional impact than those in Iraq. Because far fewer U.S. troops are in Afghanistan than in Iraq, effort there has greater effect than equal effort in Iraq—a brigade (3,000 people) in Afghanistan is worth a division or more (10,000–12,000) in Iraq, in terms of its proportionate effect on the ground. Regardless of the outcome in Iraq, Afghanistan still presents an opportunity for a positive long-term legacy for Western intervention, if it results in an Afghan state capable of effectively responding to its people's wishes and meeting their needs.

Conversely, although the American population and the international community are inured to negative media reporting about Iraq, they are less used to downbeat reporting about Afghanistan. Most people polled in successive opinion surveys have tended to assume that the Afghan campaign is going reasonably well,[11] hence Taliban successes or sensational attacks in Afghanistan may actually carry greater political weight than equivalent events in Iraq, a campaign that is so unpopular and about which opinion is so polarized that people tend to assume it is going less well than is actually the case.

During the summer and autumn of 2006, and again in the spring of 2008, I led field assessment teams in Afghanistan. In each case, the aim was to conduct an independent expert review of the Afghan campaign so as to identify best practices and challenges. My activity in late 2006 also sought to capture best practices and counterinsurgency techniques that had been developed under the U.S.-led Combined Forces Command Afghanistan, as that headquarters closed and control of the campaign passed to the NATO-led International Security Assistance Force (ISAF). Many of these techniques (some of which I discuss below) informed our approach in designing the tactics we applied at the ground level in Iraq the following year, during the "surge" of 2007. The 2008 assessment took place in the lead-up to a major NATO summit meeting at Bucharest and a change of command at ISAF, and sought to assess ISAF performance and identify key issues needing to be addressed. It also afforded me a personal opportunity, after spending virtually all of 2007 focused on or deployed in Iraq, to revisit earlier impressions and get a feel for trends and developments over time.

During 2006 and 2008, my team conducted numerous debriefings, round tables, structured interviews, and analysis sessions with U.S. and Coalition military, diplomatic, intelligence, aid, and counternarcotics (CN) personnel. I delivered counterinsurgency training to Afghan and Coalition staff at the Afghan National Army (ANA) Kabul Military Training Center, and held detailed discussions with leaders responsible for developing the ANA and the Afghan National Police (ANP). I also met many Afghans—officials from the government of Afghanistan (GOA), provincial governors, local officials, intelligence officers, police and military officers, tribal and community leaders, and recently captured or reconciled Taliban. I spent time with senior commanders of ISAF, representatives of the United Nations, commercial firms, aid agencies, and nongovernmental organizations (NGOs) working in rural Afghanistan. My team also conducted field activities with Regional Command East (based in Bagram) and South (in Kandahar). We worked with CN teams, intelligence and regional affairs officers, special operations forces, combat maneuver and aviation units in the field, and Provincial Reconstruction Teams (PRTs).

These assessments built on earlier work in Afghanistan, Pakistan's North-West Frontier Province (NWFP), and the Federally Administered Tribal Areas (FATA) during summer of 2006. This included field activities and discussions with U.S. and NATO commanders, GOA ministers and officials, ANA and ANP commanders, government of Pakistan (GOP) ministers and officials, Pakistan army, Frontier Constabulary, Police and Frontier Corps commanders and units, political agents and tribal elders in the FATA, elected political representatives, aid agencies, CN officials, and local journalists in NWFP. Taken together, the two activities provided opportunity for trend analysis and field verification of both intelligence and open-source media reporting. I hesitate, for methodological reasons discussed in previous chapters, to talk about objective "truth" in the field reporting of such complex and dangerous activities as guerrilla wars, but in bureaucratic shorthand, these were "ground truth" assignments designed to better inform decision-makers in coalition capitals.

All this fieldwork has led me to the view that the Afghan campaign is at a strategic crossroads, and may indeed be approaching a tipping point. In my view, the conflict remains winnable, but the overall trend is extremely negative and a concerted long-term effort is needed—lasting 5–10 years at least—if we are to have any chance of building a resilient Afghan state and civil society that can defeat the threat from a resurgent Taliban and an increasingly active sanctuary in Pakistan. The problem in Pakistan, as I shall show in a subsequent chapter, is even more complex and demanding, and it is probably not an overstatement to suggest that Pakistan is now, and will be for the foreseeable future, the epicenter of global *takfiri* terrorism, making Afghanistan a frontline state.

AFGHANISTAN IN 2008

Instability in Afghanistan is a far broader problem than insurgency. It also derives from the activity of globally focused terrorist organizations such as al Qa'ida, interference by neighbors, institutional weakness, a rapidly expanding narcotics trade, a weak economy, and a lack of confidence on the part of the Afghan people in their government and the international community. The essential strategic problem for Western intervention in Afghanistan is therefore less about directly defeating the Taliban and more about building an Afghan state that can handle the Taliban, among many other problems, without permanent large-scale international assistance. District and local level governance—building political legitimacy, delivering essential services, enacting the rule of law, improving economic conditions, and countering corruption and drugs—is the key contested space. Extending an effective, legitimate government presence into Afghanistan's 40,020 villages is the principal challenge, as government weakness, corruption, misrule and perceived lack of legitimacy at the village and district level allows militias, warlords, and criminals to reassert themselves.[12] Failure to deliver services, widespread corruption (Afghanistan was ranked 172 out of 180 in a July 2007 worldwide corruption survey),[13] poor coordination between central, provincial, and local authorities, abusive behavior by some local officials and lack of government presence creates space for nonstate armed groups and criminal networks.

One example suffices to illustrate this situation. By mid-2008, the Taliban were operating 13 guerrilla law courts throughout the southern part of Afghanistan—a shadow judiciary that expanded Taliban influence by settling disagreements, hearing civil and criminal matters, and using the provisions of Islamic shari'a law and their own Pashtun code to handle everything from land disputes to capital crimes. Local communities often cry out for external mediation in settling local disputes: along with security for person and property, dispute resolution is the public service that tribal and community leaders I have asked about this issue most ardently wish for. Meanwhile, the international community is training Supreme Court judges and seeking to build an Afghan legal system based on the post-2001 constitution, but local judges, prosecutors, and police are often known for their love of bribes, and locals see them as giving phony "justice" to whoever can pay most handsomely. The Taliban may be cruel—everyone acknowledges this—but they are seen as fair. Too often, local people who are asked "If you had a dispute with a neighbor, to whom would you turn to resolve it?" answer, if they are being honest: "The Taliban."[14]

As of mid-2008, the insurgency was increasing its geographic spread and level of violence. According to statistics released in March 2008,[15] insurgent-initiated violence in 2007 followed an almost identical seasonal pattern to that of 2006, but there was an overall increase of about 35 percent, with August and September 2007 the most violent months since 2001. According to UN assessments, the insurgency also spread into much of western Afghanistan, particularly Baghdis Province, and into interior provinces like Lowghar, Kapisa, and Wardak that used to see very little insurgent activity. In 2007, the insurgents suffered tactical defeats but made strategic progress. The failure to take Kandahar City, the failed "spring offensive," and increasing casualties all set them back tactically. ISAF disrupted Taliban operations in some provinces, and the enemy lost a record number of leaders, including the talented and influential Mullah Dadullah Lang in May.[16] But they expanded their control over the Afghan population, and actively contested more territory across the country—so these setbacks seem to have done little to halt the insurgency's spread.

I discuss counternarcotics (CN) operations in detail below, but in general it seems fairly certain that the drug trade is now consolidated into networks with significant political backing, aligned geographically with areas of heavy insurgent activity. Indeed, we are seeing an increasing congruence of interest between corrupt officials, narcotics traffickers, and insurgents, and a failure to address this problem has led to the emergence of a narco-state in at least some parts of Afghanistan. In the meantime, counterinsurgency operations (especially in the south, most notably in Helmand and Kandahar provinces) have effectively become CN operations, and vice versa.

UNDERSTANDING THE THREAT

Although often described using the aggregative shorthand term "Taliban," the insurgent coalition in Afghanistan is actually a fragmented series of shifting tactical alliances of convenience, especially in the East. Insurgents in the South are comparatively unified under the Taliban Quetta *shura*, the core leadership group of the old Taliban regime, now based, as a de facto government-in-exile, in Pakistan's Baluchistan Province, while in the East, extremist groups—such as Lashkar e Tayyiba (LeT), Hizb-i Islami Gulbuddin (HIG), and Tehreek-e-Nafaz-e-Shariat-e-Mohammadi (TNSM), as well as al Qa'ida, Tehrik e-Taliban Pakistan (the "Pakistani Taliban,") under leaders like Beitullah Mahsud, and the Haqqani network in Waziristan—are loosely cooperating toward roughly similar objectives. Paradoxically, their disunity makes them harder to counter—they have no central leadership that can be dealt with, co-opted, or eliminated.

How large is the Taliban movement? I estimate on the basis of field reporting and open-source data, and calculating total strength province by province, that as of mid-2008, between 32,000 and 40,000 insurgents were operating inside Afghanistan at any one time.[17] This includes 8,000–10,000 full-time fighters or "core" Taliban, or about 25 percent of the total, typically on the order of 200 to 450 full-time Taliban per province (though this varies widely across the country). The remaining 22,000 to 32,000 fighters are local, part-time guerrillas who, as I shall show, operate on a temporary, ad hoc basis. In addition, several thousand individuals operate in loose networks as part of to the clandestine village underground, and a sympathizer and supporter base exists in both Afghanistan and Pakistan. This total matches most Afghan estimates, but is substantially higher than that released officially by NATO, and is indeed higher even than the estimate made by Antonio Giustozzi as part of his comprehensive, excellent assessment of the Taliban calculating 17,000 core Taliban and 2,000 foreign fighters, in his 2008 book *Koran, Kalashnikov and Laptop*.[18] Nevertheless, I believe my calculation represents a reasonable best guess as of mid-2008, and I account for the difference between my figures and Giustozzi's on the basis of two factors: first, the insurgency has continued to grow substantially since the end of 2006, when Giustozzi completed compiling his figures, and second, my total includes Taliban-allied religious extremist movements as well as the recent spike in infiltration of Pakistani Taliban into Afghanistan, following a series of deals between the Pakistani government and tribal leaders in the FATA in late 2007 and 2008.

All but the full-time Taliban (and even potentially some of them) are reconcilable under some circumstances, in my view.[19] Perhaps 3,000–4,000 fighters, therefore, or about 10 percent of the total, are hard-core fanatics who are not reconcilable under any circumstances and thus have to be dealt with through police and military security measures. The remaining 90 percent, in my judgment and that of most Afghans I have asked, are actually or potentially co-optable, though any such attempt at cooption would have to be conducted from a position of strength lest insurgent leaders (or, more importantly, local communities) interpret this as a Taliban victory. The Afghan governor quoted in the epigraph to this chapter, who believes that 90 percent of so-called Taliban are potentially reconcilable,[20] shares this view, as did a recently surrendered Taliban leader who defected to the government side in early 2008 and whom I interviewed, along with 11 local and tribal elders from his district, in March 2008.[21]

The core Taliban movement, through much of 2006–2007, appeared to be applying a three-track strategy blending information operations (IO), guerrilla tactics, and asymmetric attacks (including terrorist-style bombings). The movement's key strength was its leaders' ability to integrate guerrilla warfare (insurgent attacks and guerrilla shadow government) with asymmetric attacks (suicide bombings and assassinations) to support an overall political strategy. During 2006–2007 they tended to switch from one form of activity to another in order to maintain political momentum. In this respect, the Taliban's key strength mirrored the Coalition's key weakness—the capacity to synchronize physical activity in support of a unified information strategy. (I discuss this in detail in the next section.)

It is a mistake to see the insurgency as primarily focused on over-throwing the Afghan state. This might be one objective, but the insurgents' actions indicate that it is probably not their primary aim. The overall Taliban movement, though relatively fractured, may end up controlling the Pashtun regions of both Pakistan and Afghanistan. For example, the insurgents ignored several opportunities to directly threaten Kabul and the central government in 2005–2006. Instead, they sought to control the Pashtun South and East, while simultaneously building control in Pashtun regions of Pakistan (primarily northern Baluchistan, the NWFP, and the Northern Areas). Similarly, in 2007–2008, although attacks were mounted closer to Kabul and in the city itself, they continued to push to the west and north of the country, as if aiming to encircle the cities through controlling rural areas and tribal allies.

The Taliban's relationship with local tribal allies is important in this pattern of conflict, and arises largely from opportunities created by the Afghan government. President Karzai, as a compromise candidate during the Emergency Loya Jirga after the fall of the Taliban, lacked a strong tribal support base and had only a modest personal following. Thus, according to the veteran Australian observer of Afghan affairs, William Maley, he showed "an inclination to pacify potential trouble-makers (in both Kabul and beyond) by offering them positions in the state, which naturally annoyed those who argued that disloyalty was attracting rewards and that Karzai had devalued competence as a criterion for advancement."[22] Maley points out that this pattern of installing former warlords, potential rivals and competitors in positions of authority, treating administrative authority as "political goods"[23] to be traded for loyalty, had sharply negative effects on government legitimacy:

> An insidious—although not widely publicized—consequence of all this has been that elite politics has been marked by ferocious rivalries, competition for the president's attention and favor, and denigration of

opponents as a way of reducing their influence. As a result, some very gifted Afghans have left government... Beyond Kabul, the results have been even more destructive. It cannot be said too often that awarding offices to undeserving figures at the provincial and local levels is a recipe for dramatically poor governance and the progressive erosion of the legitimacy of the state.[24]

There is a tribal aspect to this: President Karzai, as a member of a prominent family in the Popalzai tribe, has tended to appoint provincial governors who would be unlikely to threaten his influence by building strong tribal bases of their own. Thus, especially in the south, he appointed tribal outsiders or members of minority tribes as provincial governors, leaving the stronger majority tribes disenfranchised—a situation that was exacerbated by the failure to hold promised district-level elections. Provincial governors have also, at times, had an incentive to channel or divert state benefits (construction contracts, development assistance, security, goods) to their tribal or personal supporters, further alienating the majority tribes. This dynamic has been most noticeable in the flatter south of the country while, in the east, the mountainous terrain restricts settlement patterns so that tribes tend to be smaller in numbers and cover less ground. Because these smaller, fragmented tribes are more fractured, there was less risk of a rival developing a strong competitive power base in these areas, and so the central government tended to appoint local strongmen or members of majority tribes.

The Taliban exploited this, posing as defenders of the local tribes against misrule by unrepresentative appointed provincial and district governors, and seeking alliances with dispossessed and disenfranchised tribal power brokers. In the east these were minority tribes while in the south they were the majority. This difference in the insurgency's tribal base (small minority tribes in the east, larger more unified majority tribes in the south), may partly explain why the insurgency has been weaker and more fractured in the east and stronger and more cohesive in the south.

In areas where the local Afghan government representatives have shown themselves to be efficient, have governed with genuine care for the welfare of the people or represent majority tribes this Taliban approach has had limited success. But in areas where the local government is seen as illegitimate, oppressive, corrupt or weak, there has developed a governance vacuum at the local level that the Taliban have been able to exploit, while tribal leaders who have allied themselves to the Taliban have largely done so for reasons of self-interest and disillusionment with the government, not from any strong ideological commitment to the Taliban agenda.

Even without these tribal dynamics, this is in any case not a classical Maoist *protracted warfare* insurgency. A Maoist approach seeks victory through a *displacement strategy* of building what classical counterinsurgency theorists call "parallel hierarchies"—a competitive system of control tantamount to a guerrilla counter-state in permanently liberated areas—which then spread across the country and seek to defeat the government in, eventually, a relatively conventional war of maneuver. Rather, the Taliban appears to be applying an *exhaustion strategy* of sapping the energy, resources, and support of the Afghan government and its international partners, making the country ungovernable and hoping that the international community will eventually withdraw in exhaustion and leave the government to collapse under the weight of its own lack of effectiveness and legitimacy.

The Taliban, in other words, are highly unlikely to overthrow the government by force of arms. A much more likely failure mechanism might occur if northern ethnic groups—Uzbeks, Tajiks, Hazaras—should, in frustration at lack of progress, withdraw their support for the Pashtun-dominated Kabul government and take matters into their own hands in fighting the Pashtun Taliban. This would lead to an ethnic civil war with ISAF left holding, at best, an enclave around the capital and the Government of Afghanistan becoming an isolated and ineffective figurehead, as international support for it collapsed. Perhaps not coincidentally, this strategy aligns very well with the broader AQ global strategy discussed in earlier chapters.

All of this means that the Taliban is neither a purely internal Afghan problem nor solely a crossborder insurgency threatening Afghanistan from Pakistan. Rather, our enemy appears to be a confederated movement that blends insurgency with terrorism and information operations, and threatens both Afghanistan and Pakistan. Its ultimate achievement, if unchecked, may be the emergence of an Islamic emirate in "Greater Pashtunistan," along with the destabilization or even collapse of both the Afghan and Pakistani states. Given the presence of core AQ leaders and nuclear weapons in Pakistan, this makes the Taliban an extremely serious strategic threat to the international community and to our entire strategic position—a judgment that tends to suggest that we should give far greater priority to this theater than we have done to date.

Despite its importance as a terrorist safe haven, Pakistan is *a* problem, not *the* problem. The FATA is an active sanctuary, along with Quetta and parts of Pakistani Baluchistan. Reducing insurgent sanctuary in Pakistan is thus a key campaign objective. But the problem is not solely Pakistan. If this were so, we would tend to see shallow-depth, short-duration cross-border raiding by Pakistan-based insurgents. Instead, we see local guerrilla cells cooperating with mobile insurgent columns that draw supplies and recruits from Pakistan, but can operate for extended periods deep inside Afghanistan, drawing on local support. (I describe in detail below this "Taliban operating system," as I have called it, and expand on it in the Kunar Province case study that follows.) Thus, "fixing" Pakistan would help but not solve the Afghan problem. The key to the Afghan insurgency lies in Afghanistan, not Pakistan.

Unfortunately, the Taliban have consistently benefited from our tendency to underrate them. Today's enemy represents the third generation of Taliban that we have encountered (the first generation was the irregular "conventional force that operated in a linear fashion using light cavalry tactics,"[25] which we destroyed in 2001–2002; the second generation was the embryonic guerrilla force that emerged from the remnants of the first in the Pakistan safe haven in 2003–2004 and began raiding in earnest into Afghanistan in 2005). In contrast to previous generations, today's Taliban are an extremely proficient, well-organized, and well-equipped insurgent force. They combine cynical, experienced, hard-bitten leaders with extremely well-motivated, disciplined fighters and a new capacity for terrorist attacks.

But they have significant, exploitable weaknesses. Their Pashtun tribal base limits their appeal; the southern provinces of the Taliban heartland make up only about 12 percent of the Afghan population. In essence, the Taliban are masters at mobilizing and exploiting their ethnic and social base, but are not good at winning over the uncommitted, fence-sitting swing voters outside the Pashtun ethnic group—giving them a strongly Pashtun-specific, but therefore limited, appeal. Consolidating and broadening the GOA support base, provided due emphasis is given to instituting the rule of law, countering corruption and building administrative practices that meet the people's needs and make them feel safe, thus has a good prospect of ultimately marginalizing the Taliban or containing their influence. This is easy to say, but extremely hard to do.

ASSESSING THE TALIBAN AS A FIGHTING FORCE

On the basis of my field experience in 2005–2008 in Iraq, Southeast Asia, Afghanistan, and Pakistan, I assess the current generation of Taliban fighters, within the broader Taliban confederation (which loosely combines old Taliban cadres with Pashtun nationalists, tribal fighters and religious extremists), as the most tactically competent enemy we currently face in any theater. This judgment draws on four factors: organizational structure, motivation, combat skills, and equipment.

Taliban organizational structure varies between districts, but most show some variation of the generic pattern of a local clandestine network structure, a main force of full-time guerrillas who travel from valley to valley, and a part-time network of villagers who cooperate with the main force when it is in their area. In districts close to the Pakistan border, young men graduating from Pakistani *madrassas* also swarm across the frontier to join the main force when it engages in major combat—as happened during the September 2006 fighting in Kandahar Province, and again in the 2007 and 2008 fighting seasons. (I will describe the elements of this structure more fully in the Kunar case study.)[26]

These multifaceted motivations provide Taliban fighters with a strong but elastic discipline. Although opportunities may arise for us to "divide and conquer" elements of the enemy, in practice local ties tend to far outweigh government influence. Thus we need to induce local tribal and community leaders who have the respect and tribal loyalty of part-time elements to "wean" them away from loyalty to the main force Taliban. Appealing to the self-interest of local clandestine cell leaders may also help isolate them from the influence of senior Taliban leaders who are currently safe in Pakistan.

Clearly, the weakest motivational links within the Taliban confederation are those that are based on the accidental guerrilla syndrome (discussed in the previous chapter) and that draw local part-time fighters to fight alongside the main force when it is in their area. Local security measures such as neighborhood watch groups and auxiliary police units, creation of alternative organizations and life-pathways (including jobs and social networks) for young men, protection from Taliban intimidation, and alternative economic activities are potential approaches to detaching these individuals from main force influence. The main force itself is highly cohesive in most districts, and relatively invulnerable to direct penetration or infiltration. But, as I shall show, the habit of recruiting part-time local fighters to join the main force, including forced recruitment, might expose the main force to indirect infiltration.

In terms of combat skills, reporting from units in the field, as well as my participant observations, suggest extremely high competence in some areas, but some equally significant lapses in others. Key areas of skill include ambushing, use of improvised explosive devices (IEDs), sniping, field defenses, and reconnaissance. Weaknesses include a tendency to operate in a set routine, lack of communications security, poor indirect fire skills, dispersed tactical movement, and sloppiness in the security of crossborder infiltration.

Insurgent groups have mounted ambushes using up to several hundred fighters (as in Uruzgan on May 19, 2006, the example that began this chapter), including coordinated mortar, rocket and sniper fire to engage coalition troops in the killing area, and the use of L-shaped or T-shaped layouts to catch troops in crossfire. They have shown good fire discipline, marksmanship, and tactical control during these activities. Though in many cases they have suffered significant casualties, they have shown an aggressive spirit, and a marked willingness to accept severe losses in order to press home an attack.

Careful mine placement, good camouflage, employment of unexploded or modified ordnance, use of decoy and secondary devices, baited attacks (to draw first responders or military and police columns into a trap), and use of covering observation and sniper posts and ambushes are all features of insurgent IED technique, which has shown substantial improvement (especially in the South) over the past several years, including an extremely significant rise in the prevalence of Iraq-style suicide attacks using suicide car bombs, suicide vests or limpet mines. Although IED attacks are still less intensive than in Iraq before the surge, in most cases this is probably explained by lower population density and scarcity of military-grade ordnance, rather than lack of skill. In any case, since the success of the surge in reducing violence in Iraq in 2007–8, Afghanistan has overtaken Iraq as the main source of coalition casualties from IEDs.

Proficient use of snipers, operating in pairs and coordinating their activities by radio both among pairs and with maneuver forces, are a key feature of improved insurgent tactical proficiency since 2005. Camouflage, stalking, use of high-powered optics, and coordinated engagement are all signs of increasing professionalism by enemy snipers, who have graduated from the category of "marksmen" to become true sniper pairs in the professional military sense. This bespeaks at least some training by professionally qualified military snipers, or by foreign fighters (such as Chechens) with previous operational sniping experience. It also shows an emphasis on training and preparation that was absent from some of the ad hoc Taliban efforts of previous years.

The field defenses of Pashmul and Panjwai during Operation Medusa in 2006, in an area of fertile farmland, small fields, orchards, and hedgerows that the Soviets called the "green belt" and where they lost many casualties, showed intensive preparation and skill. Equally professional field defenses have been encountered in several subsequent operations. Good use of terrain, pre-registration of killing areas and firing points (a technique by which mortar and heavy weapons crews walk the ground before a battle and adjust their aim points for maximum effectiveness), and the use of bunkers, crawl trenches, tunnels, caches, and obstacle plans highlight this tactical proficiency. During the 2006 fighting, because a large number of fighters were inexperienced Pakistani *madrassa* graduates, dozens were killed every day by Coalition air power on the approaches to the battle. But once dug into their defensive zones, these fighters proved extremely difficult to extract.

Finally, in terms of strengths, the insurgents have shown great skill in scouting and intelligence collection, using local villagers and clandestine cadres for close target reconnaissance and conducting stand-off observation from dominating hills and by means of night and day movement in mountainous and vegetated areas (particularly in the eastern hills and the "green belt" in the Helmand and Arghandab river valleys). Some insurgents have also been very effective in using local informants and illegal vehicle checkpoints to gain and exploit information about the population.

Insurgent tactical weaknesses include the tendency to follow set routines. Because some senior leaders have been operating in the same areas for many years, and because the terrain limits maneuver options (as noted, most valleys have only one route in and out, for example), some insurgent groups have begun to set patterns and operate in a routine and repetitive fashion. This creates exploitable vulnerabilities. For instance, as mentioned earlier, local guerrillas typically wait for a Coalition convoy to enter a valley, and then seek to ambush it on its way back out at a series of "traditional" attack points. This tendency, also noted by observers of *mujahidin* operating against the Soviets[27] in the 1980s, appears to be widespread and could be exploited by working with local partners ahead of an operation to identify the traditional ambush sites in a given valley, and then sending a force into the valley, waiting until enemy fighters move into ambush sites, and engaging these positions with air and indirect fires. Similarly, despite some proficiency in the use of rockets and rocket propelled grenades (RPGs) in a semi-indirect fire mode, insurgent skills in mortar work seem relatively less developed than in other areas. In some districts (particularly those along the Pakistan border) their proficiency is better, but in general this is one area where they still have room to improve. Because mortar work is a fairly technical skill, future improvements in this area might signal a higher level of assistance from sponsors located in Pakistan.

There have been several recent instances of insurgents massing in large numbers (up to 250 fighters) in the open, often at night, only to be engaged by indirect fire or air power and suffer significant losses. Again, during the September 2006 fighting around Pashmul the insurgents lost hundreds of fighters who were moving openly in pickup trucks toward the scene of the fighting, while in autumn 2008 there were several coordinated large-scale attacks on British bases and population centers in Helmand province. Such engagements typically kill young, inexperienced guerrillas rather than older cadres who tend to hang back in the fighting, directing the fanatical young fighters while not exposing themselves to risk.

A final key weakness is in crossborder movement, where infiltrators have typically taken little trouble to disguise their movement or activity, in some cases infiltrating in broad daylight under the noses of Pakistan army checkpoints, or even with direct assistance from Pakistani Frontier Corps troops. If we could convince the Pakistani government to actually take action against infiltrators, we could exploit this lack of skill in crossborder movement so as to ambush infiltration parties or deny specific routes, channeling the enemy into locations where we could engage them using air and indirect fires without significant risk to the local civilian population.

Finally, insurgent equipment has improved substantially over time. By 2005 and 2006, small arms and RPGs being carried by the Taliban were generally of much better quality than ANA or ANP weapons, though government weapons have improved in quality since that time. Other insurgent weapons capabilities (especially rockets and IEDs) continue to improve in sophistication. Handheld radios, satellite phones, and cell phones have become common. Some infiltrators wear items of camouflage uniform, and some even have rudimentary badges of rank. Vehicles are of better standard than most ANP or GOA vehicles, and the supplying of food, water, and ammunition is very effective. But the Taliban still tends to travel more lightly, with far less reliance on the road network or logistic resupply, than the ANA/ANP or the Coalition, giving the enemy greater tactical mobility in rural parts of the country, especially where a measure of popular support exists for their agenda.

TALIBAN PROPAGANDA

The insurgents treat propaganda as their main effort, coordinating physical attacks in support of a sophisticated propaganda campaign. Given its importance, this aspect of the campaign is worth addressing in some detail.

Throughout much of 2005–2006, the enemy appeared to be succeeding in their information operations primarily because they made propaganda (including "armed propaganda"[28] and intimidation) their main effort, while coalition forces tended instead to treat information as a supporting activity and did not doctrinally recognize armed propaganda as a form of IO. According to officers of the National Directorate of Security (NDS)—the Afghan intelligence service, with whom I discussed this issue several times in 2006–2008[29]—the Taliban adopted a five-line information strategy, in the form of a series of slogans, in early 2006. These were "Our party, the Taliban"; "Our people and nation, the Pashtun"; "Our economy, the poppy"; "Our constitution, the Shari'a"; and "Our form of government, the emirate." These slogans provided a rudimentary political platform for insurgent activity and were used as a guide to structure messages to the population and manipulate public perception of the movement. Insurgent leaders organized their physical operations efforts around these simple but effective propaganda concepts.

The key strength of this approach is that it provides a series of unifying "rallying calls" that appeal to a broad base of popular support by speaking to a wide range of aspirations and discontents—Pashtun nationalism, religious conservatism, the desire of narcotics traffickers to be left alone to pursue their activities, impatience with foreign occupation. Each slogan is also vague enough that it can be interpreted in numerous ways by different components of the population, and can serve as a tool to create a united front among groups that are not natural allies (for example, religious radicals and traditional tribal elders, who are traditional rivals for tribal loyalty).

A key weakness is the close linking of this Taliban agenda to poppy cultivation and, by extension, narcotics trafficking. Only a very small proportion of the Afghan population (about 11 percent according to 2006 polling data)[30] consider poppy cultivation legitimate under all circumstances. The majority consider it either totally unacceptable or acceptable only if those involved have no other way to make a living. By tying themselves to the poppy economy, the Taliban thus open themselves to two possible lines of attack. First, as some insurgent leaders (and, in some cases, local narcotics figures posing as Taliban) have pressured local people to grow poppy, there has been an implied contract—"we can protect your poppy." The government or coalition could thus use increased eradication or interdiction to discredit local Taliban and undermine popular confidence in them. Second, the Taliban's current support of the poppy economy is inconsistent with their previous antiopium stance when in power. That stance was actually driven by a desire to drive up prices on the world market and exploit their large stock-on-hand of opium paste, though their public stance was based on the un-Islamic nature of drug cultivation. Their new attitude thus undermines their claim to Islamic rectitude.

Regarding propaganda, the Taliban have shown skill in using word of mouth and rumor, and in "pitching" local officials using a combination of coercion and persuasion. These skills equate to what was classically known as "armed propaganda." One good example of Taliban armed propaganda is the use of "night letters" (shabnamah).[31] Taliban leaders have pressured local farmers in several provinces (Helmand, Uruzgan, Kandahar, and elsewhere) to grow poppy instead of regular crops, using night-time threats and intimidation to punish those who resist and to convince waverers to convert. They also use object lessons, making examples of people who do not cooperate. For example, dozens of provincial-level officials were assassinated in 2005–2006, again as an "armed propaganda" tool—not just because the enemy wanted to target individual officials but also because they wanted to send every local official the message "We can reach out and touch you if you cross us." Field reporting from the eastern provinces in 2008 suggested a similar approach of intimidation through assassination of government representatives.[32] This is classic armed propaganda.

In essence, effective counterinsurgency is a matter of good governance, backed by solid population security and economic development measures, resting on a firm foundation of energetic IO, which unifies and drives all other activity. Security, political (governance and institution-building), and economic measures are built in parallel to gain control over the environment. The government must de-energize the insurgency and break its hold on the population, rather than seeking solely to kill insurgents. Fighting will be necessary, and cannot be avoided: counterinsurgency is not peacekeeping, and there is no known method of conducting it without using armed force to kill or capture insurgents. But as the classical counterinsurgency theorist Bernard B. Fall pointed out, a government that is losing to an insurgency is not being outfought, it is being outgoverned.[33]

Counterinsurgency expertise is somewhat lacking in the Afghan government. This may be counterintuitive, since Afghanistan after all has experienced more or less continuous insurgent warfare since the 1970s. But most Afghan army, police, and civil administration officials are either relatively newly recruited or are old hands with experience as insurgents (*mujahidin* against the Soviets) or in the civil war after 1992. Neither of these experiential backgrounds is a sound basis for counterinsurgency operations.

In my experience, insurgents generally do not make good counterinsurgents without extensive retraining, since the task of the insurgent is to attack an easily identified but much more powerful enemy, and then fade into the background to avoid retaliation. Conversely, the counterinsurgent's hardest problem is to find the enemy among the population: destroying him once found is easier by far than finding him in the first place.[34] This arises from the fundamental asymmetry of insurgency, in which the government is strong but visible and the insurgent weak but hard to find. The insurgent wins by avoiding defeat, creating disorder, maintaining a force-in-being that challenges the government's monopoly of authority, and preventing the population from cooperating with the government. Conversely, the counterinsurgent's fundamental task is to secure and control the population, as a means to marginalize and ultimately destroy the insurgency. This involves countering an enemy who is weaker but much harder to find, and creating order and good governance in order to control the environment.[35]

Similarly, commanders who grew up fighting in an anarchic civil war sought to co-opt the local population in their area and counter their opponents' military and political moves, rather than to create order and build functioning government institutions, perpetuate human security, and seek the consent of the governed at the national level (as distinct from within their own partisan groups). Thus, many of the governance and administrative skills fundamental to counterinsurgency are lacking in these commanders' backgrounds.

In the case of the ANA, this tendency is compounded by the fact that the Afghan operation was originally conceived as a reconstruction mission rather than a counterinsurgency campaign. Hence, many of the ANA battalions and commanders recruited since 2002 received little or no initial training in counterinsurgency, and essentially picked up their skills on the job—in some cases, learning wrong lessons. Coalition instructors at the Kabul Military Training Center (KMTC) in 2006 were not specifically trained in counterinsurgency, until mid-2007 there was no counterinsurgency course or doctrine for the ANA, and advanced counterinsurgency skills were restricted to special units or locally recruited groups. The overall base level of competence in counterinsurgency skills across the force is therefore relatively low, though it has improved rapidly in recent years.

The ANP are even worse off, with no courses in counterinsurgency, no formal counterinsurgency doctrine, and few trained personnel with counterinsurgency skills. Counterinsurgency policing is substantially different from policing in a peacetime environment. The three key components required for effective police work in a counterinsurgency environment are community police officers, who act to secure and protect population centers and deliver basic public order and rule of law; field police (paramilitary organizations sometimes called constabulary or gendarmerie units), who conduct normal police duties but in a higher-threat environment and typically are better armed and more mobile than community police; and a police intelligence or police special operations capability (sometimes called a "special branch") that specifically targets and arrests insurgent underground cells. An additional element sometimes required is local police auxiliary forces, consisting of "home guard" or "neighborhood watch" groups whose members are enrolled as special constables or sheriff's deputies and conduct local protective work under the control of the community police service. None of these components was originally put in place in the ANP, which was created following the Bonn Conference under German oversight, but eventually taken over by the United States military in 2006. The establishment of the Afghan National Civil Order Police (ANCOP) in mid-2006, following poor performance by the regular police during riots in Kabul and Jalalabad, created the beginnings of a field police capability. As noted, according to local community leaders I interviewed during my fieldwork, some ANP officers have the reputation of being corrupt and unprofessional, though there are notable exceptions. In some cases, particularly during the early period, individuals with criminal or insurgent links who failed the necessary background checks to enter the ANA joined the ANP instead, and the level of equipment is extremely poor. There is no police special operations capability or special branch, but this is not necessarily a bad thing: experience (including in Iraq) has shown that attempting to create such a capability before a robust community and field police capability is in place can result in "death squads" or "secret police" activity, which (besides being morally repugnant) is fundamentally counterproductive in this environment. Rather, police intelligence analysts are a good first step, and the police intelligence capability should grow naturally to include informant networks, undercover police officers, and joint police-military intelligence centers. Effective police work, however, is of little use without judiciary and detainee systems, which are also embryonic at this point, especially at the village and district level. And, as noted, we have tended to employ the police on counterinsurgency tasks to the exclusion of local law-and-order and rule of law activities, creating a governance vacuum at the district level, which the Taliban have filled.

Afghan civilian officials currently receive no training in counterinsurgency and, apart from whatever understanding they pick up on the job, have little counterinsurgency expertise. This is relatively easy to remedy, since good governance is the key civilian task in counterinsurgency. But civilian officials also need an understanding of the use of military force and police forces in support of the civilian authority, and in the application of population control measures and economic controls within the framework of the rule of law. The other key requirement is for anticorruption measures, which reduce the population's perception that it is being exploited by corrupt government officials. A course in what we might call basic "opposed governance," including an understanding of the proper employment of military and civilian security forces in a counterinsurgency environment, would substantially remedy this.

COUNTERNARCOTICS IN THE CONTEXT

OF THE AFGHAN INSURGENCY

When the international community designed an Afghan CN strategy in 2002 and the United Kingdom was given the lead in executing it, the Afghan campaign was considered primarily a reconstruction and nation-building problem. This is no longer the case: as noted, resurgent Taliban activity over the past several years now presents a significant threat to GOA control of the Pashtun south and east of the country. Thus, CN efforts need to be understood in the context of counterinsurgency efforts, not in a stand-alone fashion. It does not matter how good CN efforts are, if we fail to defeat the insurgency: there will be no Afghan state or civil society to benefit from CN programs unless the counterinsurgency succeeds. Conversely, however, given the increasing emergence of a narco-insurgency in the South, addressing narcotics is critical to counter corruption and build a state that can defeat insurgents while governing its people in a way that meets their needs.

In this context, the often-quoted problem is that eradication of poppy crops and other CN measures tend to alienate the rural population, increasing support for the Taliban and thus strengthening the insurgency.[36] This is a commonly held perception and may partly explain the reluctance some nations have shown to engage fully in CN programs; they may believe that such efforts will only make the counterinsurgency effort harder by alienating the bulk of the population, thus putting their deployed forces at greater risk. (To be frank, this was also my view before deploying to Afghanistan and observing the situation in more detail.)

But the facts do not support this view. According to UN Office on Drugs and Crime (UNODC) figures, only about 12.7 percent of the Afghan population was engaged in poppy cultivation in 2006.[37] Since that time, while the proportion of Afghans involved in narcotics has grown, areas of major narcotics activity have increasingly become geographically aligned with areas of Taliban influence. Thus, even the harshest efforts to eradicate the poppy would be highly unlikely to alienate anything like the majority of the population, except in areas that already firmly support the Taliban and are therefore already alienated anyway. Similarly, by far the largest areas of cultivation in 2006 were Helmand and Badakshan provinces. Together, these provinces accounted for 49.9 percent of poppy cultivation (82,290 hectares out of a total cultivation of 165,000 hectares in 2006) but only 5.6 percent of the Afghan population (1.7 million out of a total population of 31 million). The largest pockets of cultivation—in rural northern Helmand Province—are thus in the least populated areas of Afghanistan, so that increased CN efforts would directly affect only a small minority of Afghans.[38]

As Antonio Giustozzi rightly points out, the size and importance of narcotics in funding the insurgency remains a matter of controversy.[39] Nevertheless, qualitative judgments by intelligence and finance officials I interviewed in 2006 suggested that poppy cultivation may account for just under 50 percent of Taliban funding, with another approximately 25 percent deriving from extortion and protection racketeering associated with narcotics smuggling.[40] This would make the drug trade a secondary but important revenue source for the insurgents. These figures, though imprecise, suggest that reducing poppy cultivation would at least partly reduce the funds available to the insurgents. Better CN efforts might also substantially reduce corruption, by reducing the corrupt incentives represented in the enormous amounts of illicit money currently flowing around the Afghan government system. Aid agency officials with whom I spoke estimated the value of the narcotics trade at around $4 billion in 2008, of which about $800 million goes to the farmers who grow the poppy.[41] This leaves about $3.2 billion for middlemen and traffickers, an enormous amount of money in any society and with even more value in Afghanistan, since government salaries are very low and unemployment is extremely high. Officials pointed out: "3.2 billion dollars buys you a lot of provincial and district governors, police chiefs, and other officials."[42] The corruption fueled by this opium bonanza hampers all efforts at reconstruction and counterinsurgency in Afghanistan, so improved CN would have a knock-on effect of reducing corruption, which would in turn help the counterinsurgency campaign.

Some people my team spoke to in 2006 suggested to us that purchasing the poppy crop would be one way of reducing drug cultivation without alienating the population. The same approach has been suggested by the Senlis Council, an NGO that has argued for the legalization of opium cultivation in Afghanistan.[43] After examining this proposal in detail and discussing it with local Afghan and coalition officials on the ground, I believe that the money paid to farmers would still find its way (through landowners and creditors, extortion and intimidation) to the Taliban, thus this approach would probably be ineffective, on balance, in a counterinsurgency sense. The Taliban would still get their poppy funding, but from us. Moreover, creating a government market for narcotics would potentially result in an increase, rather than a decrease, in poppy production; giving the population an incentive to grow opium for government purchase would not reduce the overall acreage under poppy. In any case, since the value of the crop as paid to farmers is currently about $800 million, purchasing the crop every year would be an extremely expensive proposition, potentially unsustainable over the long term.

Nonetheless, by linking themselves so closely to opium, the Taliban have created a vulnerability we can exploit. As noted, the Taliban have tied themselves to the poppy, by means of both propaganda and intimidation of farmers; yet only a minority of Afghans consider poppy cultivation acceptable.[44] This suggests that potential public support for CN could be substantial—if handled correctly, that is, with due attention to alternative livelihoods and support to ensure the continued economic wellbeing of the affected population.

Reports from the U.S. Government Accountability Office indicate that lack of security in key parts of Afghanistan severely hampers CN efforts.[45] This is another way of saying that CN must be conducted as part of an overall counterinsurgency campaign, not as a stand-alone activity. This in turn suggests that the international community should focus CN efforts on key insurgent regions and conduct them as part of a comprehensive counterinsurgency campaign—with supporting IO, short-term "surge" security operations to support eradication efforts, and long-term security and development assistance to support and protect alternative livelihoods. We should perhaps adopt an "oil-spot" approach: working district-to-district on CN as part of a comprehensive counterinsurgency effort that integrates it, instead of treating as an activity outside the mainstream counterinsurgency campaign.

Conversely, improving counterinsurgency is among the most effective CN measures we can take, particularly in Helmand Province. Here, as in several other provinces, areas of poppy cultivation are extremely closely aligned with areas of Taliban presence; the poppy-growing population tends to be located in enemy-controlled areas. Clearly, for these people, concepts such as alternative livelihoods, education, and information are entirely academic unless and until some form of effective government presence and control is established and the enemy is driven off. This would first require a security presence of Coalition and Afghan military and police units. As one provincial governor from the South put it to me in March 2008, "you have enough troops to secure the province. You really do. All you have to do is to get out among the people, off the FOB [Forward Operating Base]."[46] In the absence of a forward-deployed presence—of troops working in partnership with local communities to protect them from insurgent influence and ensure government officials treat them decently—increased eradication efforts will simply punish the friendly population in government-controlled areas by removing their poppy crops while leaving untouched those belonging to corrupt government officials, or people who live in Taliban-controlled areas. (Indeed, unfairness and lack of consistency has been one key criticism of eradication efforts to date.)[47] In this sense, much as improved CN efforts can help the counterinsurgency fight, improved counterinsurgency performance is potentially a very effective CN tool. More broadly, the current close geographical alignment between areas of insurgent activity and areas of poppy cultivation tends to render the distinction between CN and counterinsurgency somewhat moot, as in a very real sense the two efforts are now the same fight.

DEVELOPMENT ASSISTANCE, PRESENCE OPERATIONS AND POPULAR SUPPORT

Because the Afghan campaign was originally conceived as a reconstruction rather than a counterinsurgency effort, some countries initially adopted a "pure" development approach, treating governance and economic assistance as politically impartial, needs-based activities. Such an approach is appropriate for NGOs and for official aid agencies operating in an unopposed environment, but less suitable for official development agencies in a counterinsurgency—government aid agencies under these circumstances are not impartial actors but are representatives of one side (the government) in an armed conflict. They are certainly not regarded by the population as impartial,[48] and should not pretend to be. Counterinsurgency theory, as well as field observation,[49] suggests that a minority of the population will support the government come what may, and another minority will back the Taliban under any circumstances, but the majority of Afghans simply want security, peace, and prosperity and will swing to support the side that appears most likely to prevail and to meet these needs, and that most closely aligns with their primary group identity.[50]

It is extremely important, in analyzing an insurgency, to be able to put oneself in the shoes of local community leaders. In insurgencies and other forms of civil war, community leaders and tribal elders find themselves in a situation of terrifying uncertainty, with multiple armed actors—insurgents, militias, warlords, the police and military, terrorist cells—competing for their loyalty and threatening them with violence unless they comply. They tend to seek what we might call "survival through certainty," attempting to identify consistent rules they can follow in order to keep their people safe. If these rules, or an actor capable of enforcing them, are not consistently present, then they tend to swing to the side of whichever force is present at any given moment.[51] Thus, the natural tendency of the Afghan population is to triangulate between the government and the Taliban—phenomena known in civil war literature as *attentisme*, free riding, or simply "fence-sitting"[52] Unfettered development assistance allows local communities to do this: but since a fundamental element in counterinsurgency is gaining political control over a disputed population and denying that control to the enemy, counterinsurgency measures (including official development assistance) must be designed to help the population to choose between the government and the insurgent, and to enforce that choice once made. This also implies the paramount moral obligation to protect and defend populations that have made the dangerous choice to side with the government: thus the symbiosis between politics, governance and security in insurgency warfare.

Governance and development, tied to a security and information strategy that gives the population incentives to support the government, are thus extremely powerful counterinsurgency tools we cannot afford to neglect. Orienting aid agencies (including those of NATO countries) to this aspect of the problem has been difficult in Afghanistan, as many began the campaign under different circumstances and have institutional cultures that, rightly under normal circumstances, value impartiality and eschew political conditionality. There is also a belief, unfounded in reality, that development assistance generates gratitude, or "hope," in the population and thereby of itself encourages them to support the government. Field experience in both Afghanistan and Iraq, however, has shown that insurgent intimidation easily overcomes any residual gratitude effect,[53] while historical studies[54] have shown that in civil wars and insurgencies, popular support tends to accrue to locally powerful actors rather than to those actors the population sees as more congenial: the more organized, locally present, and better armed a group is, the more likely it is to be able to enforce a consistent system of rules and sanctions, giving the population the order and predictability it craves in the deeply threatening, uncertain environment of insurgency. As Stathis Kalyvas puts it:

> as the conflict matures, control is increasingly likely to shape collaboration [with the principal locally present armed actor] because political actors who enjoy substantial territorial control can protect civilians who live in that territory—both from their rivals and from themselves— giving survival-oriented civilians a strong incentive to collaborate with them, irrespective of their true or initial preferences. In this sense, *collaboration is largely endogenous to control* though, of course, high rates of collaboration spawned by control at a given point in time are likely to reinforce it in the future.... In the long run, military resources generally trump prewar political and social support in spawning control.[55]

It is important to remember, however, that population groups in a traditional society exercise choices collectively, not individually—unlike Western societies, which tend to be relatively atomized and in which individuals exercise a relatively greater degree of personal choice independent of their social groups. In traditional societies, choices tend to reflect group consensus based on what military sociologists and anthropologists call "primary group cohesion."[56] This tendency is even more pronounced in tribal societies under the stress of insurgency, when an individual decision to go against the group consensus could prove fatal. In helping the Afghan population choose to support the government rather than the insurgents, we have a natural tendency to focus on incentives to the individual, hoping that individual Afghans will perceive their interests as best served by supporting the government. This is evident in several of our development and governance extension programs, and in the Alternative Livelihoods Program. This is fine as far as it goes, but we must also recognize that in a tribal, traditional society, choices are made collectively (by family, section, clan, tribal, or village units), not by single individuals. If we focus on winning over key traditional leaders, we can win the support of an entire village or lineage group at one time, rather than piecemeal. As noted above, the enemy has followed this approach very effectively in some areas, forging alliances with disaffected tribes and posing as defenders of the population against misrule. Similarly, Coalition forces have tended to experience greater success in parts of Afghanistan where we have done the same (as my Kunar case study here demonstrates).

Synchronizing community engagement with maneuver and development assistance is fundamental. As Lieutenant General Karl Eikenberry, the insightful commander of Combined Forces Command Afghanistan pointed out to me in late 2006, in conventional maneuver no commander will commit forces to a combat operation without first shaping the conditions for the engagement (using intelligence, fires, or supporting maneuver). Similarly, once the initial phase is completed, any competent commander will have an "exploitation" force cued to capitalize immediately on initial success and prevent enemy counterattack. However, some commanders in counterinsurgency neglect these fundamentals of operational art. The equivalent of "shaping maneuver" in counterinsurgency is engagement with local community leaders, seeking their commitment to support one's activity, and establishing measures to hold them to this commitment. Occasional security breaches are an inevitable cost of doing business, but can generally be avoided through appropriate deception measures (attempting to divert enemy attention from proposed operations) and tactical psychological operations (influencing tribes and local enemy groups), just as in conventional combat. In this context, influential local tribal leaders and village chiefs—regardless of whether they formally support the government—are the key. The equivalent of "exploitation" in counterinsurgency is rapid follow-up with humanitarian and economic assistance, and rapid establishment of long-term security measures to protect the population and confirm them in their decision to support the government. Any combat operation in counterinsurgency must therefore be preceded by community engagement and focused IO, and followed by rapid targeted development assistance and permanent population security measures. Failure to correctly synchronize these activities equates to poor maneuver, however well combat forces conduct actual engagements. I observed several excellent examples of the proper approach being applied by both conventional and Special Forces units in both eastern and southern Afghanistan in 2006, including extremely close participation by provincial and local leaders in planning and conduct of operations.[57]

An example is Operation Al Hasn, conducted during November 2006 in the Tagab valley, east of Bagram. My team and I had the opportunity to observe and participate in the planning for this operation, which represented best practice in engagement with local communities, focused IO, and cooperation with local and provincial GOA officials. Although this was a Special Forces operation, we observed several instances of conventional units (notably Task Force Spartan in the East and U.S. elements of Task Force Aegis in the South) adopting very similar approaches with good effect. The key features of this operation were the extremely close involvement from the outset of Abdur Sattar Murad, the governor of Kapisa Province, and his staff (including ANA, ANP, NDS, and civilian provincial government officials) in planning the operation; vetting and approval of all targets by responsible GOA officials ahead of time; and the forward deployment of Murad and his staff to the tactical operations center to control the operation from the third day. The operation used IO (based on local radio stations, with Governor Murad as the central player) to generate popular support, while ANA, ANP, and Coalition units operated together to create a two-week "surge" in their presence, which enabled them to dominate the environment, expel enemy forces, and marginalize local guerrilla cadres. The ANA and ANP forces then garrisoned secured areas, creating a permanent presence once the "surge" operations began to wind down. Hallmarks of this operation were close cooperation with allied special operations forces, prepurchase, prepositioning, and rapid distribution of humanitarian and civilian assistance using emergency funds (from the Commander's Emergency Response Program; CERP), and rapid exploitation, using development and governance activities. This approach capitalized on maneuver successes, and involved very close cooperation with the local PRT.

This approach represents best practice, and as the Kunar case study will show, this type of approach has been relatively successful in eastern Afghanistan, and has simultaneously confirmed the existence in Afghanistan of the same dynamics we have identified in other theaters, namely those of local alliances, accidental guerrillas, and global terrorist groups.

Case Study: Road building in Kunar Province

In spring 2008, I spent some time out on the ground with coalition and Afghan units in eastern and southern Afghanistan, and spent a short time with a PRT and its associated Brigade Combat Team in the Kunar River valley. Since my last visit, in 2006, this area has seen a significant improvement in security, despite ongoing fighting in some parts of the province (notably the Korengal and Watapur areas) and against the background of a generally downward trend in security across the country as a whole. The fact that Kunar has bucked the general trend seems largely to be the result of a consistent U.S. strategy of partnering with local communities to separate the insurgents from the people, bring tangible benefits of governance and development to the population, and help the population choose their own local leaders through elections. Road building has been a key part of this effort.

What has made this program successful is not the road per se, nor does this case study suggest that the *presence of the road* is solely responsible for improvements in security, since it is obvious to anyone that a road, as an engineering project, can have both positive and negative effects. Rather, this project seems to be succeeding because people have used the *process of the road's construction*, especially the close engagement with district and tribal leaders this entails, as a framework around which to organize a full-spectrum strategy—an approach I call "political maneuver"—to separate insurgents from the people, win local allies, connect the population to the government, build local governance capacity, modify and improve government behavior, swing tribes that had supported the insurgency onto the government side, and thereby generate progress across the four principal dimensions of counterinsurgency (security, governance, development, and information). The road itself matters less than the construction process, which helps focus and organize a broader security strategy.

SETTING THE SCENE

On a small-scale map,[58] Kunar Province looks like a wedge-shaped block, lying on its right-hand side along the Afghan-Pakistan border northeast of Jalalabad, with the province of Nangarhar lying to its south, and to the east, across the Durand Line, lying the Mohmand and Bajaur agencies (administrative divisions) of the FATA and the districts of Chitral, Swat, and Dir (a rumored location for Usama bin Laden), in the Malakand Division of Pakistan's NWFP. But to conceive of Kunar Province as a solid block of undifferentiated territory and regularly administered population would be entirely mistaken.

Topographically, Kunar is not a block but a tree, its trunk running from southwest to northeast along the Kunar River valley on the province's eastern edge, anchored by the towns of Jalalabad (capital of Nangarhar Province) to the southwest, Asadabad (the Kunar provincial capital) in the center, and the large village of Asmar (in Bar Kunar District) in the northeast. The branches of the tree are tributary valleys of the Kunar; they run west into Afghanistan and east to Pakistan, each dividing into smaller branches in a twig-like capillary drainage system. The Kunar River, about 480 kilometers long, rises in Pakistan (where it is called the Chitral) and flows south into the Kabul River just east of Jalalabad. It is a perennial, shallow braided stream system, not navigable except by small boats, and—until recently—rarely and poorly bridged outside major towns, with a rocky stream-bed and high gravel banks, fed by snow-melt from the ranges (the Hindu Kush to the west, Hindu Raj to the east). Tributary creeks and streams are intermittent; some flow in the spring and early summer, while others are dry *wadis* that only experience occasional flash flooding during storms or the spring thaw. Although there are some glaciated landforms in Kunar, in general the valleys are V-shaped, with steep, bare, craggy mountains sloping down to narrow basins dominated by the rivers and their flood plains (less than 500 meters wide in most places, much narrower in others). The province is rich in natural resources, especially timber, in which there has long been a lively crossborder smuggling racket, prompting a recent moratorium on timber movement by the provincial governor, Fazlullah Wahidi. I saw several overstocked lumber yards in March 2008.

In its human geography the province is also tree-like; its population is clustered in villages on the valley floors and along the tributaries of the river system, like leaves on branches. Most villages and all towns are in valleys, while the mountainous interstices between the valleys are barren and largely unpopulated. The total population, last estimated in 2006, is approximately 390,000[59] across the province's 15 districts.

Since almost all these people live in villages along the valley floor, and securing the province means securing them where they live, operations tend to focus on securing valleys, not hills. And because each valley feeds into the next, parts of the population are isolated from the rest, and movement from a minor capillary valley to the main Kunar valley, or further to Jalalabad or Kabul, requires passing through multiple terrain compartments and chokepoints. (Areas like the Korengal or Watapur districts, for example, have traditionally been very isolated because of this: their populations have a general clannishness and suspicion of outsiders as a result and, at least in the Korengal, the population has long been vulnerable to religious indoctrination by extremists, sometimes described by outsiders as Wahhabi in orientation.)[60] Thus, securing routes is also critical. Holding the valleys and routes is not the whole security problem, though: critical

Figure 2.1 Afghanistan, March 2008—Fortified houses in the Kunar province. Note the watchtowers and firing positions.
Photo: David Kilcullen

points in the hills also have to be held because they dominate routes and allow observation and fire onto populated areas; it is a tenet of mountain warfare on the frontier that whoever holds the high ground at dawn has the upper hand.[61] But mountain picquets and outposts are supporting activities for the main security effort, which is to create a protective "bubble" around each population center and then link each bubble to the next with measures that hold and protect the valleys and the routes along them (traditionally unimproved dirt tracks, more recently paved roads).

In counterinsurgency the population is the prize, and protecting and controlling it is the key activity. The war, therefore, is where the people are: you win or lose it a village at a time, and you secure villages and gain access to the people by controlling valleys, roads, and the heights that overlook them, in that order of priority.

Politically, also, the province is a tree not a block, with political power centering in the major towns, and state influence attenuating sharply with distance from the main valleys and their population centers. Changing the metaphor, we might consider towns and their associated valley-based infrastructure as magnets that draw in population, information, resources, and also predators, with a field of attraction and influence that weakens with distance. This has always been so, and indeed the state has never been particularly influential in this part of the country. As my colleague Chris Mason has argued, most Afghans have historically had little interaction with the central state, and they like it that way.[62] Recent World Bank governance assessments support this view,[63] as do detailed analyses spanning many years by the highly respected Afghanistan analysts Thomas Johnson[64] and Barnett Rubin.[65]

ETHNOGRAPHY OF KUNAR PASHTUNS

Apart from Naray District in the far northeast of the province, which borders Nuristan and is peopled principally by people of Nuristani origin, the rest of Kunar (approximately 95 percent of its population) is Pashtun. The principal tribes are the Pashai, of Bar Kunar and Dangam districts in the east; the Safi, who dominate the center and west of the province in Asadabad, Marawara, Narang, Darya-e Pech, Chawkay, and Chapa Dara districts; the Mohmand, a major crossborder tribe dominant east of the Kunar River; the Ghilzai of Nurgal and Sirkanay districts, and the Khugiyani (a Ghilzai subtribe) of Khas Kunar District. Most of these tribes speak eastern Iranian dialects, including the Tarkanri of central and eastern Kunar, whose tribal territory extends into Bajaur across the Durand Line (an area discussed in detail in Chapter 4) and includes important border-crossing subtribes of the Mohmand, Salarzai, Zamani Khel, and Shinwari lineages.

Like other societies in the Pashtun culture area, Kunar's social structure is based on what anthropologists call a "segmentary kinship system," with tribes divided into subtribes, clans, sections (usually inhabiting one or sometimes several villages), and subsections (extended families) based on lineage segments that are defined by descent from a common apical male ancestor. Balanced opposition between lineage segments of approximately equal size (as the anthropologist Philip Carl Salzman has described for Arab and Baluch tribes),[66] in which each group member must side with the closer against the more distant relative, and with locals against outsiders, defines and enacts the social order. This balanced opposition is often expressed through agnatic rivalry—competition between male relatives within and among family groups.[67] As Salzman emphasizes, cultural norms of collective responsibility and generalized reciprocity promote clan and group cohesion: each tribal member is collectively responsible for the actions of every other, and each kinship group supports other groups in the expectation that the tribe in turn will support it when it needs assistance. In the Pashtun case, cultural institutions such as revenge, feud, hospitality, honor toward enemies, and highly restrictive protectiveness of women are prevalent, though tribal institutions have been eroded through Soviet occupation, civil war, population displacement, economic collapse, the rise of the Taliban, and the current conflict. Akbar Ahmed, the famous anthropologist, diplomat, and former political agent of Waziristan, described the key institutions of Pashtun ideal-type behavior (known as Pashtunwali, "acting like a true Pashtun") as courage (*tora*), revenge (*badal*), hospitality (*melmastia*), generosity to a defeated enemy (*nanawati*), and heeding the voice of the *jirga*, the tribal assembly. He also considers *tarboorwali* (cousin or agnatic rivalry) and *tor* (literally "black," the protection of women's honor, a concept roughly equivalent to that of *'ird* in Arab society) as key additional institutions.[68]

Ahmed divides Pashtuns (all of whom are in some sense tribal, in that they self-identify within the world's largest segmentary lineage system) into two categories: *nang* Pashtuns (those driven by *nang*, honor), who typically live in low-production zones, mountains, and areas distant from the reach of the state and tend to be warlike and predatory, and *qalang* Pashtuns (those who pay *qalang* or *kandar*, taxes or rent), who typically live in richer, fertile irrigated lowland areas under greater control of the state. Like mountain peoples everywhere in the world, *nang* Pashtuns look down on lowlanders and have traditionally regarded them as fair game for raiding and pillaging. In Ahmed's framework, remoter tribes are *nang* Pashtuns; lowland people in the main Kunar valleys might be considered *qalangi*. Except for the *kuchi* (nomadic Pashtuns, of whom there are virtually none in Kunar)[69] all Pashtun tribes—even the most honor-driven, remote *khel* outside government control—tend to make their livelihood as sedentary agriculturalists (crop-growing house-dwellers tied to their villages and fields) rather than nomadic pastoralists (mobile tent-dwellers who live by their flocks). This means that the traditional recourse of lowland or desert nomadic tribes when threatened by the encroachment of enemies or state authorities on their independence—to escape into inhospitable terrain where adversaries cannot follow—is not open to hill-tribes, tied as they are to households, fixed landholdings, and immobile crops.

Thus when threatened they tend to stay and fight, banding together to resist intrusion and reestablish their independence from external control (a hallmark characteristic of tribes as distinct from peasants) through violent resistance rather than withdrawal: desert tribes run, mountain tribes fight. This cultural ecology perspective, though somewhat simplistic and perhaps subject to charges of environmental determinism, may at least partly account for the extremely warlike nature of Pashtun tribes, as well as for their tendency to fragment (or "fission") into feuding subgroups when the unifying "fusion effect" of an external threat is withdrawn. One coalition commander who worked in the Kunar area in 2006–2007 made the following observation:

I always thought it was a better sign when the locals were getting after each other rather than getting after us. This didn't, in our minds, mean the beginning of civil war, but rather the acceptance of us as part of the landscape and a consequent return to normalcy—which includes "getting after each other." Of course, we didn't let it just go on—damaging to overall order, of course. Additionally, it gave us the chance to get the district administrators to mediate between the tribes—thereby increasing the stature of the governmental official, as well as continuing to "practice habits of governance." CPT Jody Hansen did incredible work with M. Rahman (Monogai District) in this way; I remember one issue when one town cut another's tree, and it went all the way to lashkar [tribal war parties, with] (200 guys heading up into the hills after the others), but Rahman and Hansen talked them down from it—and, of course, became heroes. The issue of lashkar brings to mind something else. Most societies engage only reluctantly in blood feuding—it's simply too costly. Not surprisingly, then, the whole system of Pashtunwali and Pashtun social interaction can sometimes be seen as a series of ways to prevent needing to execute "badal." In fact, it is often a system of systematic escalation, with an almost-endless string of negotiation and a long sequence of "off-ramps"—a form of institutionalized brinksmanship. Lashkar, for example, is arrived at only after extensive consultations and warnings, and then has a bunch of built-in restraints—how much do other tribesmen want to send their boys off to your lashkar, etc. Also, Lashkar begins by the lashkar showing up in the target area, and demanding to be quartered. Then they sit in the houses for a few days, while the "hosts" become weary of feeding all the extra mouths. . . . and then begin to provide information on the objects of the lashkar. This fascinating form of economic warfare was explained to me by several Pashtuns.[70]

The martial character of Pashtun tribes is something of a clichéd stereotype, though it is rarely remarked on in contemporary conflict literature (where most analysts rightly tend to focus on the war-weariness of Afghans after decades of conflict). Still, over the years the warlike nature of Afghans has become very evident to me, over the course of repeated activities and operations in Afghanistan between tours in Iraq and visits to other war zones. At the risk of reinforcing cultural stereotypes I would be remiss if I failed to record my observation that while the Iraqi insurgents I encountered liked to win, and they certainly enjoyed killing people who could not hit back, they did not particularly like to fight. They didn't exactly dislike fighting, and would do so willingly in protection of relatives or hope of plunder or profit, but it was a rare Iraqi insurgent who loved the fight itself. The Afghan insurgents and former insurgents I have encountered *do* love the fight: they like to win, and are certainly not averse to killing, but what they really love is the fight, *jang* (battle), for its own sake. For example, the local farmers in Uruzgan who took part in the Taliban ambush I described at the beginning of this chapter did so not because they supported the Taliban politically or hated the Coalition but for reasons of honor, adventure, and love of the fight.

Traditionally, patterns of political authority in Pashtun tribes reflected a shifting internal balance of power, conditioned by these phenomena of balanced opposition, generalized reciprocity, honor (*nang*), extremely warlike behavior, the fusion-fission cycle of response to external threat, primary group cohesion, and a desire for partial or total independence from government control, enacted through the warlike repulsion of intruders into tribal territory. The authority system was well adapted for maintaining social order and collective security in an inhospitable frontier environment that typically saw little, if any, government presence. Like other forms of tribal organization, this was in essence a self-regulating social system for governance without government.

The Tribal Governance Triad

This informal power system had three poles of authority, perhaps best understood as a tribal governance triad. These were the *khan* or, collectively, the *jirga* as a group of tribal elders; the *mullah* as a member of the

Islamic religious establishment (the *'ulema shura*); and the government intermediary or representative (the government-approved political agent, in parts of Pakistan, or the *wali* or district governor, in Afghanistan). It might be tempting to liken these functions to those of a modern democratic state, with the *jirga* representing the legislative branch, the *wali* the executive, and the *mullah* the judiciary. Some Pashtuns do this: one tribal leader I met in mid-2006 asked why Americans want to bring democracy to Afghanistan through the medium of national elections: "We already have democracy," he said, "but at the level of the tribe, not the central state. How will elections improve things?"[71] The analogy is a limited one, since women and children are excluded from this governance system and it does not cover the full range of state functions, but for male Pashtuns tribal governance is in principle very egalitarian; in ideal terms, except when appointed as a temporary war leader in time of conflict, no adult male Pashtun can tell another what to do. All have a theoretically equal voice in the *jirga* and a right to be heard.

Actions of leaders are sharply circumscribed by group consensus and judgments about what tribal public opinion will bear. In this sense, public opinion is the ultimate sanction, a potent force indeed in one of the most inhospitable regions on earth, where withdrawal of tribal protection can literally be a death sentence. But in theory, all hold themselves equal and independent members of a free association based on lineage, rather than slaves of the state or followers of a *khan*. (This is one of the cultural features that distinguish Pashtuns from Baluchis: the Bugti and Murri tribes of Pakistani Baluchistan near Quetta have a much more centralized, hierarchical way of life, with tribal leaders exercising much greater or at least less publicly questionable authority. The career of Nawab Akbar Khan Bugti—tribal leader, sometime Pakistan government leader, and ultimately rebel and insurgent chief, a "great man" by any measure and one whose tribe followed him without question—is a case in point.) Similarly, Arab tribes tend to be much more ordered and hierarchical than Pashtun tribes, as discussed in the next chapter. Winning over the *sheikh* of an Arab tribe implies, to some extent, the making of an agreement which the *sheikh* can enforce and the tribe will honor; this is far from the case with Pashtun tribes.[72]

Indeed, far from considering themselves part of an ordered hierarchy, members of Pashtun tribes traditionally positioned themselves for advantage by shifting allegiances and rebalancing among the three competing poles of authority—like middle children in a large family. In addition, tribespeople participated in business, governmental, party-political, and religious hierarchies, simultaneously occupying rungs on multiple ladders (a phenomenon the anthropologist Max Gluckman described as "interhierarchical roles" in his studies of African tribes,[73] and something I also observed in the Torricelli Ranges of western Papua New Guinea, and among Makassae and Mambai tribespeople in East Timor in the late 1990s).[74] This system of inter-hierarchical roles allowed individuals to deploy supporters and resources from one hierarchical system (say, tribal kin) to neutralize a challenge emerging from another hierarchy (perhaps an overeager district governor) but then to shift opportunistically as power relations changed (later making an ally of the governor to outmaneuver a pushy business rival). As Gluckman showed elsewhere,[75] such patterns are very common in "eroded" or "detribalizing" systems where traditional authority patterns are disrupted, as in Afghanistan.

A similarly eroded system exists in Waziristan, across the Durand Line in Pakistan's FATA. In this area Akbar Ahmed developed a broadly similar construct which he designated the "Islamic District Paradigm" and which, like my tribal governance triad model, posits three overlapping systems of authority (lineage-based authority, central government authority and religious authority) within Pashtun tribal areas on the Pakistani side of the frontier.[76] In this structure, Professor Ahmed noted that religious leaders tend to emerge and assume greater leadership roles and political prominence in times of external threat (from colonial forces, the Soviet occupation in the 1980s, or indeed today with the intrusion of external armed actors into tribal territory).[77] Such behavior allows religious leaders to sideline both tribal leadership and central government authority.

In the Afghan case, the traditional authority structure can be represented graphically (see fig. 2.2).

In Kunar, this traditional authority structure has been especially heavily corroded through war and its attendant social chaos, with the introduction of new actors (religious extremists, foreign fighters including the Coalition, and the Afghan government) and the growth of an unemployed, traumatized, deracinated youth population vulnerable to recruitment by groups like Gulbuddin Hekmatyar's HiG, the Taliban Peshawar shura, associated networks like those led by Jalaludin and Siraj Haqqani, or by AQ itself. This in turn has marginalized tribal elders, government representatives, and sometimes also mullahs (though in many

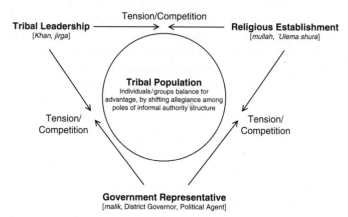

Figure 2.2 Tribal governance triad diagram

cases extremists have cooperated with the traditional religious establishment in alliances that have superempowered the *mullahs*).

Traditionally, the *mullah*'s authority derived from his status as a sanctioner of social practices, an arbiter of faith and morals, and a provider of religious and educational services, dispute resolution, and mediation to the tribe. As Akbar Ahmed shows, the *mullah* (unlike the *syed*, a person with traditionally ascribed authority deriving from his lineage as a descendant of the Prophet, similar to a *sharif* among Arabs—Governor Wahidi of Kunar is a *syed*) had little traditional prestige, but *mullahs* frequently sought to achieve authority by building a personal following through a network of dyadic patron-client relationships with followers, often provoking rivalry with tribal elders, whose authority derived from different sources and who sought to resist religious leaders' economic or political self-aggrandizement.[78]

A Pashtun of a respected family from Swat in Pakistan, an educated 40-year-old man now living in Peshawar, with whom I discussed changing authority relationships within the tribes, put it this way:

> Previously we would respect the *mullah*, we would offer prayers
> and stand beside him, but we would never marry our daughters to
> him. He was like a musician: we love music, we love to listen to it,

we respect the musician as a traditional craftsman but he has a low social status, we would not give our daughter to him. But now the *mullah*, as a result of the war with the Soviets, has been elevated to high influence and status. Now the *mullahs* have become honored, they are the commanders. The *maliks* now are herded, like animals.

I was in [my home village] one month back, in Swat, in Buner district, and I wanted to go to the mosque to see people and socialize. So the *mullah*, he was looking at me, and he was prolonging his *khotba* [sermon] and after speaking he said, "Nobody is to leave the mosque, because now we have a talk by the *tablighi jamaat* missionaries." After a while I left, and there was a line of people following me out, because they were afraid to go out until I did. This is how the *mullahs* intimidate them now. My family [in Swat] own one *imam* [prayer leader] for fifteen days [in a month] and my cousin's family owns the *imam* for fifteen days, we feed him, we have a dispute [sic—agreement?] with them—we know this system, we are familiar with it, but now there's only one *imam* for the village, and he's an Afghan. The elders have lost power, influence, and authority and the mullahs have gained the upper hand.[79]

Another Pashtun said:

The *mullahs* are approaching women to get their men to become more extremist. They tell the women to say that unless the men grow their beards [an outward symbol of radicalization] then the women will shave their heads. This would be more than an insult. Women come up with their jewelry and even their sons to [give them to] the *mullah*.

The *mullah* is telling people in the *jirga* what to do, giving the prayers and giving the orders—but he is just a village schoolteacher, not a leader! *Pashtunwali* has been neglected, because of radicalization: they don't know our code of life because they only know the *madrassa* and how to make more *madrassas*.[80]

This process of change in the internal authority dynamics of tribes can be represented graphically (see fig. 2.3).

This process of disruption is critical for the security situation, since many tribal elders and some relatively moderate religious leaders in Kunar have felt dispossessed, giving them a motivation for revenge and a strong desire to get "back into the game" by driving out extremists and recovering

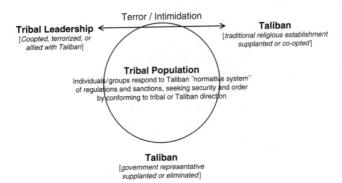

Figure 2.3 Disrupted governance triad diagram

their traditional authority. A series of Coalition commanders—going back to Colonel Mick Nicholson, who commanded the highly effective Spartan Brigade in this area in 2006–2007, Lieutenant Colonel Chris Cavoli, battalion commander of the equally tough and professional 1–32 Battalion of Tenth Mountain Division in the Kunar valley, along with PRT leaders like navy commanders "Doc" Scholl and Larry Legree at Asadabad—have worked closely with tribal leaders on this basis. Meanwhile, projects like the road provided a source of patronage, employment, and income to the tribes, which traditional leaders, in conjunction with representatives of the Afghan state, were able to disburse to the people, thus cementing their positions of influence, reestablishing tribal cohesion and social norms, and undermining radicals in the tribal power structure and their external extremist sponsors. The road—not the road itself, but the process of constructing it (like the bridge that saved the regiment in David Lean's 1961 film *Bridge on the River Kwai*)—became for some the means of restoring and reintegrating the tribe's honor and cohesion, regaining their status, and redressing the erosion of social structure caused by war and extremism.

This general description of the physical, human, and political terrain of Kunar gives a context within which we can begin to understand how the insurgents operate in this and similar environments, and how the accidental guerrilla syndrome emerges.

THE TALIBAN OPERATING SYSTEM

As described in general earlier, the Taliban are far from unified: they include competing or cooperating factions and, especially in Kunar, are not the only threat, since religious extremists like HiG or AQ and more recently the breakaway Tora Bora Front are also important. Moreover, the term *talib* ("students" or "seekers") applies broadly in Pakistan and Afghanistan to people with varying motivations and characteristics. So any attempt to describe a "Taliban operating system" is to some extent a caricature, a snapshot of one stage in the constant and rapid evolutionary process of a highly adaptive social movement. But it is possible to identify general patterns: this description reflects the operating patterns that I and others have observed in Kunar, Khost, Uruzgan, and parts of Kandahar and Helmand since mid-2006.[81]

There are seven basic elements in the system, three located inside Afghanistan ("in-theater") and four in Pakistan (the "active sanctuary"). In-theater elements include full-time fighters (operating as a "mobile column"), local guerrillas (who typically operate on a part-time basis in their local area only), and village cells (providing a clandestine infrastructure for the movement and linking local guerrillas to full-time fighters). The active sanctuary elements, located in Pakistan, include training and logistics support systems, political and religious leadership, the recruiting base for full-time fighters, and external sponsors and financial backers. Terrorist cells operate semi-independently on both sides of the frontier.

The in-theater system works like this: full-time fighters, recruited in either Afghanistan or Pakistan but usually trained in Pakistan, move around the area in groups of varying size (sometimes a dozen or fewer but sometimes up to several hundred, with the ability for small groups to concentrate into larger columns within hours or days). They operate as a mobile column, working in one valley for a period of days or weeks and living in villages or compounds alongside the people, or (only when absolutely necessary) out on the hills. They do this until the security forces' response to their presence becomes too intense, at which point they disperse into smaller groups and melt away across the hills into the next valley, where they reassemble at prearranged points and start the process again. Their main activities are political and religious indoctrination, armed propaganda, intimidation and killing of those who support the government or breach their extreme interpretation of *shari'a* law (e.g. schoolteachers educating girls, active local officials, or tribal leaders working with the government); public killings of criminals and corrupt or oppressive local figures, in the manner of vigilante violence; attacks on symbols or infrastructure of the coalition or the GOA; collection of taxes; levying of support in kind; and laying of ambushes and improvised explosive devices (IEDs) against government projects or infrastructure. These fighters operate almost entirely on foot, though pack animals are also sometimes used, and they almost always avoid roads, preferring to move across country, usually by night, and relying on the local knowledge of their part-time guerrilla guides to find neglected passes or mountain trails. Long-distance transport of supplies sometimes is done by road, but generally the Taliban use of the road system is incidental, occasional, and light. They communicate using radios and cellphones or satellite phones, and they carry small arms (rifles and machine guns), rocket launchers, sniper rifles, mortars, mines, explosives for IEDs, and sometimes antiaircraft weapons. In some cases (as in Nuristan in 2006), a better class of fighter has emerged, appearing to have benefited from professional military training and equipment and operating in a more "regular" fashion; other fighters operate in a looser, less technology-enabled manner. The groups of fighters function as "flying columns," the technique pioneered by the early IRA in the 1920s:[82] working at a high level of intensity for several months (a typical "tour" for Pakistan-based full-time fighters is four to six months)[83] before returning to Pakistan for rest and refit, to be replaced by another mobile column as it comes on line.

Full-time fighters (sometimes called Tier 1 Taliban) are usually therefore foreigners in any valley where they operate, unless it happens to be their actual home valley, and a mobile column is usually made up of people from several tribes, reinforced by foreign fighters (often Uzbeks, Tajiks, Chechens, Arabs, or Pakistanis) acting as embedded trainers or advisers. These embedded foreigners often hang back in the fighting, directing the column's operations, coordinating heavy weapons or logistic support, and generally avoiding direct contact with Coalition or government forces, though their presence is well known. Some Afghan tribal leaders I spoke to said that since many full-time fighters come from refugee communities or originate outside Afghanistan, they don't really fit into the tribal structure: "their tribe is the Taliban."[84] This might create difficulties for the full-time column in terms of local knowledge and support were it not for the next element in the system, the local guerrillas.

Local guerrillas (also known as Tier 2 Taliban) are like the farmers I described in the Uruzgan ambush example: they fight almost entirely in their home valley, usually within a day's march of their village, close to the roads, on a relatively casual "pick-up team" basis, and almost always in support of the full-time column—rarely on their own. The arrival of the mobile column in a valley tends to serve as the signal for a general activation of local guerrillas, who fight in support of the column while it is in their valley, and then go back to farming as the column melts away and the full-time Talibs depart in the face of reaction from the security forces. Local guerrillas seem mainly to act as guides, conduct reconnaissance, carry ammunition and supplies, support full-time fighters during combat, provide guards and sentries for full-time fighters, and gather intelligence. They are normally motivated by economic self-interest (the Taliban leaders pay local guerrillas for specific activities such as attacking a road or placing an IED); desire for excitement, honor, and prestige; fear of retaliation if they fail to support the Taliban; and tribal and local identity (supporting locals or relatives against outsiders). Some exhibit individual motivation along these lines; others fight out of tribal loyalty, as in the case of the Mahsuds (a legendarily well-organized, dangerous, and cohesive tribe whom the British colonial administrator Sir Olaf Caroe described as a "wolf-pack")[85] in Waziristan, where tribal elders told me that the tribe had decided to allocate a certain number of their young men, two per family, to fight with the Taliban—in this case the motivation is tribal solidarity, while the tribal leaders themselves are driven by more instrumental motivation.[86] Religious extremism and support for the old Taliban regime are rarer motivations, according to Afghan intelligence officers and local officials with whom I discussed this;[87] desire for revenge (badal) and anger arising from the loss of relatives in the fighting or from killing of bystanders and destruction of property through "collateral damage" are more common.[88]

The connective tissue between local guerrillas and full-time fighters, and a key coordinating mechanism in the overall operating system, is the third in-theater element: the village underground. This varies in sophistication between villages but usually consists of a cell of a few people, perhaps led by an elder with a traditional or personal connection to the old Taliban regime, along with a few relatives. The cell operates clandestinely, gathering intelligence, reporting on Afghan government or Coalition activities, intimidating those who support the government (often, as discussed earlier, via threatening night letters—as well as intimidatory visits and assassinations or beatings), managing caches of explosives and ammunition in the local area, and sometimes functioning as a shadow governance structure with the cell leader acting as the "guerrilla mayor" of the village. (Indeed, in some cases I observed, the leader of the local cell was the actual former Taliban mayor of a village.) The cell rallies local fighters to meet the "flying column" when it is in the valley, coordinates local support work for the full-time fighters, conducts armed propaganda, and provides leadership for local guerrillas. As such, the village infrastructure is the key link in the in-theater system.

Students of Mao will recognize this as a standard, classical guerrilla structure, which would have been familiar to any Cold War counterinsurgent. Unlike Maoist protracted warfare, however, Taliban fighters tend to adopt the "focoist" strategy popularized by Che Guevara and later Régis Debray, according to which the presence of a roving armed band is supposed to arouse opposition to the government and ultimately instigate a popular uprising or revolution through inspirational violence.[89] As Julian Schofield pointed out in a 2006 study, this approach to guerrilla warfare is culturally familiar to Pashtuns, mirroring their preferred traditional modes of conflict, and Pakistani-sponsored insurgents in Kashmir during the 1990s adopted a very similar approach, even though a Maoist protracted warfare model might have served them better. As Schofield further demonstrates, the focoist approach has since been endorsed as the official Pakistani special forces doctrine for sponsoring insurgents in the conduct of guerrilla warfare.[90]

This "coincidence" is perhaps an appropriate point at which to discuss the external, active-sanctuary components of the Taliban operating system, as these are located in Pakistani territory—though they require only a brief mention here since they do not directly affect the situation inside Kunar. Out-of-theater elements include training and logistic systems (training camps; supply and infiltration routes and depots; contracting and purchasing arrangements for weapons, ammunition, and other supplies; medical support for wounded fighters; and recreational/leave services); political and religious leadership (including the Quetta *shura*, the Peshawar *shura*, the leadership of the Tora Bora Front, the HiG, the Haqqani network, Tehrik-e-Nafaz-e-Shariat-e-Mohammadi, LeT, and other Taliban or associated leadership groups); the recruitment base for full-time fighters (largely drawn from crossborder tribes, large-scale Afghan refugee communities in Pakistan, and *madrassas*); and sponsors and financial backers. This last category includes both private and unofficial sponsors, and sponsors associated with governments outside Afghanistan. The degree of official endorsement of such sponsorship has been the subject of debate; the fact that members of the Pakistani armed services, civil armed forces,[91] and other government agencies have directly and indirectly supported the insurgency (whether on their own initiative or under official direction) is not disputed. Whether the insurgency inside Afghanistan is now self-sustaining or would wither without its active sanctuary on the Pakistani side of the Durand Line is something of an open question. In my view, since there is very little practical prospect of the active sanctuary diminishing any time soon, the point is somewhat moot: the sanctuary's role in enabling the insurgency is a fact of life.

On the basis of this understanding of the environment and how the Taliban operate in it, I can now begin to evaluate the approach that U.S. and Afghan forces and civilian agencies are taking in Kunar.

ROADS IN KUNAR

There have always been tracks, or dirt/gravel roads, linking villages in Kunar. During the Soviet-Afghan War, the *mujahidin* made extremely frequent use of mines and IEDs along the roads, aided by the ease of emplacing explosives in the soft shoulders and along the roadways, culverts, and stream fords of what were basically dirt tracks throughout the province.[92] However, Coalition commanders who worked in the area told me that not 1 kilometer of paved (i.e. "hard-top," all-weather) road existed in the province in 2001, and local Afghan officials I spoke to confirmed this. The Soviets built roads in Afghanistan in the 1960s and 1970s before the Soviet-Afghan War, including the famous 2-kilometer-long Salang Tunnel in the North, and were responsible for the major ring-road system linking Afghanistan's key cities. (Note that this was a peacetime aid project rather than a wartime operation—the Soviets carried out road maintenance during the campaign, but no major new roads were constructed.) In addition, Kunar, as an outlying frontier province, never received the kind of engineering attention that was directed to the main ring-road, and even during the war the Soviets never constructed hard-top roads in the province, and only carried out limited road maintenance in direct support of their own operations.[93] In short, there was never a Soviet "road construction program" of the sort the Coalition has carried out since 2006.

Figure 2.4 Afghanistan, March 2008—USAID-funded road construction project, Kunar province.

Photo: David Kilcullen

According to Carter Malkasian, who served as a civilian counterinsurgency expert with the Asadabad PRT during this period, the paving of the Pech Road was begun in earnest in the spring of 2007 and completed in March 2008, and was paid for by the Asadabad PRT at a cost of $7 million.[94] An earlier road project had been attempted in 2005–2006 by a local contractor working with the PRT and the local U.S. units (3/3 and 1/3 Marines), but construction had failed due to lack of funding (the project was initially costed at only 1.5 million) and intimidation by local Taliban who burned the contractor's equipment. In April 2006 the road project was re-started by Colonel Chris Cavoli's unit, 1–32 Battalion of 10th Mountain Division, as part of the Lines of Communication security project to support Operation Mountain Lion, a major counterinsurgency presence operation mounted by Colonel Mick Nicholson's Spartan Brigade.[95] Commanders on the ground rapidly found that permanent security was needed to protect the project. Security presence, in the form of several platoon-size outposts, had already been established when roadwork started. Following the construction of the road, IED activity decreased. Malkasian commented:

> Security in the area now is such that Afghan government officials are able to stay at the district centers at any time, as are the police. Officials get out into most areas of the districts easily. It's the upper reaches of the tributary valleys that are problematic, as was the case before the road was constructed: the difference was that officials had difficulty getting to and from places because of the road conditions, whereas now their movement is easier. There has been little popular backlash to the roads. The biggest problems are when outside workers are hired or when the road has to destroy a home or a shop. The former has been resolved by hiring locals, the latter through negotiations. Each road contractor has a "social organizer" whose job is to bring together elders to handle problems of this type, while the PRT has to oversee the social organizer's work.[96]

Lieutenant Colonel Cavoli confirmed that the road from Jalalabad to Asadabad was still dirt in November 2005 (as was Highway 1 from Khyber to Kabul); by March 2006, the Jalalabad-Asadabad road was being cut and flattened, but was not paved at all. This road was a USAID project. The Pech River Road was highly problematic, according to him—local commanders (of the First and Third battalions of the Third Marine Regiment) desperately wanted the road, but the contract had been let at around $1.5 million by the Asadabad PRT at the time, and "was going nowhere." A few other road projects existed, but were ad hoc projects that one commander described to me as "give a couple thousand bucks to this guy to fix up his dirt road." As a consequence, no paved roads existed.[97]

In terms of the overall effects of the road program, Lieutenant Colonel Cavoli commented:

> When I arrived in Afghanistan, it took 5.5 hours to drive from Jalalabad to Asadabad. The last time I drove it, it took less than 2. Along the way, there used to be one gas station up around Narang where I'd stop and make a satcom [satellite communications] shot. When I drove it in June 2007, there were twenty-three. . . . This progress, of course, brings issues with it, but those just provide more chances to work with the population to connect them to the government (again: Bill's roads have led to traffic safety issues; but Bill [Ostlund, the current coalition battalion

commander in this area] responds by using this as a chance to do a new info campaign, further connecting people to government). When Operation Mountain Lion started, it took 4–7 hours to drive Pech road (depended, literally, on enemy). Now it's 45 minutes or so, and probably most of that time is traffic. Concept of a gas station was amusing; by the time we left, there was one near the bridge to the Korengal and one east of Watapor. Now, I think Bill's counting seven. Hotel started going up in Nangalam in late 2006—now complete, I believe. Surplus crops are growing and being sold along roads.[98]

The following two extracts from my field notebook for March 2008 describe the project:

[Field Notes, 2 miles southwest of Asadabad, Kunar Province, 10:30 AM, March 13, 2008]

The PRT's main project at present is the opening up of the Korengal valley, to assist in clearing out a former major stronghold of the enemy, and to bring development and governance to the area. The main push is centered on driving a paved road through the valley to allow forces to secure the villages, driving the enemy up into the hills . . . and affording freedom of action to civilian agencies so that they can work with the people to extend governance and development.

The road project involves a series of negotiated agreements with tribal and district elders—the approach the PRT is taking is to make an agreement with the elders to construct the portion of the road that runs through their tribal territory. This has allowed them to better understand the geographical and functional limits of each elder's authority, and to give the people a sense of ownership over the road: since a local workforce has constructed it (and is then paid to protect it) they are more likely to defend it against Taliban attacks. Also, the project generates disputes (over access, resources, timing, pay, labor, etc.) that have to be resolved between tribes and community groups, and this allows Afghan government representatives to take the lead in resolving issues and negotiating settlements, thereby connecting the population to the provincial and local administration and demonstrating the tangible benefits of supporting the government.

The PRT tracks the current rate the Taliban are offering as payment for attacks against the road or vehicles traveling on it, and ensures they pay more than the enemy (though only just). Once the road is through and paved, it is much harder to place IEDs under the tarmac surface or on the concrete verge, and IEDs are easier to detect if emplaced. The road provides an alternative works project to prevent people joining the Taliban, the improved ease of movement makes business easier and transportation faster and cheaper, and thus spurs economic growth, and the graded black-top road allows friendly troops to move much more easily and quickly than before, along the valley floor, helping secure population centers and drive the enemy up into the hills where they are separated from the population—allowing us to target them more easily and with less risk of collateral damage, and allowing political, intelligence, aid, governance, education, and development work to proceed with less risk. Road building is not a panacea, but the way this PRT and the local maneuver units are approaching this project is definitely a best practice.[99]

[Field Notes, 8 miles northeast of Asadabad, Kunar River valley, 11:35 AM, March 13, 2008]
We exited from the PRT base in a four-car Humvee convoy, through a rough HESCO-and-razorwire gatehouse, then bumped down a rough dirt track to the main Kunar valley road, a two-lane asphalted roadway, well graded and with a deep concrete monsoon drain on the left (west, or hill-ward) side to catch runoff, frequent culverts made of concrete, a stone retaining wall on the downhill (river) side, and yellow steel road hazard markers. This road is newly completed and very good—the best I have ever driven in rural Afghanistan and a real feat of civil engineering. It was mainly constructed by an Indian contractor using local labor and Indian government aid money. The area south of Asadabad is even newer, and was a multimillion dollar USAID project.

The tactical advantages of the road, as well as the economic benefits, are much as I described earlier, and in this case the road (which parallels the border 5 kilometers away) also provides a strategic advantage for lateral movement of forces along the frontier, and to interdict Taliban infiltration routes—though Colonel Preysler [commander of the 173rd Airborne Brigade Combat Team currently deployed in this area] said that parties of enemy still infiltrate in this area, coming down by night from the hills on the Pakistani side, crossing the river on truck inner tubes, spending a few days attempting to do armed propaganda work in the villages on the Afghan side of the river, and then moving up into the hills to avoid our patrols. Many of them congregate northwest of the river, just beyond the [next] valley, in a district that we rarely visit and that remains a pocket of insurgent activity—one the Brigade tolerates because there is no access from that isolated valley to the rest of the population; their focus is on securing the bulk of the population rather than clearing terrain; and they lack the forces to secure every part of the province and have therefore sensibly "triaged" their [area of operations].

We moved fast along the road... as we drove, Preysler and I were discussing key development issues. His two main concerns are water—the river is low this season after only light snowfall over the winter (by Afghan standards), and he is worried about irrigation and crop rotation issues—and electricity generation capacity, which is now the key limiting factor on development as basic infrastructure problems begin to be solved (roads, bridges, etc). Like the other Regional Command–East commanders, he is all about development and governance. Having fought a hard kinetic fight [i.e. a fight using lethal or potentially lethal force] to gain control of the province in 2005–2006, during Mick Nicholson's time, the focus has now shifted to economic and political issues, with the ANA and ANP doing the bulk of the security work, supported by a smaller U.S. footprint and by local agreements and neighborhood watch forces.

The PRT operates a "10-kilometer rule" which stipulates that 80 percent of unskilled labor on any project has to come from within 10 kilometers of it—this helps build community jobs and ownership over projects, and gives the people a stake in defending them against the enemy....

Alison Blosser, the State Department representative, later pointed out to me that it has become a widespread PRT practice to have local communities construct at least part of the projects themselves, especially the perimeter and security fences and walls, to give them a sense of pride and ownership in the project (as well as longer-term employment—rather than build many projects simultaneously, they space the work out over time to generate long-term jobs). She said this makes it more likely that the population will defend the facility, prevent their men being involved in attacks on it, or at the very least give early warning to the government and security forces if they become aware of insurgents' plans to attack the project. In this sense, community involvement is a source of both economic development and strategic (or indirect) force protection.[100]

COUNTERING THE TALIBAN SYSTEM IN KUNAR

In describing their strategy in relation to this road construction program, American commanders in Kunar tend to refer back to the approach established by Colonel (now Brigadier-General) John "Mick" Nicholson, mentioned earlier, who commanded the brigade in this area in 2006–2007. He based his strategy on the delivery of four key operational effects: securing the people, separating them from the enemy, helping them choose their own local leaders, and connecting them to the government via those leaders.[101] One of the aspects of this approach that, in my observation, has made it so successful is its consistency. Rather than the phenomenon I have observed in the south of Afghanistan, where successive Coalition commanders have sought to "make their mark" by changing and rethinking the strategy at the start of their six- or eight-month tours (resulting in inconsistency over time), in Kunar successive commanders have fallen in with the strategy established several years earlier and have treated consistency as a key operational effect in its own right. Lieutenant Colonel Chris Cavoli, battalion commander of 1–32 Infantry in the Kunar valley in 2005–2006, commented on this factor in relation to his successor, Lieutenant Colonel Bill Ostlund (commanding the experienced and capable 2–503 Parachute Infantry Battalion in the Korengal), in terms that strongly echo the findings of the key analytical studies (Peterson, Kalyvas, Jackson) referenced earlier:

> I think if you build an overall picture, you'll see maybe a bigger point even than road building—the quest for continuity. Without putting words in his mouth, I think Bill O. understood deeply that the effect

of Coalition operations *on the people* was the key question; and that one of the things people (like investors) need before they commit to something is predictability; so a key factor in success would be to ensure that the people perceived continuity of efforts, decisions, power structures, etc. I think this led Bill to begin by accepting what we left for him, despite many, many obvious deficiencies and mistakes, and to make that "set" the baseline for evolutionary change, rather than "rotation disjunction." [Since that time, by the way, Bill and I have become quite close and often talk about the area.] Bill's effort to create a perception in the population of continuity by employing evolutionary improvement (which has been of such a magnitude as to approach "revolutionary" improvement in the aggregate) has, I would imagine, been one of the most insightful and effective things I've seen any commander do.[102]

I identify six key elements in this approach, which I christened the Kunar model in late 2006, when I studied it in detail as part of a field assessment project sponsored by Lieutenant General Karl Eikenberry, before applying several of its aspects in Iraq during the "surge" of 2007. These elements are: securing the people where they live; disaggregating the Taliban system; building local allies; denying the enemy access to the population; linking the people to their government; the "persistent presence" approach; and full-spectrum political maneuver. Taken together, they add up to a comprehensive system designed to address the specific environment of Kunar.

Securing the people is fundamental to effective counterinsurgency. As I have shown, in Kunar this involves securing villages, valleys, routes, and the heights that overlook them. Population centers need to be secured 24 hours a day; otherwise, the enemy reinfiltrates the area and intimidates or co-opts the population, and only once security is consistently established can the population be won over and induced to provide information about local clandestine cells of the enemy, who can then be dealt with by police or intelligence services. In Kunar, the imperative to secure the population where they slept led Coalition forces to set up a series of local outposts, partnering Coalition and Afghan forces and police, so as to create a protective "bubble" around each population center. The road construction project enabled them to link each bubble to the next. Lieutenant General Eikenberry, who was instrumental in creating this system, described the

Figure 2.5 Afghanistan, March 2008—Dr. Carter Malkasian (center) and members of the Asadabad Provincial Reconstruction Team preparing for a patrol, Kunar province. Photo: David Kilcullen

roads as "ink lines" (a variation on the "ink-spot" method of traditional counterinsurgency)[103] while Colonel Cavoli commented:

> We've talked about the important rhetorical effect of the road-building technique—how it constructs fights that leave the enemy away from populated areas and subject to all our "toys" without high chances of collateral damage; how the people can see our bullets going away from the road, enemy bullets coming toward it; etc, etc. [But] one of the most important things a road does that no other technique can do is to convey a sense of long-term commitment to the people. You can drill a well in a day, and build a school in a month...but it takes a long, long time to build a road. When you start a road, you send a message that this isn't a month-long partnership—it's for the long haul. This is very important for all the reasons you can dream up, but let me highlight one: when you mix this sense of long-term commitment with a persistent-presence methodology, it becomes apparent to everyone that

U.S. and ANA forces are going to be in the towns for a long, long time. The U.S. isn't going away tonight and leaving the elders to cope with the Taliban on their own. This *forces* the enemy's hand. He cannot abide that much contact between the government and the people while he has almost none—staying out of the towns while we're in them would render him irrelevant to the people, a fate worse than death for insurgents. Therefore, he has to dislodge us; therefore he comes to us to fight; but now when he gets there, the whole fight is constructed physically, visually, rhetorically to put him at a military and informational disadvantage. While our people are in the valley, daily demonstrating that we don't eat babies and that we care for the people... [and showing] concern from the government for the people, the enemy's only response is threat, intimidation, and physical attacks that conclude with the government forces still among the people and the enemy going off to pull slivers of metal out himself.[104]

Cavoli contrasts this "permanent-presence" methodology with the "repetitive raiding" that has characterized operations at some other times and places. He argues that persistent presence is essentially a "counterpunching" strategy that relies on a cycle of defense and counterattack, in which the presence of the road and Coalition forces protecting and interacting with the population draws the enemy into attacking defended areas, causing him to come to the population and the government—the opposite of the "search-and-destroy" approach in which security forces "sweep" the countryside looking for the enemy within the population, as if for a needle in a haystack, and often destroy the haystack in order to find the needle. More particularly, search-and-destroy operations tend to create a popular backlash and contribute to the "antibody response" that generates large numbers of accidental guerrillas and pushes the population and the enemy together. The persistent-presence method avoids this. Cavoli commented that:

This seeming "defensive" orientation, then, is actually a great way to steal the initiative from the enemy. It may seem on the surface to be less offensively oriented than repetitive raiding, but if you establish persistent presence in the correct places, the enemy has to come fight you. After a period, you know and understand these fights better than he does, and whip his ass in them (my god, look at 2–503's use of echeloned fires in known areas). And the enemy is like a moth to light—he has to come fight you for so many reasons. So, persistent presence, correctly done, can force the enemy to come to you on your terms—this is true initiative. And it's asymmetrical—he wants you to come track him down on his own turf, but rather than do that, you build a road; your building of the road drags him to you, where you suddenly have the ability to use your second asymmetrical advantage (money and construction being the first), good ol' firepower. This is my way of explaining what I think we all understand intuitively: that an increase in fighting doesn't necessarily indicate a loss of initiative or, more to the point, momentum gathering for the enemy. It is also a way of explaining why "who initiates each [combat engagement]" is less meaningful sometimes than the very fact that they're happening. Persistent presence, over time, robs the guerrilla of advantages and gives them to us. After a year of fighting in Kunar, I'd venture that Bill [Ostlund]'s guys are going to know the area better than the enemy that'll come in this spring. Likewise for [PRTs]—after time, Larry LeGree certainly knew more about the local politics than someone from outside (whether Kabul or elsewhere).[105]

Persistent presence is not a panacea, as those involved in the fighting in Kunar readily acknowledged. The method ties forces to areas, and any movement becomes difficult. "Surging" forces elsewhere for temporary missions brings opportunity costs in the vacated area, as forces can only be concentrated in one area at the expense of other areas. When an area no longer requires forces, or when another area requires them more, there is a "breakup" between the population and local Coalition forces, often a very delicate matter. Men and commanders can become wedded to local ways of doing things, and must be encouraged not to believe their method is the only method, lest they become less effective when eventually moved. And—a point not often mentioned by those on the ground but perhaps most important—persistent presence, done effectively, requires a relatively large number of troops (as in the Iraq "surge" of 2007, which enabled persistent presence in Baghdad and the surrounding areas) or conversely demands a relatively ruthless triage in which commanders decide to protect some areas and leave others outside government control. As such, it is not a sustainable long-term strategy for an overall campaign, but rather a method for stabilizing key areas on a temporary basis.

Building local allies, both military and political, is a critical aspect of this approach. In Kunar, this developed in stages: first, U.S. and ANA soldiers spread out along the roads that were under construction in patrol bases to monitor construction and to guard road-building equipment and work crews. The road-building contractor originally took several weeks in the spring of 2006 to begin work, because of poor security: it took a platoon dedicated to guarding the road contractor's work sites to get him going, as well as a troop presence all along the road. In the next stage, the road created an opportunity for the creation of an auxiliary police force, which district chiefs had been trying to get the government in Asadabad and Kabul to authorize; once these chiefs were able to justify the need for local police as a guard force for the road, the GOA gave its approval to raise five men from each population center to act as police along the road. The U.S. forces created a program to equip, train, and jointly operate with these local police; Cavoli commented that "they were the only thing remotely like police out there, so we jumped in with both feet. Doc Scholl [the PRT commander] bought them red caps so we could identify them, I made my B Company commander give over a bunch of handheld radios, we gave them flashlights and sandbags and Afghan flags, and C Company trained them and interacted with them and planned patrol schedules with them."[106]

Like the raising of local security forces in Iraq (which is discussed in the next chapter and was partly modeled on this Kunar program), this method was successful in improving security and establishing the beginning of a governance system. Just as in Iraq, however, providing consistent, long-term funding to support local auxiliary forces is a critical requirement, such that the Kunar project almost ended in disaster: after approving the raising of the local police force, the authorities in Kabul refused to release funds to pay the men in it, who would go for months at a time without pay, creating very significant problems. In the autumn of 2006, with the formation of the Afghan National Auxiliary Police, this local force was rolled into it, in order to give them centralized training, uniforms, and equipment, place them on a permanent payroll, and make them a recruiting base for the ANP (which each man had the option to join after a year). This approach, which Colonel Mick Nicholson and his commanders on the ground originated with support from the 10th Mountain Division commander (Major General Ben Freakley) as well as from General Eikenberry, was very influential as an example of best practice in raising local forces and integrating them into national institutions. It formed a mental model of best practice to which I often referred when I came to design the framework for raising and employing local security forces in Iraq (Sons of Iraq, Sahawa al Anbar, concerned local citizens groups, etc.) as part of General David Petraeus's staff the following year. Cavoli again:

> [This]put uniforms and governance all over the valley. And it all started because we needed guards on the road ("we" is not just my battalion—Col Nich[olson] and other commanders were starting this elsewhere.... after early Fall of 06 when he put a firebase into Kamdesh, Mike Howard (3/71 Cav) had a very similar situation up in Nuristan, trying to create a police force to guard the roads he was trying to build). [Another way in which road building] related to security: Doc Scholl wrote the [road-building] contract so the contractor would hire hundreds of security guards for his equipment, etc., from the local area. We trained and interacted with them—they had uniforms, radios, the whole schema. This put even more people on the road who were interested in keeping the project going and who were under the control of the government.[107]

ROAD BUILDING AND IEDS

As noted, the road construction resulted, over the long term, in dramatically reduced placements of IEDs along roads,[108] primarily because IEDs were easier to spot and harder to emplace on paved roads than on dirt tracks.[109] Coalition commanders initially spent a long time considering how paving would affect IED emplacement. They expected at first that paving would simply lead to side-mounted IEDs in the cliff faces (an escalating response-counterresponse situation). In some places, the road contractor understood this and cut a wide shoulder, but on balance, commanders decided that side-mounted IEDs would still be easier to spot than ones buried in the roadway, and that they would still therefore be better off on balance with paving.[110]

While the roads eventually brought a drop in IED placement, on the Asadabad-Jalalabad road the construction process (including the digging of more than 200 culverts under the roadway, the presence of piles of loose dirt and gravel along the roadside, and the need to park road-building machinery on site overnight) prompted a temporary spike in IED emplacements. This was not always entirely a bad thing, as Cavoli recalled:

> Once one big one was put in under [local Taliban leader] Ahmed Shah's direction.... it blew up during emplacement just a bit before

I crossed it with my [tactical headquarters], down there south of A[sada]bad near Narang, and it ruptured the road. It turned the concrete pipe into a field-expedient cannon, and the dudes putting in the bomb suffered.... one foot was about 100m away. Interesting thing, though: the locals poured out [of] their houses and began to repair the road immediately—and utterly loaded us with information about who they thought did it. They didn't want the road broken. We designed a culvert grate and put together a plan to put grates over all culverts on the J[alala]bad-A[sada]bad road—don't know if the plan was ever fully executed, but I remained wary of the potential to put big bombs in the culverts. There was one period, winter 07, when we had 17 IEDs...14 turned in by locals or found by our guards, 3 found by our Huskies (all 3 in places where there was no population to see the IEDs and turn them in), zero exploded. Just before [the end of our tour], we lost some ANA to an IED (case noted above). Significantly, it was in an unpopulated area where there was road construction going on.... ground turned up, lots of metal on the ground.... Then Bill and I saw successful IED #2 on our first outing together.... location met same description, precisely. So, the road helped us get the population to help us with IEDs, but where there was no population, that didn't work. However, overall, the effect of the road building—the activity, the guards, the community buy-in, the hard surface—on the IED threat was a dramatic [improvement].[111]

The reduced IED threat also means that security forces can adopt a lower threat posture, allowing them to interact more closely and in a more friendly and collaborative manner with the local population. I observed this firsthand in March 2008, as highlighted in this extract from my field notes of the time:

[Field Notes: 12 miles northeast of Asadabad, March 13, 2008]
After about 35 minutes of fast road move, in a disciplined, well-spaced patrol formation along the valley floor, we came to a ford where the road crossed a big tributary of the river, running across a weir as the creek came into the left (northwest) side of the river. There was a quite significant backlog of traffic—8–10 cars and taxis and a jingle-truck—waiting in line to cross the ford in both directions, and a watchful crowd of small children from the local

areas, as well as vehicle drivers who had dismounted while waiting to cross, standing and sitting on both sides of the road, though mainly on the left (higher) side.

This was the only point on the move where I saw a U.S. security presence (as distinct from ANA or ANP). A four-vehicle Humvee patrol was at the ford, with two vehicles in overwatch and two at the ford itself and troops dismounted along with an ANP detachment at the crossing point and mixed in with the crowd. The mood was friendly and relaxed, with the crowd accepting the presence of the police and soldiers and children hanging close in around the patrol. This would have been incredibly dangerous for all concerned if this were Iraq (or even Kunar last time I was here in late 2006), but the enemy in this area—Taliban from the Peshawar shura and Haqqani network, plus some HiG in the northern part of the province—tend to avoid targeting the civilian population indiscriminately except in unusual circumstances, so perhaps the mix of civilians and military was safer for everyone on this occasion.

Nonetheless, this was an excellent ambush spot—as we approached, the lead vehicle of the patrol stopped, and we closed up to about 10 meters behind it, and so did the cars behind us—meaning that 10 civilian vehicles, 8 U.S. vehicles, about 60 people, and a major piece of infrastructure were all bunched up in about 100 yards of road. A sniper pair on the far (Pakistan) side of the river valley could have pinned us down while a heavy mortar team one ridgeline back worked us over—[and we could not have done anything about this] short of calling for air (which could not have engaged across the border anyway and would have taken some time to arrive). This is exactly the sort of ambush that the Taliban were very capable of in 2006 and 2007.[112] The fact that nobody took the threat of such an ambush seriously enough to do anything about it is probably an indicator that not only is the province relatively safer now, but people (civilians especially) also *feel* safer, which is of course mostly what matters, since it is the "well-founded feeling of security," to quote the Briggs Plan, not just the existence of security per se, that has the desired influence effect of bringing the people to the government side in [counterinsurgency].[113]

In essence, the positive effect of road paving on IEDs seems to derive primarily from the fact that the paved surface makes IEDs harder to emplace and easier to detect, because insurgents have to choose between digging through a hard, clean surface layer (which takes time and a larger emplacement party, making it more likely the emplacers will be caught, and disturbs the road surface, making the IED easier to spot) or surface-laying the IED, also making it easier to spot. This, in turn, reduces IED casualties for both security forces and the friendly civilian population and gives the population greater confidence in the security of the roads, increasing their feeling of deriving tangible benefit from the government, and encouraging them to invest in crops or other economic activity because the likelihood of produce reaching market safely is increased.[114]

OPERATION BIG NORTH WIND, AUTUMN 2006

Separating the people from the Taliban and connecting them to the government was also a key aspect of the Kunar approach. As noted, unlike in a conventional development scenario, in a counterinsurgency environment it is much less effective to apply governance and development assistance on a purely needs-based or universal basis. This soaks up resources with minimal political effect, and does little to counter the accidental guerrilla phenomenon.

In contrast, local commanders in Kunar, after a series of extremely difficult and costly operations that failed to make significant headway in breaking into the Korengal valley in the summer of 2006, mounted Operation Big North Wind during that autumn—an operation my team was able to observe during its planning and early execution stages. This operation was part of Operation Mountain Fury, under the control of Major General Ben Freakley, commander of Combined Joint Task Force 76 (CJTF-76), responsible for eastern Afghanistan.[115]

Commanders on the ground assessed that the enemy clandestine network and local guerrilla force structures overlapped so much with tribal and community networks in southern Korengal that it would be too difficult to immediately separate the enemy from the people in that part of the valley. The operation therefore set out to initially exacerbate regional and district divisions within the population, separating groups from each other, and then to use this political maneuver as leverage to separate the population from the enemy. To do this, units focused on securing and improving conditions in the northern sector of the valley only, while deliberately ignoring the south (due to the strong enemy presence there). The U.S. and Afghan forces established persistent presence in the village of Omar and further north on the east wall of the valley, realizing that this area had tribal and family connections to towns in the south of the valley, so that word of events there would rapidly spread to the southern area, which was receiving no assistance. In the vicinity of Omar, Lieutenant Colonel Cavoli's 1–32 battalion constructed a footbridge, a school, and a water scheme, refurbished a mosque, built a bridge across the Pech river into the Korengal valley, and restarted the construction of the Korengal Road, which had been stalled. At the same time, they mounted high-intensity kinetic operations against Taliban fighters operating in the southern area,[116] with the assistance of an extra one and a half infantry companies (about 200 soldiers), provided by Colonel Nicholson, the Spartan Brigade commander, for this purpose. Simultaneously, the Afghan government administrator of Monogai, Mohammed Rahman,[117] applied strict resource and population control measures to villages in the valley, preventing anyone but people needing medical assistance from entering or leaving the area, unless and until local Korengali leaders would begin serious negotiations with him about allowing government access to the population. This extract from media reporting of the time illustrates the governor's approach:

For Rachman, ending the fighting in his area does not depend on a military solution alone. Negotiation and politics can play a role as well. "I selected the elders from each village. Those people who are educated, who have tribal powers. So we use these elders against the bad guys," says Rachman. "We signed an agreement with the people saying that they will not allow bad guys to use their villages or territory." But some areas, such as the Korengal, remain outside his influence. To bring the area under government control, he has implemented a new tactic—sanctions. Barring the movement of items such as tea, sugar, or cooking oil into the area, Rachman is hoping to show the people that supporting al Qaeda and other anti–Afghan government insurgents may not be worth the cost. "The Korengal people are subsistence farmers. They grow their own food, but they are going to need sugar, oil, cooking oil," says Hansen. "They are going to need all those things that make their lives just a little bit better. We are providing them with the hard decision. Either you work with the government of

Afghanistan or you have the effects of not working with them. It's in their court."[118]

This was the governor's own decision, not that of military commanders on the ground,[119] and serves to emphasize that the key aspect of this operation was political maneuver. Indeed, in this case, a political plan devised by local Afghan government officials was the necessary starting point for all operations in the valley. Cavoli recalled:

> In fact, Rahman came up with the political plan first, and then we decided we needed to support it kinetically, and we developed Operation Big North West around it, as a kinetic/nonkinetic complement to his efforts. [The] intent of OpBNW was to make life tough in the south, good in the north, so that southerners would look toward Omar and say, "My elders suck." Was pretty successful—character of N[orthern] part of valley changed *greatly* (probably still better even today, I hope). We were getting results in the south, too, we saw the population's unity starting to crack—but then the enemy launched a great political smear campaign against Rahman and got him fired.[120]

In this example, U.S. forces combined kinetic operations with engineering activity, civil development assistance, route and population control, and targeted humanitarian and economic assistance, in cooperation with Afghan government officials who applied political negotiations and civil population control measures, all in support of a political strategy to extend government control into an enemy-dominated area. This disrupted the Taliban operating system I have described earlier, separated the enemy from the people, and gave the population incentives to support the government. In response to this full-spectrum political maneuver, the enemy mounted their own political maneuver: a campaign to remove the effective local district administrator. Cavoli described the sequence of this operating method in relation to Operation West Hammer, January 2007, as follows:

> We followed the same principles: went in, met the locals, set up shop, provoked a reaction, used ISR [intelligence, surveillance, and reconnaissance assets] to find enemy, did a mortar-a-thon for a couple of days, held a *shura* [for negotiating purposes] and the governor said, "OK, we'll stay here and get rid of more of these guys, just like you've seen the past couple of days, and then we'll keep police here and build

you a road." We built a firebase, loaded it with ANA and ANP, initiated contracting for a road, and left a U.S. platoon there. Same model: go in, hit the enemy, create a space, establish a permanent presence organized around doing something good for the people, and then use the projects to create habits of cooperation between the government and the tribes/people.[121]

As noted by Malkasian, Eikenberry, Legree, and Cavoli, road construction in this area and elsewhere served the key function of connecting the government to the people. Roads give government representatives greater access, and allow NGOs and other assistance to reach the population. The Pech and Kunar valley roads, constructed in 2006–2007, made policing, meetings with community leaders, and visits to local *shura* and *jirga* meetings much more possible. An example quoted by Cavoli was that of Haji Zalmay, the district chief of Watapur District in 2006, who lived in the Chowkay area. To visit his district before the road was constructed, he had to travel across country and disappear for days at a time; after the roads were improved, he could "commute" on a daily basis, allowing much greater interaction with the population.

I have already discussed the role of local Afghan officials, and the quality of these officials—especially provincial governors and district administrators—is central. Governor Wahidi has played an extremely important leadership role in Kunar Province, similar in some ways to that of Mohammed Rahman, as described earlier. Previous governors in this district, Governor Wafa and Governor Didar, had less of a positive reputation among local people; some saw them as lacking in energy and prone to corruption. During 2006–2007, Haji Zalmay (Watapur District) and Mohammed Rahman (Pech District) played the main role in road construction along the Pech River valley. Cavoli commented: "it remains very humbling to me how much of any success we may have achieved was really the result of good Afghan politics. When it was absent, we just fought." This succinctly sums up the central role of political strategy in effective counterinsurgency, and the central role of local leaders in developing that political strategy. The "human capital" of indigenous civilian district administrators is thus a critical aspect of the effort, and one that it is almost impossible for Coalition military commanders to compensate for if absent. Building such administrative capital is therefore a key part of an effective strategic approach to Afghanistan.

Figure 2.6 Afghanistan, March 2008—Police patrol vehicles near Kandahar.
Photo: David Kilcullen

FULL-SPECTRUM STRATEGY

Summarizing this approach, one can see that it is founded on a detailed understanding of the population in terms of local culture, politics, ethnic and sectarian makeup, and geographical, demographic, and economic spread. This understanding is used to build reliable local alliances and partnerships with key leaders and influencers in the population. These partners, in conjunction with the intervening force, then develop a political strategy designed to improve governance, security, and economic conditions and so extend government control over the population and the environment while marginalizing the enemy in a physical and political sense. The political strategy drives an influence strategy that applies kinetic and nonkinetic measures, using civilian and military assets of both the host nation and the intervening force to enact the political maneuver required by the overall political strategy. In the Kunar case, due to the specifics of terrain, tribal structure and economics, roads and bridges became critical infrastructure elements that formed leverage points as part of the political strategy. The key, as local commanders recognized, was effective integration of all measures within a unified, full-spectrum strategy.

In my judgment, based on personal observation and discussions with Afghan and U.S. civilian and military leaders in the field, where we have succeeded in Kunar our success has resulted from the effective application of this approach. Where we have failed, our failures have usually been due to inadequate knowledge of the local environment, unreliable or ineffective local allies, or poor coordination and synchronization between kinetic and nonkinetic, civil and military, and Afghan and Coalition aspects of the strategy.

GENERALIZING FROM THE KUNAR CASE

How possible is it to generalize from this example? On the face of it, road-building appears to be a generally recognized form of force projection and governance extension; hence the extreme frequency of its historical use by governments, colonial administrations, occupying powers, and counterinsurgency forces through history. It is also worth recognizing that there is little that is specifically American (or Afghan) about the engineering aspects of the approach I have described.

Nonetheless, the effects I have described in this case study accrue not from the road itself but from a conscious and well-developed strategy that uses the road as a tool, and seizes the opportunity created by its construction to generate security, economic, governance, and political benefits. This is exactly what is happening in Kunar: the road is one component, albeit a key one, in a broader strategy that uses the road as an organizing framework around which to synchronize and coordinate a series of political-military effects. This is a conscious, developed strategy that was first put in place in 2005–2006 and has been consistently executed since. Thus, the mere building of a road is not enough: it generates some, but not all, of these effects, and may even be used to oppress or harm the population rather than benefit it. Road construction in many parts of the world has had negative security and political effects, especially when executed unthinkingly or in an uncoordinated fashion. What we are seeing here, in contrast, is a coordinated civil-military activity based on a political strategy of separating the insurgent from the people and connecting the people to the government. In short, this is a political maneuver with the road as a means to a political end.

We might also note that, as emphasized earlier, terrain, climate, demographics, and ethnography play a key role here. The terrain is mountainous: indeed, this is one of the most topographically forbidding operating environments in the world. Most valleys in this area have never in recorded history possessed more than a single dirt track along the valley floor; some lack even that. The climate is brutal: valleys are snowed in for several months of the year, so that a hard-top, all-weather road such as has been constructed in Kunar brings a major change in the seasonal pattern of life in the hills. The population is tribal, with a traditional way of life that balances tribal elders against religious leaders and representatives of a distant, scarcely noticed government; this tribal governance triad has been heavily eroded by religious extremists and the Taliban, who have threatened the traditional dominance of the elders, creating tension and giving traditional leaders an interest in partnering with an outside actor who can restore their authority.

CONCLUSION—ROADS AIN'T ROADS

In summary, like other counterinsurgents through history, U.S. forces in Kunar, in a close and genuine partnership with local communities and the Afghan government (most especially, a highly competent and capable provincial governor, courageous district administrators, and others), have engaged in a successful road-building program as a tool for projecting military force, extending governance and the rule of law, enhancing political communication, and bringing economic development, health, and education to the population. That this has happened against the backdrop of a sharply deteriorating security situation in the rest of the country is even more remarkable. The roads in the frontier area that are patrolled by friendly forces and secured by local allies also have the tactical benefit of channeling and restricting insurgent movement and compartmenting terrain across which guerrillas could otherwise move freely, and the roads' political and economic effects are even more striking.

All of this seems to suggest, in effect, that "roads ain't roads." To generate the effects just listed, a road-building project probably needs to be consciously approached as an integrated form of political maneuver, and the approach taken also probably needs to take into account the human, topographic, political, cultural, and economic environment in which that maneuver will occur. All this is happening in Kunar today, with substantial positive effects on the counterinsurgency campaign in the province, despite a generally downward trend in the overall Afghan campaign. But replicating this limited, local success in other places is likely to demand detailed study of the environment and an understanding of political maneuver as a counterinsurgency technique.

Let me reiterate the key observation: what has made this program successful is not the road per se, nor am I arguing that the presence of the road is solely responsible for improvements in security. Rather, the project succeeded because people used the process of the road's construction, especially the close engagement with district and tribal leaders this entailed, as a framework around which to organize a full-spectrum strategy to separate insurgents from the people, win local allies, connect the population to the government, build local governance capacity, bring tribes that had supported the insurgency onto the government side, and thereby generate progress across all the dimensions of counterinsurgency.

Conclusions: An Effective Afghanistan Strategy

This chapter has examined the Afghan situation in considerable detail, considering the campaign in its strategic context, the key elements of the situation, and key problems and issues in its conduct. It has highlighted the complex interplay of terrain, population, Taliban, and terrorists that makes Afghanistan such a difficult, dangerous, and complicated environment. This has allowed us to identify some of the key features of the accidental guerrilla syndrome: global terrorists exploiting accidental guerrillas, societal antibodies emerging in response to Western intervention, the risk of playing into an AQ exhaustion strategy. The Kunar case study shows the importance of consistency and a full-spectrum approach in the east of the country, where a road-building program integrating civilian and military effort into a single political maneuver has proved surprisingly effective since 2006. As the case study demonstrates, this program's success has had relatively little to do with the road itself and much more to do with insightful American and Afghan leaders' use of the road construction process as a vehicle for political maneuver designed to drive a wedge between the local people, the local guerrillas, and the hard-core Taliban leadership in this area and thus undo the accidental guerrilla phenomenon that had hampered previous efforts.

On the basis of all this, it is now possible to see what an effective Afghanistan strategy probably looks like. I would not suggest that our current strategy is ineffective: in fact, it is difficult to be sure that we (the international community in partnership with the Afghan government) actually have a single strategy. Rather, there appear to be several campaigns occurring simultaneously in Afghanistan, across different regions of the country, by different coalition and Afghan forces, and functionally across counterinsurgency, CN, counterterrorism, economic development, and state-building categories of effort. These efforts are loosely coordinated at best, through a Coalition command-and-control system that is byzantine in its complexity and hence much less than responsive. Nonetheless, this analysis makes it clear that the seven principal characteristics of an effective strategy would be primacy of political strategy; a central role for the Afghan government; a region-wide strategy; a population-centric approach to security; a comprehensive (or "full-spectrum") approach; effective, legitimate local security forces; a focus on local government effectiveness, presence, and local partnerships; and prioritization: nation-building first, then counterinsurgency, then CN.

Primacy of political strategy is most important of all. Building the political legitimacy and effectiveness of the Afghan government, in the eyes of its people and the international community, is fundamental. This requires, first and foremost, genuine improvements in governance, reducing corruption and abuse, and putting in place local administrators who govern in the interests of their populations and give them a well-founded feeling of security. In parallel, the political strategy is designed to undermine support for insurgents, win over their sympathizers to the government side, and co-opt local community leaders to ally themselves with the government. Political reform and development represent the hard core of our strategy, and as the Kunar example shows, provide a framework onto which programs and initiatives can be fastened. Without it, we risk incoherence or, worse, the perpetual dependence of the Afghan state on international security assistance, which will not be forthcoming forever. Events at the national level (such as the September 2009 elections) are important, but reforms targeting local and provincial government effectiveness are indispensable.

Best-practice strategy puts the host government genuinely and effectively in the lead, via integrated "campaign management" planning and consultation mechanisms. These apply Coalition expertise to cover local gaps, build the host government's capacity, respect its sovereignty, and leverage its local knowledge and "home-ground advantage." Part of our difficulty resides in the accidental guerrilla phenomenon, including both the local backlash against large-scale U.S. military presence and the unpleasant reality that U.S. leadership is unpalatable to many key players in this process, including regional actors and some European allies. Meanwhile, the complexity of NATO strategic decision-making and national caveats make planning much harder. The solution is to develop a strategy that puts the Afghan government genuinely and effectively in the lead, while encouraging that government (even forcing it, where necessary) to govern its people fairly and well. While the international community would almost certainly play a major role in drafting such a strategy, and our assistance would be fundamental to its execution, asking contributing partners and regional actors to sign up to it would be a far easier diplomatic task than asking them to support a strategy that seemed primarily to support American interests. Building the planning and oversight capability of the Afghan government would be a key component of this approach.

A region-wide approach is key. Because of the active sanctuary that insurgents rely on in neighboring countries, and the support they receive from transnational terrorist organizations and crossborder criminal networks, an integrated, region-wide strategy is essential. It must focus on disrupting insurgent safe havens, controlling borders and frontier regions, and undermining terrorist infrastructure in neighboring countries, while building a diplomatic consensus that creates a regional and international environment that is inhospitable to terrorists and insurgents. Integration with Pakistan strategy is also fundamental, given the major influence of the active sanctuary in Pakistan on events in Afghanistan, and the transregional nature of the threat. What we need is not an Afghan strategy as such but an integrated Afghanistan-Pakistan strategy. The Taliban are not primarily an Afghan movement targeting the Afghan state but should be seen instead as a loose alliance of Pashtun nationalists, dispossessed tribes, and Islamist extremists that seeks to control the Pashtun-majority parts of both Afghanistan and Pakistan. Therefore, and because of the active sanctuary the Taliban rely on in Pakistan, an integrated crossborder strategy is essential. Without one, even a military victory in Afghanistan will simply shift the problem a few miles to the east. Clearly, current events have destabilized Pakistan, but this represents opportunity as well as danger. Options that were unthinkable or infeasible for the Musharraf government in 2007 may no longer be so difficult, as Pakistan continues processes of reform. To be sure, initial signs from the new government in Islamabad are not promising—but this only further underlines the need for a comprehensive regional approach to the problem.

Population-centric security is also critical. We must focus on providing human security to the Afghan population, where they live, 24 hours a day. This, rather than destroying the enemy, is the central task in counterinsurgency. It demands the continuous presence of security forces that protect population centers, local alliances and partnerships with community leaders, the creation of community-based security through local councils, neighborhood watches and guard forces, and small-unit ground forces that operate in tandem with local security forces, developing pervasive situational awareness, quick response times, and unpredictable operating patterns that keep the enemy off balance. As several examples in this chapter have shown, if we can brush the enemy out of the way, marginalize them politically, root out insurgent infrastructure, and make local communities self-defending, we can inoculate the Afghan population against the Taliban and prevent their return. The contrary, enemy-centric approach simply wastes lives, time, and firepower on the pursuit of an adversary who has no fixed installations to hold and can therefore melt away to fight another day.

Effective, legitimate local security forces are an important aspect of this approach. Effective counterinsurgency requires indigenous security forces who are legitimate in local eyes, operate humanely under the rule of law, and can effectively protect local communities against insurgents. Building such forces takes vastly more time and resources than is usually appreciated. While they are being built, the Coalition must be willing to close with the Taliban in direct combat, thereby minimizing insurgents' pressure on local institutions. Direct combat (not remote engagement) is essential to minimize collateral noncombatant casualties, ensure flexible responses to complex ground environments, and allow rapid political and economic follow-up after combat action.

Comprehensive, or full-spectrum, approaches have the best chance of success. Counterinsurgency encompasses political, security, and economic tracks, with an underpinning information function (intelligence and "hearts and minds") that integrates all the elements of a campaign. Best-practice counterinsurgency closely integrates political, security, economic, and information components. It synchronizes civil and military efforts under unified political direction and common command-and-control, funding, and resource mechanisms. Synchronization of security, development, and governance activity is important, because timeliness and reliability in delivering on development promises is critical in winning popular support. This requires careful cueing of security operations to support development and governance activities, and vice versa. In turn, counterinsurgents must synchronize all these activities to support the overall political strategy through a targeted information campaign. This requires a shared diagnosis of the situation—agreed on by civilian and military agencies and by Coalition and host nation governments, and updated through continuous, objective situational assessment. In addition, an effective Afghan strategy must integrate counterinsurgency with nation-building, border security, and CN. This "integrated conflict management" function is essential but often neglected; building an indigenous Afghan government capability to manage the conflict is the key to achieving such integrated management.

Local government effectiveness, presence, and local partnerships are fundamental. Due to tribal dynamics and the accidental guerrilla phenomenon, insurgents are able to mobilize populations locally, and the Taliban rely on local part-time guerrillas working in partnership with local village political cells and "flying columns" of full-time fighters. Therefore, establishing effective local governance is more critical than national-level politics. This requires continuous presence by Afghan government and security forces, with coalition forces where possible to monitor and prevent abuses; we cannot achieve such presence everywhere, so we must "triage" key areas. We must also emphasize locally legitimate and effective arrangements; a genuine partnership with local communities is fundamental.

Prioritization is also critical, given the underresourcing of Afghan efforts in comparison to those in Iraq and elsewhere. Our fundamental problem in Afghanistan is building an effective state structure, for the first time in modern Afghan history. Insurgency, corruption, economic weakness, governance problems, and the narcotics trade are all symptoms of underlying state weakness exacerbated by opportunistic spoilers. Thus, our strategy must seek first and foremost to build the Afghan state. Our second priority must be to keep the insurgents, warlords, infiltrators, and other security threats from overwhelming the state while it is being built. Our third priority must be to keep the drug trade within acceptable limits. We must not lose sight of our ultimate strategic goal, which is not for the international community to solve Afghanistan's problems but rather to build an Afghan state that is capable of managing its own problems.

Pashtun tribal dynamics are critical to understanding the insurgency—but we must appreciate the limits of our ability to influence them. The Taliban remains fundamentally a Pashtun movement, based on a confederation of religious extremists with tribal leaders and Pashtun nationalists. Tribal dynamics at the subtribe, *khel*, clan, and section level are critical to understanding the insurgency. The traditional Pashtun disdain for government, the acephalous segmentary structure of Pashtun tribes, the conception of a *nang* (honor)-based society, and the overlap of individual and clan rivalries with Islamist ideology and nationalist fervor are keys to insurgents' behavior. There is no substitute for understanding this cultural terrain: we cannot defeat the insurgency unless we understand what drives it. But we must be keenly aware of the limits of our ability to "play" in this tribal game. Rather than directly meddling ourselves, we must use our knowledge to build, support and enable trusted Afghan partners whose grasp of these dynamics is instinctive. We must seek a form of indirect influence through trusted intermediaries, rather than applying too direct an approach. This may seem a neo-colonialist approach, until it is remembered that while colonialism was exploitative and was intended to be permanent, this is a temporary expedient only and is a means to deliver to Afghans the assistance promised by the international community, only until such time as they can handle their own problems without such assistance.

As a concluding thought, it is worth reemphasizing that nothing described in this chapter is particularly new or controversial in conceptual terms. Much of the best strategic work by the State Department, defense departments of contributing powers, and NATO planners conforms exactly to these prescriptions. But the collective efforts now being made by a multitude of policy players are complex, overlapping, and poorly integrated, with duplication in some areas and gaps in others. The ideas are not new; implementing them effectively would be.

Chapter 3

"The Twenty-First Day": Iraq during the Surge, 2007

It is so damn complex. If you ever think you have the solution to this, you're wrong, and you're dangerous. You have to keep listening and thinking and being critical and self-critical.

Colonel H. R. McMaster, quoted in George Packer, "The Lesson of Tal Afar," *New Yorker*, April 10, 2006

When the bomb exploded, I was in the helicopter's forward left passenger seat, behind the door gunner.[1] I had loosened my safety harness and was leaning out into the slipstream to see better. It was late on a hot afternoon in May 2007, and we were flying fast and low about 200 feet above Shula, a Shi'a militia stronghold in northwest Baghdad. The IED went off with a hollow boom a hundred yards directly ahead, the blast wave smacked into us, the Blackhawk shuddered, seeming to stagger in midair, and the pilots jinked sharply up and to the right to avoid the oily black pillar of smoke that suddenly rolled upward in our path. The abrupt movement pitched me violently forward out of the canvas seat, and my gloved hands clutched the door's edge, my heart thumping, just in time to stop myself plummeting out. The trail aircraft, another Blackhawk to our right rear slightly above us, squawked urgently on the radio and made a sharp evasive turn as we suddenly came dangerously close.

The two Blackhawks—helicopters always work in pairs in Iraq—were ferrying me to the Iraqi counterinsurgency school at Taji, a small town just north of Baghdad. I was to give a field orientation brief to the command group of 2nd Brigade Combat Team, Third Infantry Division, an army brigade of about 5,000 people under Colonel Terry Ferrell that had just deployed into the Iraqi theater of operations as part of the "surge." But since we were first on the scene, responding to this incident took priority.

For 10 minutes, we orbited low above the blast site, the door gunners squinting over their sights into the smoke, as a row of market stalls with blue plastic awnings caught fire, panicked civilians fled the scene, and others moved furtively (or innocently but fearfully—it is always hard to tell from a moving helicopter) around the rubbish-strewn streets, through the white dust our rotors kicked up, or amid the tangle of power lines and grey satellite dishes that clutter most Baghdad roofs. There was rifle fire, some directed at us, some at targets on the ground; but it was impossible to identify who was shooting, or from where, in the cluttered jumble of flat-roofed houses and narrow alleyways. Without identifiable targets, none of us fired back. An Iraqi Army (IA) patrol in four camouflaged vehicles reacted quickly, moving in a well-spaced column from its earth-work-fortified base two hundred yards away across the putrid brown Shula Creek, negotiating a dilapidated concrete bridge under our cover, setting up a cordon, and starting to help the injured. Once they were in place, we popped flares to confuse any insurgent antiaircraft teams who might have targeted us as we loitered, then rolled out and continued on our way.

To see better through the smoke, I had torn off my helmet, radio head-set, and splinter-proof sunglasses when the IED went off, and had gotten a face-full of car-bomb as we worked over the attack site. The pungent stink of sudden unexpected death—scorched wood, melted plastic, cord-ite, gasoline, burnt rubber, and barbecued flesh—stayed in my nostrils for hours. That night, alone in the blast-protected steel trailer that served as my temporary quarters at Taji, it took me 10 minutes in the shower to scrub the stench off my skin.

Saving Ourselves from a Disaster of Our Own Making

This chapter builds on the theory outlined in chapter 1, and on the Afghanistan case study in chapter 2, to explore the accidental guer-rilla syndrome in Iraq. It examines how, during the surge in 2007, we turned around a war that many believed had already been lost, through a strategy of protecting the people from intimidation, forging genuine partnerships with local communities, co-opting "accidentals" (includ-ing reconcilable Sunni insurgents and Shi'a communitarian militias), and killing or capturing the few on the extreme fringes (such as hard-core AQ in Iraq) who proved themselves irreconcilable. The success we and the Iraqis achieved in the Surge during 2007 was substantive and significant: in saving tens of thousands of Iraqi lives and restoring the possibility of political progress, it is correct (though perhaps immod-

Figure 3.1 Iraq, May 2007—Brigadier General Ali Jassim briefs the author on his brigade's operations in the "triangle of death" south of Baghdad.
Photo: 10th Mtn. Division

est) to say that we and the Iraqis together pulled their society back from the brink of total collapse. Yet the progress we made on the ground during the Surge is fragile, and highly vulnerable to being undermined by political leaders (in Iraq or at home) who may not understand how it was achieved.

Despite the undeniable tactical success of the surge, in the final analysis this study suggests that the large-scale, high-profile, unilateral, *über-blitzkrieg* manner in which the Coalition invaded Iraq (and the inherent strategic concept of the Iraq campaign itself) was deeply flawed. In my view the war, in grand-strategic terms, was a deeply misguided and counterproductive undertaking, an extremely severe strategic error, and a model of exactly how *not* to do business. In 2007 we seem, therefore, to have saved ourselves from some of the more egregious consequences of a bad decision to invade Iraq in 2003. This does not detract in any way from the efforts, sacrifice, and skill of the troops who held the line in 2006 and earlier and who saved us from disaster in Iraq in 2007. These men and women were dealt an incredibly difficult hand, and they played it bravely and well. But we asked those troops to rescue us from a disaster of our own making, and thus Iraq is an example of exactly the type of conflict we need to avoid, if we seek to succeed in the broader long-term confrontation with *takfiri* extremism.

This chapter follows the first few months of the Iraq campaign of 2007, during the so-called Surge, when I served in Baghdad as senior counterinsurgency advisor to Multinational Force–Iraq (MNF-I), commanded by General David Petraeus. This is not a comprehensive analysis: no definitive account of the Surge has yet been written,[2] and my part in it was, in any case, brief and incidental. But my position—reporting directly to General Petraeus, spending a third of my time in the International Zone (IZ) as part of the small team that designed the campaign and the other two-thirds out on the ground with U.S. and Iraqi units, civilian aid and reconstruction agencies, and diplomats—gave me an unusually good opportunity to understand both the intent behind the Surge and the way it played out on the ground in the critical first few months as the tide began to turn. I was thus in the unusual position of being a participant observer of events at both the center and periphery of the campaign. And as this chapter will show, the events of this period closely followed the pattern of the accidental guerrilla syndrome that I have already described in Afghanistan.

The key theoretical difference, indeed, is that in the case of Afghanistan the *infection* and *contagion* phases occurred first and were followed (after 9/11) by Western *intervention* and then, after a period, the local *rejection* of our presence in some areas. By contrast, in Iraq, *we* started the cycle by intervening, and the rejection of our presence opened the way to infection of the conflict by radical *takfiriin* empowered by chaos and popular backlash against foreign presence, and paved the way for a broader contagion effect (within Iraq, in attacks in Jordan, Syria, Lebanon and Turkey, and even further afield in London and Madrid). Thus the same accidental guerrilla syndrome appears to be operating in both cases, but from different start points in the cycle. In Afghanistan the enemy started it and we responded; in Iraq we started it—the Surge of 2007 was an attempt to arrest a vicious cycle that we ourselves had begun.

The first half of the chapter relies heavily on my field notes to create a sense of what the environment was like during the Surge, while the second half presents a detailed case study of the Iraqi tribal revolt against al Qa'ida (AQ), which transformed the environment during 2007.

But to understand the significance of the Surge, and the part that ordinary Iraqi civilians played in it, it is crucial to first understand the environment of Iraq in the preceding year, 2006.

The Surge

"THERE'S BEEN A BOMB IN A MOSQUE"

On February 23, 2006, I was attending a conference at Fort Leavenworth, Kansas, cosponsored by Lieutenant General David Petraeus, then commanding the U.S. Army Combined Arms Center, and Sarah Sewall, director of the Carr Center for Human Rights Policy at Harvard University. It was a detailed public interagency review of the new doctrine, laid out in Field Manual (FM) 3–24, *Counterinsurgency*, which General Petraeus and a writing team under his West Point classmate Dr. Conrad Crane had been putting together for almost a year.[3] I was attending as a State Department representative, as chief of strategy in the Office of the Coordinator for Counterterrorism. The conference brought together the leading intellects of the counterinsurgency community, along with human rights experts, area specialists, lawyers, intelligence officials, diplomats, media experts, development specialists, and representatives from all the key U.S. government agencies involved in counterinsurgency.[4] Allied governments and military forces were represented also. It was a landmark event, unprecedented in scope and extremely influential in redesigning counterinsurgency doctrine.

I missed most of it. Around lunchtime on the first day, my office in the State Department telephoned: "There's been a bomb in a mosque. We need you to go to Baghdad as soon as possible." Our office had been scheduled to hold regional counterterrorism talks with the political staff, intelligence officials, development agencies and defense staff from U.S. Embassy Baghdad and other U.S. embassies in the region, in Kuwait in mid-March. Now Ambassador Hank Crumpton, my boss, felt I needed to get out to Iraq rapidly, ahead of the meeting, to develop a sense of conditions on the ground.

A few days later, my helicopter touched down at Landing Zone (LZ) Washington, in the International Zone next to Saddam Hussein's old Republican Palace, now the U.S. Embassy and MNF-I headquarters. I landed into a rapidly escalating crisis of sectarian violence, as Iraq's

Shi'a community reacted with lethal fury against the bombing by al Qa'ida in Iraq (AQI) of the al-'Askariyya shrine at Samarra, a pilgrimage town on the east bank of the Tigris river about 125 kilometers north of Baghdad. The mosque, one of the two holiest sites in Shi'a Islam, holds the tombs of the tenth and eleventh *imams*, known as al-'Askariyyain, as well as a shrine to the twelfth,[5] the Hidden Imam, Muhammad al-Mahdi, who disappeared as a boy in a cave complex near the mosque and is believed by "twelver" Shi'a Muslims to be the ultimate savior of all humankind, occulted by God until the right moment shall arise.[6]

The AQI attack almost completely destroyed the dome of this ancient sanctuary. It was a cultural atrocity that attacked Shi'a primary group identity on a deep level, and was perfectly calculated to provoke an intense and violent backlash from the Shi'a population against Iraqi Sunnis.[7] This as it turned out, was exactly what happened: between the bombing of the mosque on February 22 and the end of March, 600 Sunni bodies turned up in the streets of Baghdad; many of these victims (including young children) had been brutally tortured before being executed.[8] The locally employed Iraqis in the embassy were too frightened to go home, and sat quietly, talking nervously among themselves. One of them said, "Please, you have to understand: this is a disaster, it changes everything. This will be civil war."[9]

A few days later, though, I discovered that the impact of the bombing had not yet sunk into the perceptions of military officers or civilian officials in MNF-I headquarters.

DIALOGUE OF THE DEAF

In late February 2006, I was invited to a meeting with Dr. Sa'afar A. R. Hussein, deputy to Dr. Muwaffak al-Rubai'e, the national security advisor of Iraq. After meeting in his office, Dr. Sa'afar asked me to sit in on the national security advisor's daily brief. This meeting was emblematic of relations between U.S. and Iraqi officials at this time, toward the end of the Iraqi Transitional Government under interim Prime Minister Ibrahim al-Jaafari. It is therefore worth recounting at length:

> I waited in the corridor for a few minutes until it was time for the national security advisor's daily brief, given by the U.S. military with Coalition, IRMO [Iraq Reconstruction Management Office] and State representatives and six senior Iraqi bureaucrats from the INSA [Iraqi National Security Agency] present.... The meeting

was a dialogue of the deaf. The American briefers gave a detailed, very jargon-filled, and intricate powerpoint brief on the latest trends, followed by a strictly quantitative assessment of progress, based on numbers of various types of incidents over time. Some of the metrics could have made sense and been useful if carefully interpreted, but there was little analysis given. In any case, the Iraqis had great [difficulty] in following the brief in military English with highly detailed, and colorfully busy powerpoint slides. Their eyes glazed over, and the interpreter translated only a few phrases. Tellingly, these were about trends in attacks on civilians and drew the most attention by far from the Iraqis, while the Americans were mainly interested in active "kinetic" op[eration]s against insurgents and terrorists (known in a quite Orwellian phrase as "AIF"—Anti-Iraqi Forces). The [Americans] all looked satisfied.

Then the roles were reversed. The key Iraqi bureaucrats now raised a series of questions, complaints, and points, admittedly often in Arabic and sometimes devolving into somewhat grandstanding speeches.... They showed a clear priority focus on population security and protecting the Sh'ia majority from Sunni terrorism, a point not actively picked up by the Americans.... The [Americans] now were silent, eyes glazed, looking into the middle distance. The senior IRMO officer present... showed visible signs of impatience, rolling his eyes and hopping about in his chair, but he was only the most frustrated of a group of [Americans] who looked bored and gave the impression they were "handling" the Iraqis rather than being straight with them. This impression was reinforced after the meeting when I asked [X] about the members of the [National Security] Council and he was unable to identify any of them, let alone their political affiliations or personal histories. Yet he or another officer attends these meetings daily.[10]

A day-by-day analysis of the battlefield update analysis (BUA) powerpoint slides from 2006, the record of the daily official briefing given to the commanding general of MNF-I (then General George W. Casey), indicates that it took approximately four and a half months, from the Samarra bombing until mid-July 2006, for these slides to begin reflecting what the Iraqi political staff (who worked less than 50 yards from the briefing room but were not allowed into it) had told me the very week of the bombing: that Samarra was a disaster that had fundamentally and irrevocably altered the nature of the war.[11] No mention was made of the danger of civil war during the formal MNF-I discussions of most of this period, even though an Iraqi officer told me later that this fear was foremost in the minds of most Iraqis at this time.[12] While the BUA slides do not reflect everything that is said to or by the MNF-I staff in this key daily briefing, they represent the official record of deliberations and as such reflected the priorities of the multinational force and the thinking of the Baghdad embassy under Ambassador Zalmay Khalilzad. To the extent that the BUA slides accurately reflected the mission's focus, they suggest that the overwhelming emphasis during this period was on putting together the new Iraqi government (eventually headed by Nuri al-Maliki), a process that was expected to take a few weeks at most and to result in an immediate reduction in violence: a top-down model that repeatedly featured in Coalition thinking right up until 2007. The high priority given to this effort was reflected in the fact that the State Department sent one of its leading authorities on Iraqi élite politics, the deservedly famous Tom Warrick whose deep regional expertise, along with that of other experienced and dedicated diplomats like Robert Ford, Ryan Crocker, David Pearce and Molly Phee, had played a major part in establishing the initial Iraqi government structure against terrible odds in 2003–4. Tom sat opposite me, hunched in the nylon sling that passes for an aircraft seat on a C-130 transport aircraft, during my flight into Baghdad and we talked at length about the risks and issues involved in putting the cabinet together, something which Tom expected to take a month or more. Eventually, of course, the process took almost five months, absorbed enormous energy and attention, and the establishment of the Iraqi cabinet resulted in no significant reduction in violence—because the killing was a mass social phenomenon, driven from the bottom up rather than from the top down.[13] Iraqi civilian deaths climbed sharply throughout this period and kept climbing, right up until early 2007 when, under General Petraeus and Ambassador Crocker, MNF-I and the Embassy finally began to adopt a bottom-up policy of securing neighborhoods and populations first and breaking the cycle of violence at its origin, instead of continuing to wait for top-down political accommodation as a means to reduce tension.[14]

WAITING TO EXHALE: THE FOCUS ON TRANSITION AND DISENGAGEMENT

The other focus throughout 2006 was on transition and disengagement. Key metrics related to how fast the force was handing provinces over to Iraqi

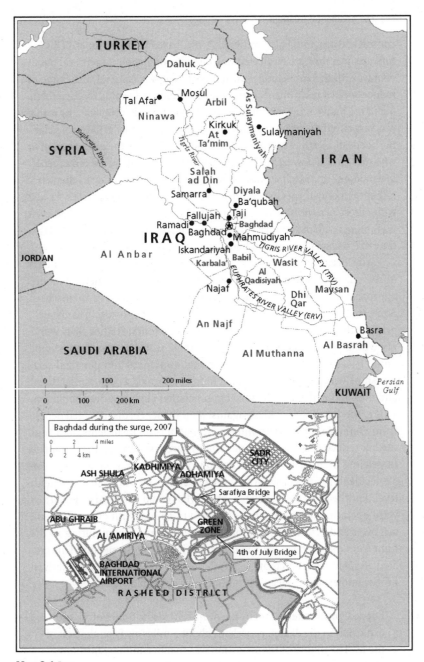

Map 3.1 Iraq

control and assuming an "overwatch" role, based in large "super-FOBs"— forward operating bases located well outside population centers and out of contact with the population—an approach that was believed at the time to reduce popular resentment against the occupation by keeping foreign troops out of the Iraqis' faces.[15] While this made good sense in principle, the reality was very different: because troops did not live in the muhalla, the Iraqi neighborhoods, they saw very little of locals, did not know them, had no notion of who to trust and how far, and adopted what Chris Cavoli would call a "repetitive raiding" approach, as discussed in the Afghan case study in chapter 2, rather than one of "persistent presence." Special operations forces, tasked with Direct Action to kill or capture High Value Targets (HVTs), had even less contact with the population. One Special Forces operator told me at this time that he had never met an Iraqi who wasn't in handcuffs.[16]

Partly because of this lack of situational awareness, some units I observed in the field in 2006 tended to take an extremely "kinetic" approach to completing their mission, and to protecting themselves. Some (though by no means all) seemed as if they were "waiting to exhale": gritting their teeth and getting through their tours. Rather than working with the population so as to protect them from the insurgents, some units, because of their lack of situational awareness and personal relationships with the people,[17] tended to treat all Iraqis as a potential threat and thus adopted a high-handed approach that alienated the population. This exacerbated the backlash against their presence, discouraged people from coming forward with information about the insurgents, and thus further reduced these units' situational awareness, leaving them trapped in a vicious cycle of intervention and rejection. This, indeed, was the classic accidental guerrilla syndrome at work at the "tactical" (i.e. battlefield) level. For the most disassociated units, what could be called a "FOB (forward operating bases) mentality" tended to coexist with overreliance on airpower and artillery and an operational pattern of commuting to the fight from out of town, instead of getting in among the people. This created accidental guerrillas at every turn, as I noted somewhat petulantly in my field notes after a sleepless night in early March 2006:

I dozed until woken again by the deep kettledrum boom of a large explosion in the distance, perhaps about 2 miles away on the east of the IZ. The timbre of the explosion was that of a military [artillery] shell in a confined space, and I heard later that a massive car bomb had exploded in a South Baghdad market area, killing about 30. As soon as the echo of the explosion died away, I checked the luminous dial of my watch—it was 02:16. Within about a minute, two small helicopters—perhaps AH6's—were airborne from LZ Washington making a series of runs over the IZ.... This is a standard procedure: the helos carry snipers and often spot or engage insurgent rocket or mortar crews shortly after an explosion—though they are almost always too late.

C. W. told me later that this is a major issue around many camps that follow the same drill—the choppers will arrive on the scene 6 or 7 minutes after the mortar team has fired, literally an age too late, and then either call in Apaches [armed attack helicopters] or guns to blast the baseplate area or even, if they are lucky enough to follow the shooters to a house, they will simply blow up the house. Since the insurgents usually choose residential houses or streets as firing points, this almost always results in civilian deaths or destruction of innocents' houses—thus progressively alienating village after village around major U.S. bases over time, by creating a pool of people who hate the U.S. at best, or have an active blood feud obligation [tha'r] against us at worst. A better approach—sending ground patrols to follow up and investigate shootings, or just accepting the occasional mortaring as the cost of doing business in Iraq—is not followed because there is a desire for revenge if someone is hurt by the mortaring, or a feeling that U.S. prestige demands a visible and lethal response. Once again the kinetic, offensive approach to force protection, and the placing of force protection at a higher priority than winning popular support.... The ultimate effect is to alienate the population, the only real strategic "force protection" we have. The helicopter flights continued all night, with the little birds [AH6 light attack helicopters] being joined later by Apaches and Blackhawks.[18]

During the rest of that year, an immense tide of blood washed over Iraq. Large parts of Baghdad were "ethnically cleansed"; entire populations were killed or driven out. Hundreds of Iraqis died every week—Shi'ites in AQI and insurgent terrorist attacks, Sunnis in death squad executions by Shi'a communitarian militias retaliating for those attacks. Civilian deaths peaked between September 2006 and January 2007, with between 2,700 and 3,800 civilians killed per month, every month.[19] In December 2006, the worst month of the entire war for civilian casualties, killings peaked at around 125 per night, more than half of whom were people killed inside Baghdad city limits.[20] Iraq was falling apart, from the center out, before our eyes. Why?

In my view, one key reason was that at this time government institutions were heavily penetrated by Shi'a sectarian extremists who used them to deny services to members of the Sunni community, or to actively kill or drive out Sunnis. This in turn drove the Sunnis into the arms of extremists, whose violence further convinced the government that it needed to continue suppressing the Sunnis. Our counterinsurgency strategy at the time relied on handing over to the Iraqi government the responsibility for population security, but the terms of the conflict had changed: the government was a sectarian combatant in the civil war that started after Samarra, not a politically neutral "honest broker" that governed in the interests of all Iraqis. Thus, increasing our support for the government, or improving the Iraqi state's capacity, without also maintaining sufficient leverage to ameliorate its sectarian tendencies, simply increased the violence. And because our focus was on transition rather than stabilization, on getting ourselves out no matter what the situation was on the ground, we lacked the presence or relevance to generate that leverage.

For example, the bank in Ameriya District in central Baghdad, (an area that was almost completely taken over by Sunni extremists during the course of 2006 and was named as the capital of AQ's Islamic State of Iraq in October 2006)[21] was repeatedly attacked and robbed until it closed down, after which the Shi'a-controlled Ministry of Finance refused to reopen it, even though 95 percent of banks in Shi'a areas were open.[22] This meant that to go to a bank, a Sunni from Ameriya carrying money had to leave this beleaguered Sunni enclave and pass through several checkpoints manned by Shi'a sectarian militia, who (if he was very lucky) would merely steal his money and, if he was a little less lucky, would simply kill him.[23] If he chose instead to stash his money under the mattress, he would make himself vulnerable to AQI intimidation and extortion or to opportunistic crime. A simple matter of banking services could thus mean the difference between life and death, and the same was true of health, electricity, sewage, and other essential services, which sectarian members of government ministries (with or without central government approval it is difficult to say) were denying to certain communities—especially Sunnis in Baghdad. For example, in towns and villages in the so-called triangle of death south of Baghdad at this time, Shi'a communities regularly received between 20 and 24 hours per day of electricity supply, while Sunni areas were lucky to get six.[24] Iraqi police were no help: when I asked one member of a Baghdad Sunni community about rumors that death squads dressed in Iraqi National Police uniforms had been picking up Sunni men from the street, torturing and killing them, and then dumping the bodies as a warning to Sunni communities, he laughed. "What do you mean, 'dressed in Police uniforms'?" he replied. "Call them what they are—the Police."[25]

By the end of 2006, therefore, the Sunni community had been driven into a corner, had closed ranks against outsiders, and believed that only AQI and the other *takfiri* extremist groups stood between it and oblivion at the hands of the Shi'a-dominated government.[26] For national reconciliation to take place, a measure of bottom-up population security was essential: the Sunnis had to feel the boot come off their necks, and confidence between the communities had to be restored, before they could feel able to engage in dialogue, let alone reconciliation, with the Shi'a community and the government. Moreover, a straight counterinsurgency approach would not work, because the government was not a legitimate or neutral actor being threatened by an insurgency but rather a belligerent on one side of a sectarian civil war.[27] We would have to not only support the government's authority but also significantly modify its behavior if the whole population were ever to accept it as legitimate.

This, then, was an accidental guerrilla syndrome run riot, with very few fighters taking part in the violence for religious or political reasons, let alone because of support for a global *takfiri* ideology.[28] On the contrary, apart from a tiny minority of extremists, most fighters (around 70 percent, based on detainee motivation surveys) participated in the violence defensively, out of a sense of threat and because of a belief that they had no alternative but to fight to the death to protect their communities in a terrifying and brutal environment. These were the very same dynamics identified by Stathis Kalyvas in his seminal study of the logic of violence in civil war, which I discussed in Chapter 2.[29] Pulling out at this point was simply not an option: it would have been morally and strategically unthinkable— ourselves having triggered this horrific, near-genocidal cycle of violence through our ill-judged intervention and failure to stabilize the country in the wake of the 2003 "victory"—to now simply walk away leaving the

Iraqis to their fate. To do so would have left our moral credibility in tatters and our strategic position in serious jeopardy.

Our first task, therefore, was to protect the people and thereby give them a viable alternative to violence. Only then would we be able to pursue reconciliation, and only after restoring a measure of peace and order could we contemplate returning to the pre-Samarra agenda of transition and disengagement. If we wanted to end the war—and our group, composed mainly of people who had opposed its conduct all along, desperately did want to end it—then the path to peace and withdrawal lay through a hard fight to secure the population first.

PUTTING THE SURGE TOGETHER

On January 10, 2007, in an address to the nation, President Bush announced a "Surge" of troops for Iraq. Much discussion in 2007 centered on these additional forces, which increased U.S. personnel in the theater by 21,500 (rising to about 28,500 over the course of the year). This focus on the additional troops missed much of what was actually new in the strategy—its population-centric approach. Here are the two core paragraphs from the President's speech, outlining the strategy:

> Now let me explain the main elements of this effort: The Iraqi government will appoint a military commander and two deputy commanders for their capital. The Iraqi government will deploy Iraqi Army and National Police brigades across Baghdad's nine districts. When these forces are fully deployed, there will be 18 Iraqi Army and National Police brigades committed to this effort, along with local police. These Iraqi forces will operate from local police stations—conducting patrols and setting up checkpoints, and going door-to-door to gain the trust of Baghdad residents.
>
> This is a strong commitment. But for it to succeed, our commanders say the Iraqis will need our help. So America will change our strategy to help the Iraqis carry out their campaign to put down sectarian violence and bring security to the people of Baghdad. This will require increasing American force levels. So I've committed more than 20,000 additional American troops to Iraq. The vast majority of them—five brigades—will be deployed to Baghdad. These troops will work alongside Iraqi units and be embedded in their formations. Our troops will have a well-defined mission: to help Iraqis clear and secure neighborhoods, to help them protect the

local population, and to help ensure that the Iraqi forces left behind are capable of providing the security that Baghdad needs.[30]

What was new here was not the mere addition of extra troops (though the strategy would not have worked without a certain minimum force size) but their tasks. The key element of the plan, as outlined in the president's speech, was to concentrate security forces within Baghdad, to secure the local people where they lived. Troops were to operate in small, local groups closely partnered with Iraqi military and police units, with each unit permanently assigned to an area and working its own local "beat."

This was a very different approach from early strategies (roughly from the start of the war until early 2005), which had been enemy-centric (focusing on killing insurgents), or more recent approaches (in 2005 and 2006) that had emphasized training and supporting Iraqi forces, transitioning to full Iraqi control as quickly as feasible, and expecting Iraqi forces to secure the population, with the Coalition in an "overwatch" role. Note that this is a discussion of strategy, not tactics: many units engaged in operations like the Battle of Baghdad or Operation Together Forward in 2006 applied sound counterinsurgency tactics and performed heroic efforts under extremely difficult circumstances at the tactical level. The problem lay not in the troops or their performance but in the strategic framework of the campaign (a problem that originated even higher than MNF-I headquarters, in the guidance given by Coalition capitals). In essence, we had surrendered control to the Iraqis over certain key levers, giving them responsibility for critical tasks that had to be performed in order to stabilize the environment. But they had no intention of doing what we needed done, and we simply lacked the leverage to make them, and so the environment remained highly unstable.[31]

The new strategy, as announced by President Bush, finally began to reflect counterinsurgency best practice as demonstrated over dozens of campaigns in the last several decades. In essence, enemy-centric approaches that focus on the enemy, assuming that killing insurgents is the key task, rarely succeed. Population-centric approaches that center on protecting local people and gaining their support succeed more often. Population-centric approaches do not always mean less fighting; they may actually involve more violence in the short-term, as security forces get in at the grassroots level and compete for influence with insurgents, sectarian militias, and terrorist gangs. But the aim is different. In a population-centric strategy, what matters is providing security and order for the population, rather than directly targeting the enemy—though this type of strategy will also effectively marginalize them. And by engaging directly with the people, building local allies at the grassroots level, we could re-create the leverage we needed to stabilize the environment.

The extra forces in Iraq were needed because a residential, population-centric strategy demands enough troops per city block to provide real and immediate security, and because regaining leverage required a firm demonstration of resolve and a definitive break with the policy of transitioning at any cost (which my colleague, the brilliant and iconoclastic Colonel H. R. McMaster once described as a strategy of "handing the Iraqis a flaming bag of feces").[32] A population-centric strategy demanded the ability to "flood" areas, and so deter enemy interference with the population. This was less like conventional warfare and more like police work: cops patrolling a beat to prevent violent crime. Committing the extra troops was also a political act—a demonstration of the Coalition's commitment to the fight, and willingness to stand alongside Iraqis for the long haul, which had a significant impact on the mindset of Iraqi community leaders, especially Sunni tribal leaders considering turning against AQ (as I shall show).

Why the focus on Baghdad? Because as noted above, during 2006 about 50 percent of the war in Iraq was happening inside Baghdad's city limits: the level of violence in the capital and the belts around it roughly equated to the violence in every other district of Iraq combined. Improving security in the capital therefore made a huge difference, physically and psychologically. Not that the enemy meekly rolled over and accepted this—hence the need for more troops and a reserve to deal with the inevitable enemy response, which brought major spikes of activity outside Baghdad in the outlying rural belts and in neighboring provinces, even as security in the city began to improve.

Thus, finally, in early 2007 the strategy in Iraq began to switch to an emphasis on population security and a residential, high-force-density, long-term approach designed to regain our lost leverage. But it took a substantial effort to turn the president's speech and the relatively brief think-tank and review papers that informed it into an executable campaign plan.

BACK TO BAGHDAD

By early 2007, as I flew again into Baghdad on a C130 transport aircraft to take up my appointment as General Petraeus's senior counterinsurgency

Figure 3.2 Iraq, May 2007—Lieutenant General Ray Odierno, Baghdad airport.
Photo: David Kilcullen

advisor, it was immediately clear to me that the situation had deteriorated very substantially: in the general's words, the ethnosectarian violence of 2006 had torn apart the very fabric of Iraqi society.[33] As the aircraft landed at Baghdad International Airport, fighter jets were strafing targets within 1,200 meters of the embassy compound, and a major firefight had just been concluded along Haifa Street, barely a five-minute drive from the Green Zone. I noted in late March: "the embassy is under pretty much constant mortar and rocket fire, with rounds striking the building on six of the last seven days. We had two killed and one seriously wounded on Tuesday night [just outside the dining facility during dinner] and several slightly hurt on other nights, so the embassy is no safe haven."[34]

Lieutenant General Ray Odierno, commanding MNC-I, captured the dynamic and deeply unforgiving nature of this operating environment in a comment to the newly arrived command group of the Third Infantry Division in April 2007. Major General Rick Lynch, the Third Division Commander, was a tough and highly competent man, who seemed gruff and cynical at first encounter but later proved capable of enormous compassion for his soldiers, their families, and ordinary Iraqis. He knew Iraq very well from several previous tours. But in this briefing, early in the Surge, General Odierno emphasized the unpredictability of the environment. "Everything can seem fine," he said, "for day after day after day—twenty days in a row. But it's that twenty-first day, when you go out, something happens and suddenly all hell breaks loose. The twenty-first day is what makes this fight so challenging."[35]

It's difficult to remember now just how bad things really were, but Iraq in early 2007 was the most dangerous place in the world: a pitiless environment that punished the tiniest tactical error, where finding the enemy was far harder than killing or capturing him once found, we often seemed to arrive just seconds too late to protect the local population, and innocent noncombatants bore the brunt of violence that was often savage quite literally beyond belief, from an enemy who was used to benefiting from our self-imposed restraint. The war's complexity matched its tough and demanding character. Unsurprisingly, the hardest thing for a counterinsurgency operator in Iraq in 2007 was to work out exactly what was going on: trying too hard to find out could get you killed, but so could *not* knowing.

As General Petraeus told me the day I arrived in Baghdad, this was the big league: we had essentially six months to turn the campaign around, rescue Iraqi society from tearing itself apart, and put the enterprise of stabilizing Iraq onto a sustainable footing, as an undertaking the Iraqis could take over and run themselves with some chance of success. Doing this meant, fundamentally, protecting the population, breaking the stranglehold of extremists, and—no less a challenge—achieving sufficient progress, by the time General Petraeus and Ambassador Crocker were due to brief a hostile Congress in September, to prevent a catastrophic collapse of popular support in the United States and elsewhere. That first day, in a note to myself in my field notebook, I defined the fundamental problem as a runaway chain reaction of intercommunal violence, carried out by terrified ordinary Iraqis—in effect accidental guerrillas—who were being exploited by small factions of extremists:

> The cycle of violence is fairly straightforward, and reflects the strategy first outlined in 2004 by then AQI leader Abu Musab al-Zarqawi (though he did not live to see it). In this pattern, Sunni extremists target Shi'a communities with large-scale, and often very deadly, car bombings and suicide attacks, which then provoke Shi'a

death squads to run amok, killing Sunni families and sparking Sunni militia reprisals. This cycle cements the power of both Sunni and Shi'a armed extremists, intimidates moderates and ordinary community members, and impels large-scale refugee flows as people seek to escape.

Iraq was locked into this pattern throughout 2006, and Coalition forces did little to prevent it because U.S. policy then was to transition to full Iraqi control as soon as logistically possible, and to minimize casualties by staying on the large FOBs established outside major cities. Thus we made ourselves irrelevant to the local power struggle, lost our leverage, and (through the constant drip-drip of U.S. casualties for no appreciable gain) lost the support of the U.S. people and congress—hence our current time/leverage crisis.[36]

THE JOINT CAMPAIGN PLAN

To begin that process of turning the tide and regaining our lost leverage, General Petraeus had assembled a team of 24 hand-picked experts, known as the Joint Strategic Assessment Team (JSAT), and tasked them with developing an integrated civil-military campaign plan, known as the Joint Campaign Plan 2007–2008. This team, jointly led by Colonel H. R. McMaster and David Pearce of the State Department, included intelligence, diplomacy, development, military, economic, information, and counterinsurgency experts, most of whom had done several previous tours in Iraq and all of whom had strong opinions on the way forward, leading to robust argument and debate—unsurprisingly, given the contentiousness and difficulty of the problem. In just over a month, the JSAT thrashed out a campaign plan that began with a detailed political strategy for achieving reconciliation from the bottom up, based on confidence-building measures and improved security in 2007, putting factions in a position to begin negotiating toward a national reconciliation or a power-sharing agreement in 2008. To enact this political strategy, we then designed an influence strategy to bring the key actors—AQI, the Shi'a militias, the Sunni nationalist insurgents, the government—to the table, by co-opting and reconciling with any willing parties and simultaneously targeting the extremist fringes (AQI in 2007 and then Jaysh al-Mahdi [JAM] in 2008) to deny them the ability to exploit the rest of the population. Developing sufficient leverage to compel the Iraqi government to begin acting as a government for all Iraqis, instead of as a sectarian Shi'a fiefdom, was also a key part of the influence strategy. Finally, a military strategy based on security, governance, development, and information operations was developed to enact the influence strategy. A focus on tribal and community engagement, reform of media operations, and a comprehensive focus on counterinsurgency best practices—emphasizing the need to place the operation on a sound long-term footing, heading toward sustainable security—were other key aspects of the plan. While it may not be obvious to some readers, the fact is that this method—starting with a political plan, then devising an influence plan to achieve it, and only then developing military, economic, and governance activities to enact it—reversed the normal military planning process and put political strategy firmly at the center of the effort.

While there was a great deal of rigor and detail in the campaign plan, which ran to more than 300 pages and was comprehensively briefed at each stage of its development to both General Petraeus and Ambassador Crocker (who had replaced Ambassador Khalilzad in March 2007), in truth the real "magic" in the planning process for the Surge had nothing to do with the JSAT and everything to do with the relationship between the two principals. Petraeus and Crocker were both intelligent, consummate professionals who were seized with a sense of urgency and an understanding that it was "now or never" in Iraq. Both had long experience in Iraq and a detailed understanding of the environment, and their strengths and insights were complementary. Both, like many members of the JSAT, had been dissidents early in the war: Petraeus had famously asked "tell me how this ends?" at the time of the invasion, while Crocker had criticized the invasion plan as likely to create a "perfect storm." Neither had any personal ambition for his next job; as General Petraeus told me once, "If we fail here nobody will ever care what we did next. If we succeed it won't matter. So we need to act like this is the last job we will ever do." Most important, both took responsibility for the whole problem, approaching it as a joint endeavor. According to a colleague who served in Iraq in 2006, this contrasted sharply with the situation under the previous leadership team: "No one in Iraq is personally responsible for victory," she had said. "Khalilzad handles the diplomatic political maneuverings to do with Iraqi government formation only, Casey does military COIN [counterinsurgency] and security only. No one is in overall command of both aspects."[37]

This was certainly unfair to both General Casey and Ambassador Khalilzad, who had had to work with the marching orders they were given and the situation in which they had found themselves. General Casey, in particular, had already introduced very significant reforms, establishing a counterinsurgency school at Taji, and bringing on board the exceptionally talented Dr. Kalev Sepp as his personal counterinsurgency advisor (pioneering the role I later filled for General Petraeus).[38] Casey had also initiated many counterinsurgency programs under Operation Together Forward, which commanders and troops at the brigade and battalion level had executed well in many cases. Still, Petraeus and Crocker had an even greater level of integration in their approach: they were in each other's heads to a large extent, and jointly approached every aspect of the campaign as a common challenge.

WALKING THE IRAQI STREET

By late March 2007, troops had shaken out into a series of joint security stations (JSSs) and combat outposts across Baghdad, with more being built every week (and eventually more than 32 in place, several times more than originally envisaged). A sense of security was gradually returning to the local population. The problem of language, culture, and situational awareness, which had hampered our unilateral operations in 2006, was breaking down. Troops were closely partnered with Iraqi units down to the company and platoon level, and always left their patrol bases accompanied by Iraqis who could understand the local environment and act as a conduit to the population, with Americans in support. Meanwhile, the Americans acted as umpires, monitoring the behavior of Iraqi security forces toward the population and preventing sectarian or abusive behavior by local units in their area.

Still, some American units—especially those who were in midtour, had served some time in Iraq in 2006, and needed to adjust their mindset to the new approach—took a little time to adapt, and I frequently went out with battalions, companies, or advisor teams who needed a little on-field coaching to understand the new approach. Some vignettes from my field notes of patrols during this period indicate our adaptation challenges:

> Five women approached us, wailing and shouting, with their long flowing black headscarves and *abayas* waving, gesticulating and complaining. They said their husbands had been arrested by the police, that there was no evidence against them, and demanded we investigate and seek their release. The brigade officer who was with us simply waved them off. . . .

We drove slowly in a six-vehicle HMMWV convoy, using sirens occasionally to blast a way through traffic—a highly visible, intrusive, and disruptive presence in a way that foot patrols are not. I was also concerned about the way the up-armored HMMWV affects our operations. As Steve [Miska, the insightful deputy commander to Colonel J.B. Burton of Dagger Brigade Combat Team, 2nd Brigade, 1st Infantry Division responsible for northwest Baghdad] pointed out, this is truly an "urban submarine"—we drive around in an armored box with three-inch-thick windows, peering out through our portholes at the little Iraqi fish swimming by. They can't see us, and we don't seem human to them. We are aliens—imperial stormtroopers with our Darth Vader sunglasses and grotesque and cowardly body armor. [Again, as Steve said], the insurgents have done to us what we said we would do to them—isolated us from the population by using the IED, and [by leveraging] our penchant for technology and fear of casualties. And we gain nothing in the process—the latest EFP [Explosively Formed Projectile] and underbelly attack IEDs will blow right through an uparmored Humvee like a breeze.

The alternative is foot patrolling—but foot patrolling done properly, not walking about in one big tightly bunched group (as we did, to my horror), which just creates an obvious, big target. Instead, you make use of small teams—bricks or fire-teams of five or six that move about 1–200 yards apart—far enough from each other that they do not become a single target, but close enough to support each other in the event of an incident....

We drove along [the] street for a few blocks, passing through an Iraqi Army checkpoint. The Iraqi soldier at the VCP [Vehicle Checkpoint] was waving at us frantically to stop (he seemed to be trying to warn us of something). [It turned out to be an ambush just up the road.] I was in the lead vehicle, and the vehicle commander simply leaned out the window and said casually to the frantic Iraqi soldier "Hey buddy, we don't stop for you people," as the convoy rolled slowly past.[39]

PATROLLING WITH PETRAEUS

During this period, General Petraeus was constantly out on the ground, observing, encouraging, coaching, and directing, stamping his authority

Figure 3.3 Iraq, March 2007—General Petraeus, in soft hat, walks the ground with local Iraqi commanders.

Photo: MNF-I

on the force as the new style of operations took hold. He also used "battle-field circulation" activities to engage directly with the Iraqi people. Here is an account of one such activity in early April 2007, out on the ground with an escort from 1st Battalion, 5th U.S. Cavalry, in a narrow crowded street in Ameriya, still at this time a major AQI stronghold:

> I was struck, as on a couple of occasions before, at how fully Petraeus gives his entire attention to the person speaking with him.... For example, on this occasion he was standing at the back of a parked car talking animatedly to a middle-aged man, eating an ice cream from a local shop with him, spreading out a map and blueprints to discuss the district's future.... Meanwhile the man's wife and small daughter were sitting in the front passenger seat of the car, the child smiling and happy but her mother looking bored, uncomfortable, keen to be gone, and quite frightened—of us, with our machine guns, helmets, body armor, and sunglasses, and also of the risk to the family in being seen in public talking in a friendly way with the general....

The other Americans stood around in their helmets, mirror sunglasses, and body armor, looking robotic rather than aggressive, but not engaging the population at all. . . . With my few words of Arabic I told the people it was OK to go past, and told a young man who was wheeling his motorcycle cautiously past that he could ride off. But there was still a large crowd gathering—about 40 people in the narrow confines of a single-lane street. About half were the local children who, realizing I spoke a little Arabic, came up and asked cheekily if I would buy them a soccer ball from the local shop. By now we had been here about half an hour, and I felt we were making ourselves quite a target, and, more important, putting at risk all the people in the street, either from a direct attack on us or from follow-up intimidation.

So I decided (against my normal rule of keeping kids at arm's length) to use the children to spread the crowd out and break the target up. So I went into the shop (followed by five beaming 10-year-olds) and bought a red soccer ball for them. The shopkeeper and I had exchanged a few words earlier, and he was friendly. . . . Back in the street I kicked the ball as hard as I could; the 20 or so children followed it with great shouts of glee, and we kicked the ball up and down the street. I took my helmet off (technically a no-no, but you can't play soccer against 20 ten-year olds in a helmet and body armor), and the game spread the crowd out. . . . General Petraeus looked up after 10 minutes or so, smiled, and came over to play. The interpreters followed, and the game went on for another 10 minutes . . . we then mounted up and moved off.[40]

This focus on local community engagement and generating bottom-up buy-in from ordinary Iraqis, entirely typical of General Petraeus's approach, was a key part of our methodology. But, as this example highlights, it was not without its risks, and his direct, hands-on leadership style also caused us on his personal staff considerable anxiety at times. On one occasion later in the year, I discussed this with Colonel Pete Mansoor, the general's incredibly energetic and intelligent executive officer, who later published a classic account of his tour as a brigade commander in Iraq in 2004–2005, *Baghdad at Sunrise*.[41] This was during the "surge of operations" (described below) when units needed lots of on-field coaching and both General Petraeus and myself had separately been out on the ground almost constantly. As Pete and I discussed, because of the enormous political and military emphasis being placed on General Petraeus—by the media, Congress, and the president—as being himself the key to victory in Iraq, his safety had become a strategic issue. If one of us on the staff, myself for example, was killed while out on the street with a unit, this would obviously be unfortunate for us, but it would not matter at all at the strategic level. But if the General were killed or even wounded, the effect it would have on public opinion and morale (in both Iraq and the United States) would be such that we could lose the war at a stroke. A belief in his competence had become, to some extent, our psychological center of gravity at the strategic level. So we tried to convince him to travel less and expose himself less to risk. We failed utterly in this, and I was struck, not for the first or last time, by the calm, courageous and measured way he handled what must have been almost unbearable stress and pressure.

JOINT SECURITY STATIONS

Out on the ground, units were now deployed in and operating from JSSs all over the city. Officers and NCOs from 1st Battalion, 325th Airborne Infantry Regiment with whom I worked with in the Kadhimiya area in March told me how happy they were to finally be out on the ground, doing their job. This tough and competent battalion, commanded by Lieutenant Colonel Mike Richardson, had been based at a FOB in Taji, north of the city, through most of 2006, supporting Special Forces raiding and time-sensitive targeting operations against AQ, before adopting the population security mission in March 2007 and deploying forward into JSSs and combat outposts. Before forward-deploying, battalions had lost many troops who had been killed and injured while "commuting to the fight"—running the gauntlet of IEDs and ambushes to get into their operating area every day, and then running the same gauntlet home at night. Now 1–325 Airborne Infantry were living in their area rather than visiting it—they could simply step out of the front door and be at work, and by avoiding the deadly commute and always working with Iraqi partners including police, army and the local Ghaydat tribe, they had managed to reduce their casualties substantially since the beginning of the year.[42]

Another JSS, in al-Jamiah, part of the al-Khadra neighborhood north of Ameriya and Hateen in downtown Baghdad, was in the area controlled by Lieutenant Colonel Dale Kuehl's 1st Battalion 5th Cavalry, another outstanding unit. It was typical of the set-up in central Baghdad:

After again winding our way through shabby streets, we found ourselves at the battalion's JSS, which is constructed in what looked like a disused school building, surrounded by T-walls and high guard towers. The streets around it are flooded with sewage—the sewage is pumped electrically and backs up when the power stops, which is about half the time in Baghdad. The people simply get on with life. As we turned into the gateway of the JSS perimeter, there was a huge explosion about two blocks away. It was getting dark by now, and we saw the flash against the twilit sky; the puddles of sewage rippled briefly, and dust came off the buildings. A large amount of [rifle] fire then broke out from the direction of the explosion—many of the shots coming our way with a "crack" overhead.... We parked the HMMWVs in the courtyard then went into the JSS, where the Iraqi garrison (a company) were struggling into their kit and climbing the stairs to their rooftop fighting positions. The American CSM [command sergeant major] explained what had happened.

About two blocks over, on "phone card road" as it is called, the Iraqi battalion had a vehicle checkpoint manned by a platoon. The insurgents had targeted it with a truck-bomb VBIED [vehicle-borne IED] killing several, including an Iraqi senior officer. The firing was not part of an ambush but rather the Iraqi battalion hosing down anything that looked likely to have been the spotter's location for the IED.

[The JSS] is a two-story concrete and brick building, heavily sandbagged but still with a glass-walled entrance foyer. The second floor houses the dining facility, offices, and the Joint Ops Center (JOC) which is manned by the U.S. battalion, Iraqi army battalion, and Iraq police. It has a large aerial photograph showing individual houses, marked up as a battle map on one wall, and a row of desks with watchkeepers and communications kit on the opposite wall. In between is a conference table at which the IA, IP and the U.S. battalion do joint planning. It is pretty steam-driven [i.e. rudimentary and Spartan], but looks effective for its purpose, which is basically to run a two-company urban patrol base.

The next floor up is the Iraqi sleeping accommodation, a series of steel double bunks, footlockers, and military equipment in piles. The floor is dark due to lack of electricity and the sandbagged windows. The same floor is the U.S. accommodation, sleeping a company (+) in very similar conditions to the Iraqis.[43]

BREAKING THE CYCLE OF VIOLENCE

By April, the components of our counterinsurgency approach were beginning to take shape, with Coalition and Iraqi forces working together in a more integrated fashion, including both civil and military organizations. We were now in a position to start reining in the cycle of violence described earlier. As noted, the cycle was a runaway variant of the accidental guerrilla syndrome, and worked as follows:

- Extremists, particularly those linked to AQ in Iraq, infiltrated Sunni communities and established base areas by intimidating the people. They sought to create a pall of fear over the community to prevent people turning them in to the authorities, so that they could plan and prepare attacks using these areas as bases.
- They then mounted attacks on neighboring Shi'a communities, often targeting markets, parks, and public places with suicide bombers or car bombs, and killing many innocent citizens in these districts.
- This provoked a response from militias and vigilante groups, who attacked their Sunni neighbors in "retaliation." They were not really retaliating against the true guilty party, the extremists, who simply went to ground. Rather, they conducted extrajudicial killings, kidnapping and killing ordinary citizens, or "sectarian cleansing," driving Sunnis out of their homes.
- These sectarian attacks polarized and split the community, created tensions that made it extremely difficult to make progress on political reconciliation, and further intimidated the Sunni communities, which closed ranks in the face of the external threat. This created further space and opportunity for extremist intimidation, and so the cycle went on, around and around again.

The cycle did not always start with AQ, although provoking exactly this kind of intersectarian violence was a long-standing element in their strategy (as noted). Sometimes it started with Shi'a extremists, including the so-called secret cells or extremist terrorists linked to JAM or to Iranian-sponsored groups. But in essence this was the vicious circle that had done so much damage in Iraq. There were number of "accelerants" in this process—people or conditions that intensified the cycle of violence, making the vicious circle run faster, and killing more innocent people. These accelerants included AQI terrorists, members of other terrorist groups, foreign fighters, infiltration, or interference by neighboring countries (especially Iran), and crime and unemployment.

Of course, this is an oversimplification, and there were many other causes of violence in Iraq in 2007. But this vicious circle was the main cause of the extreme violence that did such damage to Iraqi society in the 12 months between the Samarra mosque bombing in February 2006 and the implementation of the new strategy in February 2007. So it was the main dynamic we needed to address. In essence, the component parts of the joint counterinsurgency approach were designed to address it by breaking the cycle at each stage in the process.

- First, we sought to make it harder for extremists to infiltrate Sunni communities, or to find safe haven in them. We did this by securing the population by means of emplacing among them JSSs with both a U.S. and Iraqi presence, including police and military units, often based on an Iraqi police station. We also sought to dominate the rural belts on the city's outskirts, to control access to Baghdad and make it harder for what we called the "commuter insurgency" to function. The "commuter insurgents" based themselves outside Baghdad proper and operated by "raiding" into the city. Civil programs led by the Iraqi government and supported by our embedded provincial reconstruction teams (EPRTs) also helped protect communities and render them resistant to infiltration.

- Second, even if extremists did manage to infiltrate, we sought to make it harder for them to attack neighboring Shi'a communities. We did this partly through a system of "gated communities," access controls that meant we knew who was supposed to be in any part of the city and who was not. These included perimeter security measures such as barriers, walls, and checkpoints, so that there were only a limited number of controlled access points. This meant that if extremists did succeed in creating a base in a Sunni community, it was much harder for them to sneak a car bomb or suicide bomber out or for that bomber to sneak into a neighboring district. We also protected communities by "hardening" markets, shops, and public places with blast walls, concrete barriers and other bomb-proofing measures, and by using JSSs to establish a permanent presence to protect the people.

- Third, if a terrorist attacker still did manage to get through, we deterred retaliation or sectarian backlash, again through gated communities protecting innocent Sunnis that made it hard for death squads to target them. And our JSSs and patrol bases established a permanent, 24/7 presence (most extrajudicial killings occurred at night-time) to protect people in their homes.

- All of these measures were designed to reduce the feeling of intimidation and lift the pall of fear from communities so that people would become willing to give information to the government about the extremists, and able to avail themselves of economic opportunities. As the cycle of violence was reduced, this also created more space for political compromise and reconciliation.

Finally, we conducted operations to support the rule of law, which helped deal with the "accelerants," and we introduced what we might call "decelerants" such as political reconciliation and building competent, nonsectarian governance and national institutions, which helped slow and reduce the intensity of the violence.

By May, we had reoriented the force to the new way of operating, shaken out into JSSs and patrol bases across the city and the surrounding belts, installed 11 "safe neighborhood" systems to break the cycle of violence, and completed the surge of additional personnel, now numbering almost 28,500. I had studied the tactics needed and prepared detailed counterinsurgency guidance, which I then revised in close cooperation with General Odierno's senior adviser, the acerbically witty and phenomenally competent Englishwoman Emma Sky, a true Iraq expert and a highly valued colleague who knew Iraq like few others. General Odierno then issued this guidance in both Arabic and English to all Iraqi and coalition forces in MNC-I.[44] We had trained and oriented incoming brigades, established EPRTs as part of the "civilian surge" of aid agency and State Department personnel, and completed the "surge of forces." We were ready to take the offensive.

ONTO THE OFFENSIVE

On June 15, 2007, Coalition and Iraqi forces kicked off a major series of division-sized operations in Baghdad and the surrounding provinces. As General Odierno said at the time, we had finished the build-up phase of additional troops that had been brought into the theatre to support the Surge, and we

Figure 3.4 Iraq, June 2007—Troops taking cover during a sniper attack, central Baghdad.

Photo: MNF-I

were now beginning the actual "surge of operations." These operations were qualitatively different from what had gone before in Iraq, and therefore are worth examining in some detail, insofar as they bear on the relationship between local insurgents and global terrorists in Iraq in 2007.

The intent of these operations, collectively known as the Arrowhead series, was to clear several of the insurgents' safe havens simultaneously, in order to prevent terrorists (primarily AQI) from relocating their infrastructure from one to another, and to create an operational synergy between what we were doing in Baghdad and what was happening outside the city in the belts, the term used to describe the populated areas of farmland, and the rural villages aligned with the major river valleys and communications routes on the outskirts of Baghdad. Although we had not done so on previous occasions, this time we planned to stay in these areas once they were secured. These operations ran over months, throughout most of 2007, and the key activity was to establish viable local security forces in partnership with Iraqi army and police, as well as political and economic programs, to permanently secure areas after clearing them. The really decisive activity in this type of operation was police work, registration of the population, and counterintelligence in cleared areas. The aim was to comb out the insurgent sleeper cells and political cells that went quiet as our forces moved in and tried to survive through the operation and emerge later. This type of approach took operational patience, and it had to be intelligence driven and Iraqi government–led. Such efforts rarely if ever make the news (the really important stuff almost never did in Iraq in 2007), but in a campaign like this they were the truly decisive action.

In counterinsurgency terms, "clearing" an enemy safe haven does not mean *destroying the enemy* in it but *rescuing the population* in it from enemy intimidation or, more clinically, separating the enemy from the population. Destroying the enemy is strictly secondary and, in fact, not always necessary. Just as important, we operated in such a way as to try and separate local-focus groups that were potentially reconcilable (the accidental guerrillas) from irreconcilable extremists. We did not expect to destroy all, or even most, enemy cells in the initial operation. Rather, the point of the operations was to lift the pall of fear from population groups whom terrorists had intimidated and exploited, win them over, and work with them in partnership to clean out the cells that remained—as occurred in Al Anbar Province in 2006–2007 and later elsewhere in Iraq as well.

The "terrain" being cleared was human terrain, not physical terrain. Our operations focused on marginalizing AQ, Shi'a extremist militias, and other threat groups from the population they had long preyed on. This is why claims, repeated in the media, that "80 percent of AQ leadership have fled" in response to our entering Diyala Province did not overly disturb us: the aim was not to kill every last AQ leader but to drive off AQ from the population and keep them away, so that we could then work with the community to prevent their return.

This was not some sort of kindhearted, soft approach, as several armchair war-hawks claimed at the time from behind the safety of their desks in Washington and other distant cities.[45] It was not about being "nice" to the population and hoping they would somehow see us as the "good guys" and stop supporting the insurgents. On the contrary, our approach was based on a clear-eyed appreciation of certain basic facts,[46] to wit:

- *An insurgent enemy needs the people to act in certain ways.* He needs their sympathy, acquiescence, and silence, or simply their reaction to provocation, in order to survive and further his strategy. Unless the population acts in these ways, both insurgents and terrorists will wither, and the cycle of provocation and backlash that drives the sectarian conflict in Iraq will fail.

- *The enemy is fluid, but the population is fixed.* (The enemy is fluid because he has no permanent installations he needs to defend, and can always run away to fight another day. The population is fixed because people are tied to their homes, businesses, farms, tribal areas, relatives, and so on.) Therefore—and this was the major change in our strategy in Iraq in 2007—protecting and controlling the population is doable, but destroying the enemy is not. We can drive him off from the population, introduce local security forces, resource and population control, and economic and political development, and thereby "hardwire" the enemy out of the environment, preventing his return. But chasing enemy cells around the countryside is not only a waste of time but precisely the sort of action he wants to provoke us into. That was why AQ cells leaving an area as we moved in were not the main game—in strategic terms, they were a distraction. In Iraq, we had played the enemy's game for too long. Not any more. By focusing on the population instead of the enemy, we forced him to play our game.

- *Being fluid, the enemy can control his loss rate and therefore can never be eradicated by purely enemy-centric means:* he can just go to ground if the pressure becomes too much. But because he needs the population to act in certain ways in order to survive, we can asphyxiate him by cutting him off from the people. And he cannot just "go quiet" to avoid that threat. He has either to come out of the woodwork, fight us and be destroyed, or stay quiet and accept permanent marginalization from his former population base. That puts him on the horns of a lethal dilemma.

- *The enemy may not be identifiable, but the population is.* In any given area in Iraq in 2007, there were multiple threat groups but only one, or sometimes two, main local population groups. We could do (and did, in the past) enormous damage to potential supporters, "destroying the haystack to find the needle," but by taking a population-centric approach we found we did not need to: we knew who the people were whom we needed to protect, we knew where they lived, and we were able to protect them without unbearable disruption to their lives. More to the point, we were able to help them protect themselves, with our forces and Iraqi security forces in a backup role.

Of course, during the series of major operations of 2007 we still went after all the terrorist and extremist leaders we could target and find, and life became increasingly difficult for this group. Al Qa'ida in Iraq suffered severe damage and proved unable, at least in the short term, to reconstitute itself in the face of the pressure we had generated through a combination of our own operations, partnerships with local communities who turned on the enemy, and the Iraqi government and its security forces. But at the strategic level, we realized clearly that such operations were just a shaping activity in support of the main effort, which was to secure the Iraqi people from the terrorists, extremist militias, and insurgents who had been exploiting them.

Was there a strategic risk involved in this series of operations? Absolutely. Nothing in war is hazard-free, and in this case we had barely sufficient troop numbers, in classical counterinsurgency terms, to pursue the operations we conducted. But we chose to accept and manage this risk, primarily because a more timid option simply would not have generated the operational leverage the strategic situation demanded, and certainly not in time to regain domestic confidence in the United States. We had limited time, we knew that no more troops would be forthcoming, and we had to take dramatic action to regain the initiative and stabilize the situation in time to convince a hostile Congress to continue supporting the mission. So we chose to play the hand we had been dealt as intelligently as possible, and did what had to be done, even though in an ideal world such measures might not have been the preferred option.

The practice, as always, was mixed. Rather than summarizing it myself, it is more appropriate that I draw on the assessment of Colin Kahl, a leading Iraq war expert who, far from being a Bush administration partisan, was principal adviser on Iraq strategy to President Barack Obama during his presidential campaign, is no uncritical supporter of the Surge, and has traveled in Iraq several times and written numerous detailed analyses of progress there. In Kahl's words:

> There has been significant and meaningful improvement in the security situation since the Surge began. The clearest evidence for this is the declining level of Iraqi civilian casualties.... Civilian deaths skyrocketed in 2006 after the February bombing of the Golden

Shrine in Samarra tipped Iraq into sectarian civil war. In early 2007, violence began to decline somewhat, albeit unevenly, before dropping dramatically beginning in August.... The total number of all types of attacks on U.S. forces, Iraqi Security Forces (ISF), and Iraqi civilians have significantly decreased since the Surge began, eventually declining to 2005 levels. Falling American casualty rates also suggest an improvement in the security environment. Overall, 2007 was the deadliest year in Iraq for the U.S.... but casualties fell substantially in the latter part of the year. From a peak three-month total of 331 U.S. troops killed in April–June 2007, the numbers declined by 70 percent to 98 in October–December, the lowest three-month total of the entire war. Fatalities have increased somewhat thus far in 2008, but are still at levels not seen consistently since 2003. Finally, U.S. and Iraqi forces have made great strides against AQI [and] the organization's fortunes are likely to decline further.[47]

It was a long, hard summer, with much pain and loss, and at times it seemed as if things could still go either way. But the population-centric approach that infused these operations was the beginning of a process that sought to put the overall campaign onto a sustainable long-term footing. The political dimension of the matter could then be decisive, provided the Iraqis used the time we had bought for them to reach the essential accommodation: an inter-communal balance of power policed by a central government capable of maintaining a stable internal environment and governing in the interests of all Iraqis rather than one sectarian group. So far, there are limited signs that this is occurring, and indeed there are indications that in the event of a precipitate withdrawal from Iraq, the situation might slide back into the civil war situation of 2006 and early 2007. Fundamentally, however, this is something that only Iraqis can resolve: our role so far has been to provide an environment in which it becomes possible.

Here, then, is a brief field-based account of some aspects of the environment in Iraq in 2007 and the way the campaign progressed. It is now appropriate to consider the war from a more analytical perspective.

HYBRID WARFARE IN IRAQ

During 2007, as noted, through the application of population-centric counterinsurgency techniques, building local partnerships, and reconciling communities, U.S. and Iraqi forces under General Petraeus succeeded in stabilizing a security situation that had been fast spinning out of control.

As also noted, Iraq is much more than solely a counterinsurgency campaign, so what happens there cannot be fully understood through a classical counterinsurgency lens. Like other campaigns since 9/11 it is a hybrid conflict that involves not only a domestic insurgency including accidental guerrillas and local fighters but also elements of sectarian and ethnic conflict, international terrorism, foreign fighters (including, of course, the Coalition), and regional nation-state rivalry relating to the "Islamic civil war" and "Shi'a awakening" models described in chapter 1. The conflict is therefore an example of the type I have examined in some detail in chapters 1 and 2: hybrid warfare, with elements of "unrestricted warfare" and nation-building alongside counterterrorism and counterinsurgency.

The framework[48] I am going to suggest for thinking about hybrid warfare in Iraq is a model, not a strategy. That is, it is a systematic oversimplification, designed to clarify an extremely complex, rapidly changing reality. It is derived from thinking that was suggested to me by Professor Erin Simpson of the U.S. Marine Corps Staff College, in discussions about hybrid warfare and the problems of intervening powers in foreign complex counterinsurgencies. The model does not tell us what to do in Iraq, but is a basis for evaluating options. It is wrong—by definition, in a strictly theoretical sense, all models are—but applied tentatively, with skepticism, and with constant and rigorous firsthand observation in theater, I have sometimes found it useful. Of course, reality is neither so neatly nor so dispassionately described, with the broken lives, butchered children, smashed communities, homeless refugees, and baroque acts of cruelty and communal vengeance that have cracked the very foundations of Iraqi society. But the violence is far from random: each instantiation of the conflict seems to emerge from deeper drivers, and broader trends can be observed. Figure 3.5 expresses the model graphically.

This model suggests that hybrid warfare in Iraq consists of four strategic problems: an underlying *capacity-building* problem, resulting from the fact that Iraq is a weak and fragile state; and three overlapping security problems that sit above that underlying problem, and make it harder to get at it. The three problems are:

- *Terrorism*—that is, the presence of terrorist entities including (but not limited to) AQI, who seek to exploit the situation and manipulate the population to further extremist or transnational aims
- *Insurgency*—the Sunni rebellion against the new post-Saddam order in Iraq, including rebellion against both the Coalition presence and the

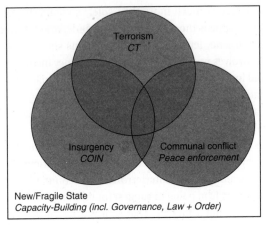

Figure 3.5 Iraq as a four-problem set diagram. The fundamental problem is control— of people, terrain, and information.

new Iraqi government, as well as the Shi'a radical rebellion against established authority, which is more in the nature of a social revolution

- *Communal conflict*—including sectarian conflict between Sunni and Shi'a elements of the Iraqi population, and ethnic conflict between Kurds, Arabs, Turkmen, and other ethnic groups

These three security problems overlap: any given incident on the ground may involve elements of more than one dimension—for example, some terrorism is pure AQI activity, while other terrorist acts are locally motivated, and yet others also incorporate a sectarian or ethnic dimension. Most incidents in fact include elements of two or all three of these dynamics. One might think of the three problems as a Venn diagram of overlapping circles, each constantly changing in size, such that any incident can be plotted somewhere within the interaction of the three dynamics, affecting the underlying dynamic of national capacity-building.

These problems prevent us from getting at the underlying issues (crime, weak infrastructure, economic and social alienation, weak governance, poor border security, corruption, inadequate institutions of law and order, lack of civil legal and regulatory frameworks, unemployment, public health, the process of recovery from decades of Ba'athist dictatorship, and so on) that must be addressed in order to build effective and legitimate institutions for the Iraqi state and foster a robust civil society in Iraq. The difficulty of getting at this underlying problem perpetuates and exacerbates the security dynamic.

The three security problems are also mutually reinforcing. Terrorism provokes communal conflict, which in turn makes the insurgency more intractable, which in turn gives rise to terrorism, and so on. Ironically, the solutions to these problems also tend to be countervailing—solutions to one problem tend to worsen the others. For example, defeating the insurgency requires building indigenous security forces. But in a society with weak national institutions, divided along sectarian lines, this can exacerbate the communal conflict, as we saw in 2006. Resolving the communal conflict in 2007 required that we reach out to reconcilable leaders within all community groups, including those (such as some Sunni groups in Anbar in 2006) who supported the terrorists. But this in turn can create safe havens for terrorists. Countering terrorist cells implies disrupting these safe havens, but that can alienate the population and thus make the insurgency worse—and so on.

THE REGIONAL DYNAMIC

This "four-problem set" of hybrid warfare sits within a regional instability complex that straddles an Arab world (Arabia and parts of the Levant) that is 90 percent Sunni and a Persian Shi'a world (primarily Iran, but also Iranian proxies and allies in other countries) with a long history of internal and intraregional conflict and tension. As General Anthony Zinni remarked in 2006, in toppling Saddam the United States and its allies created the first Shi'a Arab state in modern history, with profound implications for the long-standing regional dynamic, and the global relationship between Sunni and Shi'a Islam, that Western political leaders are only just starting to appreciate.[49]

This regional dynamic implies two things. First, conflict within Iraq that threatens to spill into the broader region or drag Sunni Arab states into increased confrontation with Iran is, by definition, more strategically ominous than conflict that remains within Iraq. By this measure, the model was already predicting in 2004 that communal conflict, exacerbated by terrorist provocation, would turn out to have broader strategic significance than the insurgency itself[50] (though this tends to change over time—in 2006 the intense sectarian violence following the Samarra bombing had major regional implications as well as influencing global perceptions of the war).

Second, the regional conflict dynamic suggests that it is critical that the United States and its allies conduct the campaign in Iraq within a broader regional campaign (diplomatic, economic, and informational), not running it as if Iraq were an island somewhere in the Indian Ocean but rather recognizing the reality that it is a central puzzle-piece in a complex regional system. We have to approach the region as a region, and maintain a realistic appraisal of the limits on our own ability to shape events. This is obvious, though not everyone seems to have always recognized it, especially early in the war.

"COUNTERINSURGENCY PLUS"

Iraq, then, is not a pure insurgency problem but a hybrid war involving what we might call "counterinsurgency plus." Classical counterinsurgency theory per se does not provide any comprehensive answers for the conflict. Rather, prosecuting the campaign demands an agile mixing of counterinsurgency, counterterrorism, border security, nation-building, and peace enforcement operations, all of which must be underpinned by a robust political strategy. Civil and military efforts must be tightly integrated. And local operations must be conducted within a regional and global perspective. Effective counterinsurgency is a sine qua non for success, but it is still only one component within a truly hybrid conflict.

In this sense, U.S. secretary of defense Donald Rumsfeld was partially correct in 2003 when, during press conferences on the Iraq War, he denied that the enemy was an insurgency and rejected the media's comparison of the campaign with Vietnam.[51] This was almost true, in that Iraq is not just an insurgency, it is an insurgency plus a terrorist campaign plus a sectarian civil war, sitting on top of a fragile state within a divided, unstable region. And Vietnam is indeed not an apt comparison. The insurgency component of the Iraq War may resemble the Vietnam War to a limited extent, but insurgency is only one part of a much bigger problem in Iraq. If we were to draw historical analogies, we might say that operations in Iraq are like trying to defeat the Viet Cong (insurgency) while simultaneously rebuilding Germany (nation-building following war and dictatorship), keeping peace in the Balkans (communal and sectarian conflict), and defeating the IRA (domestic terrorism). These all have to be done at the same time, in the same place, and changes in one part of the problem significantly affect the others.

Thus, Iraq represents a fiendishly difficult, complex, and constantly changing set of problems whose dynamic interaction drives the conflict.

This is one reason, among many, that Coalition forces found it so difficult to stabilize the country after the fall of Saddam Hussein's regime in April 2003. The problem is incredibly tough, and requires constant adaptation and agility of response. Indeed, Iraq—in common with other examples of hybrid warfare—could be called a "wicked" problem, according to the very specific way planners and systems theorists use that term to refer to a class of problem that has no single solution and no "stopping rule" that indicates when it is solved, and where the very act of trying to solve it changes its nature, so that attempts to solve it are not repeatable and there is no possibility of success through trial and error. Such problems are actually very common in the public policy arena, and include gang warfare, antidrug programs, town and infrastructure planning, and public health programs. Incidentally, there is a solid body of research into this type of problem, which I and others have found very helpful in thinking about Iraq.[52]

From a practitioner's standpoint, the interaction of these multiple problems means that improvements in counterinsurgency technique and capability, while important in addressing the insurgency part of the problem, are not enough to deal with the broader strategic issue in Iraq. On the contrary, approaches that emphasize counterinsurgency technique to the exclusion of other problem dynamics may actually be counterproductive, elevating tactics to the level of strategy. Instead, in implementing the Surge in 2007, we found ourselves needing solutions that dealt with all four problems strategically and simultaneously in an integrated fashion, as we attempted to impose order on an extremely complex overall environment.

Where a hybrid warfare model of the sort just outlined makes a difference is not so much at the tactical level (where the standard techniques of counterinsurgency, counterterrorism, and peace enforcement are being applied effectively by local commanders—most of whom understood them very well by the middle of 2007—and had already been applied by some commanders in 2006) as at the strategic level, in prioritizing actions to address each of the campaign's component problems, deciding whether and where to expend resources, and, most important, developing metrics to "read the environment" and understand how it changes over time. In a sense, models like this, and other examples of Hybrid Warfare concepts such as those advanced by leading thinkers in this area like Frank Hoffman, provide a prototypical "operational design" for the Iraqi theater.[53] In terms of evaluating options, such a model allows commanders to develop metrics to understand the second- and third-order effects of a given action. Does it help us get at the underlying problem? Does it exacerbate the other security problems? Does it address more than one security problem simultaneously? Does it help prevent spillover of conflict to the regional level? Does it advance a nation-building agenda? The questions are different each time, but the model helps frame them and work out which factors matter most in a given situation, as for example during the "surge of operations" in mid-2007.

Case Study: The Iraqi Tribal Revolt

As noted, some aspects of the war in Iraq in 2007 were utterly typical of historical insurgencies, but others were harder to fit into classical counterinsurgency theory and were better understood as part of a "counterinsurgency plus" or hybrid warfare campaign. And the accidental guerrilla syndrome was well in evidence on the ground.

One of the most striking aspects of the Surge was the growing tribal uprising against AQ, which in late 2006 and 2007 began to transform the war in ways that had not been factored into the neat "benchmarks" developed largely by the U.S. Congress, many months before and thousands of miles away. As noted, I spent time out on the ground during May and June, in Baghdad and the surrounding districts, working with U.S. and Iraqi units, tribal and community leaders, and fighters engaged in the uprising. Listening to them talk, watching their operations, and participating in planning and execution alongside American commanders supporting them gave me some insight into their motivations and thought processes. Moreover, in this process of participant observation I was able to gather some field data on the relationship between globally oriented terrorists (primarily AQ) in Iraq, and the local-focus fighters who found themselves fighting as accidental guerrillas in the early part of the war, only to turn on the terrorists in 2007.

To understand what follows, one needs to realize that Iraqi tribes are not somehow separate, out in the desert, or remote: rather, they are powerful interest groups that overlap with and permeate all parts of Iraqi society. More than 85 percent of Iraqis claim some form of tribal affiliation; tribal identity is an informal but powerful sphere of influence in the community. Iraqi tribal leaders represent a power center in competition with the formal institutions of the state, and the tribes themselves are a parallel hierarchy that overlaps with formal government structures and political allegiances at every level. Most Iraqis wear their tribal selves alongside other strands of identity (religious, ethnic, regional, socio-economic) that interact in complex ways, rendering meaningless the facile divisions into Sunni, Shi'a, and Kurdish groups that distant observers sometimes perceive. The reality of Iraqi national character is much more complex than that, and tribal identity plays an extremely important part in it, even for urbanized Iraqis. Thus, the tribal revolt was not some remote riot on a reservation: it was a major social movement with the potential to significantly influence most Iraqis where they live.

THE NATURE OF TRIBAL LEADERSHIP IN IRAQ IN 2007

The key players, both in the revolt and in the series of local agreements and alliances that it involved, were Iraqi tribal sheikhs. The Arabic word *sheikh* literally means "old man" (the feminine equivalent is *sheikhah*). Since increasing age confers respect in Arab culture, the term has come to have an honorific significance and can be applied as a mark of respect to any old person. In addition, Arabs use the term *sheikh* in a tribal context to indicate a position of leadership within a tribe or local community (akin to the notion of a "tribal elder" in Pashtun society, discussed in the previous chapter, though as we have seen Iraqi tribes are much more ordered, responsive and hierarchical than Pashtun tribes). Thus, in dealing with Iraqis one frequently encounters individuals who self-identify or are identified by their group as sheikhs (*shuyukh*).

There are more than 350 tribes in Iraq, with at least 162 leaders claiming sheikhly status in northern Babil Province alone.[54] Because of this complexity, it is not always obvious to outsiders what criteria enable someone to call himself a sheikh. For the purposes of this discussion, in the Iraqi tribal context, a sheikh can be conceived of as a senior male member of a tribal lineage group who exercises informal authority (subject to boundaries delimited by tradition) over members of that group. A sheikh's authority is rarely completely uncontested, and may be functionally defined in categories like dispute resolution, management of tribal businesses or criminal activities, war leadership, or expertise in *aadat* (tribal customary law). Thus, each tribal group may have many *shuyukh*, and a given group of Iraqis may have overlapping relationships of varying strength with several *shuyukh*. Those of us who dealt with tribal fighters during the sahawa (the "awakening," as Iraqis initially called the tribal uprising) rapidly found that we could not expect a line-and-block diagram in which each fighter was under the command of one, and only one, sheikh. Tribes are extended families, after all.

A sheikh is also not a *malik* (king), a term that implies ownership and hereditary authority that many Arabs reject. Neither is he necessarily an *emir* (prince), a concept that implies military command or governmental authority and, in the Iraqi context, is tainted through its use by *takfiri* terrorist groups such as AQ or the Islamic State of Iraq (ISI). Sheikhly status does not necessarily imply religious authority, although an *imam* may sometimes be addressed as "Sheikh" in an honorific sense, and some tribal *shuyukh* may also happen to hold positions of religious authority. The sheikh's status therefore does not imply ownership or command, but his standing, based on personal prestige and lineage, allows him to influence (to a greater or lesser degree) the actions of individuals within his sphere of authority. A sheikh's primary role is to care for his tribe.

Different tribes select leaders using slightly different approaches, but the common feature is that once chosen, group members accept the sheikh's authority and submit themselves to his judgment. He retains his authority unless he steps down, is deposed by a rival, or is forced aside by public rejection following disloyalty or incompetence. His authority theoretically dies with him and, unless his descendants have shown themselves worthy, there is no absolute guarantee that they will inherit his authority. Should they achieve prominence through their own personal qualities, their ability to claim lineage connections to a famously competent or prestigious ancestor may enhance their status. But birth in itself is no guarantee of authority, and tribal lineages are often fictive anyway, as when tribes attempt to cement a contemporary political alignment by means of reference to a presumed, but rarely historical, common ancestor.

The qualities my Iraqi informants said they most admired in a tribal leader were energy, loyalty, wisdom in settling disputes, a talent for gaining benefits for the tribe through negotiation with the government or other tribes, generosity, hospitality, unrelenting pursuit of blood feuds or vendettas, and consistency. In practice, a sheikh's authority is measured by the affirmation of his leadership in the eyes of tribal public opinion and his ability to make decisions "stick"—things that can only be judged on his record of performance over time.

Tribes tend to keep disputes within the confines of the tribal polity: this is because public disagreement shows weakness that may undermine both the sheikh's prestige (*wasta*) and the resulting prestige and cohesion of the tribe. For this reason, informants told us, disloyalty to the tribe, and by extension to the tribal leadership, is the worst offense a tribal member can commit.

This is one reason why shame, loss of face, or failure to meet commitments on the part of coalition commanders are so offensive to Iraqi leaders—each of these has a corrosive effect on a leader's unbroken record of success, which is the foundation for his power. A sheikh is only as good as his record of achievements, and his honor is closely linked to his perceived reliability, his ability to deliver. This is also why a sheikh may be extremely reluctant to press a decision until he is sure it will be accepted by his group; tribal leaders become expert in judging how far they can go without provoking disobedience, which would undercut their authority. For this reason, they tend to trim their sails to the winds of tribal public opinion as they understand it. Some coalition commanders find this frustrating, but it is understandable if one realizes that a sheikh is first and foremost a local politician whose power derives from his group's support. Tribal government is no less "democratic" for being informal, and *shuyukh* represent one of the few types of leader in Iraq today with real constituents whose interests they have to take into account.

Iraqis often describe themselves as "sheikh of the X *fakhdh* [clan]," "sheikh of the Y *'ashira* [tribe]," or "paramount sheikh of the Z *qabila* [tribal confederation]." Because the Iraqi tribal system has been corroded over decades by the Ba'ath dictatorship, sanctions, war, and insurgency, these claims are often extremely difficult to verify, and in many cases are exaggerated or boastful. I have often been astounded by the number of individuals, claiming sheikhly status, who emerge when a tribal agreement is to be negotiated and whose status is accepted (often with reservations, snide comments, or eye-rolling condescension) by other sheikhs. In practice, the authority an individual sheikh exercises, and therefore the reliance we can place on his commitments, can only be determined through trial, error, and relationship-building.

Many urban Iraqis look down on the tribes. In particular, they regard nomadic or seminomadic *bedw* ("bedouins"—also called *arab* in Iraq) who graze flocks on the desert fringe as little better than savages. This contempt may lead townspeople—particularly members of religious or political parties—to belittle a *bedw* sheikh, treating him as a second-class citizen. In some meetings, I observed urban Iraqi officials waiting patiently while a sheikh spoke, but then passing comments behind his back about the stupidity and parochialism of tribal leaders.[55] Commanders found that they had to be wary of this when working with interpreters or officials of nontribal origin.[56]

Tribal authority is also only one form of influence, though a pervasive one, in Iraqi society. In any district or population group, there are several competing centers of authority, including tribal structures, insurgent or terrorist networks, local mosques, business and criminal networks, Iraqi government structures, political and religious parties, and official and "unofficial" security forces. Many individuals occupy places of authority in several of these hierarchies: as noted in the Kunar case study in chapter 2, they cultivate what Max Gluckman called "interhierarchical roles"[57] that allow them to survive threats from rivals within one power structure by mobilizing support from another. For example, an Iraqi tribal leader may also be a business leader or local employer, have links to a crime network, have a relative in the Iraqi security forces, and sit on a town council. He can therefore mobilize tribal, criminal, police or governance authority to defeat a business rival or deploy business and military authority to defeat a tribal rival. Clearly, the more networks a leader straddles, and the more effectively he can mobilize support within them, the more resilient a "survivor" he will be. We found it particularly useful to identify such individuals, who were often key influencers in communities.[58]

Finally, in Iraq in 2007, tribal leadership was war leadership. The Iraqi tribe has been described as a "mobile ministate" in which the sheikh combines the functions of lawgiver, administrator, judge, strategist, negotiator, deal-broker, foreign minister, and commander-in-chief.[59] This is true in general terms, but in current circumstances, the authority of a given tribal leader rests primarily on his ability to assemble and arm a group of fighters and direct them in warlike tasks. This may be why, in conversation, shuyukh often describe their authority in terms of the number of fighters they can field. Though (as in every other category of tribal leadership) the sheikh naturally exaggerates his authority, and other shuyukh may have competing claims on "his" fighters, a sheikh's convening authority is a useful observable measure of his weight in tribal affairs.

THE TRIBAL REBELLION AGAINST AL QA'IDA

In Iraq in 2007, we experienced a spreading social movement, expanding along kinship lines, that could best be described as a tribal rebellion against AQI by accidental guerrillas who had formerly allowed the *takfiriin* to exploit them. Only a naïf or someone unaware of our history of disappointed expectations regarding Iraqi tribes since 2003 would interpret this rebellion as necessarily indicating support for the Iraqi government or for Coalition forces. The tribes were not pro-Coalition, much less pro-Government but were anti-AQ. That said, our experience showed that the tribes, if correctly handled, could often be brought to see that their best interests lay in supporting the government and cooperating with the security architecture of the new Iraq. But this was not an integral part of their original motivation and required time, careful negotiation and confidence-building.

The rebellion against AQI was motivated, according to my informants, by a backlash against AQ's exclusive emphasis on religion and disregard of custom. One key informant put it this way:

"What you have to remember is that there are two things in Iraq, custom [*aadat*] and religion [*deen*]. Sometimes they go hand in hand, sometimes they clash. When they go hand in hand all is well, but when they clash they create discord [*fitna*]. When you think about tribes, you almost take the religion out of it. The tribes care about *aadat*. For example, if you ask a Shammari "What religion are you?" he will say "I am a Shammari."

"There are two types of sheikh. There are legitimate sheikhs of clans, and there are what we call the sheikhs of the nineties, who Saddam gave money and power in the 1990s. The tribes know who is real and who is powerful. The most powerful sheikhs are only one or two hundred people in Iraq. A good sheikh has time for the people, so the people come to him.

"In Anbar, the tribes are Dulaim and Zobai. The Zobai are an 'ashira of the Shammari [confederation]. The Zobai did not support Saddam 100 percent, though they got lots of money from him. He paid them to guard the roads and the oil pipelines. But they went their own way when they wanted to. When you [Americans] invaded, the Qa'ida came to the tribes and said "We are Sunni, you are Sunni. The Americans are helping the Shi'a, let's fight them together." And so the tribes fought the occupation forces alongside the Qa'ida.

"Now, after awhile, the tribes fell out with the Qa'ida. This happened last year. This is what happened. They began to argue over their women. The Qa'ida would come to the sheikh and say 'Give me your daughter' or 'Give me your sister.' I mean in marriage. The sheikh would say no, because in the tribal custom they protect their women and do not give them to outsiders. I mean, sometimes two tribes exchange their women as wives to settle a dispute, but they don't just let outsiders, who are not of the tribe, marry their women. The Qa'ida started arguing with them, saying "You must give me your daughter because this is sanctioned by religion, and in the Qur'an it says that tribal customs are ignorant." So the sheikhs became angry and clashed with the Qa'ida because they were not giving any role to tribal custom, and were giving it all to religion.

'Then the al-Qa'ida killed a tribal leader because of an argument over this. Then the tribes turned against them because they believed they were trying to rule over them and tell them what to do. The Qa'ida killed a sheikh's sons, and killed other people, and attacked the fuel smuggling that the tribes use to make money. Then more and more leaders turned against the takfiriin, and now the tribes are fighting al Qa'ida."[60]

The Zobai (Zoba') tribe mentioned here is a major tribal section of the large Shammari confederation (Arabic شمّر Šammar), a very powerful confederation with more than a million members in Iraq, and branches in Sa'udi Arabia and Kuwait. It has been closely associated with the 1920s Revolutionary Brigade and the Islamic Army of Iraq (al Jaysh al Islami). Tribal leaders have fought against the Coalition since 2003, and the tribe has often shown a high degree of unity, but by mid-2007 it appeared to be turning against AQI in most of its tribal area.

Indeed, there often seemed to be a "Zobai connection" somewhere in tribal groups opposing AQI. For example, one rural farming district in the southern belts experienced constant low-level warfare between Zobai and AQI fighters, with AQI or Zobai corpses turning up in the canals most mornings.[61] The conflict oscillated in terms of who had the upper hand, and the Zobai did not directly approach Coalition commanders, but local sheikhs requested permission to raise an armed neighborhood watch and began policing their own area against AQI, and seeking to cooperate with Coalition forces.[62]

Similarly, one group of fighters in an urban district in Baghdad was non-tribal, with leadership provided by imams of local mosques opposed to AQI.

These *imams* drew on local urban youth to police their streets and fight the terrorists, but their military adviser and "technical expert" was a Zobai clan leader with previous insurgent experience who was called in to help by one of the local *imams* who was related to him through a tribal connection.[63]

Likewise, Zobai tribesmen in Abu Ghraib District, west of Baghdad, were fighting AQI for most of 2007 and demonstrated increasing willingness to cooperate with Coalition forces, though not initially with the government of Iraq.[64] Several informants stressed the need to move quickly to demonstrate to the tribal leaders that there are benefits in cooperating with Coalition forces—something that our bureaucratic processes, and the reluctance of Iraqi government officials to sanction the relationship, made harder.

Tribal fighters who negotiated or engaged with Coalition commanders in 2007 tended to make very similar demands and requests—in one case, as follows:

- Local security must be led by local forces, which must have the right to run their own checkpoints and neighborhood watch organizations.
- Local leaders must have a role in deciding who is to be detained, and must have the power to detain and question suspects themselves and to give amnesty to individuals who promise not to fight for the terrorists any longer.
- Coalition forces were requested to help smooth any issues of deconfliction (i.e., preventing accidental "friendly fire" incidents) with Iraqi security forces, and in some areas locals asked for some form of recognition symbol so that they would not be mistaken for terrorists.
- Some leaders asked for logistical support (typically food, fuel, and propane for cooking) from Coalition forces.
- Local leaders and their forces almost always wanted to be integrated into the Iraqi government structure as a local police force, legitimately employed under the Iraqi government but responsible for security in their own districts.
- Some leaders requested that Iraqi police and army units, regarded as sectarian, stay out of their area. In some cases, they were willing to accept Iraqi security forces, provided these were accompanied by Coalition forces.[65]

In most areas where local groups began working with Coalition forces, they behaved responsibly. In one incident in Sadr al Yusufiya, a southern belt district, the local neighborhood watch discovered two terrorists (thought to be AQI) in the act of emplacing a roadside IED. They forced the terrorists to dig up the IED, then brought them to Coalition forces with the IED and handed them over for questioning. In this area, IED incidents dropped precipitously over several months, from several per day along the main road (through a farming community in canal country) in 2006 and early 2007 to zero by the middle of the year. This period coincided with the development of a close working relationship with local *shuyukh* on the part of Captain Palmer Philips, commanding Company B of the 2nd Battalion, 14th Infantry, an extremely energetic and competent officer who was given very solid support by his battalion and brigade commanders in 2nd BCT, 10th Mountain Division, and benefited from a highly capable group of platoon commanders and senior NCOs whose application of counterinsurgency techniques was exemplary. Indeed, this BCT, operating under Colonel Mike Kershaw in AO Commando south of Baghdad, one of the toughest operational areas in the country, performed extremely well throughout the Surge, a performance due in part to their efforts to establish close and genuine partnerships with local communities and with their partner Iraqi Army unit, 4th Brigade of 6th Iraqi Army Division under Brigadier-General Ali Jassim Muhammad Hassan al-Frejee.

Captain Phillips' initiative also led to the formation of a neighborhood watch to guard local villages, roads, and bridges. The main issue in this area was that the tribes wished to be recognized as a provisional police unit (PPU) and provided with recognition symbols that would allow them to work against local terrorist groups without being mistaken for insurgents and accidentally fired on by Coalition forces.[66]

In the Zaidon district, a farming and canal area west of Baghdad that had long been noted for the presence of extremist groups who had dispossessed the tribal establishment and radicalized the district's youth,[67] the 2/7 Marines, under the energetic and entrepreneurial Lieutenant Colonel Joe L'Etoile, found themselves in the middle of a complex intertribal conflict. Local tribes backed the 1920s Revolutionary Brigade, a Sunni secular nationalist insurgent movement, in a fight against extremists from AQI. Each group fought both the other group and the Coalition, dispersing when confronted by superior Coalition firepower and contracting into small defended localities (houses and compounds) when confronting each other.[68] The violence between the two groups was exceptionally bloody throughout the first half of 2007. But L'Etoile, through a skillfully arranged series of political maneuvers and careful targeting, successfully played the two groups off against each other, devising a strategy he described as "fighting AQI to the last 1920s guy."[69] After a period of time in which AQI so eroded and damaged the 1920s brigade that the local insurgents were desperate, expecting annihilation, and willing to ally with almost anyone in order to get back at AQI, L'Etoile made a clandestine approach to talk with them through a local tribal intermediary—again, a Zobai—in partnership with the local Iraqi army battalion.[70] This joint Iraqi-U.S. approach immediately brought the 1920s insurgents to a ceasefire agreement, and they ultimately partnered with U.S. and Iraqi forces, joined local security force units, and cooperated to defend their communities against both Shi'a sectarian militias and AQI extremists. This brought a remarkable turnaround in the Zaidon situation over only a few months in mid-2007.[71]

In another incident, in an urban district in Baghdad, forces operating under a tribal leader allied to the *imam* of a local mosque raided five houses during June 2007, in an overnight operation that U.S. forces loosely deconflicted: we tasked patrols to isolate an area while local fighters captured suspected terrorists. The operation was conducted over several hours with no casualties, and without a single shot fired. Tribal forces took five suspects for questioning; two of them were released unharmed within 24 hours, a third was released a day later after promising not to work again with AQI, and two were handed over to Iraqi and Coalition forces, along with a dossier of evidence against them.[72] This extremely high hit rate—a very small number of arrests, of whom three out of five were guilty and the other two were released rapidly and without harm—represents a far more subtle and less intrusive method for rooting out local terrorist cells than the wholesale arrests and clumsy cordon-and-search operations conducted unilaterally by U.S. forces in the same area early in the war, and thereby provoked much less alienation among the people. It also avoided the radicalization effects of detaining large numbers of Iraqis who later turned out to be innocent, but in the meantime had been radicalized by the experience of detention, as occurred in previous years. Indeed, rather than a rejection or radicalization response, this operation generated a closer relationship between coalition forces and the community. What we saw in this district, therefore, was an informal, community-based police force attempting to secure its own streets but behaving responsibly in terms of both human rights and its relationship with the Iraqi government.

Another example of a responsible attitude on the part of local leaders was apparent in their approach to amnesty and parole. Community leaders tended to draw a distinction between terrorist leaders and the rank and file. As one respondent pointed out, "they want the terrorist leaders gone, but the followers and ordinary fighters are their own children, so they want them freed of terrorist leaders, not killed or driven away."[73] This is indeed a classic statement of the distinction between accidental guerrillas and externally focused extremists.

Local leaders who captured rank-and-file terrorists originating from the local district typically held them in custody until they agreed to sign an undertaking never to work with AQI again. The local leaders then summoned their parents to collect them, and they were released into their parents' custody, with their clan or tribe undertaking to enforce the agreement and ensure the signers never worked with the terrorists again.[74]

Importantly, in all these cases, precisely because the tribal fighters were accidental guerrillas, and thus their motivation was to protect their community from terrorism, we did not see examples of torture, extortion, execution, or killing of families by local fighters. These tactics remained exclusively the preserve of *takfiri* extremists such as AQI on the one hand and religiously motivated sectarian militias such as JAM, the militia loyal to the radical Shi'a cleric Muqtada al-Sadr, on the other. Local fighters engaged the enemy in battle, and sought to kill or capture terrorists in their local area, but did not appear to engage in torture or other atrocities. Local leaders were typically motivated by the desire to preserve good relations with Coalition forces, and realized that if they committed human rights abuses it would be impossible for us to work with them. They therefore handed off captured terrorists to us, for processing through the Iraqi judicial system.

This tribal process involved clear political dangers. For one thing, the Shi'a-dominated government was suspicious of a movement that had so far largely occurred within Sunni-majority districts, and saw local fighters as temporary allies at best, tomorrow's enemies at worst. For another, the tribes themselves (particularly the Zobai leaders) sometimes talked as if they saw their actions as a precursor to expanding their influence to regain control of formerly Sunni-majority districts in Baghdad.[75] Third, at least some (though as yet undetected) human rights abuses were probably occurring and might have been laid at our door if we had cooperated with local forces but then failed to act adequately to prevent abuse. Finally, the existence of armed security forces, however informal, operating outside the Iraqi government chain of command might be seen as a precursor to warlordism, or as compromising Iraq's sovereignty.

In my judgment, as of early June 2007, these concerns were real but manageable. An armed and organized Sunni population was not necessarily a destabilizing political factor. It created an informal authority structure that helped build political unity and social coherence within the Sunni community, moving away from the situation of hundreds of fragmented and independent insurgent groups, with community leaders unable to control them, that had plagued our initial attempts to deescalate the Sunni insurgency. Moreover, the existence of an armed local movement of Sunnis created a "balance of power" effect: it deterred Shi'a extremists like JAM who might otherwise have thought of "cleansing" Sunni communities, and reduced the fear of permanent victimization that had caused Sunni leaders to avoid involvement in the new Iraq. It also contradicted the AQ propaganda claim that AQI was all that stood between Iraqi Sunnis and a Shi'a-led genocide. These factors, correctly handled, made local security forces a key element in a balanced, self-regulating, self-sustaining local security architecture that could potentially survive without Coalition supervision. And a mechanism to enroll tribal fighters into legitimate security forces, as local police—which was, after all, what the tribes most wanted—had the potential to bring these forces under government control, thus preventing the development of nonstate forces that could undermine sovereignty.

Key lessons for Coalition forces and commanders emerged from this process. We found that we had to do the following.

- Treat local tribal irregular fighters as local allies, or a local "coalition of the willing," not as "our new employees." They began this rebellion because AQ tried to push them around; we had to make sure we did not make the same mistake. Local fighters were not under our command; this was "tribal diplomacy."
- Build a personal partnership relationship, based on honor and trust, with local leaders.
- Expect leaders to act primarily in accordance with their group's interests, not the leaders' formal undertakings.
- Expect overlapping and sometimes conflicting spheres of authority within tribal groups, not a military-style chain of command. One group might respond to several different sheikhs to different degrees.

- Look for leaders who occupied positions of authority within several local power networks (tribe, mosque, business, governance, etc.). These were likely to be survivors who could influence others.
- Be wary of nontribal Iraqis looking down on tribal sheikhs and treating them as ignorant or of no account.
- Avoid pushing a sheikh to make commitments before he was sure his tribal group would support him.
- Channel assistance to a tribal group through the local sheikh, in order to cement his patronage power and increase his authority, thus making it easier for him to make agreements stick.
- Develop coordination mechanisms and communication channels connecting with local leaders that enabled deconfliction between local "neighborhood watch" organizations and our forces.
- Work to persuade local leaders of the benefits of supporting the Iraqi government—we found we could not expect support for the government to be part of their initial motivation, which was opposition to AQ.
- Expect tribal leaders to distrust Iraqi security forces to some degree, and be prepared to act in the role of honest broker in promoting cooperation between local fighters and Iraqi forces.
- Develop mechanisms for handing over locals who had been detained by neighborhood watch groups, including the observance of clear human rights standards and clear standards of evidence before an individual could be taken into the hands of the Iraqi or Coalition judicial system.

Another key set of lessons related to reconciliation in tribal society.

TRIBAL RECONCILIATION PROCESSES (SULH)

Iraqi Arabic does not have a word that directly corresponds to the Western notion of "national reconciliation," in the sense of both dispute resolution and the restoration of friendly relationships between communities after a breach. Some Iraqi politicians in 2007 used the phrase *at taswiya wataniya* to indicate a "national settlement," while the terms *al musalaha* ("mutual agreement") and *al wifak* ("agreement" or "compact") were also used.[76] But these terms imply settling or agreement and the pragmatic resolution of a dispute, not a process of restored friendship among Iraqis alienated by sectarian conflict, terrorism, and insurgency.

At the tribal level, however, many Iraqi tribes do have a reconciliation process, the *sulh*, which incorporates elements of both dispute resolution and relationship restoration. Traditionally, such a process only occurs within or between tribes and involves no government participation. One key informant argued that it was embarrassing and shameful for a tribal leader to involve the government in a dispute. Resolution was to take place between the tribes themselves. Another key informant described the process of reconciliation as follows:

"Imagine that a member of one clan or tribe kills another. This creates a fight between the tribes. The tribe that is wronged must take revenge [tha'r], unless the dispute is resolved by paying the blood-price [diya]. This happens even if the killing is accidental. The diya would be lower then. The guilty party immediately goes into hiding. He has to do this because if the other tribe sees him they will kill him. This has nothing to do with their feelings; it is an obligation on them. Even if he is their friend, they will kill him. It is a duty.

"So the guilty send a broker [mashaya] who is respected by both. They do not send the broker to the victim's family, because they will be too emotional and will refuse to see him, or they might even be violent, which would make the fight worse. So the broker goes to the victim's sheikh. Choosing the broker is extremely important. It must be someone who is trusted and respected by both tribes, maybe an older sheikh who has a good record of settling disputes, or maybe someone who is known as an expert in tribal customs [aadat]. Because the choice of mediator is so important, it might take days or a week to choose him. Also he will have to agree, which he may not want to, depending on how serious the case is, or what his relationship is with the tribes.

"The broker goes to the victim's sheikh [and] announces that he is there as mashaya to settle the dispute. He takes off his cloak and sits down outside. He asks for permission to bring the people to discuss the dispute. I mean the guilty people, not the guilty man himself but his clan and their sheikh. The victim's sheikh then goes to the victim's family, and says the guilty clan wants to pay the diya. They will refuse at first, and he must argue with them and convince them to accept the blood-money instead of taking tha'r. Even if they are willing to take the diya they must argue. It shows their honor and allows the sheikh to show his wisdom by convincing them.

Once they agree to the *diya*, there is an unwritten law that sets how much must be paid for different events. For example, the amount is higher for a man than a woman, and for if some animals are killed or damage is done to houses or crops. There are experts who know this; there are books about it. Also they remember the price paid in past disputes and they know what is fair. The price varies, but it is usually lower than you would pay in a court of law.

"The *mashaya* then brings them all together to discuss the case. He brings the criminal's family, not the guilty person himself—he is still in hiding. He brings the family and their sheikh to "sit on the rug" and argue the case to resolve the issue. At first the victim's family will be very emotional, they will express their anger and hurt, and the guilty family will be angry also. The sheikhs and the *mashaya* control the discussion so that it doesn't get out of hand, but they let the family express their feelings to help them recover from the hurt.

"After the emotions are expressed, the two sheikhs get the families to agree to accept their decision, and then they get down to business. Sometimes they will remove themselves a little distance from the families so they can discuss in private. They negotiate the amount of *diya* to be paid, and any other compensation or other arrangements. Both know what is a fair price, and the *mashaya* is there also. Eventually they reach an agreement.

"Until this time, there is no food or drink served, not even water. Even if it is offered by one side, the other side will not accept it because it would be shameful. Also eating together can end the dispute before the correct *diya* is paid. Now the two sheikhs return to the group and announce that they have reached an agreement. Now water, and sometimes tea, is served. Once the two families accept the decision, they hold a big dinner together. Sometimes if it is particularly serious, they might exchange women for marriage between the tribes.

"After this, no one can take revenge, so the dispute is over. If they do take revenge, it would be considered a new dispute, and they would be guilty. The guilty man can come back, but this may not happen straight away. No one will break the deal because if they do they might be banished from the tribe, in which case they would die. They might not like it but they can't take *tha'r*.

"Just like the revenge debt had nothing to do with people's feelings, the sulh may not change feelings either. They might not like the other family but they can't take action. It is like a legal process. The tribes would never involve the government in this, though. That would be shameful."[77]

Strictly speaking, Coalition forces were not able to use this approach in reconciling with Iraqi fighters, because sulh does not traditionally involve government officials, much less foreigners. On the other hand, there was a clear need for a reconciliation process between Coalition forces and tribal groups, either following a specific incident (such as the accidental killing of a noncombatant, or damage to houses or crops) or when moving into an area that had suffered from fighting or damage over an extended period.[78] A reconciliation process, leading to a compact with local community leaders, was also an essential precondition for many reconstruction and security programs.

Some Coalition commanders benefited from awareness of key elements in tribal reconciliation, because a "sulh-like" process, though not a formal sulh, was more recognizable to Iraqis as a genuine attempt at reconciliation, hence was more readily accepted. Some coalition commanders (notably army and Marine Corps commanders in al-Anbar Province and, earlier, army commanders like Colonel H. R. McMaster in western Nineveh Province) also consciously emulated the behavior patterns expected of a responsible sheikh in Iraqi tribal society, which helped gain community respect and build peer-to-peer relationships with local leaders.[79] Coalition commanders could never actually be sheikhs, but some gained an advantage by acting in ways Iraqis recognized as being in the tradition of "good sheikhly behavior." One key informant observed:

"You cannot do a sulh with Iraqis because you are not Iraqi. But if you know what is a sulh, what the stages are, then you can make them understand you are serious to reconcile. Say you accidentally kill some people in a village. The tribe will want revenge and their honor is touched. They must become your enemies unless you resolve the dispute and pay the diya. Even if you pay them compensation from the government they will still be your enemies because there is no sulh for your action.

"So you should do this. You should find a local sheikh who is in charge over that district. You approach him quietly and explain that you want to resolve the problem with the tribe, and pay the appropriate diya for the deaths. He will then act as your broker. He will not tell the people that he has been approached by you. Instead, he will say to them "this happened in my area, and so I will take it up with the Americans to resolve it." He will then negotiate with the victim's sheikh on your behalf. You would not attend the negotiations. Maybe right at the end, once it has been resolved, you would go to pay the diya.

"The benefit is that you will pay less than if you try to pay directly. Also, the sheikh's prestige is built up because he has resolved the dispute, so now he is your friend. And the tribe cannot take revenge on you because the incident is now finished."[80]

Key components of tribal-style reconciliation that we identified in Iraq in 2007 included:

- The central role of a trusted mediator, respected by both parties, as a broker for reconciliation
- Avoidance of direct contact between the perpetrator of a crime and the victim's family—instead, family and clan leaders represent their group
- Investment of time in choosing the right broker, negotiating for a settlement, and allowing tempers to cool—several days as a minimum
- The role of the sheikh as moderator, adviser, and representative in negotiations
- A negotiation process that first allows both sides to express emotion in a controlled environment, after which each side's representative engages in private discussion to settle issues of compensation
- The role of social pressure from tribal "public opinion" in enforcing compliance with agreements reached through this process—pressure that does not always succeed in enforcing agreements
- Reliance on a body of traditional knowledge and tribal custom (aadat) to determine what represents a fair compensation for given events
- Tribes' strong preference for this form of reconciliation rather than formal legal processes involving the government

Reconciliation within a tribal context, as a means of marginalizing extremist "unreconcilable" elements (often terrorist groups with a global focus) from more mainstream accidental guerrillas who often proved willing to reconcile, was thus a key factor in our handling of the tribal revolt in 2007.

THE BIRTH OF THE REVOLT

The uprising began in 2006, far out in western Anbar Province, but by May it was affecting about 40 percent of the country. It spread to Nineveh, Diyala, Babil, Salah-ad-Din, and Baghdad, and—intriguingly—began filtering into Shi'a communities in the South. The Iraqi government was in on it from the start; our Iraqi intelligence colleagues predicted, well before we realized it, that Anbar Province was going to "flip," with tribal leaders turning toward the government and away from extremists.[81]

As noted, some tribal leaders with whom I spoke told me that the split started over women. This is not as odd as it sounds. One of AQ's standard techniques, which (as noted) they have applied in places as diverse as Somalia, Pakistan, Afghanistan, and Indonesia, is to marry leaders and key operatives to women from prominent tribal families. The strategy creates a bond with the community, exploiting kinship-based alliances, and in this way embeds the AQ network in the society. Over time, this makes AQ part of the social landscape, allows them to manipulate local people, and makes it harder for outsiders to pry apart the network and the population.

This time, the tactic seems to have backfired, in part because "marriages" were often forced and so violent that they were tantamount, even in tribal eyes, to rape. We often use shorthand to refer to the enemy as "al Qa'ida," but in Iraq the primary Sunni terrorist group is Tanzim Qaidat al-Jihad fil Bilad al-Rafidayn (QJBR). This organization was founded and led by Abu Musab al-Zarqawi until his death in 2006 and swore allegiance to bin Laden in 2004; it is now taking strategic direction and support from AQ central. Its archaic name literally means "the qai'da organization for jihad in the land of the two rivers," that is, al Qa'ida in Iraq, abbreviated AQI. Its foot-soldiers are 95 percent Iraqi, but its leadership is overwhelmingly foreign. The top leaders and several key players in 2007 were Egyptians, and there were Turks, Syrians, Saudis, Chechens, Afghans, and others in the leadership cadre. Moreover, the group was heavily urbanized, and town-dwellers—even urban Iraqis—may as well be foreigners as far as some tribal Iraqis are concerned. So there was a cultural barrier and a natural difference in outlook between the tribes and the AQI terrorists.

These differences need not have been fatal to the symbiotic relationship between them—indeed, for years the tribes treated the terrorists as "useful idiots," while AQI in turn exploited them for cover and support.[82] But this alliance of convenience and mutual exploitation broke down when AQI began to apply the standard AQ method of cementing alliances through marriage. As informants noted, in Iraqi tribal society, custom (*aadat*) is at least as important as religion (*deen*), and its dictates, often pre-Islamic in origin, frequently differ from those of Islam. This was highlighted in the aforementioned comment by my informant that "if you ask a Shammari what religion he is, he will say 'I am a Shammari' "—the Shammari being a confederation which, like many Iraqi tribes, has both Sunni and Shi'a branches.

Islam, of course (as I will discuss in chapter 4), is a key identity marker when dealing with non-Muslim outsiders, but when all involved are Muslim, kinship tends to trump religion. In fact, most tribal Iraqis I have spoken with consider AQ's brand of "Islam" utterly foreign to their traditional and syncretic version of the faith. One key difference is marriage custom. The tribes only give women in marriage within the tribe or (on rare occasions to cement a bond or resolve a grievance, as part of a *sulh* process) to other tribes or clans in their confederation (*qabila*). Marrying women to strangers, let alone foreigners, is just not done. For their part, with their hyper-reductionist version of "Islam" stripped of cultural content, AQ discounted the tribes' view as ignorant, stupid, and sinful.

As noted, some informants believed that the violence erupted when AQ killed a sheikh over his refusal to give daughters of his tribe to them in marriage, creating a revenge obligation (*tha'r*) on his people, who attacked AQI. The terrorists retaliated with immense brutality, killing the son of a prominent sheikh in a particularly gruesome manner, witnesses told us. This was the last straw, they said, and the tribes rose up. Neighboring clans joined the fight, which escalated as AQI (who had generally worn out their welcome through high-handedness) tried to crush the revolt through more atrocities. Soon the uprising took off, spreading along kinship lines through Anbar and into neighboring provinces.

Other tribesmen told me women weren't the only issue. The tribes had run smuggling, import-export, and construction businesses that AQI had shut down, taken over, or disrupted through violent disturbances that were "bad for business." Another factor was the widespread belief (with at least some basis in fact) among the tribes that AQI has links to Iran and has received funding and support from it. In these informants' view, women were simply the spark—AQI already "had it coming." Out in the wild western desert, things often tend to play out in a manner that is considered brutal even by other Iraqis but in this case, AQI changed the rules of the game by adding roadside bombs, beheadings, death by genital mutilation, baking of children alive, raping of women and children to death, and torture. Eventually, enough was enough for the locals.

THE AWAKENING

By mid-2007, several major tribes were "up" against AQ, across all of Anbar, Diyala, Salah-ad-din, parts of Babil, and Baghdad (both city and province). Some in Anbar and Diyala formed "salvation councils," looking to well-known leadership figures (like Sheikh Abdul Sattar Eftikhan al-Rishawi ad-Dulaimi, son of the chief of the Albu Risha tribe of the Dulaimi confederation, another extremely important tribal grouping, who led the awakening in Anbar until murdered by AQI on September 13, 2007) or to local community leaders. In other provinces, events tended to unfold quite informally, based on the authority of local elders. In Anbar, as we have seen, the movement acquired the name as-Sahawa, "the Awakening."

Combined with the counterinsurgency operations outlined earlier, the tribal uprising against AQI led to dramatically improved security through the second half of 2007. In Ramadi, Hit, Tikrit, Fallujah, and other centers, the rate of civilian deaths dropped precipitously, and overall attacks dropped and stayed far below historic trends and as low as almost nothing in some places. For anyone familiar with these places from earlier in the war, it became quite disorienting to watch Iraqis walking safely and openly in streets the mere crossing of which, a year before, would have required a major operation.[83] This change initially seemed to escape some observers' notice, but it was one of the truly significant developments in Iraq up to that time. Other provinces experienced patterns similar to that in Anbar, and by mid-June some Shi'a tribes in the South began approaching us, looking to cooperate with the government against Shi'a extremists.

Of course, this was motivated primarily by self-interest, and in particular by a nascent split between local-focus accidental guerrillas (the tribes) and the globally oriented terrorists (AQI) who had exploited them. Tribal leaders realized that the extremists were leading them on a path to destruction, and had seized the opportunity to dump the terrorists and come in from the cold. They were also, naturally, looking forward to the day when Coalition forces were no longer in their districts, and wanted to ensure that themselves, not AQI, were in charge once we left. And many of the tribal leaders realized for themselves what our army, marines, and special forces commanders had told them for years: "If you don't like having us around, and you want us to get off your backs, the solution is staring you in the face: just get rid of the extremists, reduce the violence, and cooperate with the government to stabilize your area, and we're out of here."[84]

Internal tribal dynamics also played a part. Many older leaders, who consider themselves the true heads of clans or tribes, fled Iraq in 2003 because they were implicated in dealings with Saddam, and are now in exile in Syria or Jordan. The on-the-ground leaders are a younger generation, concerned to cement their positions vis-à-vis the old men in Damascus who may one day want to return. By joining forces with the government, these leaders acquired a source of patronage, which they redirected to their people, cementing themselves in power and bolstering their personal positions.

Again, this is utterly standard behavior for tribal leaders anywhere in the Arab world: you can trust a tribal leader 100 percent—to follow his tribe's and his own interests. This is fine: self-interest, group identity, and revenge are reliable motivations. In Iraq, these motivations have proven very robust, especially when reinforced by bonds forged in fighting a common enemy alongside Coalition forces and the government. Provided they are under Iraqi government control (a nontrivial proviso), neighborhood watch groups motivated by community loyalty and enlightened self-interest are not necessarily a bad thing. Indeed, since the tribes' uprising resulted in an extremely significant drop in violence and a substantial increase (on the order of 95,000 people) in the number of Iraqis actively lining up with the government and the Coalition to defend communities against extremists, it may turn out to have been a very good thing indeed.

THE BAGHDAD VARIANT

An interesting variation on the general theme arose in Baghdad city. Baghdad, of course, is not tribal as such. But urbanization in Iraq is a relatively recent phenomenon, having occurred mainly over the past 20 years or so. For example, around half the people living in Baghdad today belong to families that came to the city since the 1980s. This means many urban Iraqis still have close kinship relationships with rural tribes, and still have relatives living in their ancestral villages with whom they keep in touch. In several districts, community leaders (often the Sunni imams of local mosques) turned against AQI in their areas around the middle of the year. In these districts, which included Ameriya, Ghazaliya, Abu Ghraib, and others, communities formed neighborhood watch organizations, established access controls to prevent people from outside the district coming in without proper authorization, and drove out terrorist cells. They began providing information to the Iraqi and Coalition security forces, protecting their own families and conducting joint patrols and operations alongside the Iraqi army and police, both by day and night.[85] This happened most often in Sunni-majority districts, and locals partnered with Shi'a-dominated security forces in most cases. (This somewhat gives the lie to assertions that Sunni populations would never work with Shi'a-dominated security forces: they often would, but the conditions had to be right: primarily, some kind of honest broker, a relationship of trust between key individuals, or formal safeguards.) Coalition forces provided support to the community and to Iraqi forces operating in the area, hence tended to play the role of honest broker.

Clearly, in Baghdad the revolt was not exactly tribal, but was based on informal district power structures that evolved through the intense period of sectarian cleansing that so damaged the city and its population in 2006. But we often found that leaders acting in a community capacity also had family ties or other links to the tribes who rebelled against AQI. In one district, Sunni imams were constantly being targeted for intimidation and violence by AQ. There was a spate of mosque bombings in May and June, for example, targeting imams the takfiriin deemed too moderate. These imams, working with local elders, banded together to drive out AQ. To do so, they brought in a military adviser from another district, known to them through his tribal connections, who was also connected to one of the main tribes currently fighting AQI outside Baghdad.[86] So while the surface level of activity in Baghdad was not so obviously tribal, clan connections, kinship links, and the alliances they fostered still played a key underlying role.

The government of Iraq was initially extremely wary of these community groups, even more so than the tribes operating against AQI outside the city. This is understandable. A rebel Sunni tribe out in Anbar Province was one thing; an armed Sunni militia in central Baghdad was quite another. One Iraqi official told us, "You have taken a crocodile as a pet"; to which a very senior coalition officer replied, "It's not our crocodile: it's your crocodile."[87] But with some persuasion from the Coalition, the government seems to have eventually chosen to work with these groups as a means to secure key districts and build partnerships with communities. This took a great deal of political courage, since many of those now fighting AQI were former adversaries of the government or even current political opponents of the Da'wa

Party and the Maliki cabinet. Part of the government's motivation was almost certainly a desire to take credit for security progress, and there is still a degree of suspicion among some Iraqi political leaders (for good reasons discussed below). But in practical terms, on the ground, the government's cooperation with local groups resulted in fewer civilian casualties, a drop in the number of attacks, a much less permissive operating environment for terrorists, and the freeing-up of Iraqi army and police units who would otherwise have been tied down in static guard duties. On balance, the results were broadly positive.

PROSPECTS

Despite its demonstrably beneficial effects on the security situation in 2007, and the continued benefits the Awakening and the associated growth of local security forces have brought about since 2007, it is clear that the Iraqi tribal revolt could still go either way once the Coalition begins a process of drawing down in Iraq.

The strategic logic, from our point of view, remains relatively straightforward. Our dilemma in Iraq is, and always has been, finding a way to cre-

Figure 3.6 Iraq, April 2007—Coalition vehicles passing through an Iraqi checkpoint south of Baghdad. Note the warning sign on the rear of the vehicle.
Photo: David Kilcullen

ate a sustainable security architecture that does not require the Coalition to be "in the loop," thereby allowing Iraq to stabilize and the Coalition to disengage in favorable strategic circumstances. But taking the Coalition out of the loop and into "overwatch" requires balancing competing armed interest groups, at the national and local level. Even with the success of the 2007 Surge and the associated political progress in Iraq, these are currently not in balance, due in part to the sectarian bias of certain players and institutions of the new Iraqi state, a bias that continues to promote Sunnis' belief that they will be permanent victims in the new Iraq. This belief has historically created space for terrorist groups, including AQI, and these groups in turn have driven a cycle of sectarian violence that keeps Iraq unstable and prevents us from disengaging. Even with the dramatic reduction in AQI activity and capabilities, this remains a potential threat to stability.

As noted, AQI's "pitch" to the Sunni community in 2004–2005 was based on the argument that only AQ stood between the Sunnis and a Shi'a-led genocide. The presence of local Sunni security forces—which protect their own communities but do not attack the Shi'a—gives the lie to this claim, undercuts AQI's appeal, and reassures Sunni leaders that Sunnis will not be permanently victimized in a future Iraq. The presence of local Sunni security forces may thus make such leaders more willing to engage in the political process, functioning as an informal confidence-building measure, and may help marginalize AQ. This might represent a step toward an inter-communal "balance of power" that could potentially be quite stable over time. On the Shi'a side, AQI represents a bogey-man that extremist groups like JAM have long exploited in order to gain public cooperation: their pitch has been "We are all that stands between you and AQI." By reducing the AQI threat, the tribal uprising also therefore undercuts JAM's appeal. And as mentioned, Shi'a tribes in some areas in 2007 began to turn against JAM as well as other Shi'a extremists, creating the potential to further reduce the level of intracommunal violence and bring nonsectarian Shi'a into the political process, marginalizing extremists and Iranian agents.

All this meant that correctly handled, with appropriate safeguards, and in partnership with the Iraqi government, the spontaneous social movement of Sunni communities turning against AQI proved able to provide one element in the self-sustaining security architecture we had been seeking. Ultimately, on the positive side of the ledger, some benefits of the tribal uprising were that it did the following:

- It relieved Coalition and Iraqi forces of garrison and local security requirements, freeing up forces for maneuver against insurgents and terrorists, and thus redressing to a significant extent our lack of coalition force troop numbers in Iraq.
- It may help create a self-regulating security architecture, making population groups "self-securing" and thus providing a stable platform for withdrawal of Coalition forces from these districts with less risk that insurgents might reinfiltrate into them once we leave
- It provided the Sunni population with a security guarantee that helped marginalize AQI, while deterring the Shi'a extremist groups that sought to attack Sunni districts
- It tapped into traditional approaches based on social and political structures that many Iraqis were comfortable with—community-based security went with, not against, the grain of Iraqi society.

But there are also clear and continuing risks. The process may lead to the forming of armed groups outside government control, which, as noted, might engage in human rights violations that could be blamed on the government or Coalition forces. In fact, we have yet to see any significant human rights violation by tribal forces—indeed, they typically apply a very measured approach, probably because the people they are securing are their own families, and their local knowledge allows them to get things done without having to apply force, as an outside force might need to. Nevertheless, risks remain, including the following:

- Some government ministries oppose arming the Sunni population, sometimes on sectarian grounds but also on the basis of legitimate concerns about future government control over Sunni-majority areas, and some Iraqi army commanders have expressed concern about the potential for regional warlordism.
- There is an outside chance that tribes that have "flipped" from supporting AQI could simply flip back, or go their own way once the Coalition begins to withdraw—especially if they believe the government is not effectively supporting them or taking their interests into account.
- Unless reintegration measures are formally established, some tribes may come to see their security forces as a permanent entitlement, which would make control over their areas more difficult for any future central government.

Having watched the tribal revolt develop at close hand over several months, I believe the risk mitigation measures that we and the Iraqi government began putting into place in mid-2007 stand a better than even chance of preventing major negative side-effects from the uprising, until such time as Coalition combat forces begin a serious drawdown. The risks are still significant, but with appropriate mitigation they are probably manageable. The key mitigation measures I proposed at the time, some of which were eventually adopted, included:

- Developing programs, from the outset, to disarm, demobilize, and reintegrate (DDR) tribal forces in Iraqi society
- Ensuring that the government did not provide weapons to any group until its loyalty was demonstrated and members had sworn allegiance to the new Iraq
- Conducting biometric registration of tribal fighters, and registering their weapon serial numbers (to discourage side-switching, detect infiltrators, and reassure the Iraqi government of its control)
- Linking tribal loyalty to local governance structures, and then directly to the central government, through traditional tribal control mechanisms such as *deera* (tribal boundaries—tribal forces could not work outside these without an agreement with the neighboring sheikh) and *sulh*, (traditional tribal reconciliation processes leading to compacts within and between communities)
- Vetting and training tribal security forces as a precondition for their enrolment in paid, government-sponsored organizations like the police and army
- Providing advisers, liaison officers, and support infrastructure (ideally from the Iraqi government with our help) to prevent human rights abuses and enforce appropriate operational standards

IMPLICATIONS

The tribal revolt represented very significant political progress toward reconciliation at the grassroots level, and major security progress in marginalizing extremists and reducing civilian deaths. It also did much to redress the lack of Coalition forces that had hampered previous counterinsurgency approaches, by throwing tens of thousands of local allies into the balance, on our side. For these reasons, the tribal revolt was arguably the most significant change in the Iraqi operating environment in several years. But the significance of this development was initially overlooked to some extent, because it occurred in ways that were neither expected nor accounted for in our "benchmarks" (which were formulated before the uprising began to really develop, and which tend to focus on national legislative developments at the central government and political party level rather than grassroots changes in the quality of life of ordinary Iraqis).[88]

One obvious outcome of the uprising is the political bandwagoning effect we saw throughout 2007 and 2008: tribal leaders saw the benefits other tribes had gained from turning against terrorists, and wanted the same benefits themselves, so they, too, turned against extremists in their own areas. At the same time, the government of Iraq saw benefits in terms of grassroots political reconciliation and reduced violence, and was keen to take control of, and credit for, the process. Provincial governments also saw the benefits of self-securing districts, freeing up police and military forces for other tasks. This dynamic has the potential to help Iraqi society coalesce around competent, nonsectarian (albeit informal) institutions.

From my point of view, the strongest positive developments are that the revolt has begun to help create a self-sustaining local security architecture, and has had what we might call a "reblueing" effect on the police. One of our problems all along, as noted, has been that some police have behaved in a sectarian manner, a few have engaged in outright sectarian atrocities, and sectarian extremists have intimidated or co-opted others. Police bias and brutality is a standard problem in counterinsurgency: it occurred in campaigns as different as those in Palestine, Northern Ireland, Cyprus, Malaya, and Vietnam. It typically takes a long time to remedy (almost 10 years in the case of the Royal Ulster Constabulary). The creation of new tribal forces as a result of the uprising could accelerate police reform by changing the police recruiting base from a heavily Shi'a to a more balanced one, as Sunni tribal recruits join the Iraqi police. "Weeding out" bad sectarian actors in police services is a slow and difficult process; changing the recruiting base, as the uprising has done, can help move the process along more quickly.

There are also economic benefits. Enlistment of tribal fighters in police units creates employment beyond the 90-day jobs based on the Commander's Emergency Response Program (CERP) funding model of the past. It also reduces the manpower pool for the insurgency, and is thus a form of "soft DDR." Increased security in rural areas boosts agricultural and market activity (by making fields safe enough to cultivate crops, and making roads and markets safe enough to transport goods). Salaries earned by newly enrolled auxiliary policemen inject capital into the goods and services economy, while vocational and educational training under DDR programs diversifies the labor pool and builds the absorptive capacity of local economies. Assistance to families channeled through tribal Sheikhs restarts the traditional patronage system, and although this involves risks of smuggling or black marketeering these can be mitigated through proper oversight. And such programs provide a "safe" outlet for CERP funds without corroding Iraqi government budget execution processes, as has sometimes happened in the past.

Another key benefit is to force ratios and Coalition troop numbers. It has become a truism to argue that we have too few troops in Iraq for "proper" counterinsurgency. This claim is somewhat questionable: there is indeed a requirement, in counterinsurgency theory, for a certain base level of troops in order to conduct effective counterinsurgency. However, this is a threshold: once you reach the minimum level, *what* the troops *do* becomes the critical factor, not *how many* there are. And as Robert Thompson pointed out more than 40 years ago, force ratio in counterinsurgency is an indicator of progress, not a prerequisite for it. You know things are starting to go your way when local people start joining your side against the enemy, thus indicating a growth of popular support, and changing the force ratio as a result. Merely adding additional foreign troops cannot compensate for lack of local popular support—the British lost the Cyprus campaign with a force ratio of 110 to 1 in their favor, while in the same decade the Indonesians defeated Dar'ul Islam with a force ratio that never exceeded 3 to 1, by building partnerships with communities and employing them as village neighborhood watch groups, in cordon tasks, and in support functions. So we could deploy many more U.S. troops to Iraq, and it wouldn't necessarily fix the problem. On the other hand, the fact that 95,000 former insurgents and tribal fighters are now on our side and fighting the enemy is worth a great deal, because it indicates that more Iraqis are lining up with the government and against extremism. It simultaneously increases our forces, improves our reach into the population, reduces the enemy's recruiting pool and active forces, reduces the number of civilians who need to rely on protection from Coalition troops (hence cuts the demand for our security services), and erodes the enemy's ability to intimidate and control the population. All these things have a positive effect on the overall correlation of forces in the theater.

The negative implications are easy to state, but potentially far-reaching. For one thing, we have spent the last several years carefully building and supporting a top-down Iraqi political system based on nontribal, national-level institutions. Indeed, the Coalition Provisional Authority deliberately sidelined the tribes in 2003 in order to focus on building a "modern" democratic state in Iraq, which we equated with a nontribal state. There were good reasons for this at the time, but we are now seeing the most significant political and security progress in years, via a bottom-up structure outside the one we have been working so hard to create. Does that invalidate the last five years' efforts? Probably not, as long as we recognize that the vision of a Jeffersonian, "modern" (in the Western, industrial sense) democracy in Iraq, based around entirely secular nontribal institutions, was always somewhat unrealistic. In the Iraqi polity, tribes' rights may end up playing a similar role to states' rights in some other democracies. That is, they will remain a power center in competition with the religious political parties, hence will probably never be popular with Baghdad politicians; but if correctly handled, they have the potential to actually enhance pluralism in Iraq over the long term, by restraining the excesses of any central government or sectarian faction.

Another important implication is that the pattern we are seeing runs counter to what we expected in the Surge and therefore lies well outside the "benchmarks" established by Congress with little awareness of field conditions. As noted, the original concept of the Joint Campaign Plan was that we (the Coalition and the Iraqi government) would create security, which would in turn create space for a "grand bargain" at the national level. Instead, in 2007 we saw the exact opposite: a series of local political deals displaced extremists, resulting in a major improvement in security at the local level, and the national government then began to jump on board with the program. Instead of Coalition-led, top-down reconciliation, this process is Iraqi-led, bottom-up, and based on civil society rather than national politics. Oddly enough, it seems to have worked better than anyone expected. This does not necessarily invalidate the Surge strategy: we are indeed seeing improved security, and political progress—but at the local, not national, level. This was not what we initially expected; but the improvement in Iraqis' daily lives and the willingness to talk rather than fight is a real improvement nonetheless.

TENTATIVE CONCLUSIONS

As we all know, there is no such thing as a "standard" counterinsurgency. Indeed, the basic definition of counterinsurgency is "the full range of measures that a government and its partners take to defeat an insurgency." In other words, the set of counterinsurgency measures adopted depends on the character of the insurgency: the nature of counterinsurgency is not fixed, but shifting; it evolves in response to changes in the form of insurgency. This means that there is no standard set of metrics, benchmarks, or operational techniques that apply to all insurgencies or remain valid for any single insurgency throughout its life-cycle. And there are no fixed "laws" of counterinsurgency, except for the sole and simple but difficult requirement to first understand the environment, then diagnose the problem, in detail and in its own terms, and then build a tailored set of situation-specific techniques to deal with it.

With that in mind, it is clear that although the requirements for counterinsurgency in a tribal environment may not be written down in the classical-era field manuals, building local allies and forging partnerships and trusted networks with at-risk communities seems to be one of the keys to success. Perhaps this is what T. E. Lawrence had in mind when he wrote that the art of guerrilla warfare with Arab tribes rested on "building a ladder of tribes to the objective." Marine and army units that have sought to understand tribal behavior in its own terms, to follow norms of proper behavior as expected by tribal communities, and to build their own confederations of local partners have done extremely well in this fight. But we should remember that this uprising against extremism belongs to the Iraqi people, not to us—it was their idea, they started it, they are leading it, it is happening on their terms and their timeline, and our job is to support where needed, ensure that proper political safeguards and human rights standards are in place, and ultimately to realize that this development will play out in ways that may be good or bad but are fundamentally unpredictable.

Conclusions

This second detailed case study, building on the previous Afghanistan example, shows what a runaway accidental guerrilla syndrome can look like on the ground, the immense damage it can do, and the enormously time-intensive, labor-intensive, and capital-intensive efforts that are needed to stop such a cycle once it is fully under way.

Yet the Iraq example differs significantly from that of Afghanistan, in that Iraq's particular accidental guerrilla syndrome was self-inflicted. As noted at the start of the chapter, in Afghanistan the cycle began with the infection of a preexisting societal breakdown (prompted by the Soviet invasion of Afghanistan, among other things) and was followed by contagion, most notably evidenced in the 9/11 attacks and other AQ-sponsored terrorist incidents worldwide. The intervention the West mounted after 9/11 generated a rejection response from Pashtun society and the creation of accidental guerrillas. In Iraq, an initial intervention by the West led to a rejection response that created space for the extremist infection of a nationalist and former regime–loyalist resistance warfare struggle against occupation. That extremist infection then created the accidental guerrilla cycle of sectarian violence that tore Iraq apart in 2006 and had to be so slowly, painfully, expensively, and carefully dealt with in 2007. In terms of the theory I have outlined, this difference between the two cases indicates that the accidental guerrilla syndrome can begin at almost any point in the cycle, and will run and accelerate until interrupted.

In terms of strategy, the Iraq example indicates that for us to invade foreign countries with large-scale unilateral military intervention forces simply plays into the AQ exhaustion strategy already described, creates space for the infection of societies by extremism, and prompts contagion to the wider world. (As successive intelligence estimates have shown of Iraq, the conflict has exacerbated extremism worldwide, and as noted actual violence has spilled over into neighboring countries, and further afield, as has radicalization.) Thus, Iraq represents a cautionary example of exactly the type of conflict we need to avoid if we wish to successfully defeat the threat of *takfiri* terrorism.

The Iraq campaign is far from over. Whether or not U.S. combat forces remain on the ground in large numbers over the long term, the conflict (with or without foreign intervention) is likely to continue for at least a decade from now, though perhaps at a reduced level of intensity, if the conflict follows the normal pattern of insurgencies over the past century which have tended to last between 15 and 40 years. In 2007, we successfully turned Iraq back from the brink of total disaster by applying a strategy of protecting the population, co-opting and winning over the reconcilables, expanding the "center" of Iraqi politics, marginalizing the extremes, and eliminating the irreconcilables. That this was ultimately successful was due to the extraordinary leadership of General Petraeus, the skill and dedication of Coalition forces who had already begun to master the environment even before his arrival, and the courage of Iraqis who proved willing, in large numbers, to turn against extremism—a sort of reverse immune response in which they rejected AQI groups whose behavior proved them to be even more alien to Iraqis than the Coalition.

The Surge worked: but in the final analysis, it was an effort to save ourselves from the more desperate consequences of a situation we should never have gotten ourselves into. The next chapter examines several comparative examples that, taken together, indicate a better way forward for the future.

Chapter 4

"Terrain, Tribes, and Terrorists": Conflicts from Indonesia to Europe

For the Pathan saying is: "First comes one Englishman, as a traveller or for shikar [hunting]; then come two and make a map; then comes an army and takes the country. It is better therefore to kill the first Englishman."

Colonel G. J. Younghusband, *The Story of the Guides* (1908)

In the dim red glow of the crowded C130 transport aircraft, my soldiers' faces were guarded and withdrawn.[1] We were minutes away from landing, and all expected a serious firefight before the day was out. Some retched from turbulence or checked their rifles, grenades, and combat equipment for the tenth time. A few gamely gave me the "thumbs-up" as I struggled along the fuselage to the flight deck, holding the wall for support, and pausing occasionally for a quiet word with someone who seemed to need encouragement. Two snipers played cards across a rucksack, while my always-carefree radio operator tranquilly turned the tattered pages of his well-traveled science fiction novel, calmly closing his eyes for especially severe bumps before serenely opening them to read again. After five hours' flying, we were finally approaching Komorro airfield, outside East Timor's capital, Dili. It was early Monday morning, September 20, 1999, and we were the seventh plane in a continuous stream of aircraft stretching all the way to Australia, 350 nautical miles to the southwest. The first combat troops had landed 40 minutes before, linking up with an advance party that had been on the ground since before dawn. Our battalion was first in, with others following by air and sea; my company of 179 light infantry specialists was crossloaded in four aircraft. The mission was to stop the violence that had torn Timor apart since its people had voted three weeks earlier for independence from Indonesia. But our brigade, a rapid deployment force specializing in airmobile and air assault operations, had a simpler task that first day: seize the airfield and port for the heavier forces behind us.

As I fought my way to the flight deck, we were already turning onto final approach. Conferring with the copilot, I glanced through the windscreen and stared in surprise. We were descending through a forest of smoke plumes, Jack-and-the-Beanstalk growths sprouting insanely from the city and the hills, merging high above into a ceiling of black haze. Dili was burning; the sky was murky, and the sun was ochre through the smoke. I counted 19 fires in quick succession, struggling to recognize the terrain I had only seen before in maps and air photographs: jungle hills south of the city, the main coast road running east-west through town, warships closing in on the harbor from the north, assault troops fanning out behind a C130 that had just touched down, the whole downtown district on fire, and behind us as we turned, aircraft evenly spaced to the horizon. Scanning the skyline one last time, I returned, heart hammering, to my nylon-mesh seat for the sudden bump, bump, and deceleration of landing.

A few minutes later, I was sitting in the Indonesian airfield commander's office, outwardly calm but sweating in my camouflage uniform, drinking sweet tea from a chipped glass, and trying to smoke a lip-numbing Javanese *kretek* without coughing. In the background, my radio operator tried quietly but urgently to raise Headquarters and tell them we had secured the control tower without a fight. As one of few Indonesian linguists in the force, I had led my team straight to the tower, only to find the commander standing forlornly outside with his staff, shading his eyes, and craning his neck to the sky. Arriving at this unexpected scene with my heavily armed troops behind me, aircraft after aircraft touching down with a turboprop roar, and a pair of Australian fighter jets streaking through the smoke haze above the airfield, I decided on a spur-of-the-moment gamble: "I'm here to accept your handover," I said, using an Indonesian word that can mean "surrender" or merely "transfer of control." The colonel looked at me. Then he smiled wanly, said "Of course," and extended his hand.

After tea, which we sipped in a slightly surreal silence against the noise of aircraft, vehicles, and running feet outside, we climbed into the commander's jeep and toured the airfield defenses together while the air-landing operation continued around us; we spoke with the Indonesian troops at each perimeter strong-point, confirming that there had been a peaceful transfer of control and that they were to remain in position, weapons on safe, until relieved by incoming units of the international force (International Force East Timor; INTERFET). A dozen handshakes and five more clove cigarettes later, the airfield was ours, with nobody killed and only a few shots fired.

I found later that my gamble had been less than reckless. Brigadier Ken Brownrigg and Major General Jim Molan, Australian officers attached to the embassy in Jakarta, had laid the foundation for us. Experienced Indonesia hands and former mentors of mine, both men had paved the way with detailed liaison and reconnaissance, alone in the dark at considerable risk, as violence exploded and the city burned around them, to ensure a peaceful entry rather than an opposed assault.[2] We had also arrived to a skillfully orchestrated reception by Special Forces under my subsequent friend and colleague Tim McOwan, commanding the Special Air Service Regiment (SASR). None of us in the assault aircraft had known this: the mission was "capture," and our commanders had given orders for a fight.[3] As it turned out, we had a few near misses and tense moments, but by week's end INTERFET had occupied Dili, secured what survived of population centers without major clashes, and turned its attention to the militias—irregular armed groups sponsored by Indonesian intelligence and sometimes led by Indonesian Special Forces—who had committed most of the violence and still posed the threat of insurgency.

Why examine East Timor, a conflict that began almost two years before 9/11 and which subsequent campaigns have dwarfed? Because in key ways, Timor was a transitional conflict: the last of the old century, the first of the new, and overlapping with the "War on Terrorism." Many dynamics that emerged after 9/11 were already evident in Timor, and the differences in how they were handled are highly instructive.

Previous chapters have described the accidental guerrilla syndrome in Afghanistan and Iraq This chapter gives brief comparative accounts of three smaller conflicts, in East Timor, Thailand, and Pakistan. The chapter is far from comprehensive; in a book of this length there is no space for the systematic studies these campaigns deserve, let alone for the many other examples—Somalia, Chechnya, Algeria, Darfur, the Philippines—that could be discussed. But the conflicts I describe in this chapter, occurring outside the spotlight of Western attention, demonstrate that the patterns of hybrid warfare I have identified in Iraq and Afghanistan hold true for other parts of the world. These conflicts also highlight cases in which indirect approaches achieved better outcomes than unilateral intervention. Finally, the chapter briefly examines Europe, to show that the accidental guerrilla syndrome is not restricted to remote hill-tribes in the developing world but can also be seen in the urban immigrant communities and developed societies of the West.

The Dog That Didn't Bark: East Timor, 1999–2000

The East Timor campaign seems to contradict the pattern of external intervention, backlash, and rejection that I have described as the accidental guerrilla syndrome. As I will explain, however, as in Sherlock Holmes's "curious incident of the dog in the night," the *absence* of a reaction in this case is an extremely important fact, since it underscores the factors that give rise to the more usual rejection response.

For me, the key question about Timor has always been how a foreign force of 10,000 troops from 22 nations[4] managed to intervene in an ongoing insurgency, amid large-scale unrest, looting, and bloodshed, and stabilize the situation without provoking an instant backlash. In terms of the accidental guerrilla syndrome, how did the intervention avoid a rejection? Some analysts have likened the chaotic situation in Timor to that of Baghdad in April 2003, and indeed there were strong similarities: a breakdown of law and order in the wake of regime collapse, looting, arson, rioting, and killing.[5] Some might suggest that INTERFET's extremely firm approach of immediately suppressing disorder and violence (akin to Loup Francart's "counterwar" strategy, noted in chapter 1), coupled with a culturally sensitive attitude to the population, prevented the kind of descent into insurgency that took place in Iraq. Others might argue that the Timor case simply shows that the accidental guerrilla is a phenomenon of the Muslim world, where religion and traditional authority are key identity markers and determinants of behavior, whereas the East Timorese are Catholic. The reality was more complex than either caricature would suggest.

The Timor Campaign

1999 was a watershed year. I remember drinking my morning coffee one Saturday in March 1999 in the officers' mess at Williamtown air base, where I had just finished an amphibious operations course, and reading with mild astonishment the newspaper coverage of negotiations between Indonesia, Portugal, the United Nations, and Australia on a proposal for East Timorese independence. "Anything could happen now," I thought:

Map 4.1 East Timor

it seemed that the fundamentals of Australia's foreign policy, the framework within which I and my peers had grown up, were shifting beneath my feet. For 25 years, Australia had been almost the only country in the world to recognize Indonesian sovereignty over the former Portuguese colony of Timor, which Indonesia had invaded in 1975, regarding the anti-Indonesian insurgency there as an internal matter. For policy-makers, it went almost without saying that Canberra's relationship with Jakarta mattered more than the aspirations of Timorese separatists and that a weak, independent Timor was less in our interest than a strong, stable Indonesia. This realist position had been our policy ever since August 1975, when Richard Woolcott, then Australia's ambassador to Jakarta, had first articulated it, and successive governments of both major parties had followed it.[6]

Like all Australian soldiers of my generation, I grew up with a policy of close engagement with Indonesia. After a year's intensive language and cultural training as a captain in 1993, I commanded military assistance teams with Indonesian Special Forces in 1994 and 1995, trained Indonesian officers in low-intensity conflict at the Australian jungle warfare school at Canungra, worked as an adviser with Indonesian airborne battalions, and spent long periods alone in the hills of West Java doing fieldwork for my doctoral dissertation on Indonesian insurgency. There was always a degree of caution in the relationship: Indonesians and Australians remembered all too well that their two countries had waged an undeclared but very real jungle war on each other during the Borneo Confrontation in the 1960s.[7] But even after the Soeharto government fell in May 1998, Australia was still working closely with Indonesia under the 1995 bilateral defense treaty, the Agreement on Maintaining Security.[8]

In early 1999, things started to slip. The new Indonesian government decided on a referendum, offering the Timorese a choice between independence and autonomy within Indonesia. A campaign of intimidation, unrest, and violence swept Timor, in two phases—in April–May, and in the lead-up to the August 30 referendum—in which the Indonesian security forces tried to sway the vote away from independence or even prevent it entirely. On the day, the referendum went ahead despite severe intimidation by units of the Tentara Nasional Indonesia (the Indonesian military; TNI), police, and "militias"—locally raised irregulars, in at least 16 main groups, who (contrary to subsequent popular belief) were almost 100 percent ethnic East Timorese and Catholic.[9] The vote was 87.5 percent in favor of independence from Indonesia. This provoked a total breakdown of law and order, as well as widespread arson, looting, mass killings, and population displacement. Thousands were killed in extremely gruesome fashion. (Corpses—some of people who had been thrown alive into the sea with their hands and feet cut off and left to drown—kept washing up on the beach near Batugade, a destroyed coastal town in our battalion sector, for weeks afterward.)[10]

The militias began a forced deportation of East Timorese civilians en masse to West Timor, destroying the province's buildings and infrastructure, and attacking the United Nations and other international organizations who were supervising the referendum. A RAND Corporation report later estimated that the violence "displaced close to 80 percent of the territory's population. Approximately 265,000 East Timorese became refugees; another 500,000 escaped to the interior of the country."[11] Under pressure from the international community—including Australia, but mainly the United States and the Association of South East Asian Nations (ASEAN)—Indonesia agreed to allow an Australia-led multinational force to intervene and restore order until the United Nations could assemble a peacekeeping mission. So from almost no officially sanctioned preparations, we had gone from a standing start on August 30 to a full deployment of 10,000 troops from 22 countries less than three weeks later—a major undertaking.

Dili was a ghost town as we pushed out from the airfield that first night. Hardly a living civilian was to be seen, though we saw plenty of dead animals and an occasional human corpse. There were signs of looting and forced evacuation, but otherwise the city presented a silent landscape of ruined buildings and tattered referendum posters flapping in a hot breeze that stank of ashes and excrement. The smoke columns towered over us, lit red by the flames underneath and periodically blocking the moon. Specks of ash rained down like large grey snowflakes. Distant gunfire could be heard, and all through the night, every seven minutes or so, another C130 landed with a roar back at Komorro, as the airlift continued. Small teams of Special Forces and reconnaissance patrols, some in commandeered Land Rovers abandoned when the UN evacuated in disarray after the referendum, moved furtively around the town. Patrols crept along the dark streets, and helicopters periodically rocketed low overhead. The militia fell back as the battalion advanced, and the TNI either stood aside or waited sullenly for orders. But I remember thinking "Where are the people?" The entire civilian population seemed to have simply vanished.

My company's parent unit, the Second Battalion of the Royal Australian Regiment (2RAR), spent the first few days establishing control of Dili. The major operation of this period was a security sweep, with 2RAR providing a blocking force and 3RAR, the parachute battalion under my friend and former boss Nick Welch, sweeping through what was left of the downtown area and trying to flush out militia fighters. There were some clashes with TNI and militia, but the sweep achieved little other than a show of presence—a foretaste of later events, when large-scale, unilateral, multiunit sweeps generally achieved nothing. Small-team, long-duration operations with local guides, though less spectacular, yielded far greater results. By late September, the battalion was back at Komorro, preparing an air assault to secure Batugade and Balibo, towns in the western area bordering the Indonesian province of West Timor. At dawn on October 1, 2RAR launched, quickly securing both towns. My company and battalion headquarters occupied the sixteenth-century Portuguese hilltop fort that dominates Balibo, with no opposition. This air assault was an ambitious

Figure 4.1 East Timor, October 1999—Australian troops during a firefight with Indonesian police, army, and militia, Motaain village. Lance Corporal Nathan Ross, the author's radio operator, is in the left foreground, the author (kneeling) is at the right. Photo: CPL Daren Hilder

undertaking: the largest airmobile operation since Vietnam and the largest ever undertaken using only Australian helicopters. Not for the first or last time, we were extremely fortunate not to incur substantial casualties.[12]

On the day 2RAR took Balibo, there were still almost 8,000 TNI in East Timor and about the same number of militia, most now positioned between 2RAR and the rest of the force. In the event of a major confrontation, the battalion would have been quite isolated. It was a bold maneuver, one that wrong-footed the opposition and silenced a variety of domestic and international critics who had accused General Peter Cosgrove, the force commander, of being slow to break out from Dili while the death and destruction were continuing in the outlying regions. But the first few weeks were tense, as we were on our own until the rest of INTERFET moved into position. Like Dili, Balibo was a ghost town. Other than about 40 militia fighters sighted during the air assault, who fled rapidly toward West Timor, the entire population of Balibo at this time was one old woman and about seven dogs. Whole districts were flattened by fire, the town center was smashed, and the population was gone—dead, hiding, or deported. Only the hilltop castle was relatively undamaged; it contained nothing worth wrecking.

Over the next month, there were clashes as the militia sought to escape across the border into West Timor, taking large numbers of the civilian population with them. This led to the most intensive series of combat engagements of the campaign. These included a Special Air Service Regiment (SASR) on Los Palos and a later ambush at Suai, a border incident at Motaain Bridge between 2RAR, TNI, police, and militia, another SASR engagement at Aidabasalala, and numerous smaller firefights across the brigade area.[13] Again, the most effective operations during this period were small-team, long-duration patrols working with the population. (One of the longest, lasting 58 days, was conducted by my company, working with local guides recruited through community leaders in Balibo.) The least effective operations were large-scale, unilateral sweeps: for example, an elaborate sweep-and-clear operation by 2RAR, supported by an airmobile assault, Armored Cavalry, and Special Forces, was conducted on October 18 in Aidabaleten District, north of Balibo. Planned as a surprise, it was compromised at the outset by an SASR firefight near the village of Aidabasalala. Despite this being a known militia area with a population of several thousand, the operation not only resulted in no enemy killed, captured, or even sighted, but failed even to encounter any of the local population, who were all in hiding, except for those who had already been detained following the firefight in the village of Aidabasalala.[14] Rather than a show of force, large-scale sweeps that hit nothing and secured nothing were displays of impotence.

By late October, the campaign began to settle into "steady-state" border and population security operations. These involved patrolling, surveillance, and reconnaissance, movement control, further fruitless large-scale sweeps, humanitarian assistance operations, and protecting the population as they slowly returned. There were incursions by militia from West Timor but little internal unrest or insurgency. The rest of our brigade arrived and deployed on the border. It seems that, broadly speaking, the shock of the first weeks of the campaign had convinced the enemy to bide their time, applying the "protraction" tactic (discussed in chapter 1) and simply waiting until INTERFET left. My company spent most of October and

Figure 4.2 East Timor, October 1999—The author negotiating a ceasefire agreement with Colonel Sigit Yowono, after a firefight between Australian and Indonesian troops, police, and militia near the border village of Motaain.
Photo: CPL Darren Hilder

November deployed in a jungle area right on the West Timor border that lay astride three major infiltration routes. This remote, underpopulated area was the scene of the refugee return incident discussed in detail below. It was known to us as the Salore Pocket and to subsequent generations of UN troops as the Horse's Head (due to its shape on the map).

By November, the population was returning, and political groups like Conselho Nacional de Resistência Timorense (Timorese National Resistance Council; CNRT), the umbrella political organization for Timorese resistance to Indonesian occupation, began to take charge of civil administration in the regions. Infighting and competition between local political groups started to emerge, and Forças Armadas da Libertação Nacional de Timor-Leste (East Timor National Liberation Forces; FALINTIL), the anti-Indonesian guerrilla movement, began to flex its muscles, leading to occasional violence. Both CNRT and FALINTIL had remained quiet during the intervention phase, staying in their base areas in the jungle hills, waiting out both the militia violence and the major maneuver operations as INTERFET seized control of East Timor, and then emerging in the aftermath to organize the population. Aid agencies and NGOs became more prominent, and border control was regularized through checkpoints and liaison measures. The campaign was transitioning into a humanitarian, reconstruction, and internal security operation. In mid-December, we began preparing for extraction as the United Nations returned under Sérgio Vieira de Mello, the brilliant Brazilian diplomat who skilfully supervised the transition to independence. (He was tragically killed four years later while serving in Iraq as special representative of the secretary-general, when al Qa'ida bombed the UN compound in Baghdad on August 19, 2003.)[15]

With a short Christmas interlude, when my company briefly secured the entire sector while the rest of the unit concentrated at Balibo for Christmas dinner, patrolling continued right up to the last moment. As the first unit into Timor, 2RAR was one of the first to leave, handing over to our sister battalion 5/7RAR on New Year's Day 2000 and returning by air and sealift from Dili to Darwin in February 2000, while many INTERFET units stayed on as part of the new force, the United Nations Transitional Authority in East Timor (UNTAET). Despite periodic militia violence, the work of UNTAET also proceeded without major disruption: the new nation of Timor Leste achieved full independence on May 20, 2002. Despite some unrest after independence (discussed below), INTERFET has been seen as a model for stabilization operations.[16] As the following incident shows, however, understanding local power relationships and building alliances were fundamental.

THE SILAWAN REFUGEES

Late in the afternoon of November 3, 1999, the guard commander came into the converted cellar under the sixteenth-century Portuguese fort in Balibo that we used as a command post. "Boss, there's a kid outside to see you," he said. Grabbing my rifle, I walked out the gatehouse and down the ramp to the perimeter fence. A boy of about 13 was sitting on a battered red Honda motor scooter under a huge *hali* (banyan) tree, looking anxiously at two soldiers who were offering him tea in a steel canteen cup. They shrugged their shoulders and smiled helplessly as I arrived; the kid was terrified. He held out a dirty piece of crumpled paper, looking as if it had been torn from a school exercise book. It was damp, and the ink on it had run, but I could just make out the words in Portuguese and Tetuñ, the Timorese lingua franca: "Major Kilkullen. Zona fronteiriça junto a Balibó. Belun diak povu nian" ("Major Kilkullen, frontier zone near Balibo. Good friend of the people").[17] The next line, in English, read simply "Australia soldier help us."

"Mai ho ha'u" ("Come with me"), the boy said urgently, turning his scooter downhill and revving the engine. Something about his face made me intuitively trust him, so I climbed on behind with my rifle slung and my arms about his waist, and we rode through the dusk to the edge of town. On a steep hillside among the trees, an old man was waiting. The boy led me to him and then squatted close behind him in the twilight. The man was extremely agitated, and at first I had difficulty understanding what he was saying, in a mix of Indonesian (which I knew well), Tetuñ (which I knew much less well), and Portuguese (which I barely understood at all). But eventually I got it.

He was a district leader from the outskirts of Balibo. In mid-September, the militia had forcibly deported his people to a makeshift camp at Silawan, near Motaain on the Indonesian side of the frontier. The militia had killed many in his town and during the inhabitants' move to West Timor, to keep them intimidated. Now, in squalid conditions across the border, they were desperate to escape: more had died, many were sick, there was not enough food or clean water, and some of the women were pregnant. But the militia had terrorized them, telling the elders that INTERFET troops were raping and killing returnees, separating families, and imprisoning displaced persons. Some believed this, others did not, and the people were divided as to the wisdom of returning. So they had sent the old man and the boy as scouts. Perhaps the leaders imagined that their ages, respectively too old and too young to fight, might make them less likely to be harmed if caught. The pair had crossed the border overnight between two TNI posts, waded the river, hiked through the jungle to an abandoned village where they had found the red Honda, met one of our reconnaissance patrols, and made their way to Balibo. They carried a message from their community leaders: the leaders wanted to have a clandestine meeting with me to discuss the return of their group.[18]

I met the leaders just after dawn the next morning, November 4, at the destroyed village of Maneha, in thick secondary jungle, extremely close to the border in the Salore Pocket. The trees were dripping from the overnight thunderstorm and the sun was just rising as I arrived with a reconnaissance patrol as escort, having travelled three rainy hours through the jungle in darkness to get there. Leaving my rifle and equipment outside, with the escort standing by in case of a trap, I ducked to enter a small *atap* hut, one of few surviving structures in the burnt-out village. Eleven men waited in the darkness inside; as my eyes adjusted to the light, I joined them sitting cross-legged on the dirt floor. They had made the border crossing overnight and now wanted to confirm the situation in East Timor before bringing their people across, they said. We all kept our voices low: sound carries a long way in the jungle at dawn, and we were less than a mile from the nearest TNI frontier post. During the course of a long meeting, I persuaded the two key leaders—both clan[19] elders, one a teacher—to return with me to Balibo, right then and there, to see conditions for themselves. They were extremely nervous, and I had to give them my personal guarantee of safe conduct before they agreed to come. Arriving in town, I simply introduced them to the local CNRT leaders and left them to it. A few hours later, they were back: the Balibo community had convinced them (more effectively than any foreigner could) that the militia propaganda was false, and they had seen for themselves that conditions were better than in the camps. That afternoon, we returned them to Maneha, from where they recrossed the border alone to speak with their people, while our civil-military operations teams established reception points in East Timor. Within five days, several hundred refugees from this group were recovered from the border area and brought back to Balibo to begin rebuilding their lives. This marked the start of Balibo's revival and coincided with the start of a period of mass refugee return to East Timor that proceeded apace through November and December.

This incident, along with many others, showed me the power of traditional authority structures—modified by the influence of CNRT, FALINTIL, and Força Segurança Popular (FSP), the local CNRT security organization—to affect the actions of the local people. In particular, the traditional establishment exercised immense influence on the critical choice of political allegiance: whether to remain in West Timor under the militia or return to East Timor. In my observation of dozens of cases, Timorese villagers' choices were almost always determined by their traditional leaders: in the example here, once I had won over the elders, their influence in turn ensured that the majority (about 70 percent) of the people in their village and clan groups returned. Interestingly, the elders had come to me on the basis of an endorsement from other Timorese leaders (whoever had marked their paper in Tetuñ describing me as a "friend of the people"), so that even my personal prestige with these elders ultimately derived from a tribal endorsement. The CNRT leaders in Balibo were responsible for convincing them that the militia propaganda was false. And my future close relationship with these returnees, due to their belief that they owed me a debt of honor for their escape, led this group's leaders to vouch for me with other Timorese, which in turn gave me the credentials to engage further groups. In this society, which was honor-based, placed great emphasis on reciprocity, exchange, and kinship, and was extremely warlike (despite media stereotypes of "peace-loving Timorese"), *achieved* authority based on personal actions and reputation was important, but *ascribed* authority, deriving from position in a traditional hierarchy or from a "ladder" of tribal endorsements, was essential.

Among townspeople, or in districts where traditional authority structures were eroded by conflict or population displacement, political party "elders" tended to assume some of the social-organizational functions that clan, house, and district leaders performed in other areas. Significantly, another local man, with whom I worked closely to secure the return of refugees from Leohitu Subdistrict, had worked in the Clandestine Front (the urban student underground movement), and saved many lives during the militia violence. But he could not translate this achievement into a formal leadership role, due to his lack of CNRT endorsement. Other CNRT leaders, members of the "resistance establishment," who had waited out the crisis but were older, possessed greater prestige, or had longer records as leaders of political opposition to the occupation tended to exclude others from leadership positions. In other words, creditable behavior in the current conflict might bring informal influence and prestige, but not formal political authority. Formal power was still based on traditional hierarchical roles and pedigree.[20] This "generation gap"—the traditional establishment's marginalizing of younger, more active leaders, despite their critical contribution during the emergency of 1999—sowed the seeds of later unrest and violence in post-independence Timor.

THE ROLE OF RELIGION

Religious leaders (especially local Catholic priests and members of the Salesian order) were also extremely influential. As many analysts have noted, Portuguese colonial rule operated indirectly through indigenous elites, and while the elite strata of East Timorese society were largely Catholic by 1975, the majority of the population remained animist in its beliefs.[21] Because the Portuguese colonized Timor before the arrival of Islam in the archipelago, there is no indigenous Muslim population in East Timor. Arab and Goanese immigrants under Portuguese rule and Indonesian migrants after 1975 were numerically small (but politically powerful) Muslim minorities, but these were largely centered in Javanese areas of Dili and had little influence on the population as a whole. James Dunn estimates that less than 50 percent of the population of Portuguese Timor was Catholic in 1975 but that the social and political influence of the Catholic Church increased markedly after the invasion, so that by 1995, after 20 years of Indonesian occupation, 80 percent of the population self-identified as Catholic.[22] Abel Guterres, similarly, estimated pre-invasion penetration of Catholicism at only 30 percent of the population;[23] but more than 90 percent of my contacts in 1999 claimed to be Catholic.[24]

Had people simply become more pious over the intervening time period? My field observations in 1999–2000 suggested not: rather, because most other Indonesians were non-Catholic (even the West Timorese are largely Protestant, a result of the influence of Protestant missionaries under Dutch colonial rule), Catholicism seems to have become a nationalist identity-marker, a symbol of East Timorese identity and resistance against the occupation. The locals I dealt with often exhibited traditional beliefs, and though very few small villages had chapels, most had traditional buildings (uma lulik) associated with the veneration of ancestors and the founders of local villages. The main lineage groups in my area, the Mambai, Kemak, and Makassae, had a matrilineal kinship system and used complex networks of exchange as a means of interaction between clans and social groupings.[25] Traditionally, tribes did not have centralized villages but lived in scattered hamlets based on groups who shared a common cult. These cult groups were organized, in turn, around a central "house of origin" (*fada ni fun*) that represented a historical or mythical founder of their village.[26] In my area, buildings used for traditional religious practices were often clustered on a hill specially set aside within a village, and had often been targeted for destruction by the militia.[27] These buildings often contained sacred relics or other heirlooms relating to the village founder, which were venerated and, in one case I observed near the village of Bauwai, could not be taken out of the *uma lulik* unless first sprinkled with the blood of a specially sacrificed chicken. In other words, despite a veneer of Catholicism, the locals I dealt with in 1999 were far from devoutly Catholic: pre-Christian beliefs and traditional loyalties were a much stronger predictor of behavior than Catholic doctrine. Rather, the nationalist movement had co-opted Catholic identity for political purposes, so that whatever their actual beliefs, Timorese self-identified as Catholic because not to do so was tantamount to supporting the occupation.

The militia themselves were also almost all Catholic, recruited from the rural poor and the urban criminal class, and tied by personal loyalty to specific Indonesian intelligence service or special forces mentors. Peer pressure and intimidation almost always played a part in the recruitment and behavior of these fighters, who were often extremely young. Access to money, alcohol, drugs, and a cheap "power trip" in relation to the local society, from which some militia members had felt themselves to be outcasts, also played a part, along with Indonesian nationalism, self-interest (some were employed by businessmen whose interests were linked to the occupation), and loyalty to Indonesian military patrons.[28] All the militia detainees I interviewed during the operation were Catholic, and captured militia documents included Catholic prayers and religious letters. Perhaps for this reason, the militia rarely damaged Catholic churches. Nonetheless, there is evidence—including the well-documented massacres at Suai and Liquiça—that the militia (when directly supervised by TNI) specifically targeted Catholic clergy during the violence, probably because of the priests' influence over the population and in the independence movement.

The parish priest of Balibo was born on the neighboring island of Flores and had served in Balibo for two years before being forced to flee in September 1999. Being non-Timorese, he had not developed particularly close relationships with CNRT, but he informally supported the independence movement. He exercised personal authority rather than formal political power, but his prestige was enormous and allowed him to question the actions of both CNRT and INTERFET. He tended to stand deliberately outside the formal power structure, using this position of freedom from formal political allegiance to question any action that appeared to harm the people. During a conversation with him about the syncretism of the people's religious beliefs,[29] it became clear to me that he regarded his role as one of pastoral care rather than proselytization: he was there to protect the people, not to enforce orthodoxy. Because of his personal prestige, the local CNRT/FSP leadership were at great pains to maintain a close relationship with him, and he had very considerable influence in sanctioning their political legitimacy. He also had a close relationship with our battalion's Catholic chaplain, Father Glynn Murphy.

One of Glynn's best decisions was to restart village church services in Balibo in early November, even before the population had returned in any numbers. He said mass in the Balibo church in early November, encouraging the parish priest to return from hiding on November 15. The local population began trekking in from their hiding places in the surrounding jungle-covered hill districts to go to church, and the town gradually revived around a core of tribal, local, and religious identity. The CNRT used this ostensibly religious process as a vehicle for social and political organization: the church, as a community focal point, became a means of political control and popular mobilization. For example, on the morning of Sunday, November 21, 1999, the day when the newly returned priest said his first mass in the Balibo church, I sat near the church entrance and watched three CNRT/FSP leaders whom I knew well sit on the church porch and tell each arriving adult male "Soe fatuk, soe fatuk" ("Throw a stone"), requiring each man to throw a pebble onto a pile just outside the church door; they then counted the pebbles to get a rudimentary civil census. By repeating this procedure each week, the local *conçelho* could both calculate the manpower available to it and track the process of refugee return, as well as stamping its authority on the population and determining its population base (allowing it to bid for resources from the central CNRT leadership and from INTERFET).[30]

As these examples suggest, the Timor campaign showed the critical importance of close and genuine partnerships between the intervention force and indigenous allies, building on a solid understanding of local cultures and languages. We rapidly found that we needed to build leverage by engaging local partners, including scouts, interpreters, informants, local community leaders, and civilian organizations, in order to do anything at all. At the force level, INTERFET developed close relationships with the local irregular forces of CNRT, FSP, and FALINTIL and used these relationships to generate information, create a permissive operating environment, and enhance flexibility. We found that acquiring prestige through relationships with traditional elders was important, that local religious leaders were highly influential, and that political groups used ostensibly religious institutions as vehicles for control and popular mobilization.

During INTERFET, there was no significant rejection of the foreign presence. No major popular unrest emerged until after independence in 2002, and nothing resembling an insurgency developed until 2006, when a small group of rebels took to the jungle in the aftermath of a mutiny within the East Timor military. (Interestingly enough, this unrest grew out of perceptions by younger-generation leaders from the western part of the country that members of the old FALINTIL establishment were continuing to discriminate against them in allocating positions of formal authority.) Another continuing source of grievance is a belief that older establishment politicians, many of whom spent most of the Indonesian occupation in safe and comfort exile, have not done enough to ameliorate the conditions of ordinary rural Timorese. Still, these sources of tension were internally derived, and did not reach crisis point until seven to nine years after the INTERFET intervention, and three to five years after full independence and the drawdown of UNTAET. By the standards of peace enforcement and stabilization operations, East Timor thus represents a very significant success: a smooth, nonviolent transition to civilian-led democratic government, without any significant rejection response or exploitation of unrest by external actors, and with no major internal unrest for years afterwards.

IMPLICATIONS

How did this occur? How did the intervention in East Timor succeed in stabilizing the environment without generating an immediate backlash? Why did the dog not bark, and what are the implications?

Scale and geography mattered. East Timor is small: about 5,700 square miles, the size of Connecticut, Northern Ireland, or the greater Sydney metropolitan area. Its population is also tiny: about 1 million people in 1999, of whom (as noted) almost 80 percent had been displaced by the militia violence. And except for East Timor's western enclave of Oecussi-Ambeno, and the main land border with West Timor (which INTERFET secured on day 10 of the operation) East Timor is an island, making the problems of border control and infiltration relatively straightforward, though difficult at times due to extremely rough jungle terrain and lack of infrastructure. In other words, though difficult enough for a regional power like Australia or a regionally based coalition like INTERFET, the scale of the East Timor operation was manageable within available resources.

The entry of INTERFET into East Timor was largely nonviolent, even though, as mentioned, it was not originally planned as such. But the relative size, mobility, and technological superiority of the intervention force, the fact that it entered simultaneously by air and sea across multiple points of entry and seized key population centers with great rapidity, and the active and overt presence of strike aircraft and warships demonstrated its ability to overmatch both the militia and TNI and created a shock effect on the population and the enemy. The rapid expansion of control to the border areas and other key points added to the dislocating effect on the opposition. Besides the forces actually engaged in the landing, a key asset was the amphibious assault ship USS *Belleau Wood*, carrying the Thirty-first Marine Expeditionary Unit of the United States Marine Corps, whose presence off the coast discouraged (at both a political and a military level) any attempt at interference. As RAND counterinsurgency researcher Russell Glenn has noted, the nonviolent but psychologically dislocating effect of this type of air-land-sea maneuver (known in Australian doctrine as MultiDimensional Manoeuvre) achieved a similar shock effect on opposition groups in the Solomon Islands during subsequent operations in 2003, while avoiding the popular alienation that might have resulted from large-scale killing.[32] The combination of rapid maneuver with extremely tight rules of engagement, and a series of operational choices (such as my own on day 1) that favored ruse or negotiation over bloodshed and preferred surrender or capture to killing, added to this effect.

Still, these factors would only account for the lack of a backlash during the immediate "shock and awe" of the entry phase, not for the sustained lack of popular opposition to the intervention. A second major influence was the de facto counterwar strategy the force applied from the outset. Again, this strategy combined extremely tight rules of engagement with a very energetic approach, across the whole force, to instantly suppressing all forms of disorder, violence, and lawlessness, however they originated. General Cosgrove's leadership was an extremely important factor here. His guidance, and frequent personal visits, made it clear that his intent was that, while INTERFET did not take sides in the political question of East Timorese independence, its role was to suppress any and all violence and unrest, emanating from whatever source. Individuals found using or carrying a lethal weapon such as a firearm were subject to immediate disarmament, detention, and if they resisted, to lethal force. INTERFET treated violence and instability arising from any source (rather than targeting one particular group) as its enemy. Even after the Indonesian parliament voted to ratify the vote for independence, and CNRT/FALINTIL emerged as partners in the UN-sponsored process of establishing a transitional administration, INTERFET still prevented any group, whatever its political orientation, from carrying weapons.

General Cosgrove also, wisely, did not confuse entry with victory. He regarded the successful seizure of key population centers in East Timor as the beginning, not the end, of decisive operations. Troops pushed out rapidly to secure the population, protect the people from further violence, return them to their homes, and create a sense of security and predictability to replace the violent uncertainty of the preceding months. This population-centric approach, which included very active communications and IO directed at influencing the population, allowed local community leaders to interact with the force on a confident basis. It also provided the security and certainty, the "normative system" of rules and sanctions,[33] that, as Stathis Kalyvas's work on civil war violence later showed, are precursors to the development of popular support for armed groups (including the government or an intervening force) in situations of internal conflict.[34]

INTERFET had also attained a degree of cultural understanding of the Timorese people, although, as in my own case, this was largely ad hoc and accidental, not driven by higher direction: many East Timorese live in Australia, Australian guerrillas had operated in Japanese-occupied Timor during World War II, there was a historic relationship of respect between Australia and East Timor, and there were several soldiers of Timorese origin in the force. Still, there were few Indonesian linguists and almost no Tetuñ speakers in the initial rotation. Troops in the initial landing received only limited language and cultural training: though this was the largest single component of predeployment training, the time was so short that little could be achieved. But subsequent rotations received language and cultural training, were allocated a higher proportion of linguists and a much higher proportion of intelligence analysts than normal, and conducted mission rehearsal exercises in a specially designed training environment that included a major cultural component. As an institution, the Australian government reacted quickly, establishing vastly enhanced language programs and specialized training facilities within weeks of the initial deployment. Perhaps more important, most Australian combat troops were rapidly banished to the relatively underpopulated border area, where the risk of combat engagement was highest, while Asian components of the force (from Malaysia, Singapore, Thailand, and South Korea) were assigned to secure major population centers where daily interaction with the population was greatest.

A number of situational factors (as distinct from actions under INTERFET's control) also seem to have contributed to the lack of backlash. First, unlike in Afghanistan or Iraq, no globally focused enemy group equating to AQ preexisted in Timor or was able to enter the theater after the start of the operation.[35] To the extent that the East Timorese had some global reach through the agitation and propaganda efforts of their diaspora in Europe and elsewhere, this global network was solidly on the side of INTERFET and against TNI and the militia. For similar reasons, the Indonesian security forces and the militia had an extremely limited pool of local allies. Although they had shown themselves highly adept in developing tribal and local allies during the invasion of Portuguese Timor in 1975,[36] and although the recruitment of militias had been tactically effective in 1999,[37] the Indonesian military had failed to gain any significant measure of popular acceptance from the Timorese by 1999, and the Indonesian state had relatively shallow roots in East Timor.

Indeed, to the extent that there was a backlash against intervention in East Timor, it was directed at the initial 1975 intervention by the Indonesian government, which most East Timorese always had seen as a foreign external actor. This, indeed, was a key perceptual difference that most Indonesians I spoke with never grasped: Indonesians saw themselves as essentially the same as East Timorese, brothers in the great concept of *nusantara* that covered the whole Malay archipelago.[38] They saw their actions as benefiting the Timorese, liberating them from the burden of colonialism that they themselves had escaped a generation earlier, and from the threat of communism, which they had defeated a decade before the invasion. They were well aware of Timor's unique ethnic characteristics, but discounted them as a political factor: Indonesia has 27 provinces and well over 300 ethnic groups, all of whom claim some cultural autonomy. The Indonesian educational and administrative system takes this into account: policies the Timorese saw as designed to eradicate their indigenous culture were only the same policies that applied to everyone else in Indonesia,[39] and most Indonesians found it inconceivable that Timorese would prefer to sink alone when they could be part of the Indonesian state and participate in its economy. The overwhelming rejection of autonomy in favor of independence in the August 30 referendum was therefore a slap in the face to many Indonesians, prompting conspiracy theories about Western (especially Australian) interference and contributing to the vindictiveness of the post-referendum violence.[40] Indonesia had poured aid and economic development into its province of East Timor, which was vastly better resourced than West Timor, or indeed any other province in eastern Indonesia. The perverse, ungrateful attitude with which the East Timorese seemed to reject autonomy (a more generous offer than other separatist regions like Aceh, Papua, or Maluku had received) was literally unbelievable to many Indonesians.

Thus, Indonesia's failure in Timor was political (in its inability to establish the legitimacy of its rule and to convince Timorese to see themselves as Indonesian), not military. The Indonesian military had, in fact, soundly defeated FALINTIL as a guerrilla force by the end of the 1980s and had established control over all key population centers and more than 90 percent of the East Timorese population by as early as 1983.[41] There was very little insurgent violence at any time during the 1990s, and by 1999 less than 200 FALINTIL fighters remained at large, keeping to themselves in remote hideouts in the eastern jungle. But Indonesian military methods, though in line with Indonesian counterinsurgency theory as it had developed since 1945 and had been successfully applied in Java in the 1950s and 1960s, were extremely alienating to the Timorese people, resulting in large-scale hardship, death, and population relocation.[42] Under the glare of the international media spotlight, and amid changing international norms, these methods were simply unacceptable to the international community in the 1990s.[43]

The key actors in the resistance, by the late 1980s, were the Frente Clandestinha, the urban, student-based Clandestine Front inside Timor, and the Timorese diaspora outside the country, especially in Europe. Their approach was the classic "provocation" tactic I described in chapter 1: the Clandestine Front provoked the Indonesian military (which had a natural tendency to heavy-handedness, as well as a lethally inefficient culture of lax rules of engagement and poor control by senior officers over local units) into committing a series of public atrocities and harsh security measures that alienated the bulk of the people, while the diaspora publicized these atrocities and agitated for international intervention on human rights grounds.[44] The most prominent incident of this kind was the Dili Massacre of November 12, 1991. The formation of the International East Timor Solidarity Movement in the 1990s reflected the success of these efforts, and played a role in forcing the hand of Western powers, including Australia, who were initially reluctant to intervene.[45] FALINTIL and FRETILIN were mainly important as symbols of resistance, a guerrilla force-in-being, and an alternative government-in-waiting. The real political resistance was mounted by the Clandestine Front and its international supporters, united after 1979 under the banner of the Conçelho Naçional de Resistência Maubere (Maubere National Resistance Council; CNRM), which became CNRT in 1998.

ACCIDENTAL GUERRILLAS IN TIMOR?

To the extent that the accidental guerrilla syndrome operated in Timor, then, it was directed at the Indonesian central government rather than INTERFET. In terms of the four stages of the model, the *infection* stage occurred (in Indonesian eyes, at least) when FRETILIN gained power over East Timor and declared independence, having defeated the other political parties in a brief but violent civil war after the precipitous Portuguese withdrawal from Timor in 1974–1975. The *contagion* stage never materialized, but a key Indonesian motivation for the invasion was the fact that FRETILIN was a socialist movement that the Indonesians believed was tied to Communist China. The year of the Indonesian invasion, 1975, also saw the fall of Saigon, the start of the Cambodian killing fields, and ongoing communist insurgencies in Thailand and the Philippines. A socialist state (the Democratic Republic of East Timor), unilaterally declared by FRETILIN on November 18, 1975, sitting in the middle of Indonesia and potentially spreading Communist influence, was too much for Jakarta to tolerate. The *intervention* phase resulted: a large-scale invasion by air, land, and sea in December 1975, followed by the expansion of Indonesian control to almost the whole territory and population of Timor by 1981. The heavy-handedness and violence of the Indonesian approach, well-documented in multiple sources, provoked a severe *rejection* response, which was only exacerbated by the effective provocation operations of the Clandestine Front and CNRM. Civilians in the towns and in villages in the hills, including large numbers of people who had not supported FRETILIN before the invasion, coalesced into a broad opposition front in the face of the occupation. Many took up arms or joined the Clandestine Front when they were alienated by killings of family members or notable atrocities like the Dili Massacre. Yet others, sensing the change in the wind after 1998, jumped on the CNRT band-wagon. Thus, in a sense, we can see the entire 24 years of Indonesian occupation of Timor as an extremely long-duration example of the accidental guerrilla syndrome.

The INTERFET operation, then, may have been a "counterintervention" rather than an "intervention" in the minds of most Timorese, and the local people (though clearly perceiving the international force as foreign) evidently saw it as less foreign or alien than the Indonesian government. Religion also played a part: as noted, Catholicism (along with language and ethnicity) had become a key marker of nationalist identity over time, and had been effectively exploited by essentially nonreligious political groups as a means of popular mobilization and control. INTERFET was not entirely Christian, let alone Catholic, in its makeup, but it was led by a "Christian" country (Australia). The local people in this case sided with the closer of two foreign groupings—a pattern repeated in Iraq and Afghanistan, as we have seen. A final factor may simply have been that the extremely critical environment of late September 1999 (with the country literally on fire and 8 out of every 10 Timorese dead or displaced) created such a crisis mentality that Timorese were willing to support almost anyone who provided a normative system of predictable order and security in which they could feel safe.

Perhaps the key observations here are that the definition of "foreign" and "intervention" can be highly elastic, that foreignness is relative (that is, when there are *two* intervening external actors, a population will tend to side with the less foreign against the more foreign—echoing Salzmann's concept of contingent identity described in chapter 2), and that what matters more than external actors' perceptions are those of the local people, which in turn create opportunities that can be exploited by a determined minority (regardless of ideology). The next example, southern Thailand, reinforces this conclusion.

A Flag of Inconvenience: Southern Thailand

"What do you think is driving the insurgency?" the professor asked. It was January 2006, and I was eating dinner with two respected Thai academics from the National Reconciliation Council, appointed the previous year to examine ways to end the violence in southern Thailand.[46] I had been traveling across Southeast Asia that month with Ambassador Hank Crumpton, United States coordinator for counterterrorism, responsible for America's counterterrorism diplomacy worldwide. As Ambassador Crumpton's chief strategist from late 2005 until I deployed to Iraq in early 2007, my task was to deepen our understanding of terrorism and insurgency, apply that understanding to counterterrorism policy, and work across U.S. and partner government agencies to integrate military, political, economic, intelligence, educational, development, and information efforts to reduce terrorist and insurgent violence. This involved regular field visits and consultations with counterparts, and on this visit we had spent several days meeting with Thai military, diplomatic, and intelligence officials, calling on General Winai Phatthiyakul (secretary general of the National Security Council of Thailand) and interim prime minister Chidchai Vanasatidaya, and consulting the U.S. Country Team at the embassy in Bangkok.

The main issue, of course, was the insurgency in the three southern border provinces of Yala, Pattani, and Narathiwat, which had escalated alarmingly since early 2004 and had reached unprecedented levels in the previous year: according to the National Reconciliation Commission, 2004 and 2005 saw 2,940 people killed or injured and 3,456 violent incidents—an intensity level 26 times higher than in the preceding 11 years.[47] According to figures cited by RAND researcher Peter Chalk, "between January 2004 and the end of August 2007, 7,743 incidents were recorded in southern Thailand, leaving 2,566 dead (which equates to an average of 58 per month or roughly two a day) and a further 4,187 wounded. While civilians have been the hardest hit (accounting for more than 70 percent of all fatalities), both the police and military have also suffered significant losses with respective casualty counts amounting to 711 and 689. Most attacks have taken the form of drive-by shootings and assassinations (3,253), acts of arson (1,298), and bombings (1,189) using improvised

Map 4.2 Southern Thailand

explosive devices (IEDs). For a population that numbers only 1.8 million, these figures represent a considerable toll."[48] Indeed, this level of violence makes southern Thailand's ethnoreligious insurgency one of the most intense in the world, second only to those in Iraq and Afghanistan during this period. The insurgency had sparked unrest in other parts of Thailand, and violence was beginning to bleed out into neighboring provinces.

At this time, there was intense debate within policy and analytical circles in Washington about whether the southern Thailand insurgency was driven by local issues and grievances or whether it was instead a new front in the so-called War on Terrorism.[49] On this visit we had learned a lot, but as often in traditional diplomacy, our perception had been limited by the perspectives of our interlocutors, who were mainly Thai government officials or Bangkok-based, English-speaking members of the political or intellectual elite. Their insights naturally reflected their own experience and background, which was closer to ours, I suspect, than to that of the average person in southern Thailand. And for security reasons (another besetting problem for diplomats, whose field activities are often sharply constrained by risk-averse parent bureaucracies)[50] we had been unable to visit southern Thailand ourselves or talk to the people there.

So I answered the professor's question with one of my own. How many people in Thailand were Muslims, I asked, and what was their ethnicity? "Well, overall, Thailand is about 96 percent Buddhist and 4 percent Muslim," the professor replied. "Of the 4 percent who are Muslim, the vast majority are ethnic Malay. The others are Indonesian, Pakistani, or Bangladeshi immigrants in the large cities, some Cham people and ethnic Chinese Muslims, and the rest are ethnic Thai Muslims."[51] I asked the obvious question: how many ethnic Thai Muslims were involved in the insurgency?

"None," he replied. "It's a Malay thing."[52]

Despite frequent service in the field alongside the Thai military and police over the past 25 years, I have had little opportunity to date for first-hand field research in southern Thailand. So, to preserve the approach I have adopted in the Afghanistan and Iraq case studies, this section relies on the work of researchers who follow a methodology similar to my own: Duncan McCargo of the University of Leeds, Francesca Lawe-Davies of the International Crisis Group, and to a lesser extent Zachary Abuza of Simmons College, Boston, and Peter Chalk of the RAND Corporation. Of these, I have leant most heavily on McCargo's work, given that he recently completed a year's fieldwork in the southern provinces. Although these analysts do not agree on some key issues—hardly surprising, given the complexity and difficulty of the topic—on balance their research confirms my impressions, based on a reading of open source documentary evidence, plus limited personal time in the field. As I wrote in my fieldnotes during a visit to Thailand in 2006:

> The more I look at this, the more it seems an indigenous separatist insurgency—albeit one that includes a high degree of terrorist activity [and Islamist rhetoric]—rather than a JI [Jema'ah Islamiyah-sponsored or AQ [al Qa'ida]-linked jihad. Having said that, it seems many original leaders of the [Gerakan Mujahidin Islam Patani; GMIP] movement are veterans of the Soviet-Afghan War, so there are probably personal contacts and links through shared experience. And we know that in insurgencies where religion functions as a marker for ethnic identity, [both] religious motivations and religious justifications tend to increase over time. So this is a potential future AQ theatre—a wound at risk of infection, as it were. . . . The fact is that this is an ethnic separatist insurgency, not a fundamentalist Islamic jihad. This may explain why we have seen no JI/AQ involvement in the conflict to date, though this could also be explained by the fact that the insurgency hotted up in early 2004, after JI and AQ were already under pressure. None of this means that the insurgency might not become a jihad in future if not effectively addressed: in conflicts like this, where religion is an ethnic marker, experience has beenthat the religious element becomes more dominant over time. Examples are East Timor, Cyprus, Lebanon, Northern Ireland—and, of course, Iraq.[53]

As I shall show, the evidence suggests that the insurgency is fundamentally an ethnic uprising, driven by the lethal interaction of two underlying trends. The first is a belief by local people in the South that their unique Patani identity (centered on ethnicity, language, and religion) is under threat from a Bangkok government that unilaterally interferes in their affairs, corrodes their traditional way of life, and is fundamentally illegitimate in their eyes. The second is a series of central government policies that have been at best paternalistic (treating the South as a pseudocolony with special needs) and at worst assimilationist, authoritarian, and brutal (treating all local people as potential rebels and insurgents as mere bandits). A harsh crackdown by the Thaksin Shinawatra government in 2004 significantly exacerbated the problem. Human rights abuses and atrocities on both sides have dramatically heightened hatreds, corroding the basic framework of society in the South and making the violence self-sustaining beyond its original grievances so that, as David Galula predicted in his classic *Counterinsurgency Warfare*, "as the war develops, war itself becomes the paramount issue, and the original cause consequently loses some of its importance."[54]

Zachary Abuza commented on this in February 2007, noting that entire Buddhist communities had fled the South in a "de facto ethnic cleansing" and that the "social fabric of the south [had] been irreparably damaged," an impression confirmed by Francesca Lawe-Davies, who pointed out that some remote areas in the south had become no-go zones for security forces during 2006, with insurgent groups starting to permanently control territory[55] as distinct from simply intimidating the population or mounting attacks on security forces. As Duncan McCargo's detailed field research confirms, the existence of no-go zones has been a long-standing phenomenon, such that some areas of the South have not experienced effective government control at any time since the separatist movement first flared up in the 1950s.[56] Indeed, my reading of McCargo's fieldwork data[57] suggests that in terms of the basic metrics of counterinsurgency—route and infrastructure security, access to the population, freedom of movement by government officials, collection of taxation, survivability of local officials, and the delivery of basic governance services—by mid-2008 the government had completely lost control of large areas of the South.

This escalating violence and loss of control has occurred against the background of a shift in Thai politics away from the royalist administration of Prem Tinsulanonda during the 1980s, followed by a turbulent period of parliamentary democracy under Thaksin Shinawatra's Thai Rak Thai party since 1997. Dissatisfaction with Thaksin's handling of the insurgency was one key trigger for the bloodless military coup of September 16, 2006, which led to a military-backed interim government, which was succeeded by a civilian coalition government formed after parliamentary elections on December 23, 2007. All Thai governments since 2004 have faced extremely significant challenges in dealing effectively with the insurgency. The conflict has escalated within the context of the so-called war on terrorism since 2001 and offers significant insights into the dynamics of the accidental guerrilla syndrome.

A FLAG OF INCONVENIENCE

The insurgency in southern Thailand has roots stretching back to attempts before the nineteenth century by a modernizing and centralizing Kingdom of Siam to expand its control over the pseudoindependent princely states of the Malay Peninsula, some of which had at various times paid tribute or owed nominal allegiance to Siamese monarchs, such as the kings of Ayutthaya. One of these Malay states, the Sultanate of Patani, was annexed in 1902 and formally incorporated into Siam in 1909 under the terms of the Anglo-Siamese Treaty,[58] which defined the spheres of influence of British Malaya and Siam and ultimately delineated the frontier between modern Thailand and Malaysia. The rajah and local nobility of Patani were deposed, direct rule from Bangkok was imposed,[59] and in 1931 the Siamese government arbitrarily separated the sultanate into the three provinces of Yala, Pattani, and Narathiwat, while four districts with significant Muslim populations were assigned to the neighboring province of Songkhla.[60] The southern border provinces have been the scene of calls for autonomy as well as separatist violence, banditry, civil unrest, and guerrilla warfare ever since their annexation.[61] As Duncan McCargo puts it:

> Many Muslims in Thailand's Southern border provinces are very proud of an identity that they consider highly distinctive, as Malays (Melayu; in local dialect, nayu), as Muslims, and as people of Patani, an ancient kingdom and center of Islamic learning and culture. These three identity markers clearly distinguish Patani people from the rest of Thailand's population. At the same time, Patani identity has an ambiguous relationship with the modern nation-state and notions of citizenship. Almost all Patani people are citizens of Thailand, but for many of them this citizenship is a flag of inconvenience, a formal identity that they are obliged to adopt for pragmatic reasons.[62]

The key objections of Malay Muslims against the central Thai state throughout the century since Patani's annexation have been the classic grievances of any ethnoreligious minority forcibly incorporated into the periphery of a larger, racially and religiously distinct, unitary state. They included the displacement of traditional Malay elites and their replacement with appointed ethnic Thai Buddhist officials who spoke Thai and reported directly to Bangkok, and the imposition of Thai language education and Buddhist ethical instruction in primary schools.[63] As McCargo points out, "Thailand is a highly centralized political order, in which all provinces are administered by unelected governors—sometimes characterized as a form of 'internal colonialism' "[64]; whereas a series of community and political leaders in Patani have argued that the area's unique history and culture entitles it to special administrative status, or at the very least a more representative form of government. Going further than mere calls for autonomy within Thailand, other groups—initially representing the interests of the dispossessed traditional establishment but more recently reflecting aspirations for union with Malaysia or for an independent Patani state—have taken an outright separatist line.[65]

The imposition of land taxes, alienation from traditional landholdings, and collection of revenues that went directly to the central government rather than supporting the local area were other classic grievances, as was the complaint that officials sent to administer the southern provinces were corrupt, did not understand the people, and were of lesser quality than officials elsewhere in the country.[66] As ethnic Thai Buddhists settled in the area as part of a central government economic development plan from the 1930s to 1960s, intercommunal tensions and violence periodically arose between the Patani Malays, who were a minority in the country as a whole, and the ethnic Thais who were a minority in the southern provinces. And partly as a result of their own resistance to learning Thai and participating in Thai national educational programs, people in the South have limited access to well-paying employment in the Thai economy and so tend to stay in the South rather than accessing mainstream Thai society.

The ultranationalist Phibun Songkhran dictatorship of the late 1930s imposed the "norms of central Thai culture... on the rest of the country with no deviation tolerated."[67] The government

> banned the use of Malay in government offices, forced government employees to take Thai names, forbade men and women to wear traditional Muslim-Malay dress in public, and circumscribed almost every aspect of daily life. Islamic law, which King Rama V had recognised for family and inheritance matters, was rescinded. Phibun also imposed elements of Buddhism on the Malay population. Buddha statues were placed in all public schools, and Malay-Muslim children were forced to bow before them as a patriotic act.[68]

The Phibun regime, which was allied with the Japanese during World War II, established a narrative of the Thai-nationalist unitary state that has survived to become embedded in mainstream Thai consciousness,[69] and now informs a view among some ethnic Thais that culturally divergent practices are, in and of themselves, tantamount to sedition.[70] As Francesca Lawe-Davies has argued, the

expression of non-Thai identity was not only unpatriotic in the eyes of the authorities but in itself a security threat. The fusion of national security and national identity created one of the central paradoxes of the conflict: the state saw assimilation as the key to reducing a perceived security threat posed by Malay Muslims who refused to adopt Thai culture, but the only real threat to security came from protests against assimilation policies. For Malay Muslims, the situation started to look increasingly like a choice between submitting to Thai rule and forsaking language, culture and religion, or fighting for independence to retain them.[71]

These grievances, combined with a repressively harsh intervention by the Thaksin government in 2004 following an increase in violence after 2001, ultimately gave rise to a cycle of intervention, rejection, and escalation of the insurgency. The National Reconciliation Commission noted this in its 2006 report:

The National Reconciliation Commission is of the view that whoever uses violence to harm or kill the innocents, or to destroy the property of people and the state, are committing criminal acts and must be made accountable for such acts. However, from a certain angle, *the violence that took place in the area was a reaction to the state's excessively harsh tactics and measures*, which resulted from miscalculated strategies and circumstantial assessments. Such miscalculations included the dissolution of the Southern Border Provinces Administrative Center (SBPAC) and the combined 43rd Civilian-Police-Military Command (CPM 43). At the same time, there was a conviction among the local Thai Muslims of Malay descent that they have been perceived as outsiders, marginalized or turned into second-class citizens living in a state bent on the destruction of their language and cultural traditions. Young Muslims felt they were discriminated against in making a living, and lacked participation in the administrative system. To make matters worse, some local state officials were corrupt, inefficient and lacked understanding of the local culture. Therefore, the majority of the populace, Buddhist and Muslim alike, was not prepared to assist the state in defeating the violence, either due to sympathy for the militants or fear that violence might threaten themselves and their families.[72]

The Role of Religion and Transnational Takfiri Terrorism

Some terrorism analysts have seen the southern insurgency as an Islamic jihad that forms part of the broader network of AQ-linked extremism, with Islamic theology and religious aspirations (for shari'a law or an Islamic emirate) as a key motivator.[73] This surface impression is reinforced by the facts that the violence is led by ustadz[74] and other religious teachers, that the mosques and ponoh (Islamic schools) have a central role as recruiting and training bases, and that militants repeatedly state that they are fighting a legitimate defensive jihad against the encroachment of the kafir (infidel) Buddhist Thai government. Clearly, also, the AQ affiliate Jema'ah Islamiyah (JI) has used Thailand as a venue for key meetings, financial transfers, acquisition of forged documents,[75] and money laundering and as a transit hub for operators. And AQ's leading operative for Southeast Asia, Riduan Isamuddin (known as Hambali), was arrested in Thailand in 2003, suggesting to some the possible role of AQ-linked transnational terrorists in the southern uprising.[76]

The reality, again, appears more complex. Hambali was arrested in Ayutthaya, one of the central provinces of Thailand, a majority-Buddhist area to the north of Bangkok and very far from the southern insurgency. His focus appears to have been on terrorist activities of region-wide or global significance (such as the 1993 Bojinka plot to destroy airliners over the Pacific Ocean, or the attack on the 2003 Bangkok APEC Summit, which Hambali was allegedly planning when arrested),[77] not on the Patani separatist struggle. And other JI and AQ activity in Thailand seems to have used the country as a safe haven for logistics and planning, not as an active operational theater.[78] Nonetheless, even though there is no hard evidence that transnational terrorists are directly involved in the insurgency, the continued existence and escalation of the conflict provides an opportunity for infection and manipulation by takfiri terrorist groups.

I have already examined the role of religion in the East Timor insurgency, and there are clear similarities between the situation in Timor and that in southern Thailand. Just as in Timor, for Patani Malays religion is an identity marker, a distinguishing feature that sets them apart from the rest of the country, and a source of historic pride and self-worth. One very knowledgeable Western diplomat who (unlike others) traveled frequently in the South in 2005–2008, told me that ethnic identity, Malay (Jawi) language, and Islam represented a tightly bound cluster of identity markers, with religion playing a key role but not a dominant one.[79] Just as Catholicism in Timor became a symbol of nationalist resistance to Indonesian occupation, Islamic piety (often of a very traditional, syncretic character) has become a marker of resistance to Thai hegemony. And just as in Timor, over time the level of piety and religious observance among Patani Malays has risen in line with opposition to the central government.

Still, Islam in the South seems to play primarily a traditional identity role, as distinct from representing a pan-Islamic consciousness. This is emphasized by the function of magic and superstition among insurgents. As McCargo's fieldwork with current and former insurgents showed, the use of magic (a key component in traditional Malay religious belief but extremely heavily frowned on by takfiri believers such as AQ) was widespread. Most participants in the major insurgent attacks of April 28, 2004, "had been issued with magic spells in Arabic"[80] acquired from a Malaysia-based expert in the dark arts. One participant said that a key leader, Ustadz Soh, "had taught him some Arabic spells to protect himself from bullets, which he said would also make him invisible."[81] Actions such as the use of amulets, blessing of weapons and clothing, drinking of holy water to make fighters invulnerable or invisible, and laying of "holy sand" across roads as a magical barrier against security forces represent traditional Malay syncretic practices rather than Islam—and would probably be entirely unacceptable on theological grounds to most wahhabi or salafi Muslims, though not, of course, to many Malaysians or Indonesians.[82]

Indeed, McCargo's findings echoed my own fieldwork in Indonesia with former insurgents of the Dar'ul Islam (DI) guerrilla movement, some of whose networks and descendants are now associated with JI.[83] Recent ethnographic research has again highlighted that for traditional communities in Java, as for Patani Malays, establishing a viable personal identity requires a complex negotiation between traditional societal structures and the modern Indonesian state, a negotiation in which religious institutions play a critical mediating role.[84] My fieldwork in West Java indicated a strong component of traditional magic in DI. Researchers have long noted the prominence of religious institutions as rhetorical resources and tools for social and political mobilization in insurgent organizations in Java, observing that the cultural climate of peasant revolt in traditional

Muslim societies in Southeast Asia was likely to include fetishism (the use of amulets and talismans), a cult of invulnerability, the worship of saints, and prognosticism (fortune-telling).[85] All these elements were present in varying degrees in Dar'ul Islam. Many local villagers I interviewed in 1995–1996 perceived DI members as having supernatural abilities, and S. M. Kartusuwiryo, the movement's leader, gained great prestige through his reputation for mysticism and miraculous powers. Most DI fighters carried *jimat* (amulets) for protection, and practices such as the drinking of holy water, the use of spells and the belief that specialized clothing could make the wearer invisible or invulnerable were widespread.[86] These tendencies are not, of course, unique to Islam. Members of the Timorese Clandestine Front carried a red and black amulet, similar to a Catholic scapular, confirming their membership in the front and in memory of the victims of the 1991 Santa Cruz massacre. These amulets (known as *ilas* or *kakaluk* in Timor) were treated with religious reverence.[87]

Similarly, as I noted in the Timor case study, when CNRT members have exploited church services as a means of establishing social and political control, religious institutions in southern Thailand have functioned as a social and political mobilization tool for militants. Thus, the role of *ustadz* as recruiters, the use of mosques and *ponoh* as training venues, and the reliance on religious rhetoric may reflect the social leadership role of Islamic institutions—which have tended to fill the vacuum created by the displacement of traditional secular Malay leaders after the annexation of Patani—rather than simply or solely the importance of religious ideology in the struggle.

Nevertheless, although Islam in this case shares a common social function with Catholicism in Timor, there is a clear qualitative difference between the theological content of Catholicism and that of Islam: Islam provides a well-defined, readily accessible and detailed ideology of *jihad* or holy war, which in turn provides justification and motivation for insurgency in a more robust manner than typically seen in Timor, where Catholicism was generally a force for non-violent activism only. This is seen in the actions of Ustadz Soh, a key leader in the major uprising of April 28, 2004. One of McCargo's informants

> explained how Ustadz Soh trained one group of twelve men intensively during the two or three months prior to the attacks. In nightly meetings inside the village mosque he taught them to hate police and soldiers,

partly on the grounds that they mistreated Muslim women, and also because the government was undermining Islam.... He also quoted from the Koran to illustrate that killing was not a sin, as in the case of the American invasion of Iraq: just as Iraqi people were entitled to kill Americans, so Patani people must fight the Siamese.[88]

Some may interpret these comments as indicating the involvement of transnational militant Islam in the insurgency. Clearly, Ustadz Soh was using the same appeal to Islamic jurisprudence (on the grounds of a defensive jihad, which, unlike an offensive jihad, is obligatory for all members of a Muslim society faced with the invasion of an infidel government) that AQ leaders like Usama bin Laden and Ayman al-Zawahiri use. But, as we have seen, there is no evidence for the involvement of transnational takfiri terrorists in the southern insurgency. By appealing to Islamic notions of legitimate defensive jihad (functionally akin in some ways to Christian just war theory, though different in content), Ustadz Soh was not necessarily indicating any form of connection or allegiance to bin Laden; rather, both men were appealing to a discrete body of juridical thought and judgment that was commonly available to both of them.

Thus, Islam in this conflict seems to play a powerful role as an identity marker, rhetorical resource, and tool for social and political mobilization, much as Catholicism did in East Timor. And just as in Timor, traditional belief systems, syncretism, superstition, and magic were accreted onto orthodox religious belief. But unlike Catholicism, the qualitative content of Islam also provided a well-developed "script" for militants that explained their situation, provided sanctioned pathways for violent action to deal with it, and tapped into a broader religion-wide ideology of struggle and conflict. In this sense, Islam played something of the role that Roman Catholic liberation theology[89] has played in some Latin American conflicts, but on a global scale and as a mainstream theological element rather than a heterodox doctrinal variant.

As for the presence of transnational takfiri terrorists in the South, while it would be premature to completely rule out such a presence, the balance of evidence suggests that the conflict remains local at this point. As Peter Chalk concluded in a recent RAND study:

It is certainly reasonable to speculate that at least some outside Islamist entity has attempted to exploit the ongoing unrest in southern Thailand for its own purposes. To be sure, gaining an ideological presence in this type of opportunistic theater is a well-recognized and—established practice of the JI movement and one that was integral to the institution of the mantiqi cell structure that characterized its operational development from the late 1990s onward. That said, there is (as yet) no concrete evidence to suggest that the region has been transformed into a new beachhead for panregional jihadism. Although there is a definite religious element to many of the attacks that are currently being perpetrated in the three Malay provinces, it is not apparent that this has altered the essential localized and nationalistic aspect of the conflict.[90]

What can this conflict tell us, then, about the broader patterns of hybrid conflict, accidental guerrillas, and the exploitation of local grievances by global extremists?

Accidental Guerrillas in Thailand: An Interrupted Cycle

It is clear that while certain elements of the accidental guerrilla syndrome are well evident in Thailand, the full cycle has not developed. As in Timor, there are important insights to be gained by asking why, despite the intensity of the violence and the cycle of central government intervention and popular rejection, we have not seen the infection of this conflict by transnational takfiri terrorist organizations and only a very limited and localized contagion effect from it has occurred to date.

Perhaps because the Thai insurgency began to escalate dramatically only in early 2004, after the United States and other countries were heavily committed to Iraq and Afghanistan, no party has ever seriously suggested deploying a major Western police or military presence on the ground in southern Thailand. Under the Thaksin government, as well as subsequent administrations, Thailand has resolutely regarded the southern insurgency as a domestic, internal matter and has been unwilling to countenance the deployment of Western troops (including advisers, trainers, or combat support troops) in the region in any overt fashion. The government has been equally averse to any such deployment of foreign police trainers or assistance, a point Thai officials repeatedly made to me in meetings in 2005 and 2006. Thus, there is no major overt Western presence on the ground, and this is arguably a key factor in preventing the infection of the conflict by transnational takfiri terrorist groups. The United States and Australia have indeed provided extensive police assistance to Thailand, including assistance in countering money laundering, counterfeiting, people smuggling, narcotics, sea-lane security, WMD proliferation, and illegal crossborder movement, but Australian policy in particular has been to avoid the overt deployment of any Western police into the southern border provinces, precisely in order to prevent a popular backlash against foreign presence.[91] Australian assistance under the Southeast Asia Counterterrorism Program[92] and American assistance under the Department of Justice Office of Overseas Prosecutorial Development and Training[93] has focused on training police, prosecutors, and attorneys to deal with money laundering and terrorist financing. United States military trainers have deployed in other parts of the country under the Joint United States Military Advisory Group Thailand.[94] But, again, there has been no overt deployment of U.S. personnel in the South. Thus, there is no international intervention that might intensify an existing backlash against the central government and create space for transnational *takfiri* involvement.

Simultaneously, there is some evidence that insurgents may have avoided attacking Western targets, spreading large-scale violence more broadly within Thailand, or accepting assistance from transnational terrorists, precisely because of a desire to avoid a large-scale Western intervention. "In the words of Kasturi Mahkota, the self-defined foreign-affairs spokesperson of PULO [Patani United Liberation Organization], 'There is no interest in taking operations to Bangkok or Phuket. We do not need to be on anyone's terrorist list. Once we are on that list, it is all over.'"[95] Thus, in this case, awareness of the likelihood that transnational terrorist presence could provoke a large-scale Western intervention seems to have deterred insurgents from accepting such presence.

Whether intentionally or not, we may have succeeded for now in avoiding a backlash against Western presence that could have created an opening for transnational terrorists—by working through local partners on the ground and taking a long-term, low-profile approach that regards support to Thailand as a routine development and capacity-building partnership engagement process rather than as a warlike, military-led intervention. The conflict in Thailand is tragic, but as yet it remains local rather than a front in the international *takfiri* confrontation with the West. As one of Chalk's respondents in Pattani Province remarked,

> there is a general awareness of issues currently going on in the Middle East and concern about U.S. policies in the region. However, these [actions] are not impacting on our unique way of life. But if any outside

group [in this context, the United States] tried to come in and threaten our religion, we would rise up against them—naturally.[96]

Thus, we have observed an internal intervention-rejection cycle driven by a harsh Thai government crackdown in the South, which has created a certain number of accidental guerrillas fighting alongside the insurgents—due to coercion or intimidation, in the hope of financial gain, or to defend their way of life against external encroachment; these are the classic motivations of the accidental guerrilla, as we have seen. But on a broader level, the lack of direct Western intervention in this case seems to have avoided "closing the loop" and thus starting the cycle of external intervention, societal immune response, infection by global terrorist entities, and contagion into the broader region. This does not mean that such an infection might not already be happening covertly, or might not happen in the future if the insurgency remains unresolved. At the same time, the fact that Western forces—especially ground troops and police—have stayed out of southern Thailand may demonstrate that an indirect approach, working through local partners and adopting the least intrusive approach possible, is preferable to large-scale intervention. Western partners have urged restraint on successive Thai governments, rather than pushing Thailand prematurely into large-scale military intervention or launching unilateral strikes. Unfortunately, the same cannot be said for my next example, Pakistan.

Terrain, Tribes, and Terrorists: Pakistan, 2006–2008

"The two main factors for you will be the terrain and the tribes. You have to know their game and learn to play it, which means you first have to understand their environment." It was May 2006, and the late-afternoon sun was slanting through the windows of my cluttered office on the second floor of the State Department building in Washington, where I was deep in discussion with Professor Akbar Ahmed. We were poring together over air photos, tribal gazetteers, and topographic maps, laid out across my desk and spilling onto the floor: a panorama of the Afghanistan-Pakistan Frontier at one-to-a-million scale in the muted cartographic colors of British India. These were modern Pakistani maps, but not enough has changed on the Frontier to justify redrawing the old colonial mapmakers' work.

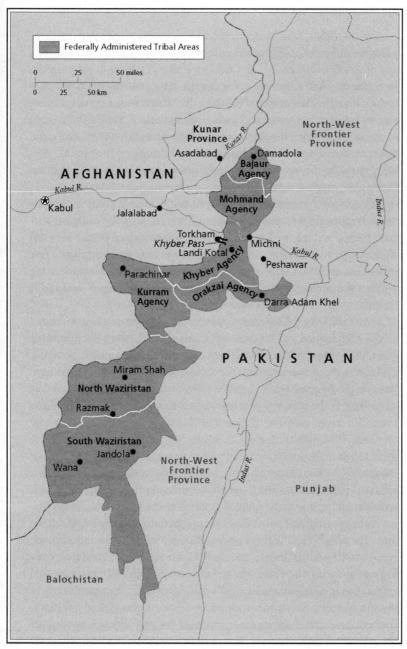

Map 4.3 Pakistan's federally administered tribal areas.

Ahmed, whom I mentioned in chapter 2, as well as being a noted anthropologist, diplomat, and filmmaker, is professor of international relations and chair of Islamic studies at American University. More to my purpose, he had served half a lifetime in the District Management Group, the elite cadre within the civil service of Pakistan that administered the tribal agencies on Pakistan's Frontier until disbanded by General Musharraf in 1999. In the 1980s—during the Soviet-Afghan War, when the United States, the Pakistani intelligence service (Inter-Services Intelligence Directorate; ISI), and groups like those supported by the young Sa'udi militant Usama bin Laden were running separate networks for the *mujahidin* from safe houses in different parts of Peshawar—Akbar Ahmed had been political agent of South Waziristan: then and now, a stronghold of insurgency and tribal warfare. He had walked the Durand Line, the still-contested border between Afghanistan and Pakistan, when Soviet troops were operating just a few miles away and MiGs were overflying the Frontier. I listened intently to his advice. I was leaving for the North-West Frontier in a few days—and a stint on the Frontier concentrates the mind.

In the field, with military and civilian teams and local people in locations across Afghanistan and Pakistan at various times through the next three years, the wisdom of Ahmed's insight came home to me again and again. The fact is that the terrain and the tribes drive 90 percent of what happens on the Frontier, while the third factor, which accounts for the other 10 percent, is the presence of transnational terrorists and our reaction to them. But things seem very different in Washington or London from how they seem in Peshawar, let alone in Bajaur, Khyber, or Waziristan—in that great tangle of dust-colored ridges known as the Safed Koh, or "White Mountains." This is a southern arm of the Hindu Kush, the vast range that separates Afghanistan (which lies on the immense Iranian Plateau, which stretches all the way to the Arabian Gulf) from the valley of the Indus, the northern geographical limit of the Indian subcontinent. The locals call the area "the hills." Their highest peak is Mount Sikaram, just under 16,000 feet—a trifling height beside the nearby Hindu Kush and Himalayas, but a big mountain anywhere else. The terrain is barely believable: razor-backed ridges, precipitous goat tracks, near-vertical foot trails, deep ravines where the sun scorches the midday rock and you seem to struggle in a furnace, rivers that are gravel gullies nine months of the year and roaring torrents the other three, winter passes deep in snow where vehicles bog, mountain winds slash your face, and pack animals sink to the belly. And yet there are lush river valleys with magnificent *chenar* trees, where the fertile green of crops and orchards and the sparkle of flowing water soothes the eyes. And there is a scent to the Frontier: a mixture of hot granite, dry grass, wood-smoke, and pine—an aromatic, dusty, sun-baked scent that never leaves you once you have smelled it.

The people, Karlanri hill-tribes of the Pashtun ethnic group, are as harsh and handsome as their hills. Most men carry rifles from boyhood; women are rarely seen and never heard in public, though some (particularly those of elite status)[97] are privately influential. Fierce pride, unyielding self-reliance, and exacting reciprocity (the Pashto word for "revenge," *badal*, can also mean "exchange") are key assets in the struggle for life. The hill-tribes regard warfare and pillage as forms of extreme sport, and tribal solidarity, the code of Pashtunwali (discussed already in the Afghan context in chapter 2) and *shari'a* law are the only standards that count. The harshness with which men treat women and adults exploit children is often simply astonishing to outsiders. Yet these are also some of the kindest, liveliest, most humorous, hospitable, and resilient people I have ever met.

Villages are tight clusters of dwellings and compounds, often located in valleys. Every house is a fortress, surrounded by its crenellated stone or mud-brick wall, with rifle loopholes instead of windows, and every approach is covered by observation and fire. Many compounds have a 20-foot–tall watchtower or thick-walled central keep, and some have a fortified gatehouse.[98] Some clans have traditional ambush sites, passed from father to son like favorite fishing spots in a Western family. The young Winston Churchill, campaigning here in 1897, wrote that "all along the Afghan border every man's house is his castle. The villages are the fortifications, the fortifications are the villages. Every house is loopholed, and whether it has a tower or not depends only on its owner's wealth."[99]

"ALL THE WORLD WAS GOING GHAZA"

Churchill was describing the operations of the Malakand Field Force around the village of Damadola, in Bajaur Agency, during the Great Frontier War of 1897—a tribal uprising inspired and exploited by religious leaders who co-opted local tribes' opposition to the encroachment of government authority (an alien and infidel presence) into their region. This intrusion was symbolized by the building of roads into Gilgit, Chitral, and Dir, bringing British military garrisons closer to Bajaur, which borders on Afghanistan's Kunar valley, which I discussed

Figure 4.3 Pakistan, May 2006—Fortified village in the federally administered tribal areas.

Photo: David Kilcullen

in the context of another road-building program in chapter 2. Ironically, this increase in government presence was driven by British fear of Russian expansionism across the Pamir ranges, not by a desire to control the independent tribes. Members of tribal society were, in effect, pawns in a classic Great Game conflict driven by a geopolitical contest between imperial Russia and British India on the one hand and on the other, indigenous religious leaders (most notably Hazrat Sadullah Khan, from Buner in Swat, known to the British as the Mad Mullah) striving to cement their positions of influence. A very similar situation applies today.

The Malakand Field Force fought several major battles in the valleys around Damadola, killed hundreds of tribal fighters, and destroyed dozens of houses in the village, many by burning and others through heavy artillery bombardment.[100] Following the military campaign, political officers accompanying the force conducted punitive negotiations with the tribes, according to Churchill's eyewitness account:

Mr. Davis [the political officer] conducted the negotiations with the Màmunds. On the 26th a Jirgah from the tribe came into camp [at Inàyat Qala, just under 3 miles from Damadola]. They deposited 4000 rupees as a token of submission, and brought in fifty firearms. These, however, were of the oldest and most antiquated types, and were obviously not the weapons with which so many soldiers had been killed and wounded. This was pointed out to the tribal representatives. They protested that they had no others.... The political officer was firm, and his terms were explicit. Either they must give up the twenty-two rifles captured from the 35th Sikhs on the 16th, or their villages would be destroyed. No other terms would he accept. To this they replied, that they had not got the rifles. They had all been taken, they said, and I think with truth, by the Afghan tribesmen from the Kunar Valley [who had participated in the battle of September 16, 1897, alongside the Mamunds]. These would not give them up. Besides—this also with truth—they had been taken in "fair war."... They admitted to having sent their young men to attack the [British Forward Operating Bases at] Malakand and Chakdara. "All the world was going *ghaza* [becoming warriors for the faith]," they said. They could not stay behind. They also owned to having gone five miles from their valley to attack the camp at Markhanai. Why had the Sirkar [government] burnt their village? they asked. They had only tried to get even—for the sake of their honour.[101]

All the elements of Churchill's account will immediately be familiar to any-one who has served in Afghanistan or Pakistan in the "War on Terrorism." Honor (*nang*)–driven behavior, tribal solidarity, cultural institutions of revenge, generalized reciprocity and balanced opposition, placement of immense value on weapons, the *jirga* pleading an inability to account for the actions of its young men or to control its tribal allies, crossborder raid-ing, advancement of religious justification for tribal militancy, coalescing of rival tribes in a temporary alliance against external intrusion, and a harsh and alienating government response—all these elements of "Frontier tradition" are strongly in evidence in Pakistan's Federally Administered Tribal Areas (FATA) today.

Indeed, the elders' comments to the British political officer in 1897 echo the words of the Afghan villagers interviewed by Americans in 2006 after the ambush I described in chapter 2, who argued that "it would have shamed them to stand by and wait the battle out." Back in 1897, negotiations eventually failed, and in consequence the British "destroyed all the villages in the centre of the valley, some twelve or fourteen in number, and blew up with dynamite upwards of thirty towers and forts. The whole valley was filled with the smoke."[102]

Punitive raiding, collective punishment, and destruction of houses and villages[103] are still features of life on the Frontier, though the means have changed. More than 110 years since being burned by the British, the same village of Damadola was the scene of an alleged CIA airstrike on January 13, 2006, using armed MQ-1 Predator uninhabited aerial vehicles (UAVs) against suspected AQ militants, which destroyed a house and killed 18 people, provoking widespread violent protests across Pakistan.[104] The strike was launched against a dinner party celebrating the Muslim festival of Eid ul-Adha, the Festival of Sacrifice, one of the two holiest feasts of the Sunni Islamic calendar.[105] Though initially there were claims that Ayman al-Zawahiri was in the house and that one of his close relatives was killed in the attack, Pakistani and U.S. officials later admitted that no senior militants were present and that only local villagers were killed, including women and children.[106]

A few months later, on October 31, 2006, the Pakistani army, again allegedly supported by multiple strikes from armed Predator UAVs, once more attacked and destroyed a madrassa outside Damadola, killing about 85 local people—most alleged to be militants—in a predawn airmobile assault led by attack helicopters. An army spokesperson later claimed the military had received "confirmed intelligence reports that 70 to 80 militants were hiding in a madrasa used as a terrorist-training facility" at Chingai, near Damadola, but admitted that "no high-value target was present at the time of the attack."[107] Some local residents and opposition politicians said that children had been in the school, and contended that American warplanes had participated in the attack.[108]

In May 2008, Damadola was hit yet again by another alleged Predator strike targeting Abu Suleiman al-Jazairi, an Algerian AQ trainer and explosives specialist involved in a range of European terrorist networks. At least 16 people, including Al-Jazairi, died when the house they were staying in, believed to belong to former Afghan Taliban defense minister, Maulvi Obaidullah, was completely destroyed. Members of Obaidullah's family, again including women and children, are thought to have died in the strike.[109]

Perhaps unsurprisingly to anyone who realizes that Western powers have repeatedly been blowing up this particular village since at least the nineteenth century, Damadola is known as a center of militant activity, a Taliban base area, and a stronghold of Tehrik-e-Nafaz-e-Shariat-e-Mohammadi, an organization that has recruited thousands of Pakistani tribesmen and militants to fight with the Taliban in Afghanistan. The entire Mamund area (tehsil) of Bajaur Agency has been a key area of militancy and crossborder infiltration into Afghanistan.[110] Damadola is also allegedly a base area for Gulbuddin Hekmatyar's Hezb-I Islami Gulbuddin (already discussed in the Afghan case study) and the Pakistani Taliban movement (Tehrik-e-Taleban Pakistan) led by Beitullah Mahsud, who is alleged by some in Pakistan to have been responsible for the murder of former Pakistani prime minister Benazir Bhutto on December 27, 2007.[111] One might argue that as an extremist stronghold, the village deserves what it gets. But which came first, the extremism or the punitive attacks by external powers? Clearly, the two are cyclic and mutually reinforcing.

A few months after the January 2006 strike, I spent several hours in conversation with a local politician from the Damadola area, associated with the Jema'ah Islamiyah (JI), a pro-Taliban, antigovernment, Deobandi[112] Islamist political party. At this time, JI had some representation in the National Assembly and held 14 seats in the North-West Frontier Province (NWFP) Assembly (though the party was subsequently trounced by the secular Pashtun-nationalist Awami National Party in the January 2008 elections). This local leader vociferously denied any possible justification for the government attacks on the village, and rejected the implicit paternalism (akin to the "internal colonialism" noted in the southern Thailand example), which he saw as inherent in the traditional government approach to the FATA:

> I live only 2 kilometers from the place [Damadola], and I was there within hours of the attack while they were still pulling bodies out of the rubble, including children. All the bodies were of innocent local people, there were no al Qa'ida. The people don't want to be ruled under the old system by the maliks. Rather they want an elected legislature at the FATA level. FATA is the fifth unit of Pakistan (the others being NWFP, Baluchistan, Sindh, and the Punjab) and the others are all governed by elected democratic representatives: FATA should be, too. The people should have the freedom to elect their own representatives. America's war against the Soviets in Afghanistan exploited and used these people then abandoned them. They don't trust America, or the central government, which has been very harsh in its operations in Waziristan.[113]

These several incidents at the one village of Damadola, extending over more than a century, illustrate some of the enduring characteristics of life on the Frontier. After 9/11, some Western planners and policy-makers approached engagement in Pakistan and Afghanistan with only a scant understanding of the colonial and postcolonial history of the area, let alone of the cultures and societies in this part of the world and the deeply corrosive impact of the Soviet-Afghan war, the Afghan civil war that followed it, and the rise of the Taliban.[114] Well-meaning attempts were made to establish control over the putatively "ungoverned space" of the FATA safe haven through a program of benevolent modernization backed by modern, high-tech military force.

But there are dozens of places, and dozens of tribes, on the Frontier with problematic histories similar to that of Damadola. To think that modern Western technology, superficial "hearts-and-minds" activities, short-term development projects, or large-scale military intervention can reverse this history overnight, win over the population, and integrate them into "modern" Pakistani society without some major political and cultural transformation is simply naïve. Moreover, the idea that extending the reach of government into the area is the solution to all its problems is misguided, since external government (as distinct from self-governance by informal but robust tribal institutions) is both alien and abhorrent to many tribal Pashtuns, and its encroachment into their culture area has been a key trigger for violence and warfare since the nineteenth century, and arguably through all of recorded history.[115] Similarly, to imagine that killing or capturing Usama bin Laden, Ayman al-Zawahiri, or any of the other AQ leaders thought to be hiding in this area will help stabilize the situation is also unrealistic: intrusive actions, especially punitive raiding and air strikes targeting AQ senior leadership, may or may not be justified on other grounds, but their effect on local stability is unarguably and entirely negative. For stabilization and reconstruction measures to have any effect at all, they would have to take place in the context of a comprehensive political solution to complex and intractable problems—something that is unlikely to occur in the foreseeable future.

THE ANCESTRAL HOME OF THE ACCIDENTAL GUERRILLA

As I recounted in chapter 1, I first began to notice the accidental guerrilla syndrome during fieldwork in West Java in 1996, but its full importance only hit me 10 years later, during a field trip to the Khyber Agency, a few

Figure 4.4 Pakistan, June 2006—Complex terrain near the Khyber pass.
Photo: David Kilcullen

miles south of Bajaur. The FATA, indeed, is the ancestral home of the accidental guerrilla and the place where the syndrome is visible in its purest and most classic form.

The majority of people who actually think in concrete terms about the whereabouts of Usama bin Laden tend to describe him as hiding, "holed-up," harried, fugitive, pinned down, in a hideout in the FATA and eking out a hunted existence in a cave. Indeed, the ideologically satisfying notion of bin Laden and the senior AQ leadership as infernal troglodytes, plotting fanatically against the West from an underground lair like demons in a mythical netherworld, seems to have entered the Western popular imagination since 9/11. The reality is very different. Movement in and out of the FATA to and from Afghanistan and other parts of Pakistan, is relatively easy, and life can be comfortable and pleasant. Most of the area is a no-go zone for government forces; the local population, while almost impossible to hide from, are also highly unlikely to turn in any fugitive to the authorities. If bin Laden is actually in the FATA, this is by choice rather than necessity: he is not hiding but veiled, cocooned in a protective network of local allies and trusted relationships.

The FATA's population is about 3.25 million, and adding the people who live across the Durand Line in eastern Afghanistan gives a population of almost 10 million along the FATA border with Afghanistan: the central sector, about 1,200 kilometers long, of the Frontier, which is 1,640 miles (2,640 kilometers) long. The FATA is theoretically governed under a loose form of indirect rule, and law and order are administered under a system called the Frontier Crimes Regulation (FCR), first established in 1848 and revised in 1901. This system works through officials called political agents, who deal with *maliks* (government-endorsed tribal representatives), and applies collective punishments when tribes overstep the bounds, but levies no taxes and imposes little law and order beyond the internal tribal governance system. Indeed, government authority under the FCR does not apply to any area more than 100 yards from a road. This traditional system has largely broken down since the Pakistani military, responding to Western pressure, began to intervene in the FATA in 2004. Several tribes straddle the Frontier, with branches in both Afghanistan and Pakistan. Most of these run smuggling or other criminal activities. South Asia analysts Thomas Johnson and Christopher Mason commented on this in a 2008 article:

> The Durand line, which was negotiated and formalized in 1893, was drawn by a team of British surveyors, led by Sir Mortimer Durand, to create a boundary between colonial British India and Afghanistan. To a great extent, the line followed the contours of convenient geographical features, as well as the existing limits of British authority, rather than tribal borders. It divided the homelands of the Pashtun tribes nearly equally between Afghanistan and Pakistan, effectively cutting the Pashtun nation in half. This largely imaginary boundary has been viewed since its inception with contempt and resentment by Pashtuns on both sides of the line. As a practical matter, the border is unenforced and unenforceable. In some places the position of the line is disputed; in others it is inaccessible to all but trained mountain climbers; in still others it cuts through the middle of villages and even through individual homes. The majority of the Pashtun tribes and clans that control the frontier zones of eastern and southern Afghanistan along the Durand line have never accepted the legitimacy of what they believe to be an arbitrary and capricious boundary.[116]

As Afghanistan expert Barnett Rubin told me in mid-2008, to think of Afghanistan and Pakistan as separate countries divided by a normal international border, or to conceive of Pakistani Taliban in Afghanistan, or Afghans in Pakistan, as foreign fighters is to fundamentally misunderstand the mental geography of the Pashtun nation. Rubin argues that Pashtuns see both the Afghan and Pakistani states as foreign interlopers in their culture area, and regard crossborder tribal cousins as fellow members of the real though yet unachieved nation of Pashtunistan.[117] As I noted in my Timor and Thailand examples, the definition of "foreigner" is elastic and rests in the eye of the beholder.

INFECTION AND CONTAGION

Al Qa'ida presence is a long-standing phenomenon here, dating back almost 30 years. The Soviet invasion of Afghanistan in 1979 eventually drew up to 25,000 Arabs to Afghanistan to fight on the side of the mujahidin. These included Usama bin Laden and the Maktab Khadamat al-Mujahidin al-'Arab (Afghan services bureau), which he supported and eventually led, and which subsequently became the nucleus of AQ.[118] Apart from a few years in Saudi Arabia and Sudan in the 1990s, the AQ leadership has been in the Afghan-Pakistan frontier region for a generation,[119] and the Arab takfiri presence in the FATA has been nearly continuous. During the same period, the Taliban—originating in Afghan refugee camps in or near the FATA and growing through a network of tribal connections, as well as support from ISI under successive Pakistani regimes—has established a strong presence in the same areas.[120]

During that time, both AQ and the Taliban, as well as AQ-allied foreign fighters, including Chechens, Uzbeks, Uighurs, and others, have burrowed deeply into tribal society, through activities such as intermarriage with local tribes, co-opting of local leaders, purchase and operation of businesses and other services, charity activities, sponsorship or partnership with madrassas, and settling of local disputes. In doing so, they have in many areas displaced the traditional tribal governance structure (described as the tribal governance triad in chapter 2) and have undermined and dispossessed both the tribal establishment and the traditional form of governance by political agents and maliks under the FCR. In parts of the FATA where the traditional tribal structure still functions, it does so on the sufferance of local Taliban or AQ leadership.

This is absolutely typical of the infection phase of the accidental guerrilla syndrome: the basic structures of tribal society, damaged and weakened by war and population movement, allowed an opening for an extremist presence. Extremists then co-opted some members of local society, intimidated others, and created a safe haven for their own activities in the area. They created resentment against themselves over time through their intimidatory behavior, but they also effectively bought off local opposition through political alliances (sometimes through marriage), bringing economic benefits to the local area, and appealing to religious identity and their status as guests and allies under Pashtunwali. Thus, by the turn of the twentyfirst century, the *takfiri* presence in the FATA was well established, with strong local allies, embedded in the fabric of local society.

According to local people and government officials I talked to, tribal fighters allied with AQ have a very distinctive appearance and manner. They typically wear their hair long, and they sport Thuraya satellite phones, load-bearing vests designed to carry grenades, and well-maintained modern weapons.[121] They often drive four-wheel-drive SUVs, sometimes of extremely recent Japanese make, are often accompanied by Arab "minders," and behave with swagger and arrogance. An illustrative incident that occurred in Kurram Agency highlights the interaction of these AQ-allied tribal fighters with local people.

In March 2006, a local staff member from the U.S. Embassy's Narcotics Affairs Section (NAS) was working in Kurram Agency with a survey team, developing a road and a microhydroelectricity program to improve government access to the area. One NAS official described the program, and the incident, as follows:

NAS supports roadbuilding in the FATA, a program the Pakistani army values greatly as it improves their mobility and access. They complain loudly any time there is talk of cutting the program, but local contractors are too frightened to actually build the roads in the more threatened areas, and so less than 20 percent of projects are on track. Also, the local tribes reject the road program because it brings government access and army presence to their areas, so NAS supports miniature hydroelectric projects to encourage locals to accept the roads—as a "sweetener," effectively. A couple of months ago, a local NAS staffer and a survey team were in the Kurram Agency working on a road and hydro program when they were bailed up [accosted] by a threatening and heavily armed group of tribesmen. These men were accompanied by several foreigners, possibly Arabs or Chechens, who were very hostile and spoke no Pashtu. The tribesmen warned the project team to leave the area, desist from planning the project, and never come back: "Otherwise we will kill you." The team left, the project is stalled, and NAS teams have not been back to Kurram since.[122]

Another NAS official told me that there were about 40 tribesmen in the group, with four foreigners who shook hands with the team but then said nothing during the incident. They carried Thuraya phones, and both they and several of the tribesmen wore vests complete with grenades. The incident occurred in the part of Kurram Agency right opposite Tora Bora, and the warning included a threat to shoot on sight any work teams seen in the area. The same official commented that the Pakistani army response took approximately 48 hours to mount, consisted of a two-battalion sweep of the area, commanded by a full colonel, and found nothing—a further example of the uselessness of large-scale sweep operations in this type of environment.[123]

Since 9/11, there has been continued growth in Taliban strength and influence in the NWFP, with some areas now completely under Taliban domination. There has also been a distinct contagion effect, with "Talibanization" of many areas in the FATA, as well as in the Frontier Regions—the portions of the NWFP that border on the FATA. Staff at the U.S. Embassy in Islamabad in mid-2006 assessed Bannu, Tank, the boundary area of Dera Ismail Khan District, and other parts of the province as effectively Taliban controlled, remarking that embassy officers "have little or no access to the field, their teams have not been able to move freely in the FATA for at least a year, they have not been able to visit an actual agency or see conditions on the ground at first hand. Their projects are lagging because local staff are too frightened to go into the field, the local tribes have become hostile and have warned them off projects, and the security situation is deteriorating."[124] Major Pakistani cities are now subject to Taliban influence, and there have been high-profile militant strikes in Islamabad (the Red Mosque siege of August 2007, discussed below), Rawalpindi (the assassination of Benazir Bhutto in December 2007), and Karachi (a series of deadly bombings). The Pakistan army has applied a heavily "kinetic," firepower-based approach to suppressing the insurgency in this area, which has alienated the tribes, helping the Taliban recruit. The Taliban have also killed hundreds of maliks and other tribal leaders in the FATA, to intimidate the others and bring local tribes onto their side. Meanwhile, extremist influence has spread into the National Assembly and other legislative bodies.

This increase and spread of Taliban and AQ influence was exacerbated and, in some ways, driven by the Pakistani army's intervention in the FATA—urged on by the United States and other Western governments—and by the societal rejection of the army's presence.

INTERVENTION AND REJECTION

In July 2002, under strong pressure to support the international community in the so-called "War on Terrorism," the Musharraf government deployed the Pakistan Army into the Tirah valley in upper Khyber Agency. The army's primary mission was to deal with AQ and Taliban remnants who had fled into Pakistan following the fall of the Taliban regime and the escape of AQ senior leaders after the battle of Tora Bora (Spin Ghar), which had occurred in December 2001 on the Afghan side of the frontier about 10 kilometers from the FATA. Following negotiations with reluctant tribal leaders, the army also entered North Waziristan, and later South Waziristan, in a similar effort to mop up AQ and Taliban remnants.

This intervention prompted an immediate societal immune response, with local tribes (especially the Zali Khel of the Ahmadzai Wazirs in Waziristan Agency, and later the powerful and well-organized Mahsuds to their south) perceiving the military presence as an attempt to suppress and control them. Attempts to force the tribes to surrender foreign militants to the government backfired badly, as did other heavy-handed tactics, so that by early 2004 the tribes were in open revolt across key parts of the FATA, in the largest tribal uprising since the Great Frontier War more than a century earlier. Heavy fighting first erupted at Azam Warsak, near Wana in South Waziristan, leading to a major pitched battle in March 2004 between the Pakistani army and up to 400 tribal fighters. Fifty-five tribal fighters were killed and 149 captured in the battle, which cost the Pakistan army 93 soldiers killed, wounded, or captured.[125]

Importantly, the Pakistan army's entry into the Tirah Valley in 2002 was the first time that the regular army (as distinct from the Frontier Corps and tribal levies) had entered the FATA on operations since Pakistan's independence in August 1947. As such, not only was it an act with extremely inflammatory potential but it also undermined the tacit social compact on which the FCR and traditional Frontier governance systems had been based. The implicit agreement that underpinned the FCR system was that if the tribes sat down quietly under the political agents, maliks, and Frontier Corps, then they would be left alone to govern themselves, and the central government and the army would stay out of their affairs. Now the army had broken the government's end of the deal, attempting (at the behest of *kafir* foreigners, no less) to force the tribes to break two key tenets of Pashtunwali: *melmastia* (hospitality to a guest) and *nanawatei* (protection of a defeated combatant seeking refuge). Tribal honor and Islamic principle, especially the Qur'anic injunction against siding with any infidel against any fellow Muslim, alike combined to ensure that the tribal leaders would utterly reject these demands. The army, also, had first broken the deal, not the tribes: why then should they remain quiet? By the end of 2004, the tribes were in a full, though undeclared, frontier war against the government. By early 2005, heavy army casualties in the FATA had forced the government to alter its strategy from confrontation to negotiation.

The Government of Pakistan signed the Shakai Peace Agreement, the first of three peace agreements with the tribes, in South Waziristan in April 2004. This peace agreement had been negotiated with former Taliban commander Nek Muhammad Wazir, but it broke down almost at once, and he was killed in mid-June 2004, allegedly by a U.S. Predator UAV strike.[126] As BBC News Peshawar correspondent Rahimullah Yusufzai reported at the time, the peace deal did not result in any lasting reduction in violence, but it altered local power structures, empowering militants like Nek Muhammad, who were seen as negotiating with the government from a position of strength, while marginalizing traditional tribal leaders:

Mohammad had his moment of glory when Lt Gen Safdar Hussain, commander of the forces battling the militants in South Waziristan, publicly embraced him in the presence of several thousand tribesmen to announce a reconciliation. Though Mohammad renounced militancy in return for an amnesty from the military, the deal raised his stature in the eyes of tribal people. The subsequent media limelight made the long-haired, black-bearded militant a familiar face and a household name in Pakistan. But it was not long before disagreement over the terms of the unwritten agreement once more pitted Mohammad against the armed forces. He said he was unable to produce fugitive foreign militants before the authorities for registration. The military retaliated by revoking his amnesty. Orders to kill or capture him were issued as the military launched its biggest operation against al-Qaeda-linked foreign militants and their Pakistani supporters on 11 June. A week later, Nek Mohammad was dead.[127]

The same pattern has been evident in subsequent peace deals, with Nek Muhammad's successor, Beitullah Mehsud, in February 2005, and in the North Waziristan agreement of September 2006. In each of these agreements, the army negotiated from a position of weakness, obtaining at best minimal temporary reductions in violence, at the cost of empowering militant leaders over tribal elders, further disrupting the fabric of society in the FATA. Such deals also increased the freedom of action for militants in the FATA, creating a de facto Taliban safe haven in the area, and resulting in a spike in Taliban infiltration into Afghanistan: seasonally adjusted, infiltration into Afghanistan from the FATA after the North Waziristan Agreement over the winter of 2006–2007 rose by 400–600 percent.[128] These peace agreements were formally abrogated in August 2007 after the Lal Masjid episode, in which militants occupied the Red Mosque in Islamabad and brought violence out of the FATA into the Pakistani capital, leading to violent protests all over the country (a further example of the contagion effect).

The broader approach, described by some as "back to the Raj,"[129] that Pakistani military and political leaders advocated—that is, falling back on "proven" methods from the colonial era to regain control of the FATA— also incorporates two strategic flaws. First, British methods were designed to preserve the FATA as an ungoverned space, in order to create a buffer zone against encroachment from Afghanistan. The British approach was not intended to govern the FATA but merely to keep it quiet by preventing tribal unrest.[130] Falling back on these methods, in the face of an organized insurgency, is unlikely to succeed by itself, since the Pakistan government's fundamental strategic aim is different. In essence, it is hard to see how one could use a system that was designed to *create* an ungoverned space as a means to *control* such a space to government control. Second, as we have seen, British methods used the regular army as an implied threat or tacit sanction. The tribes were pressured to cooperate with local administrators and paramilitary forces, or else the regular military would be deployed and crush them. This bluff has now been called; the army was deployed in large-scale operations from 2004, but has failed to crush the insurgents, destroying the deterrent effect of army operations.[131] The tactic sanction was called upon, the Army invaded the tribal areas—and far from crushing the recalcitrant tribes the Army itself was defeated. Thus, the implied threat on which the old system relied is no longer available as a means to underpin this approach.

WEAKNESSES IN THE ARMY'S
COUNTERINSURGENCY APPROACH

Why did the army do so poorly against the insurgents? Based on field assessments with the Pakistani army in 2006, and on my reading of media and unclassified analytical reporting since then, I believe there are nine key reasons.

First, Army operations have been enemy-focused, aimed at hunting down and killing or capturing key enemy personnel (high value targets; HVTs) and attacking armed insurgents in the field. Army and Frontier Corps operations are focused on insurgent fighters and aimed at eliminating HVTs and insurgent units. Protecting and winning over the population are strictly secondary to the aim of destroying the insurgents. This is contrary to best-practice counterinsurgency,[132] which is to focus on the population—an approach that, counterintuitively, has been shown to produce quicker, more effective results than targeting insurgents directly.

Second, operations have tended to be large-scale, multiunit activities. Contrary to best practice, most army and Frontier Corps operations are at least battalion size, with the majority of operations being conducted at brigade level or higher.[133] There has been little attempt at small-unit operations (i.e., company size and smaller), local patrolling, or presence operations to dominate population centers and the countryside. Instead, more attention has been given to large-scale sweeps.[134]

Third, again contrary to best practice, the majority of Pakistan army and Frontier Corps units are deployed in static garrison, checkpoint, or asset protection tasks.[135] This is exacerbated by a lack of appropriate mobility assets; there is a particular shortage of helicopters[136] and mine-protected vehicles that are proof against improvised explosive devices (IEDs). Typically, units are deployed in forward operating bases (FOBs) of half-battalion to battalion size, or larger brigade garrison positions. They adopt a defensive posture, rarely leaving their positions.[137] This leaves few troops available for operational reserves (although some local quick-reaction forces are maintained), so that Pakistani forces cannot flexibly deploy troops to deal with insurgent activity (as commanders acknowledge).[138]

Fourth, this has contributed to an overextension of military forces. The lack of reserves and the pattern of large-scale static deployment indicates that the Pakistani army is overextended—units lack flexibility, have little maneuver room, and are forced to rely on kinetic strike (using aircraft and artillery) to react to incidents or deny areas to insurgents. Simultaneously the Frontier Corps has been forced to concentrate troops in high-threat areas, leaving other parts of the FATA unsecured. Several incidences of overreliance on kinetic means, driven by lack of available manpower, were highlighted in media reporting in 2006, as well as in my discussions with Pakistani Army and Frontier Corps personnel, local administrators and community leaders in the field.[139] For example, on June 5, 2006, a Frontier Corps convoy was ambushed several miles outside Miran Shah using a rocket attack and possible IED, and the insurgents disappeared after the attack. Two Frontier Corps soldiers were killed in the ambush; the Pakistani army response was to bombard built-up areas in the town of Miranshah with heavy artillery fire, destroying several hotels, markets, and houses and killing several civilians in the process. No ground-based follow-up was mounted: the response was primarily kinetic suppression (or retaliation), leading to alienation of the population.[140] Again, this is contrary to counterinsurgency best practice and is evidence of the tactically precarious position in which the army finds itself.

Fifth, indeed, the overall pattern of operations is highly kinetic. Because the Pakistani army has little maneuver reserve, except its Special Services Group (SSG)—a "black" (covert) special operations force unit trained in direct action, that is, unilateral strike operations, rather than unconventional warfare tasks involving close cooperation with the population[141]—it tends to mount kinetic punitive raids in response to information or in reaction to incidents. The Chingai incident of October 2006, discussed above, is a good example of this. But because there is little small-unit patrolling or local presence, such information is often wrong, resulting in collateral damage and civilian casualties that alienate the population. Significant effort is going into medical civic action, school construction, road-building, and health extension,[142] but the "hearts-and-minds" benefits of these activities are continually undermined by the resentment created by this kinetic focus.

A sixth problem is the discounting, by regular Pakistani army officers, of local assets, including Frontier Corps, levies, and khassadars. This attitude arises partly from the army's kinetic approach, which leads some army officers to judge local forces as lacking capability due to their limited firepower and mobility. Regular officers have also sometimes tended to discount the value of local knowledge, cultural understanding, and local contacts. Indeed, the very local characteristics that make irregular troops effective—their close connectivity to the local community, their understanding of local people's grievances and issues, their knowledge of key local figures and cultural norms—make some regular officers doubt the loyalty of local forces.[143] While this could be ameliorated by training, regular officers have tended to exclude Frontier Corps commanders from planning and maneuver operations, leaving them to static guard duties.

Seventh, helicopters are lacking. As noted, only 19 trooplift helicopters were forward-deployed in the FATA in 2006, leaving only about 12 available at any one time because of maintenance requirements.[144] This represents a company-size airlift capability—sufficient to respond to a small-scale insurgent incident of no more than about a platoon-size enemy (30 fighters or so), but insufficient for extended or large-scale operations. It means that helicopter lift (essential in mountainous terrain with a limited road network, such as the FATA) is limited to SSG raids, because the helicopter base is located in the same place as the SSG FOB. The traditional mountain warfare security techniques of "crowning the heights," picqueting routes, and area surveillance become extremely difficult without helicopters, and are therefore rarely done, though they are recognized as essential tactics in mountain warfare against insurgents.[145]

Eighth, the lack of mine-protected or IED-proof vehicles (especially in Frontier Corps units) makes convoy movement difficult and dangerous, and is another major problem for Pakistani military operations.[146] Vehicles are frequently attacked by IEDs, and the response is usually to spray the surrounding area with "suppressive" (i.e., untargeted) fire.[147] This tendency is exacerbated by the fact that most IED attacks cause casualties, due to the lack of protected vehicles, and so troops are angry and frightened, leading to a harsher attitude toward the local population and their increased alienation because of the army's overreaction to IED attacks.

Ninth, a perhaps counterintuitive problem that has hampered the army's performance is a desire to copy U.S. methods. Army and Frontier Corps leaders I dealt with in the field frequently expressed a desire to copy U.S. methods as used in Afghanistan and Iraq. They characterized these as "sting" operations, but they seemed to be describing preplanned air assault raids, based on intelligence, rather than patrol-based area-dominance and population-security operations.[148] Army leaders argued that such operations would be better because they would "remove forces from contact with the people, decrease resentment and allow a focus on HVTs."[149] This was worrying, for several reasons: U.S. methods, as noted, rely on extremely sophisticated surveillance, intelligence, targeting, and mobility systems—none of which Pakistan has or is likely to acquire; U.S. methods such as these actually proved counterproductive in Iraq and Afghanistan, and (as noted) the United States itself has moved away from them toward a small-team, presence-based approach.[150] Pakistani officers also seemed motivated in part by the prestige involved in technologically advanced operations rather than by their effectiveness in countering the local insurgency. And given Pakistan's strategic focus on India, such capabilities were often more likely to be applied to eastern Frontier operations than to current operations in the FATA.

IMPLICATIONS

It is clear from all of this that the campaign in Pakistan, since well before 9/11 but even more so since then, is a classic example of the accidental guerrilla syndrome. During and after the Soviet-Afghan War, AQ and other extremists moved into an already disrupted social framework in the FATA, infecting an existing problem of poor governance and societal weakness. The contagion effect from their presence (most obviously the 9/11 attacks themselves) brought a Western-prompted intervention by the Pakistan army into the FATA. The use of heavy-handed, overly kinetic tactics by troops who were mainly lowland Punjabis, culturally foreign to the area where they were operating and untrained in counterinsurgency, contributed to a societal immune rejection response. The tribes coalesced and rose up to drive out the intrusion, resulting in the perpetuation of destructive patterns of what Akbar Ahmed called "resistance and control" on the Frontier, and undermining the established, if loose, local governance system. Pumping additional assistance into Pakistan, without a fundamental rethinking of political strategy, is therefore likely to be highly counterproductive in the long run.

Radicalization in Europe

I have examined the accidental guerrilla syndrome in Afghanistan, Iraq, and several other conflicts around the world, but it would be a mistake to see the accidental guerrilla as solely a phenomenon of remote, underdeveloped frontier areas. On the contrary, if we consider the situation among immigrant communities in Europe, it is apparent that a variant of the syndrome operates there also.[151]

THE ROLE OF EUROPE IN
TRANSNATIONAL TERRORISM

How does Europe fit into the broader dynamic of international *takfiri* terrorism? Europe's most obvious historical function in terms of international terrorism was as a transit and mounting base—a staging area where operatives prepared for operations; gained access to Western economies, identity documents, and transportation systems; gathered intelligence; and planned attacks.[152] Because of its geographical features (dense population, developed infrastructure, and open societies), Europe provided "excellent conditions in which to establish and sustain a complex, illicit network, and was an ideal base from which to organise a terrorist campaign directed primarily against Western targets."[153] But since 9/11, efforts by European governments and Muslim communities have made Europe a less permissive operating environment.[154]

Europe also acts as a source of intellectual capital for some *takfiri* groups. Many influential publications, spokesmen, thinkers, and media outlets are based in Europe or run by people with European backgrounds. This is partly because of Europe's historic role as a place of asylum for radicals expelled from Middle Eastern and African countries.[155] It is also partly because European school systems contribute to a better-educated, more articulate class of activist than tends to emerge in some *takfiri* extremists' countries of origin. European-educated individuals, often with qualifications in medicine or engineering, account for a high proportion of the leaders of some extremist movements.[156] Greater access to funds, information, and education may give such people leadership capabilities that allow them to perform a "cadre" function in extremist groups.

Europe also embodies grievances that extremists exploit. Issues like the French headscarf ban, lack of Muslim parliamentary representation across Europe, economic grievances, perceived exclusion from full participation in education and employment, citizenship restrictions, and the participation of European countries in U.S.-led coalitions in Iraq and Afghanistan serve to motivate and recruit militants. Extremists use images from European conflicts such as Bosnia, Kosovo, and Chechnya to inspire followers. Some grievances are exploited through organized agitation/propaganda campaigns.[157]

Europe is also a scene of conflict. Besides current and previous wars in Bosnia, Kosovo, and the Caucasus, terrorists have attacked several European countries, and riots, assassinations, and religious violence have occurred in others. Thus, events have disproved any lingering pre-9/11 impression of Europe as primarily a staging area, or the idea that other regions are at greater risk. Peter Neumann perhaps overstates the case when he argues that "there is broad agreement among scholars and analysts that Europe has evolved into a nerve centre for the global jihad, and that it is here that future attacks against Western interests are most likely to be planned and executed."[158] But the importance of Europe, European immigrant populations, and European societal conditions for the future of *takfiri* terrorism seems fairly clear.

Still, there is a very obvious difference between the Middle East and South Asia—where Western countries are engaged, as we have seen, in a series of active counterinsurgency campaigns—and Europe. Unlike Iraq or Afghanistan, Europe has little large-scale conflict. But extremists and subversive networks exploit local outbreaks of violence. Unlike the Horn of Africa, the Afghan-Pakistan Frontier, or the Sulawesi Sea, Europe has no remote "safe havens" outside state control. But it does have "micro-havens"—urban undergrounds, alienated ethnic groups, and slums where the writ of government does not always run and where police and security services' situational awareness is low. And although Europe, unlike the Middle East, does not suffer from authoritarian regimes that create unrest through human rights abuses, the very strength of European human rights legislation provides loopholes that *takfiri* cells exploit as a "legislative safe haven."[159]

Against this background, five classes of threat currently confront Europe: terrorist cells, subversive networks, extremist political movements, insurgent sympathizer networks, and the crime/terrorism overlap.

Terrorist cells include "home-grown" and externally inspired groups. Contrary to popular belief, most terrorist incidents on European soil since 9/11 have *not* been purely home-grown but have drawn on sponsorship, support, or guidance from AQ.[160] Unlike the 9/11 attacks, which, as discussed earlier, applied an "expeditionary" model (the preparation of a team remotely and its clandestine insertion into the target country to mount its attack), we are now seeing a "guerrilla" model in which local clandestine cells are recruited and trained in the target country.[161] The 7/7 London bombing and the Madrid bombing are examples of this model. Some cells are directly linked to AQ; others receive training from AQ affiliates, or are inspired by AQ propaganda. There is a trend toward smaller, looser networks that are less capable, but also less predictable and harder to detect, than the more sophisticated networks of the pre-9/11 period.[162] While AQ still seeks to strike in the United States, security improvements and an inhospitable international environment have prompted it to seek softer targets—including in Europe.[163]

Subversive networks use methods short of violence to further extremist takfiri objectives. According to the leading RAND researcher William Rosenau, such methods include establishing front groups, penetrating and manipulating political parties; infiltrating the armed forces, the police, and other institutions; and generating civil unrest through demonstrations, strikes, and boycotts.[164] Extremist networks (including Hizb-ut Tahrir, al-Muhajiroun, firqa al-najiyya, some ostensible charity groups, and others) sometimes have terrorist links. But they often cannot be countered through military or law-enforcement methods because existing laws may not cover their activities. Moreover, the present threat of takfirism arises from a political ideology that cloaks itself in religion—cynically exploiting religious tolerance to prevent democracies from acting against it.

Extremist political movements have similar goals to those of takfiri terrorist groups and subversive cells, but—though individual members may participate in terrorism or subversion—employ primarily peaceful, political means. It would be a mistake to see such movements as solely a threat: they can help aggrieved members of society seek redress through nonviolent political action. And to the extent that political extremists accept the rule of law and the primacy of democratic political processes, their activities are quite legitimate. But it would also be naïve to discount the role of such movements as a recruiting base, a radicalization pathway, and a target for subversive and terrorist cells. This makes political movements (like youth organizations in the Cold War) a potential arena in the ideological competition between open societies and takfiri groups such as AQ and its supporters.[165]

Insurgent sympathizer networks are a threat that has emerged since 9/11 as communities in Europe have reacted against Western intervention in Iraq and Afghanistan. These networks are informal groupings, often lacking fixed structures that support the flow of foreign fighters from North Africa or Europe to conflicts in the Middle East, Afghanistan, and the Caucasus.[166] Such networks have an enduring strategic significance beyond their ability to funnel fighters to today's conflicts.[167] They can be "run in reverse" to infiltrate fighters into Europe or elsewhere, from current conflict zones. As established clandestine underground networks, they have an innate capacity to threaten their host societies. And they give "strategic depth" to terrorist groups, who recruit from them to replenish losses and sustain operations.

The crime/terrorism overlap involves links between extremist and criminal networks in Europe and the Mediterranean basin—particularly those involved in narcotics, smuggling, people-trafficking, document fraud, and money-laundering. Low-level alliances of convenience between criminals and terrorists are common, as are informal arrangements whereby terrorists, insurgents, and criminals share networks and support systems.[168] Thus, though most crime bosses are wary of close relations with terrorist networks, extremists can nest within a criminal underworld that sustains them and masks their presence.

ISLAM IN EUROPE

Radicalization in immigrant communities, accompanied by increased piety, self-awareness, and consciousness of membership in a global *ummah*, which some Europeans have termed the Islamic Awakening,[169] has touched off a backlash from nonimmigrant populations. During the period since 9/11, several European societies have polarized, with leaders reemphasizing "European" as distinct from "Muslim" identity—a process evident in Dutch, Belgian, Danish, French, or German society since 2001.[170]

Several commentators have written of the "Islamization" of Europe, or of a coming "Eurabia" as European indigenous populations age and immigrant populations, primarily Muslims from North Africa, the Middle East, and the eastern Mediterranean, become demographically ascendant in Europe.[171] Is this threat exaggerated? Is Islam itself a threat? Is extremism only of concern if it becomes violent? Does radical Islam inherently involve violence and extremism? Are biographical factors more, or less, important than religious belief in determining an individual's potential for violence? Governments have tended to avoid these questions in public discussion of the terrorist threat, but they are critical for policy and therefore need to be addressed.

Islam is the largest minority religion in Europe, and Muslims form a distinct society, with greater poverty, unemployment, and welfare dependence than nonimmigrant communities. Due to their lack of elected representatives, Muslims represent a significant disenfranchised social minority. As Jytte Klausen pointed out in 2006:

There are about 15 million Muslims in Western Europe, but only about 25 have been elected to European parliaments. In ... the UK, it is estimated that about 1 million (out of 1.6 million) Muslims were eligible to vote in the May 2005 election.... In France, there are perhaps 5–6 million—some estimate only 2.6 million—Muslims, few of whom vote. The Netherlands has the highest proportion of Muslims—about 6 percent of Dutch residents, about half of whom can vote. In Germany, 0.5 million of the estimated 3 million Muslims can vote. In Italy, Muslims, like other immigrants, are overwhelmingly illegal, and so only an estimated 50,000 of Italy's 2 million Muslims can vote.[172]

Islam in Europe, with notable exceptions in eastern and southern regions, is an immigrant religion. Emigré and diaspora communities are famous for their complex, ferocious internal politics; European Muslims are no exception, bringing grievances and political divisions from their countries of origin.[173] In addition, as Olivier Roy shows in Globalized Islam, partial integration of immigrant communities into European society has contributed to a crisis of traditional authority within these communities, a breakdown in cohesion and internal governance, that is creating opportunities for extremists who offer explanations for grievances and a ready-made plan to overcome them.[174] This crisis of traditional authority, and the exploitation by external actors (including AQ) of community reactions to outside pressures from the parent society tends to operate like a version of the accidental guerrilla syndrome.

Observers of the situation are often confused by their own category errors, for example, equating liberal politics with nominal theology and nonviolence, or fundamentalist theology with extremist politics and terrorism. These traits may in theory cluster together, but are not the same thing. In fact, Quintan Wiktorowicz has argued, theology is a poor predictor for political extremism and violence. He argues that though Salafist groups share a common religious perspective, political divisions emerge when they apply enduring religious principles to contemporary problems:

Although Salafis share the same approach to religious jurisprudence, they often hold different interpretations about contemporary politics and conditions.... The different contextual readings have produced three major factions in the community: the purists, the politicos, and the jihadis. The purists emphasize a focus on nonviolent methods of propagation, purification, and education. They view politics as a diversion that encourages deviancy. Politicos, in contrast, emphasize application of the Salafi creed to the political arena, which they view as particularly important because it dramatically impacts social justice and the right of God alone to legislate. Jihadis take a more militant position and argue that the current context calls for violence and revolution. All three factions share a common [theological] creed but offer different explanations of the contemporary world and its concomitant problems and thus propose different solutions. The splits are about contextual analysis, not belief.[175]

Thus, in the Salafi case, the full range of functional and political characteristics, from quietist nonviolence (Wiktorowicz's purists) to political activism (politicos) to terrorism and extremism (jihadis), occurs within one theological category. Similarly, I observed fervent, traditionalist Islamic theology combining with both terrorism and pacifism during fieldwork among insurgents in Indonesia, and during fieldwork with Timorese guerrillas I observed nominal Catholic religious identity clustering with nonviolence, but also with terrorism, political subversion, and insurgency.[176] Likewise, in 2004, an International Crisis Group report found that Salafism and terrorism rarely occur together in Indonesia,[177] and another report made the same finding in Saudi Arabia;[178] earlier, François Burgat identified a similar pattern in North Africa.[179] Many of the most violent Iraqi groups are primarily nationalist and only nominally Islamic, as are some of the most extreme Palestinian groups.[180] And the Netherlands security service (AIVD) identified the same wide spectrum in European radical Muslim communities in 2003.[181] Hence, regardless of theological or political categorization, field evidence suggests that Islamic theology as such has little functional relationship with violence. On the basis of this demonstrated analytical weakness of theology as a predictor for violence, Wiktorowicz argues that we "should focus on the competing political analyses and interpretations and not necessarily the specific [theological] content of jihadi beliefs."[182]

If theology is a poor predictor for violence, it follows that radicalization (which includes political or theological components, or both) is relevant to counterterrorism in its political, not its theological dimension. Indeed, a focus on Islamic beliefs (equating "radical" theology with violent extremism) may be an analytical sidetrack. Rather than theology, the evidence suggests, it may make more sense to focus on recognized behavioral and sociological indicators of propensity to violence. As Marc Sageman has shown, biographical, psychological, and sociological factors are more useful predictors for terrorist activity than religion.[183] Membership in a subversive or revolutionary political group may also indicate that an individual is "primed" for violence if an appropriate catalyst emerges—but a trigger event is needed and, again, the driving factor is political, not theological.

Ethnographic studies have shown that lack of group cohesion and solidarity are good predictors for violence. Cohesive social groups with robust authority structures typically provide constructive and socially acceptable means for individuals to achieve aspirations, while providing safe institutional outlets for aggression and redress of grievances.[184] These "energy pathways"[185] reduce tension and are characteristic of stable communities. Anthropologists have identified tribal societies in postcolonial transition,[186] traditional societies undergoing accelerated modernization,[187] and immigrant communities in the process of integration with a host nation[188] as particularly vulnerable to violence and unrest, as traditional authority and grievance-redress pathways are eroded before new ones take root.

This implies that the more cohesive and robust the authority structures are within an immigrant community, the smaller is the risk of terrorism and unrest emerging spontaneously from the group. Thus, measures to strengthen communities—particularly in areas like parental authority, youth organizations, cultural mores, education systems, authority of traditional leaders, outlets for discussion of troubling issues (including contentious political and religious matters), and management of worship centers and community organizations—may help reduce terrorism risk. The specifics of a particular community's belief system may be entirely secondary.

The term spontaneously is critical, however. Though stronger Muslim communities may be less likely to produce home-grown violence, and religious radicalization may be neutral in terms of terrorism risk, such communities may still remain vulnerable to terrorists' manipulation of grievances or exploitation of radicalization processes for their own ends, a process directly analogous to the accidental guerrilla syndromw. In short, it makes more sense to see Europe's Muslim communities as a target of terrorist-sponsored subversion than as a source of threat to broader European or global society.

The touchstone of acceptable political conduct in a modern developed society, according to Fernando Reinares, is acceptance of the rule of law and democratic political processes.[189] Unacceptable behavior would include violence, incitement to violence, and political or organizational strategies that undermine the rule of law and democratic process—by definition, subversion.[190]

SUBVERSION AND COUNTERSUBVERSION

Perhaps because of our tendency to frame the confrontation with *takfiri* terrorism as a "war," subversion to date has received less attention than other terrorism threats.[191] So it is worth discussing both the concept and the evidence for subversion in Europe. I do not use the terms *subversion* and *countersubversion* here with any repressive connotation, but simply as technical terms of art in counterinsurgency and counterintelligence. Bruce Hoffman points out that "it may be more useful to re-conceptualize [the "War on Terrorism"] in terms of a global counterinsurgency"[192] and that "political subversion combined with armed action is a perennial dimension of insurgency."[193] I have argued similarly,[194] suggesting that subversion (as a standard insurgent tactic) deserves consideration as part of the repertoire of AQ and its supporters.

In an important RAND study, William Rosenau quotes a British definition of subversion as "activities short of the use of force that are intended to erode the strength of the state. Under this definition subversion can have violent manifestations, e.g., fomenting riots, and is typically part of a broader armed terrorist or insurgent campaign, but is essentially non-martial."[195] The UK Security Service Act 1989 describes the subversion threat as "actions intended to overthrow or undermine parliamentary democracy by political, industrial or violent means."[196] The U.S. military defines subversion as "action designed to undermine the military, economic, psychological, or political strength or morale of a regime."[197] And Philip Selznick's classic 1952 study of Communist subversion tactics, The Organizational Weapon, defines techniques as subversive when they are "unrestrained by the constitutional order of the arena within which the context takes place."[198] In Fernando Reinares's terms, political agitation that does not acknowledge the rule of law and democratic process is subversive by definition.

An earlier study of underground movements, prepared for the U.S. army as long ago as 1966, describes how subversion campaigns develop in terms that remain familiar today:

> the underground capitalizes upon dissatisfaction and desire for change by creating unrest and disorder and by exploiting tension caused by

social, economic and political differences. Through strikes, demonstrations, and agitation, a wider atmosphere of discontent is generated. Covert underground agents in mass organizations act in concerted effort with agitators who call for demonstrations and through subversive manipulation turn them into riots. Underground activities are directed at discrediting the police and the military and government authorities. Operational terror cells . . . operate through the selective use of threats, intimidation and assassination.[199]

Conversely, the U.S. Department of Defense defines countersubversion as "that aspect of counterintelligence designed to detect, destroy, neutralize, or prevent subversive activities."[200] Updating these Cold War concepts of subversion and countersubversion for today's conditions, we might conceive of subversion as "the conscious, clandestine manipulation of grievances, short of armed conflict, in order to weaken states, communities and organizations." Countersubversion could be defined as "measures designed to protect states, communities and organizations by preventing and defeating subversion."

Field evidence and historical analysis suggest a symbiotic relationship between subversion and countersubversion—akin to the cycle of resistance and control identified in Pakistan, or to the accidental guerrilla syndrome more broadly. The more indiscriminately a subversive movement is repressed, the more likely it is to become violent, the greater its popularity will be with sympathizers, and the more likely is the cycle of violence to be prolonged.[201] Moreover, like other aspects of counterintelligence, a countersubversion or counterpenetration operation must be extremely carefully targeted, conducted, and explained, lest it be more damaging than the subversion or penetration it was intended to counter.[202]

Indeed, subversive groups often seek deliberately to provoke a government overreaction that alienates the population, increases support for their agendas, and creates opportunities for expanded subversive activity. This was a key aspect of the Clandestine Front's urban subversion campaign in East Timor in support of the insurgency of the Forças Armadas da Libertação Nacional de Timor-Leste,[203] and featured in IRA thinking in the 1980s.[204] Provoking, then exploiting, an overreaction also featured in Ché Guevara's work on insurgency[205] and in the "urban focoist" form of guerrilla warfare advocated by Carlos Marighella (discussed in relation to Afghanistan in chapter 2).[206] Classical left-wing terrorism in Europe, as practiced in the 1970s and 1980s by the Rote Armee Fraktion, Italian Red Brigades and other far-left groups, applied a similar approach.[207] Palestinian groups in the al Aqsa *intifada* have also employed this technique very effectively.[208]

This suggests that efforts to counter *takfiri* radicalization and subversion in Europe should focus primarily on strengthening, protecting, and building networks of trust with at-risk communities (i.e., Muslim immigrant communities) and should only apply active law enforcement measures to neutralize subversive actors as a secondary task.[209] It also suggests that the "minimum force, maximum discrimination" approach that has proven effective in counterinsurgency is applicable here.[210] Indiscriminate, heavy-handed, or poorly targeted attempts to counter subversion simply play into an opponent's hands.

INFECTION AND CONTAGION:
SUBVERSION IN EUROPE

The classical concept of subversion assumes a single opponent or, at minimum, a united front of several subversive movements cooperating through front organizations, interlocking directorships, and networks of sympathizers and "fellow travelers."[211] It may also assume that subversion consists of primarily targeting state institutions. Neither of these conditions applies in Europe at present. Subversive networks often operate independently in a "leaderless resistance"[212] manner, with only loose reference to AQ-linked leaders or networks. *Takfiri* extremists exploit grievances opportunistically, rather than pursuing a unified plan. And rather than government institutions, subversive activities are primarily targeting Muslim society and its institutions.

Subversion in Europe has included penetration of Muslim community organizations, mosques, and youth groups by militants who manipulate people's grievances for the purpose of recruitment to insurgent and terrorist activity. Abu Hamza's role in London's Finsbury Park mosque is a prime example of an extremist cell penetrating, subverting, and manipulating a local community institution—the classic infection and contagion stages of the accidental guerrilla syndrome.[213] The French security service (Direction de la Surveillance du Territoire; DST),[214] the Netherlands AIVD,[215] and the Danish ministry of Justice[216] have produced reports on comparable incidents in mainland Europe. The British official account of the 7/7 bombings describes similar activity as part of the recruitment process for the bombers, who were radicalized and recruited in the UK, and received training and possibly target guidance in Pakistan.[217] The attack has since been exploited by AQ for propaganda and recruitment purposes, through a taped statement[218] that leaders in Britain's Muslim community view as an attempt to subvert parental and community authority structures.[219]

Other examples include subversive manipulation of civil unrest. Most agree that the French "riots" (actually a dispersed pattern of antisocial violence, intimidation, and arson rather than concentrated mass disturbances) in November–December 2005 were driven by poverty and youth alienation rather than deliberate incitement—though leaders did emerge, using mobile phone text messages, the internet, and email to manipulate the violence, and France expelled a number of foreign-born agitators after the disturbances.[220] But there is media reporting that about 50 of France's 1,500 mosques have been penetrated and taken over by extremist groups, and that 30 of these 50 are in regions near the area of Paris where the riots began.[221] If true, this would again suggest a similar infection/contagion pattern, while the severity of repressive measures in the wake of the riots may also have led to an intervention/rejection response.

A more complex phenomenon occurred in the Danish cartoon controversy of 2005–2006. The journal *Jyllands-Posten* may have published the cartoon images (some of which poked fun at the Prophet Mohammed) specifically to provoke Danish Muslims—part of the polarization identified earlier[222]—and widespread Muslim anger at the cartoons is not itself evidence of subversive manipulation. But "while some protests seem to have been spontaneous, others have been deliberately manipulated by Islamist elements. A Danish imam, Abu Laban, may have started the whole thing by touring the Middle East to drum up outrage, including distributing far more offensive cartoons of the Prophet (as a pig, as a paedophile), which he said had been "received" by Muslims in Denmark."[223]

Internet-based subversion surrounding the same issue was reported of

the Saved Sect (a successor organization to [the subversive network] al-Mujahiroun), which used its website to incite the murder of those who insult the Prophet and to characterize the issue as a "Christian crusade against Islam." Claiming 67,000 "hits" during the week beginning 30 January 2006, it urged readers to demonstrate in London, glorified past acts of terrorism and threatened future acts.[224]

Agitation and recruitment in prison populations is a long-established subversive technique used by extremists in Europe. Although precise evidence of trends in prison recruitment is difficult to obtain, extremist movements do convert prisoners—including high-profile individuals like the terrorist Carlos "the Jackal," who converted to a politicized form of Islam in his French prison.[225] Radicalized prisoners may go on to further subversive or terrorist activity, as seen in the high proportion of members of extremist organizations with criminal records.[226] The "shoe bomber," Richard Reid, converted to an extremist form of politicized Islam in prison, as did Jamal Ahmidan, who went on to become one of the Madrid train bombers.[227]

A more classical form of subversion is infiltration of security services. There have been at least two successful prosecutions in Europe for such activity: Ghazi Hussin, a British police officer convicted in October 2004 of leaking terrorism intelligence to a foreign power, and Outman ben Amar, a translator in the Dutch AIVD, who was convicted in December 2005 of leaking information to the Hofstad Group, which was responsible for the murder of Theo Van Gogh.[228] Typically in counterintelligence, only a few attempted penetrations succeed, only a small proportion of successful penetration agents are caught, and an even smaller proportion can be successfully prosecuted. So these two convictions may represent a larger pattern. Indeed, the British security service (MI5) reported in 2006 that it had detected several penetration attempts by AQ sympathizers—showing that this type of subversion continues to occur in Europe.[229]

A final example of subversion in Europe is the intimidation of moderates and the assassination of political opponents by members of underground groups. In this context, the activities of the Hofstad Group in the Netherlands, though usually described as terrorism, may better fit a subversion paradigm. Rather than indiscriminate acts of terror targeting the public, they seem to have been carefully planned to intimidate moderates and opponents of takfiri groups.[230] Extremist groups in the Netherlands have also focused particular effort on politicizing youth discussion groups, penetrating community organizations, and intimidating political opponents.[231]

What are the implications of this? Clearly, subversion in Europe does not pose the same level of violent, immediate threat that takfiri terrorism poses in the Middle East and South Asia. It probably does not represent today's main effort for AQ and its affiliated networks. But subversion in

Europe may serve as a source of motivation for extremism and help create a potential future theater for conflict. In the language of a previous generation, terrorist-linked extremists may believe that Europe is at an earlier stage in a protracted revolutionary struggle.

Marxist language may seem out of place in discussing Islamic extremism. But as Olivier Roy has pointed out, there is considerable overlap between the intellectual milieu of today's extremists and an earlier generation of leftists.[232] Consider this passage from the pamphlet *The Method to Re-establish the Khilafah*, by Hizb-ut Tahrir in Britain,[233] which calls for a protracted revolutionary struggle, developing from agitation/propaganda through building a vanguard party, subversion, and eventually armed insurrection against the state:

Hence the actions, in this [second] stage of the political party, would be the following:

(1) Continuing to call people to Islam not through force but intellectual discourse.

(2) Continuing to culturing [sic—cultivate?] those who respond with a strong understanding of this Deen and strong Iman in order to carry the Da'awah and shoulder the responsibilities.

(3) The Intellectual and Political struggle. This manifests itself into [sic] the adopting of the interests of the society and highlighting the corruption of the system and illustrating the Islamic system. Also by exposing the rulers and how they are not looking after the affairs of the people. In the current reality it would be exposing the plans of the Kuffar colonialists.

(4) Seeking the support from those capable of removing the present authorities and establishing, securing and maintaining the Islamic ruling i.e. militarily capable. This support must be from those who embrace Islam i.e. Muslims and unconditional.

This last point would normally be done by the Party seeking to access the military in order to take the authority. This would be after establishing the public opinion for the implementation of Islam through the intellectual and political struggle, so that the Ummah sees this as her political aim and the means of her salvation. After this the military would be capable of establishing the authority of Islam. Hence a coup d'etat would be the manifestation of the political change that the

Islamic political party had inspired in the people and the practical support in order to actually carry Islam through Da'awah and Jihad to the rest of the world.[234]

Here is a Europe-based movement publishing, in London, a classic insurrectionist approach to gaining power—initially through subversive means short of force, but eventually resulting in an armed revolutionary takeover of the state. Any Bolshevik would approve of this position on agitation/propaganda and protracted revolutionary struggle. Indeed, passages in this booklet bear a more than passing resemblance to V. I. Lenin's seminal pamphlet *Chto Delat*.'[235]

ACCIDENTAL GUERRILLAS IN EUROPE?

Clearly, then, there are elements of the environment in Europe that closely parallel the dynamics I have already described as part of the accidental guerrilla syndrome in more remote societies engaged in violent conflict. These include infection of at-risk immigrant communities by extremist cells who seek to embed themselves and manipulate grievances in order to further an extremist agenda, as well as contagion effects due to subversion of community and state institutions, and the spread of violence and radicalization. European governments have typically not engaged in heavy-handed intervention in immigrant communities, but where such intervention has occurred, those communities have tended to close ranks and adopt a siege mentality which creates further opportunity for extremist penetration and manipulation. Thus, while not a full-blown accidental guerrilla syndrome, the evidence from Europe tends to suggest that the same dynamics that occur in remote traditional societies can also occur within more developed societies, or within certain sections of the population in those societies.

If a pseudo–accidental guerrilla syndrome exists within immigrant communities in the West, it is worth asking how governments can deal with the threat of subversion without provoking a full-blown rejection response from those communities and thus exacerbating the problem. Efforts to counter subversion in this context would need to be led by elected political leaders building the support of a majority of the population, and executed by law enforcement, intelligence, and security services within a framework of the rule of law, democracy, and civil rights. This would require a concerted effort of will and commitment from European leaders, who would need to exercise leadership worldwide as well as within Europe, because of the widespread influence of Europe-based extremist organizations (Hizb-ut Tahrir being a prime example). Muslim community leaders would play a critical role in building partnerships, taking key decisions, and leading effective action. Thus, countersubversion would focus on protecting and strengthening Muslim communities, providing means to pursue legitimate objectives, while countering subversive efforts to manipulate radicalization.

Of course, a very similar approach, with certain modifications to account for its larger scale and international character, would probably therefore also be the most effective in dealing with the AQ threat at the global level—a vastly different approach from the "war on terrorism" construct adopted after 9/11.

I will return to this in the next chapter; in the meantime it is important to note that terrorists, subversive networks, and insurgent sympathizers are no longer "foreign bodies" in European society. On the contrary, as in the FATA, they are embedded within the fabric of the community, drawing on deep-seated demographic, economic, and political conditions that enable them. They feed on the rapid and, in some cases, destabilizing societal changes of the past several decades. So it would be wrong to think of countersubversion or counterradicalization primarily as "rooting out" terrorist sympathizers. The aim should be not to arrest or kill adversaries but to co-opt them—not to destroy the enemy but to win him over. Of course, as in the other examples I have examined, while most members of opposition groups can be co-opted or persuaded to reconcile under some circumstances, some extremist operatives are beyond co-option and must be eliminated (through arrest and detention by police and security services). But this must occur in a discriminating and carefully targeted manner, to minimize the rejection response, limit the damage to broader society, and forestall the creation of further grievances that extremists can exploit. Again, all these caveats make equal sense at the global level.

Doing this requires a "trusted networks" approach. This differs from traditional counterterrorism approaches, which focus on the enemy network and seek to eliminate individual nodes, break the links between them, or undermine the "system protocols" on which the network relies.[236] These methods are appropriate for some types of campaign, particularly where the terrorist network is foreign to, or easily distinguishable from, the host society. Drawing on recent efforts to rethink classical counterinsurgency theory for the "War on Terrorism,"[237] we might categorize such efforts as countermotivation, counterideology, countersanctuary, and counterorganization activities.[238]

In countersubversion, by contrast, the aim is to displace the enemy network rather than just disrupt it. This relies on building networks of trust with individuals in the at-risk society, and then extending these networks into the community, gradually displacing the extremists. By using trusted networks of partners—focusing on a "careful nurturing of local contacts and personal relationships"[239] with those who oppose the enemy, and working to support them, extend their influence, and protect them from intimidation—we gradually restructure the social environment so as to deny the enemy a role in it. Such an approach treats the destruction of opposing subversive networks as a secondary, defensive activity, designed to create a breathing space in which the construction of friendly, trusted networks can proceed.

A close (though not perfect) historical analogy is the effort to counter Communist penetration of European trade unions during the Cold War. This effort involved all elements of national power and was directed at creating a legitimate means for disenfranchised and aggrieved workers to seek social justice without resorting to Communist revolutionary warfare or furthering Soviet objectives.[240] The effort involved "destructive" measures to disrupt Communist penetration of trade unions, but these were essentially secondary. Much more important were "constructive" measures—often led by private sector or community movements—to build viable non-Communist social-democratic parties, non-Communist trade unions, youth and community organizations, and social groups. This is a potential model for a countersubversion in Europe, and the broader problem of dealing with radicalization in immigrant communities in the West, as well as for the broader global problem of takfiri terrorism.[241]

Another historical parallel, negative and cautionary, is anarchist terrorism in nineteenth-century Europe. Public hysteria emerged in reaction to massively increased lethality on the part of terrorists, who for the first time used dynamite against civilian bystanders, exploited new forms of communication (the first true "mass media" journalism), and enjoyed unprecedented ease of international movement.[242] As Richard Bach Jensen has argued, an indiscriminate government response that targeted all labor organizations and all political agitation (including peaceful protest) actually did little to quell anarchist violence and may in fact have prolonged and exacerbated the cycle of terrorism and repression from the 1890s well into the twentieth century.[243] This, indeed, would represent a full-blown example of the infection-contagion-intervention-rejection cycle of the accidental guerrilla syndrome. To avoid a repetition of this, a well-targeted, discriminating response that distinguishes between terrorism, subversion, and mere radicalism, neither overstating nor ignoring the threat, is indispensable.

Applying this to Europe, such a campaign would focus on those elements of Europe's Muslim population who can be persuaded that their interests are better served by successful integration into modern European society than by the victory of AQ and its affiliates. Note that this would have very little to do with whether such population groups were moderate, liberal, or conservative in their religious outlook. Rather, it would rest on enlightened self-interest and building common ground. By finding means to do business with these individuals and groups—focusing on strengthening those we can work with rather than eliminating the most extreme elements—we would gradually construct a trusted network of partners. Like non-Communist trade unions in the Cold War, such partners' interests would not always align with ours. They would seek legitimate means to redress the genuine grievances European Muslims feel, and would not be our proxies or puppets in any way. But they would reject extremist approaches and deny the claims of AQ and its affiliates to speak for European Muslims. Such a "trusted networks" approach would not be the only means of countering subversion in Europe, nor would countersubversion be the only form of action needed. But it would contribute significantly to inoculating Western society against the takfiri threat while avoiding a major backlash. Detailed targeting would be required in each case, based on a sophisticated understanding of the cultural, social, and sectarian makeup of the community the campaign was designed to protect. This would be impossible without full and integrated participation by the community and support and expert advice from its leaders. Therefore, close cooperative involvement with local communities—advocated for some time by European policing experts such as Bob Lambert—is a key prerequisite.[244]

Conclusions

This chapter has only touched on a few examples of the accidental guerrilla syndrome outside the "mainstream" of the conflicts in Iraq and

Afghanistan. Clearly, however, the syndrome is widely observable, and not only in the examples given here but also in places like Xinjiang in China, in the wars in Chechnya and Palestine, in Kashmir, in Lebanon, in Somalia, in Algeria, and elsewhere.

The East Timor example is important, in that it demonstrates the existence of the accidental guerrilla syndrome in a non-Muslim society, and demonstrates that an intervention force can successfully avoid a rejection response if it is able to paint itself as the less alien or less foreign of two evils. The southern Thailand example shows how local movements may reject external extremist presence if they believe that such a presence would be likely to bring an external intervention, but also suggests that one of the key reasons AQ and affiliated movements have not been able to hijack the Malay Muslim insurgency is precisely because there is no overt or large-scale Western presence on the ground there. The Afghanistan-Pakistan Frontier example shows the classic instance of an accidental guerrilla syndrome, with heavy-handed government intervention in a highly traditional and xenophobic society producing a major backlash with extremely far-reaching implications for regional security. And the European example demonstrates that many of the same dynamics and tendencies that produce accidental guerrillas in today's active war zones also apply to the threat of subversion and radicalization in Western immigrant populations, and suggests that rather than treating these communities as a fifth column or source of threat, they are more accurately seen as targets of enemy subversion, at-risk populations who require protection through a collaborative "trusted networks" approach that rebuilds community cohesion and authority structures. By analogy, a similar approach is likely to prove much more successful at the global level than the current militarized "war on terrorism" construct.

Having scanned the horizon, looking closely at Afghanistan and Iraq and more quickly at other conflicts from Indonesia to Europe, we are now in a position to consider the broader implications, for policy and strategy, of the accidental guerrilla syndrome.

Chapter 5

"Turning an Elephant into a Mouse": Beyond the War on Terrorism

The elders, tribes, and subtribes are our police. If we lose support of the elders, one hundred police will not bring security.

District governor Rahman, Kunar Province, Afghanistan, quoted by Dr. Carter Malkasian

So far, I have examined two wars, Afghanistan and Iraq, in some detail and several other campaigns in less depth. I have shown how traditional definitions of warfare need to be substantially rethought for modern conditions, and have argued that concepts such as hybrid warfare and unrestricted warfare make a lot more sense than traditional state-on-state, force-on-force concepts of conventional war. And I have shown how most of the adversaries Western powers have been fighting since 9/11 are in fact accidental guerrillas: people who fight us not because they hate the West and seek our overthrow but because *we* have invaded their space to deal with a small extremist element that has manipulated and exploited local grievances to gain power in their societies. They fight us not because they seek our destruction but because they believe we seek theirs, a belief in which they are encouraged by a cynical, manipulative clique of *takfiri* terrorists who, though tiny in number, have been catapulted to great political influence and prestige because of our reaction to 9/11. By treating terrorism as the number one national security concern and al Qa'ida (AQ) as its most important proponent, we have in effect elevated Usama bin Laden and his core leadership group, lending prestige and credibility to his claims of importance by treating him as worthy of our attention, resources, and blood. To paraphrase a Viet Cong leader interviewed by Jeffrey Race in his classic study of revolutionary conflict in a Vietnamese province, *War Comes to Long An*, we have turned a mouse into an elephant.[1] How, then, should we seek to remedy this situation? Is it possible to turn the elephant back into a mouse?

Previous chapters have explored AQ strategy and shown how it relies on provoking Western powers into a series of protracted and exhausting interventions worldwide, in order to bankrupt the financial resources, political will, and moral authority of the established international community. I theorized—and then observed in the field—the existence of an accidental guerrilla syndrome, whereby transnational extremists infect an existing societal problem, and then through a process of contagion spread instability and violence into broader society. This provokes an intervention (from the national government or the international community), which then alienates traditional societies, causing them to close ranks and to lash out in an immune rejection response that exacerbates violence, alienates social groups from the government and from each other, and further strengthens the hand of extremists. Our too-willing and heavy-handed interventions in the so-called War on Terrorism to date have largely played into the hands of this AQ exhaustion strategy, while creating tens of thousands of accidental guerrillas and tying us down in a costly (and potentially unsustainable) series of interventions.

So much for the diagnosis. What of the cure? Before we can deal with specific remedies and policy formulations, we need first to consider how best to break the accidental guerrilla cycle rather than further exacerbating it: and effective counterinsurgency technique is a key aspect of this.

Counterinsurgency: Possible, Not Recommended

BEST-PRACTICE COUNTERINSURGENCY

The Afghanistan and Iraq examples demonstrate that if we must engage in large-scale counterinsurgency campaigns, then there are certain techniques that can work when properly applied in support of a well-considered political strategy. Indeed, drawing together my observations from Afghanistan and Iraq, as well as Timor, Thailand, and Pakistan, it is possible to distill a set of principles for effective counterinsurgency. These are neither original nor unique to current conflicts, or to the United States: historically, all successful counterinsurgencies seem to have included some variation on them. But current counterinsurgency campaigns are occurring in traditional, often tribal societies, and under resource constraints that make classical counterinsurgency methods (particularly the traditionally recommended force ratio of 20 police or military personnel per thousand local people)[2] simply unrealistic. Nevertheless, the field evidence suggests that effectiveness improves exponentially when counterinsurgents apply the following eight "best practices":

1. A *political strategy* that builds government effectiveness and legitimacy while marginalizing insurgents, winning over their sympathizers, and co-opting local allies
2. A *comprehensive approach* that closely integrates civil and military efforts, based on a common diagnosis of the situation and a solid, long-term commitment to the campaign
3. *Continuity* of key personnel and policies, with sufficient authority and resources to do the job
4. *Population-centric security* founded on presence, local community partnerships, self-defending populations, and small-unit operations that keep the enemy off balance
5. *Cueing and synchronization* of development, governance, and security efforts, building them in a simultaneous, coordinated way that supports the political strategy
6. *Close and genuine partnerships* that put the host nation government in the lead and build self-reliant, independently functioning institutions over time
7. Strong emphasis by external intervening forces on building effective and legitimate local security forces, balanced by a willingness to close with the enemy in direct combat while this is being done
8. A region-wide approach that disrupts insurgent safe havens, controls borders and frontier regions, and undermines terrorist infrastructure in neighboring countries

A brief discussion of each of these principles follows.

Political Strategy

It is fundamental to build the political legitimacy and effectiveness—in the eyes of its people and the international community—of a government affected by an insurgency. Political reform and development is the hard core of any counterinsurgency strategy, and provides a framework for all other counterinsurgency programs and initiatives. Achieving it requires a genuine willingness to reform oppressive policies, remedy grievances, and fix problems of governance that create the conditions that extremists exploit. In parallel, an effective political strategy is designed to undermine support for insurgents, win over their sympathizers to the government side, and co-opt local community leaders to ally themselves with the government.

Comprehensive Approach

Best-practice counterinsurgency closely integrates political, security, economic, and information components. It synchronizes civil and military efforts under unified political direction and common command-and-control, funding, and resource mechanisms. This requires a shared diagnosis of the situation—agreed between civilian and military agencies, intervening coalition forces, and host nation governments, and updated through continuous, objective situational assessment.

Continuity, Authority, and Resources

Key personnel (commanders, ambassadors, political staffs, aid mission chiefs, key advisers, and intelligence officers) in a counterinsurgency campaign should be there "for the duration." If this is not possible, they should serve the longest tour feasible. Key personnel must receive adequate authority and sufficient resources to get the job done while taking a long-term view of the problem, so that a consistent set of policies can be developed and applied over time.

Population-centric Security

Effective counterinsurgency provides human security to the population, where they live, 24 hours a day. This, not destroying the enemy, is the central task. It demands the continuous presence of security forces that protect population centers; local alliances and partnerships with community leaders; creation of self-defending populations through community-based security measures such as local neighborhood watch and guard forces; and operation of small-unit ground forces in tandem with local security forces, developing pervasive situational awareness, quick response times, and unpredictable operating patterns that keep the enemy off balance.

Synchronization of Security, Development and Governance

Timeliness and reliability in delivering on development promises is critical in winning popular support. Security operations must be carefully cued to support development and governance activities, and vice versa. In turn, counterinsurgents must synchronize all these activities to support the overall political strategy through a targeted information campaign.

Partnership with the Host Nation Government

Best-practice strategy puts the host government genuinely and effectively in the lead, via integrated "campaign management" planning and consultation mechanisms. These apply the expertise of intervening countries or international organizations to cover local gaps, build the host government's capacity, respect its sovereignty, and leverage its local knowledge and "home-ground advantage."

Effective, Legitimate Local Security Forces

Effective counterinsurgency requires indigenous security forces that are legitimate in local eyes, operate under the rule of law, and can effectively protect local communities against insurgents. Building such forces takes vastly more time and resources than is usually appreciated. While these forces are being built, intervention forces must be willing to close with the enemy in direct combat, so as to minimize insurgents' pressure on local institutions. Direct combat (not remote engagement by air or artillery) is essential, in order to minimize collateral noncombatant casualties, ensure flexible responses to complex ground environments, and allow rapid political and economic follow-up after combat action.

Region-wide approach

Because of the active sanctuary that insurgents typically rely on in neighboring countries, and the support they receive from transnational terrorist organizations and crossborder criminal networks, an integrated region-wide strategy is essential. It must focus on disrupting insurgents' safe havens, controlling borders and frontier regions, and undermining terrorists' infrastructure in neighboring countries, while building a diplomatic consensus that creates a regional and international environment that is inhospitable to terrorists and insurgents.

NECESSARY BUT NOT PREFERRED

Iraq in 2007, and parts of the Afghan campaign in 2006–2008, demonstrated that counterinsurgency can work when done properly. But we must recognize that against the background of an AQ strategy specifically designed to soak up our resources, paralyze our freedom of action and erode our political will through a series of large-scale interventions, counterinsurgency in general is a game we need to avoid wherever possible. If we are forced to intervene, we now (through much hard experience) have a reasonably sound idea of how to do so. But we should avoid such interventions wherever possible, simply because the costs are so high and the benefits so doubtful.

In my view, as noted, the decision to invade Iraq in 2003 was an extremely serious strategic error. However, the task of moment is not to cry over spilt milk but to help clean it up: a task in which the surge, the comprehensive counterinsurgency approach, and our troops on the ground are admirably succeeding as of late 2008. This method thus represents the best approach to ending the Iraq war. When I went to Iraq in 2007 (and on both previous occasions) it was to help end the war—by suppressing the violence and defeating the insurgency: to *end* the war, not abandon it halfway through, leaving the Iraqis to be slaughtered. When the United States and the Coalition invaded Iraq in 2003, we took on a moral and legal responsibility for its people's well-being. Regardless of anyone's position on the decision to invade, those obligations still stand and cannot be wished away merely because they have proven inconvenient.

Still, like almost every other counterinsurgency professional, I warned against the war in 2002–2003, on the grounds that it was likely to be extremely difficult, demand far more resources than our leaders seemed willing to commit, inflame world Muslim opinion, making our counterterrorism tasks harder, and entail a significant opportunity cost in Afghanistan and elsewhere. This was hardly an original or brilliant insight; it was a view shared with the rest of the counterinsurgency community, one would be hard pressed to find any professional counterinsurgent who thought the 2003–2004 Iraq strategy was sensible.

The task for practitioners in the field today is not to second-guess the decisions of 2003 but to get on with the job at hand, which is what both Americans and Iraqis expect of us. In that respect, the new strategy and tactics implemented in 2007, which have relied for their effectiveness on a population-centric strategy and the extra troop numbers of the Surge, *are* succeeding and deserve to be supported. As noted, in 2006 a normal night in Baghdad involved 50 to 100 dead Iraqi civilians, and each month we lost dozens of Americans killed or maimed. In 2008, a bad night involves one or two dead civilians, U.S. losses are dramatically down—to levels not regularly seen since 2003—and security is beginning to be restored.

Therefore, even on the most conservative estimate, in the 18 months of the Surge to date, the new counterinsurgency approach has saved 12,000–16,000 Iraqis and hundreds of American lives. And we are now, finally, in a position to pursue a political strategy that will ultimately see Iraq stable, our forces withdrawn, and the whole sorry adventure of Iraq cleaned up to the maximum extent possible, so that we can get on with finishing the fight in other theaters—most pressingly, Afghanistan.

On the ground, in both Iraq and Afghanistan over several years, I have fought and worked alongside brave and dedicated military and civilian colleagues who are making an enormous difference in an incredibly tough environment. These quiet professionals deserve our unstinting support. Besides having the courage to close with and finish the enemy (an enemy capable of immense depravity and cruelty toward its own people) they have proven capable of great compassion and kindness toward the people they protect. The new tactics and tools they are now applying—protecting the people 24/7, building alliances of trust with local communities, putting political reconciliation and engagement first, connecting the people to the government, co-opting anyone willing to be reconciled, and simultaneously eliminating the irreconcilables with precision and discrimination—these techniques are the best way out of a bad situation that we should never have gotten ourselves into.

My personal position on counterinsurgency in general, and on Iraq and Afghanistan in particular, could therefore be summarized as "Never again, but . . . " That is, we should avoid any future large-scale, unilateral military intervention in the Islamic world, for all the reasons already discussed. But, recognizing that while our conventional war-fighting superiority endures, any sensible enemy will choose to fight us in this manner, we should hold on to the knowledge and corporate memory so painfully acquired, across all the agencies of all the Coalition partners, in Afghanistan and Iraq. And should we find ourselves (by error or necessity) in a similar position once again, then the best practices we have rediscovered in current campaigns represent an effective approach: effective, but not recommended.

THE STRATEGIC ARITHMETIC OF LOCAL
SECURITY FORCES

As mentioned, one of the ways current counterinsurgencies differ markedly from those of the classical era is in force ratio: that is, there are simply insufficient Western troops available to conduct traditional counterinsurgency with anything like the necessary troop numbers. But the events of the Sunni Awakening in Iraq in 2007, and especially the tribal revolt against AQ in Iraq, suggest a strategic arithmetic of local partnerships that could be very significant in future campaigns.

In Iraq in 2007, as noted, even with the extra Surge brigades we found ourselves with simply insufficient forces to secure the entire population and to be everywhere we needed to be. We did not have any additional U.S. troops available for the Iraqi theater beyond those already deployed in the Surge, but even if we had, their impact would have been quite limited—because of the massive support troops need when they come to a theatre from somewhere else. For example, imagine we had possessed an additional 50,000 U.S. troops and inserted them into the Iraqi theater of operations at the beginning of 2007. Of those 50,000 troops, approximately 60 percent (30,000 personnel) would have been tied up in headquarters, forward operating base security, logistics, maintenance, communications, rear area security, guarding lines of communication, or other noncombat tasks. This would have left about 20,000 combat troops available for operations. On a 2:1 or 1:1 rotation model (since even combat troops need to rest, refit, and recuperate between operations) this would have translated into 7,000–10,000 additional troops out on the ground, providing security or improving situational awareness, at any one time. Thus, overall, for an investment of an additional 50,000 U.S. troops, we would have gained a net improvement of 7,000–10,000 personnel in the available force ratio. The effect on the enemy's recruiting base and deployed forces would have been nil.

Consider an alternative approach. Instead of inserting an additional 50,000 U.S. troops into the theater, we attempt to win over 50,000 Iraqis to join local security forces such as neighborhood watch organizations, concerned citizens groups, local security guard forces, auxiliary police, and the like. (In fact, as of mid-2008 approximately 95,000 Iraqis, mostly former Sunni insurgents or former members of local community or tribal militias, were so employed by the Coalition or the Iraqi government.)[3] In this approach, there is no requirement for headquarters personnel, FOB security, rear area, or logistics support, since all these recruits live and work out on the ground. For the same reason, there is no "rotation model" as such, since the full number of personnel are permanently in the field. Assuming a normal rate of sickness, absenteeism, and rest, this means that approximately 40,000 additional security personnel are out on the ground at any one time. Some Coalition forces are clearly needed for mentoring, supervision, and support—approximately a 1-in-10 ratio, worst case, giving an additional Coalition overhead of 5,000 troops. But, most important, the act of recruiting these personnel has an enormous effect on the enemy's recruiting base and available manpower, denying 50,000 fighters to the insurgents, while putting all these fighters' families and local communities into the ledger on the government side. This gives a net benefit, in terms of force ratio, of 85–90,000, or 8 to 12 times the benefit of inserting an equivalent number of Western troops into the theater, even without counting the family networks involved.

Clearly, issues of loyalty, motivation, and reliability come into play in recruiting so many local people into security forces (as discussed in chapter 2). But these can be overcome through supervision, vetting, employment of forces on missions within their capabilities and skillset, and proper mentoring and advisory teams. Political measures to secure the loyalty of these personnel toward the national government are more difficult, but still feasible. And the strategic arithmetic of local partnerships is inescapable: for an equivalent investment of personnel, the benefit gained by developing local partnerships with the community being protected is on the order of 10 times greater than what is achieved by inserting Western troops into the environment. In addition to creating self-protecting communities, isolating extremists, and vastly improving situational awareness by tapping into large-scale community networks, this approach dramatically reduces the number of Coalition troops required to carry out a counterinsurgency mission. The 95,000 Iraqis now working with the Coalition represent an improvement in force ratio of more than 200,000 personnel, an improvement without which the current security gains in Iraq would have been completely impossible.

Again: counterinsurgency is feasible, though definitely not preferred in the current strategic environment. But if we do need to engage in it, especially in traditional tribal societies, then an emphasis on local partnerships and local security forces that protect communities and guard against extremist presence is likely to be an essential component of such a campaign.

At a more strategic level, such local partnerships are also a key component in coping with the threat of transnational *takfiri* terrorism.

Coping with the Threat of *Takfiri* Terrorism

AN EXISTENTIAL THREAT

The day after 9/11, the French liberal daily *Le Monde* published a now-famous editorial entitled "Nous sommes tous Américains." Its author, Jean-Marie Colombani, expressed what many felt at that instant:

> In this tragic moment, when words seem so inadequate to express the shock people feel, the first thing that comes to mind is this: We are all Americans! We are all New Yorkers, just as surely as John F. Kennedy declared himself to be a Berliner in 1962 when he visited Berlin. Indeed, just as in the gravest moments of our own history, how can we not feel profound solidarity with those people, that country, the United States, to whom we are so close and to whom we owe our freedom, and therefore our solidarity?[4]

Just over five years later, in December 2006, I was part of a U.S. diplomatic delegation headed by Ambassador Hank Crumpton, U.S. Coordinator for Counterterrorism, attending counterterrorism talks with the French Ministry of Foreign Affairs at the Quai D'Orsay in Paris. I mentioned the *Le Monde* editorial to a French colleague, asking her whether people in France still felt that way. She replied that sadly, no, "not only are we French no longer Americans, some people are beginning to wonder if the Americans are still Americans."[5] She was referring to the primary existential threat posed by transnational terrorism: not the damage inflicted by terrorist attacks themselves but the damage inflicted by the reaction from societies that terrorists attack.

Some strategists have argued that AQ or similar transnational *takfiri* terrorist groups do not pose any kind of existential threat to the United States, pointing out that even in the extremely unlikely circumstance of terrorists smuggling a Hiroshima-sized nuclear weapon into a major American city, even the worst-case casualty estimates, which would dwarf 9/11 and potentially run to hundreds of thousands of dead or injured, would neither stop the country in its tracks nor inflict an irrecoverable blow on its people, infrastructure, or economy.[6] The threat, they argue, is thus severe but not existential. Some have also pointed out that such high-casualty scenarios are very unlikely, despite our visceral fear of chemical, biological, and nuclear terrorist attack: the March 1995 Sarin gas attack on the Tokyo subway system by Japanese terrorist group Aum Shinrikyo killed only 12 people, while the 2001 anthrax attacks in the United States killed a grand total of five.

Others argue that on the contrary, the consequences of such a "low-probability, high-impact" event would be so significant that the risk of it must be completely eliminated, regardless of the second-order effects on the society that is being "protected." Ron Suskind's 2006 book *The One-Percent Doctrine* laid out, unsympathetically, a particularly hard-line version of this thesis.[7] According to a *Washington Post* review, the book

> takes its title from an episode in late November 2001. Amid fears of a "second wave" attack after 9/11, [CIA Director George] Tenet laid out for Vice President Cheney and national security adviser Condoleezza Rice a stunning trove of new intelligence, much of which Suskind reveals for the first time: Two Pakistani scientists who previously offered to help Libya build a nuclear bomb were known to have met with Osama bin Laden. (Later, Suskind reports, the U.S. government would discover that bin Laden asked pointedly what his next steps should be if he already possessed enriched uranium.) Cheney, by Suskind's account, had been grappling with how to think about "a low-probability, high-impact event." By the time the briefing was over, he had his answer: "If there's a one percent chance that Pakistani scientists are helping al Qaeda build or develop a nuclear weapon, we have to treat it as a certainty in terms of our response."[8]

It seems clear that transnational terrorism does indeed pose an existential threat to the West, but not in the way Suskind describes. Rather, as was so eloquently expressed 180 years before 9/11 by John Quincy Adams in the epigraph to chapter 1, the existential danger is that our response to terrorism could cause us to take such measures that, in important ways, we could cease to be ourselves: the Americans would "not still be Americans," to paraphrase my French counterterrorism colleague. To paraphrase a possibly apocryphal quote from the Vietnam era, we might be "destroying the village in order to save it." The threat is that a zero-risk approach to terrorism, one that seeks to drive the chances of another 9/11 attack down to zero, might cause Western countries to take well-intentioned precautionary or reactive measures that would be so divisive internationally, and so repressive domestically, that we would end up destroying our way of life in order to save it, compromising freedoms and values to guard against a relatively remote risk, undermining the functioning of the very international system the terrorists are trying to attack, and destroying our international credibility and moral authority in the process.

This is, indeed, a typical consequence of terrorism and one that terrorists and insurgents count on in planning their attacks: what hurts the targeted state (as distinct from the victims of the actual attack themselves) is not the direct effect of the terrorist attack itself but the "auto-immune response" of the threatened society and government in reaction to the attack, a response that alienates allies within and outside the targeted society, and inflicts far greater loss, cost, and damage (physical, political, and economic) than the terrorists themselves could ever directly impose.[9] As described in chapter 1, this was exactly the effect of the 9/11 attacks: for every dollar AQ spent to mount the attacks, the terrorists inflicted $544,000 of damage, and the United States has so far spent $1.4 million *per dollar of AQ investment in the attacks* on the response.

THE INADEQUACY OF COUNTERTERRORISM
AS A STRATEGY

All of this suggests that, contrary to the implications of the President's June 2002 National Security Strategy of the United States (NSS 2002),[10] which asserted a right to unilateral preemptive direct action against "terrorists and tyrants" anywhere in the world, anytime, as part of a conflict of "uncertain duration," countering transnational terrorism cannot be the organizing principle for U.S. national security policy. Instead, that organizing principle must be U.S. national interest, broadly defined to include protecting an open, democratic society. To be effective, any counterterrorism strategy must meet certain obvious and basic requirements, such as the need to build effective international partnerships, create a bipartisan consensus for a sustainable long-term approach, and ensure the support and understanding of the American people. More important and, perhaps, somewhat counterintuitive, counterterrorism strategy must protect and affirm positive objectives: it cannot simply be based on the negative objective of defeating terrorism. Most obviously, in the current so-called War on Terrorism, we know what we are fighting *against*, but what are we fighting *for*?

Failure to answer this question effectively can lead us down the zero-risk, 1 percent path Suskind identified, which effectively translates into asserting a right to make war, on suspicion, "on anyone anywhere, forever."[11] Against an enemy whose strategy (as explained in chapter 1) relies on provoking us into an exhausting series of overcommitments, in an environment where trust in our good intentions is essential for the smooth functioning of the world system, and where other countries regard with unease the already overwhelming military superiority of the West, such a maximalist approach is precisely the most harmful strategy we could possibly adopt, a strategic "own goal" of enormous extent.

Terrorism is not the only threat or foreign policy issue we have to deal with. Others include the further proliferation of nuclear weapons or WMD technology, the threat from rogue states (including the threat that they might catastrophically collapse, with significant human and geopolitical implications), the real possibility of wars between nation-states, climate change, resource conflict, managing the rise of major powers and integrating them effectively into the international community, and so on. Therefore, defeating terrorism, though extremely important, is not adequate as the sole organizing principle for our foreign or national security policy.

Moreover, organizing a national security strategy primarily around counterterrorism carries the risk that government agencies will execute the strategy without due attention to the need to minimize cost and limit activities so as to avoid being drawn into the "provoke, exhaust, and bankrupt" strategy adopted by AQ (discussed in detail in chapter 1). This, to some extent, is actually what happened in the aftermath of NSS 2002, with agencies either lumping existing programs under a counterterrorism banner in order to show they were "doing something," or engaging in spending for the sake of spending—we confused the input metric of how much money was being spent on counterterrorism with outcome metrics such as actual reductions in radicalism or *takfiri* terrorism worldwide.

Instead of countering terrorism (hence, instead of framing national security policy around a military construct such as a "War on Terror" or some semantic variation of that term) the appropriate organizing principle for U.S. national security policy is the preservation of U.S. national interests and, to the greatest extent possible, those of the international community more broadly (since a well-functioning, prosperous and just global society is ultimately in our own enlightened self-interest). A nonexhaustive list of those interests might include:

- Prevention of further major terrorist attacks (especially those potentially involving WMDs, as discussed above)
- Protecting America's territory, population, and key infrastructure;
- Preserving America's way of life as a free, open, and liberal-democratic society under the rule of law

- Containing the spillover from turmoil within the Muslim world into the rest of global society
- Promoting the effective integration of Arab and Muslim countries into the modernized world as responsible and prosperous members of the international community
- Maintaining the stability of the international system and the global economy
- Preserving the moral authority and credibility of the West

Since 9/11, the first two of these (preventing further attacks and protecting the homeland) have received almost all our attention; indeed, our actions to further them have arguably undermined the others, especially the last. Instead of asking "How can we spend more (or more efficiently) on counterterrorism programs?" we should be asking "How much effort and money can we afford to spend on the threat of terrorism before our other interests are compromised?" Our answer to this second question must consider not only the risks to an open society of a hyperactive counterterrorism approach but also the risk that such an approach will continue to play into the hands of AQ's strategy of exhaustion and overreach. Against the background of the continuing world economic crisis, such questions, which were already extremely important even before the financial crash, have assumed much more immediate urgency. We can no longer afford to neglect this critical issue.

THE NEED FOR A NATIONAL DISCUSSION
ON TERRORISM RISK

When I raise this thinking with colleagues in the intelligence community, diplomatic service, aid and humanitarian community, and the military, most respond that this is perfectly rational but—for that very reason—would never work, because no politician would be willing to accept the risk of electoral defeat implied in being perceived as "soft on terrorism." Most agree, for example, that the overhead cost to the economy imposed by transportation security measures has had major negative impacts on the airline industry and on the cost of transportation generally, with flow-on effects to the rest of the economy that negatively affect all of us. The political effects are even more significant: tens of millions of passengers enter and leave airline terminals worldwide every day; at some point in the journey, every single one of these people is forced to submit to security measures that remind them, consciously or unconsciously, of the terrorism threat and thus underline the importance of terrorists: "If the government believes terrorists are so important that all this expense, time and inconvenience is worthwhile, then AQ must be important indeed." This simply reinforces the political importance and propaganda significance of the terrorist movement and its activities. This is not to say that protecting aircraft and travelers is not a good, important thing. But it is not the only important thing, and it is not unequivocally good: we could spend so much on security, and disrupt society and the economy so much in the process, that we would shut the economy down and close our open society, thus achieving the terrorists' objectives for them. In practical terms, of course, we recognize this: transportation security measures are carefully calibrated to reduce risk to an acceptable level without disrupting the broader flow of transportation. Total openness and full security are opposite ends of a spectrum, and we apply, in practice, a risk-management approach.

Most security specialists agree that this risk-management approach (rather than a zero-tolerance approach) to the risk of terrorism attack would have made much more sense at the strategic level also, but that once we committed to a direct intervention approach in the immediate aftermath of 9/11, it became politically impossible for any new administration to walk away from it without being punished electorally.

For instance, some have pointed to Senator John F. Kerry's loss in the 2004 U.S. presidential elections, which can at least partly be traced to an appearance of softness on the issue of terrorism and national security. While President Bush was calling the "War on Terrorism" an enduring conflict that America must pursue at all costs in order to destroy AQ, Senator Kerry expressed a very different view (in conversation with the journalist Matt Bai):

> When I asked Kerry what it would take for Americans to feel safe again, he displayed a much less apocalyptic worldview [than the president's]. "We have to get back to the place we were, where terrorists are not the focus of our lives, but they're a nuisance," Kerry said. "As a former law-enforcement person, I know we're never going to end prostitution. We're never going to end illegal gambling. But we're going to reduce it, organized crime, to a level where it isn't on the rise. It isn't threatening people's lives every day, and fundamentally, it's something that you continue to fight, but it's not threatening the fabric of your life."[12]

Three weeks later, and despite the evident good sense of this argument, Senator Kerry lost the general election amid accusations of being soft on terrorism. All of this implies that one precursor to a rational terrorism policy is a national (and perhaps international) discussion on how to handle terrorism risk, one conducted outside the glare of a national election campaign or in the crisis atmosphere following another major attack.

Such a discussion would highlight the costs and benefits of counterterrorism programs, including the political and propaganda costs of overactive security measures. The aim would be to achieve a national, and to the greatest extent possible an international consensus on how to cope with the threat of terrorism. Once such a consensus was achieved, leaders could proceed on the basis of an agreed national set of priorities, and could point to those agreed priorities in the event of a future attack. This may seem entirely too rational and managerial to ever happen, and indeed what I am advancing here could turn out to be some kind of policy planner's nirvana of little relevance to real-world electoral politics. Nonetheless, something like this will be needed if we are to frame a sustainable long-term security policy that both protects against key terrorism risks and avoids the overreaction and exhaustion response the enemy relies on.

TIME FOR ANOTHER ARCADIA CONFERENCE?

As I have shown in previous chapters, our de facto strategic choice to date has been to put the needs of the Iraq campaign ahead of other campaigns, to put the Middle East ahead of other regions and to put counterterrorism ahead of other national security concerns. Even though we frankly acknowledge that any effective counterterrorism response has to be an international effort, we have rarely sought the input or views of allies on these choices: we have often sought to form and maintain coalitions based on convincing partners to join our predetermined courses of action, and only rarely allowed our partners substantive input into deciding what those courses of action should be.[13]

This is not, of course, the first time the United States and the western allies have faced the need to make tough decisions about regional priorities, choosing which of multiple threats to deal with first, and which campaigns to run as a holding action. During the World War II, the "ARCADIA" conference, held in Washington, D.C., in December 1941 and January 1942, faced critical questions on whether to deal first with Nazi Germany or imperial Japan, whether to focus first on the European theater or the

Pacific theater, how to engage and cooperate with Soviet Russia, how to organize for national defense, and how to build an international political coalition robust enough to prosecute the war effectively.[14]

These were extremely difficult choices, not least because in the immediate aftermath of Pearl Harbor, as in the immediate aftermath of 9/11, there was almost overwhelming pressure from the American people to be seen to do something about the threat. After three weeks of often tense discussion, President Roosevelt and Prime Minister Churchill agreed to make defeating Germany the top priority, pool military resources to create the European Theater of Operations under a combined Allied command, fight a holding action in the Pacific, create the Anglo-American Combined Chiefs of Staff, and issue a declaration of common purpose.[15] The 26 allied nations of the coalition joined together on January 1, 1942, to declare the foundation of the United Nations, a declaration that became the political basis for Allied cooperation in World War II, as well as the basis for the post-1945 formation of the UN as a world institution.[16]

Importantly, this was an international conference at the head-of-government level, involving all allies at various stages of the discussions but with the leading Allied powers—Great Britain and the United States—each playing a principal and complementary role. It resulted in a clear decision on which theater to put first, how to allocate resources, and where to apply the military main effort. No less important, it established a political strategy and an alliance mechanism for pursuing it. And because of the way the conference was conducted—with preparatory staff talks, interagency representation, and the heads of government playing a direct and leading role in discussions—the decisions taken at the conference were made to stick.

We have yet to hold an equivalent of the ARCADIA conference for the "War on Terrorism." That is, we have never formally sat down with allies and determined which theater in the current conflict should have priority, how to prioritize competing resource demands and strategic threats, and what our common, agreed-on political goals should be. Individual campaigns in Iraq and Afghanistan have, of course, been the subject of numerous Coalition conferences and formal meetings. But the overall "War on Terrorism" has not, and this has led—among other things—to sharp differences between allies over relative priorities, and indeed the conceptual basis for the war.

For example, when I was serving as chief counterterrorism strategist at the State Department in mid-2006 I met for lengthy discussions with my opposite number in London, an official charged with writing the United Kingdom's counterterrorism strategy, known as CONTEST.[17] After reading the draft, I asked him where in the document the strategy for Iraq and Afghanistan was discussed, and how those campaigns fitted into the broader conceptual framework for UK counterterrorism. To my surprise, he answered that the United Kingdom did not subscribe to any equivalent overarching concept such as the "War on Terrorism," and that Iraq and Afghanistan were regarded as alliance commitments rather than as part of the counterterrorism strategy.[18] Regardless of the intellectual merits of the UK position, the fact that two such close and significant allies as Great Britain and the United States could hold such divergent strategic views, almost five years into the conflict, suggests that a more rigorous form of strategic dialogue and priority-setting between allies could be very valuable, especially as the U.S. administration changes in 2009.

Perhaps we need to hold a gathering equivalent to the ARCADIA conference, in order to decide how to deal with the interrelated threats of *takfiri* terrorism, Iranian-sponsored extremism and terrorism, state fragility and weakness, and the other threats I have discussed. This would allow us to risk-manage the allocation of resources to different theaters, to determine the relative importance of military and civilian resources in each part of the world, to consult allies and affected governments, and to develop—and promulgate—a common political strategy.

UNDERSTANDING THE LIMITS
OF OUR INFLUENCE

In developing such a strategy, we would need to apply one of the principal lessons of the past seven years: understanding the limits of our own influence.

Consider our immediate strategic response to 9/11, which was to adopt a strategy of direct intervention in the heart of the Islamic world, seeking to redress the causes of transnational terrorism at source, remedy popular grievances, democratize the Middle East, gain control over "ungoverned spaces" around the world, and preemptively deal with any potential terrorism or WMD threat before it could fully emerge. This amounted, ultimately, to a policy of remedying the entire world's problems in order to prevent a recurrence of 9/11. To say that we have bitten off more than we can chew would be a gross understatement: as Michael Scheuer pointed out in 2005, the degree of hubris and arrogance involved in the assumption that we could simply restructure the world using American or Western power to suit our own interests was enormous.[19] Andrew J. Bacevich, writing in the *Atlantic* in August 2008, highlights a similar discussion within the U.S. military, with some officers accusing others of making a " 'breathtaking' assumption about 'the efficacy of American military power to shape events.' "[20]

Or, indeed, consider the assumptions we made on entering Afghanistan: that we could succeed in subduing a people who had fought tooth and nail to retain their independence from all invaders in recorded history, and in creating a governed space, in the FATA, in an area that had literally never submitted to any external government. We also assumed that it was only a matter of time before Usama bin Laden and his AQ leadership group were killed or captured, unlike the numerous fugitives who have successfully hidden out in the Hindu Kush over the past several hundred years. We assumed that pervasive surveillance, high-technology weaponry, and unlimited cash could allow us to do, in 2001, what no power in history had ever been able to achieve. Whether or not we could have actually pulled off such a daunting challenge is, of course, something we will never know—since our assumption that the job was all but done led us to begin another adventure in Iraq.

Again, in invading Iraq we set out to remake the Middle East in our own image, remove a dictator, reform and restructure a society he had dominated for decades, transform the underlying conditions in the Islamic world, and so remove a source of threat (albeit a relatively remote one). We are still, as I have shown, digging ourselves and the Iraqis out of that particular hole. And so, if nothing else, our actions to date in the "War on Terrorism" have made obvious, to ourselves and to everyone else (whether they wish us well or ill) the limits on what can be achieved by military force, by American power, and by the combined efforts of the "coalition of the willing." It is critical that, going forward, we continue to bear those limits in mind.

THE "ANTI-POWELL DOCTRINE"

Ironically, therefore, the preferred American intervention model of the pre-9/11 period, the "Powell Doctrine," can be highly counterproductive in this environment. The Powell Doctrine is so called because it was first articulated by Colin Powell, then chairman of the Joint Chiefs of Staff, in an article in *Foreign Affairs* in 1992.[21] The doctrine, also sometimes called the

Weinberger Doctrine, asserts that before the United States decides to intervene in a foreign conflict, a list of questions has to be asked, including:

1. Is a vital national security interest threatened?
2. Do we have a clear attainable objective?
3. Have the risks and costs been fully and frankly analyzed?
4. Have all other nonviolent policy means been fully exhausted?
5. Is there a plausible exit strategy to avoid endless entanglement?
6. Have the consequences of our action been fully considered?
7. Is the action supported by the American people?
8. Do we have genuine broad international support?

This doctrine is, of course, eminently sensible and rational as far as it goes. Indeed, as the events of 2002–2003 showed, it is perhaps too sensible and rational to survive contact with Washington bureaucratic politics and decision-making processes at times of crisis.

More damagingly, though, it has been used (by others, not so much by General Powell himself) to justify two corollary assertions that are deeply damaging when confronting the accidental guerrilla syndrome. The fifth question ("Is there a plausible exit strategy?") is often interpreted to mean that the United States should not become involved in peacekeeping or nation-building activities. This plays to a desire for neatness and clarity, and a preference for the "clean" application of precision military force rather than the "messy" engagement of civilian agencies in stabilization, reconstruction, or humanitarian interventions (i.e., it bespeaks a preference for the very forms of intervention that are least likely to succeed against takfiri groups in safe havens, and against the forms of intervention that are most likely to be effective in dealing with the threat in such a way as to avoid a rejection response).

Second, Powell and others have expanded on the doctrine as originally formulated, asserting that when a nation is engaging in war, every resource and tool should be used to achieve a "decisive" blow against the enemy, minimizing American casualties and ending the conflict quickly by forcing the weaker force to capitulate.[22] This implies a maximalist approach such that U.S. intervention occurs overtly on a large scale with rapid, overwhelming military force, followed by a rapid exit. This is epitomized by the notion of "shock and awe" expressed at the time of the invasion of Iraq in 2003, or in John Hillen's 1997 assertion that "superpowers don't do windows."[23] Again, this "repetitive raiding" approach, the intrusion of foreign-based forces in a highly forceful, large-scale, high-profile manner, attempting to "decisively" (that is, quickly and lethally) resolve a complex sociopolitical problem through the application of precision weaponry before heading for the "exit strategy," is precisely the most counterproductive approach possible under these circumstances.

Rather, then, the analysis of the environment that I have been developing through the past several case studies suggests what some might, perhaps unfairly, call the "Anti-Powell Doctrine." It could be summarized as follows:

> For reasons of cost, to sidestep AQ's "exhaust-and-bankrupt" strategy, to minimize any backlash from local populations against foreign presence, and to protect the sovereignty of the affected government:
>
> 1. Planners should select the lightest, most indirect and least intrusive form of intervention that will achieve the necessary effect.
> 2. Policy-makers should work by, with, and through partnerships with local government administrators, civil society leaders, and local security forces wherever possible.
> 3. Wherever possible, civilian agencies are preferable to military intervention forces, local nationals to international forces, and long-term, low-profile engagement to short-term, high-profile intervention.

If this approach is not feasible due to the scale of the problem, then policy-makers should carefully weigh the risks of nonintervention against the costs and benefits of intervention.

Clearly, the implications of such an approach would be far-reaching, and are worth discussing in detail.

Deductions and Implications

On the basis of this analysis of the security environment, AQ strategy and tactics, the accidental guerrilla syndrome, and approaches to coping with terrorism risk, it is now possible to tease out some of the implications of this security environment, which has turned out so differently from our expectations at the turn of the century. In particular, we might draw the following top 10 deductions from this analysis of the environment:

This will be a protracted conflict. Because the drivers of conflict in the current security environment (backlash against globalization, a globalized insurgency, a "civil war" within Islam, and a fundamental mismatch between our capabilities and the requirements of the environment) lie predominantly outside Western governments' control, our ability to terminate this conflict on our own terms or within our preferred timeline is extremely limited. The closest historical analogies we have for the current pattern of conflict are the European religious wars of the sixteenth and seventeenth centuries, the Cold War against communism from 1919 to 1991, and the wars of decolonization from 1945 until 1980. These analogies are not perfect, but there is no reason to suppose that the current cycle of conflicts will take a substantially shorter period of time to play out than did previous cycles. This would suggest a likely duration of this conflict of between 50 and 100 years, though within that time frame we might expect several phases of hot and cold conflict, relative peace, or acute instability. This is therefore a multigenerational conflict, with potentially dramatic consequences for the future of the entire human race.

We need to take a measured approach to national mobilization. Given the extremely long-term nature of this conflict, there is a need for a degree of national mobilization to support its conduct. In particular, the American people need to be educated and convinced of the nature and seriousness of the threat, and they need to be convinced of the efficacy of the strategy applied to deal with it. But at the same time, because AQ strategy is fundamentally designed to bleed the United States to exhaustion, there is a need to impose tight spending limits and cost ceilings on the degree of effort applied to deal with the threat. This is a marathon, but since 2001 we have approached it with spending policies designed for a sprint. As we have also seen, there is a need for a careful risk calculus that determines how much effort and money can legitimately be spent to deal with the threat, before the very level of expenditure and activity itself becomes self-defeating by playing into the enemy's strategy. This will be an extremely tough political sell, requiring high-level national political leadership and a high degree of consensus across party lines and between branches of government, implying the need for a national discussion on the issue, one that takes place outside the framework of an election campaign.

We need to disaggregate and distinguish between enemies. Western countries face an extremely diverse threat picture, with multiple adversaries who oppose each other's interests as well as those of the West. Lumping

together all terrorist or extremist groups and all insurgent or militia organizations under the undifferentiated concept of a War on Terrorism makes
an already difficult challenge substantially harder than it needs to be, while
shoe-horning a fundamentally nonmilitary phenomenon into a conceptual framework, that of conventional warfare between states, to which it
is spectacularly ill-suited. Instead, there is a need to disaggregate adversaries, separate them from each other, turn them where possible against
each other, and deal with those who need to be dealt with in sequence
rather than simultaneously. This requires a more calculating response to
risk assessment and a willingness to talk to, or deal with, players whose
ideology we may reject or who may be past (or indeed future) enemies.

We need to use military force extremely sparingly. Because of the "antibody
response" generated by deploying U.S. combat forces into direct operations against an irregular enemy within Muslim countries (especially those
whose governments are undermined by appearing too closely associated
with the United States), and because of the need to radically constrain
costs in order to counteract AQ's exhaustion strategy, the use of U.S. military forces (ground, air, or maritime) in a direct combat role in this protracted conflict must be considered a last resort. None of this means that
combat forces will not be committed in large numbers from time to time:
they undoubtedly will. But since the AQ strategy is precisely to provoke
such large-scale commitments and then use them to exhaust the United
States while inciting resentment in the Muslim world, such commitments
must be applied extremely sparingly.

The role of government agencies needs to be limited. Governments do not control processes of globalization, the rise of violent nonstate actors, or the
increasingly self-synchronized international economy and information
domain to anywhere near the extent that they did even a decade ago. For
this reason, government agencies have relatively limited leverage in certain
key parts of the threat environment, especially in the now heavily deregu-
lated and diversified information and media domain, and in some aspects
of economic and reconstruction activity. Private sector entities, working in
partnership with governments and local communities, have a substantial
role in these aspects of the struggle against extremism, and can often generate greater agility and better leverage than government agencies.

We need to take the indirect approach. Wherever possible, our interests will
be best served by working by, with, or through a local partner, adopting
an indirect approach that ruthlessly minimizes American presence. Where

such presence is necessary, a low-profile civilian presence will always be preferable to a military presence, and where a military presence is essential it should be as stealthy and unobtrusive as possible, and tied to strictly limited and defined objectives informed by a realistic understanding of the limits of what can be achieved by military force. This will assist in minimizing the resentment provoked by direct military intervention, while sidestepping the enemy's provocation and exhaustion strategy.

Nonmilitary means need to receive greater emphasis in national security. Because of the overwhelming military superiority of the United States, which drives all rational adversaries to adopt asymmetric and irregular approaches, it follows that U.S. military superiority is a given in most strategic scenarios, especially those involving direct intervention. By contrast, the scarce assets within the U.S. government system are diplomats, linguists, appropriately qualified intelligence personnel, foreign assistance teams, information officers, technical and development specialists, humanitarian assistance teams, advisers, and civilian personnel trained in stabilization and reconstruction operations. This, in turn, means that the success of a given intervention is likely to depend on the speed and effectiveness with which nonmilitary elements of national security capability can be brought to bear, and on how effectively they can be coordinated with extant military capabilities.

We need to emphasize the primacy of virtue, moral authority, and credibility. Through accusations that America supports, or itself inflicts, large-scale human rights abuses on the world's Muslim population, AQ and other opponents directly challenge the legitimacy of the United States, arguing that America exploits the rest of the world for its own purposes but applies hypocritical double standards to other countries. Because AQ acts primarily as a propaganda and incitement hub, this narrative is strengthened every time U.S. actions in the "War on Terror" can be plausibly portrayed as evil or hypocritical. Developing a "counternarrative" that contradicts AQ propaganda is necessary but not sufficient: along with other Western countries the United States must also, as a matter of priority, articulate and enact its own narrative that explains and demonstrates to what end American actions are being taken, and why the world's population would be better off participating in the international community under U.S. leadership than accepting AQ domination and the takfiri extremist agenda.

We need to rebalance capabilities. There is a demonstrated need to achieve better balance between the military and nonmilitary elements of

U.S. national power, and to balance expensive but rarely needed capabilities for conventional war-fighting with cheap but frequently needed capabilities for stabilization, reconstruction, and unconventional warfare operations. Since this asymmetry is the only major driver of the current threat environment that lies within our control, addressing this imbalance would redress some of the impetus toward terrorist and insurgent activity on the part of U.S. adversaries, while better fitting Western governments as a whole for the protracted conflict ahead.

We need to rein in unsustainable spending and consolidate. The level of activity and expenditure we have applied since 9/11 is unsustainable on economic grounds alone, a conclusion that recent developments in the United States and the global economy have only underlined. It also involves enormous opportunity cost, as funds that could have been allocated to establishing sustainable long-term approaches to the problem have been spent instead on large-scale or wasteful high-profile projects. Because the enemy's strategy is to exhaust and bankrupt the West, sharply limiting expenditure and adopting a focus on small, local, low-cost programs is likely to be much more effective. In addition, because of the over-stretch and exhaustion suffered by the U.S. military, especially general-purpose ground forces, as a result of the conflict in Iraq, there is arguably a medium-term requirement to consolidate, rein back activity, and refurbish military capabilities, while building new and complementary civilian capacity, before again engaging in large-scale intervention operations.

IMPLICATIONS FOR MILITARY FORCES

In thinking about the implications of the new environment for military forces, another historical analogy springs to mind: that of the "chateau generals" of World War I. Locked in the "riddle of the trenches,"[24] senior military leaders in 1914 understood that the world had changed and that the fighting being experienced on the Western Front was a new kind of war, but their parent societies and their militaries were ill equipped to deal with the changes. Existing tactics, organizations, communications tools, equipment, training, personnel systems, education, concepts—all were inadequate to the task of dealing with the new environment. It took years, many failures, and millions of deaths to achieve the breakthrough new concepts that underpinned the blitzkrieg-style, air-land maneuver advocated in J. F. C. Fuller's *Plan 1919*,[25] or the infiltration tactics advocated by German practitioners like Oskar Hutier.[26] Independent air forces, radio-based artillery spotting, mobile logistics, and other technological and organizational breakthroughs were also needed. Because the generals were schooled in the then "conventional" (i.e., nineteenth-century colonial) style of warfare, they had to unlearn what they knew. Civilians (for example, political leaders like Lloyd George and Clemenceau),[27] nonprofessionals (T. E. Lawrence, Sir John Monash, Billy Mitchell, Giulio Douhet), and members of "new" military branches such as aviation, the submarine service, the tank corps, or the German *sturmbataillonen*, found it easier to grasp and initiate changes than did their military superiors.

Like the chateau generals, today's military leaders (especially those who have been engaged in the field since 9/11) know that the environment has changed and our existing concepts are inadequate. But we have yet to fully "crack the code" on the breakthrough concepts and organizational and technological innovations that will allow us to fully adapt to the new hybrid form of warfare. Our "new" branches of the Cold War era (special operations forces, the covert action arms of intelligence services, specialized aviation organizations, the system-of-systems of network-centric warfare, and so on) have ceased to be initiators and some are in danger of becoming cosseted elites, like the cavalry generals of World War I—one of whom, a Russian grand duke, admitted that he mainly hated war because it "spoiled the armies."[28]

Obviously, today's issues are different. They encompass, as we have seen, political Islam, the conceptualization of intervention and stabilization, the interplay of intelligence, covert action, and overt maneuver with reconstruction, development, humanitarian assistance and political strategy, the backlash against globalization, individualized lethality, and disaggregated discontinuous battlespace. Nevertheless, the innovation challenge is very similar.

MISSION SETS

In the environment I have described, there are likely to be two key mission sets (or clusters of similar types of tasks) that both military and civilian agencies will need to be able to perform if they are to remain strategically relevant. One of these is defensive, the other offensive (or, perhaps, "decisive"). They are *strategic disruption* and *military assistance*.

Strategic disruption aims to keep today's enemy groups off balance, prevent the emergence of new terrorist threats, disrupt *takfiri* safe havens, and defeat enemy propaganda. This is defensive, not offensive. Superficially it looks offensive, because it involves direct action against terrorist targets, strikes against safe havens and the kill/capture of extremist and insurgent leaders. But it is actually strategically defensive, because it deals only with today's threat and does not contribute to preventing the next crop of enemies from emerging. To paraphrase the Arab proverb, an approach to the *takfiri* threat that solely involved strategic disruption would be akin to sweeping the sand out of our house without first closing the door. Over the long term, therefore, strategic disruption is necessary but not decisive, and will probably only amount to 10–20 percent of the military's role in countering terrorism, and perhaps will remain primarily a special operations forces task. It is of course critical, and the military has to be proficient at it, but it is not ultimately decisive.

The ultimately decisive mission set is what we might call "military assistance." This set of tasks aims to restructure the threat environment over the long term so that we hardwire the enemy out of it, deny them a role, reduce the recruiting base, and attack the conditions that generate the threat. This is the truly decisive activity, even though, as noted, we must clearly bear in mind the limits on our ability to shape events, and recognize that we will probably never be able to do more than give them a gentle nudge in our preferred direction. Clearly, military assistance lacks the glamor of "Direct action," much as building a road is less glamorous than raiding a terrorist hideout, but it is nonetheless strategically fundamental. Adjusting military assistance to modern conditions requires some conceptual rethinking: we need to redefine the meaning of military assistance; as currently defined by NATO, for example, it means "assistance *to* foreign militaries." But in future we may need to apply "assistance *by* militaries" or even by the whole of our government, to the whole of an at-risk society. If all our assistance is directed to improving the military or police performance of countries that oppress their populations or fail to govern their territories effectively and humanely, then it does not address the corruption, bad policies, poor governance, and lack of development that generate the threat in the first place. In this case, then, not only is our "assistance" not helpful but, in strategic terms, we may actually be making the problem worse. This means that cooperation with aid agencies, educators, charities, departments of foreign affairs and state, intelligence services, economic development agencies—truly full-spectrum assistance—is required.[29] This is the truly decisive activity at which we need to become highly proficient if we are to break the accidental guerrilla cycle.

Conclusion

> To hear the marines describe it, Ramadi [in 2006] is the Chernobyl of the insurgency, a place where the basic proteins of guerilla warfare have been irradiated by technology and radical Islam, producing seemingly endless cells of wide-eyed gunslingers, bomb gurus, and aspiring martyrs.
>
> David J. Morris ("The Big Suck," *Virginia Quarterly Review,* 2007)

As I discussed with reference to the ARCADIA conference, despite our rather rosy hindsight view of World War II, there was considerable dissent at the time about the war's aims, conduct, and strategy. But virtually no one disagreed that it was indeed a war or that the Axis powers were the enemy.[1]

Contrast this with the so-called War on Terrorism. Some rightly dispute the notion that the conflict can be defined as a war; others question the reality of the threat. Far-left critics blame American industrial interests, while a lunatic fringe sees 9/11 as a massive self-inflicted conspiracy. More seriously, as noted, people disagree about the enemy and the nature of the threat. Is al Qa'ida (AQ) a real threat or a creature of Western paranoia and overreaction? Is it even a real organization? Is it a mass movement or simply a philosophy, a state of mind? Is the enemy all terrorism? Is it extremism? Or is Islam itself in some way a threat? Is this primarily a military, political, or civilizational problem? What would "victory" look like? These fundamentals are disputed, as those of previous conflicts (except possibly the Cold War) were not.

In truth, as I have shown in reference to the campaigns in Afghanistan, Iraq, Pakistan, and elsewhere, the threat of takfiri terrorism is all too real. But ambiguity arises because this conflict breaks existing paradigms— including notions of "warfare," "diplomacy," "intelligence," even "terrorism." How, for example, do we wage war on nonstate actors who hide in states with which we are at peace, even within our own society? How do we work with allies whose territory provides safe haven for nonstate opponents? How do we defeat enemies who exploit the tools of globalization and open societies, without destroying the very things we seek to protect?

New Paradigms

The British general Rupert Smith argues that war—defined as industrial, interstate warfare between armies, in which the clash of arms decides the outcome—no longer exists; that we are instead in an era of "war amongst the people," in which the utility of military forces depends on their ability to adapt to complex political contexts and engage nonstate opponents under the critical gaze of global public opinion.[2] Certainly, in complex, multisided, hybrid conflicts like Iraq, conventional warfare has failed to produce decisive outcomes. We have instead adapted existing policing, nation-building, and counterinsurgency approaches—and developed new interagency tools "on the fly." Expanding on General Smith's notion of "war amongst the people," if we include the accidental guerrilla phenomenon, the presence of a transnational *takfiri* terrorist enemy seeking to exploit local fighters, the threat to homelands and populations from subversion and terrorist attack (home-grown or "guerrilla") and the propaganda offensive being mounted by AQ and its associated movements, we are truly dealing with an era of "hybrid wars" that defy easy classification under traditional paradigms.

"War" is not the only paradigm being challenged by current conditions: the notion of "diplomacy" is similarly threatened. As discussed in chapter 4, we traditionally conduct state-based diplomacy through engagement with elites of other societies: governments, intellectuals, and business leaders, among others. The theory is that problems can be resolved when elites agree, cooler heads prevail, and governments negotiate and then enforce agreements. Notions of sovereignty, the nation-state, treaty regimes, and international institutions all build on this paradigm. Yet the *takfiri* terrorist enemy organizes at the nonelite level, exploiting discontent and alienation across numerous countries, to aggregate the effects of multiple grassroots actors, many of whom are accidental guerrillas, into a mass movement with global reach. How do elite models of diplomacy address that challenge? This is not a new problem—various programs were established in U.S. embassies in the Cold War to engage with nongovernment elements of civil societies at risk from Communist subversion. The Labor Attaché position in most U.S. embassies, for example, was originally established during the Cold War as a means of countering Communist subversion within trade unions and reaching out, at the nongovernment and nonelite level, to organized labor. Some cultural and youth programs during the Cold War served a similar purpose. But many Cold War programs lapsed after 1992, and problems of religious extremism or political violence require subtly different approaches.

Likewise, traditional intelligence services are primarily designed not to find out what is happening but to acquire secrets from other nation-states. They are well adapted to state-based targets but less suited to nonstate actors—where the problem is to acquire information that is unclassified but may be located in denied, hostile, or inaccessible physical or human terrain. In the Pakistan case, public opinion in Miran Shah or Damadola may matter more to our chances of dealing with AQ senior leadership than any piece of state-based "intelligence." This information is, obviously, unclassified—but extremely difficult to come by. Similarly, in Iraq, public perceptions of Coalition and enemy operations were extremely important data for our planning and conduct of counterinsurgency missions. Again, this was unclassified data that resided in denied areas. Even against state actors, the traditional intelligence approach cannot tell us what is happening, only what other governments *believe* is happening. Why, for example, did Western intelligence miss the imminent fall of the Soviet Union in 1992? In part, at least, because we were reading the Soviet leaders' mail— and they themselves failed to understand the depth of grassroots disillusionment with Communism.[3] Why did most countries (including those who opposed the Iraq war) believe in 2002 that Saddam Hussein's regime had WMDs? Because they were intercepting the regime's communications, and many senior Iraqi regime members believed Iraq had them.[4] Why did the same agencies miss the ongoing and detailed preparations for an insurgency in Iraq after any potential coalition invasion? Perhaps partly because their resources were focused elsewhere, following analytical dead ends.

As discussed in chapter 1, long-standing trends underpin the new conflict environment. These drivers include globalization and the backlash against it, the rise of nonstate actors with capabilities comparable to some nation-states and able to attempt a globalized insurgency, the Shi'a revival leading to what some have characterized as a civil war within Islam, the asymmetric effect of U.S. conventional military superiority that forces all opponents to avoid Western strengths and migrate toward unconventional approaches, and a global information environment based on the internet and satellite communications. All these trends would endure even if AQ and its *takfiri* allies disappeared tomorrow, and until we demonstrate an ability to defeat this type of threat, any smart adversary will adopt a similar approach. Far from being a one-off challenge, we may indeed look back on AQ as the harbinger of a new era of conflict.

Adapting to the New Environment

Thus, as U.S. counterterrorism ambassador Hank Crumpton observed in 2006, we seem to be on the threshold of a new era of warfare, one that demands an adaptive response. Like dinosaurs outcompeted by smaller, weaker, but more adaptive mammals, in this new era nation-states are more powerful but less agile and less flexible and slower to adapt than their nonstate opponents. As in all conflict, success will depend on our ability to adapt, evolve new responses, and get ahead of a rapidly changing threat environment.

The enemy adapts with great speed; consider AQ's evolution since the mid-1990s. As noted in chapter 1, early AQ attacks (the 1998 East African embassy bombings, the USS *Cole* in 2000, and 9/11 itself) were "expeditionary." In response, we improved transportation security, infrastructure protection, and immigration controls. In turn, terrorists developed a "guerrilla" approach: instead of building a team remotely and inserting it secretly to attack, they grew the team close to the target using nationals of the host country. The Madrid and London bombings, and attacks in Casablanca, Istanbul, and Jeddah, followed this pattern, as did the foiled London airline plot of the summer of 2006. The new approach temporarily invalidated our countermeasures—in the case of London, instead of smuggling 19 people in, the terrorists brought one man out—sidestepping our new security procedures. The terrorists had adapted to our new approach by evolving new techniques of their own. Again, as I have shown, counterterrorism methods that work are almost by definition already obsolete: our opponents evolve as soon as we master their current approach. There is no "silver bullet": like malaria, terrorism constantly morphs into new mutations that require a continuously updated battery of responses.

Five Practical Steps

In responding to this new hybrid form of warfare, with its complex combinations of local and global threats, we have done two basic things so far. First, we have improved existing institutions (through processes like intelligence reform, creation of the Department of Homeland Security, and additional capacity for "irregular"—that is, nontraditional—warfare within the Department of Defense). Second, we have begun developing new paradigms to fit the new reality. These are yet to fully emerge, though some—like the idea of treating the conflict as a very large-scale counterinsurgency problem, requiring primarily nonmilitary responses coupled with measures to protect at-risk populations from enemy influence—have gained traction.[5]

In a sense, though, as I said in the last chapter, policy-makers today are a little like the chateau generals of the World War I, confronting a form of conflict that invalidates received wisdom just as the generals faced the "riddle of the trenches" in 1914–1918. Like them, we face a conflict environment transformed by new technological and social conditions, for which existing organizations and concepts are ill suited. Like them, we have "work-arounds" but have yet to develop the breakthrough concepts, technologies, and organizations—equivalent to blitzkrieg in the 1930s—that will solve the riddle of this new threat environment.

The accidental guerrilla phenomenon does not explain the entirety of the problem, which is so complex that it does not fit neatly into any one model. And clearly, there is no easy answer (if there were, we would undoubtedly have found it by now), but it is possible to suggest a way forward. This involves three conceptual steps to develop new models and, simultaneously, two organizational steps to create a capability for this form of conflict. This is not prescriptive, but is simply one possible approach. And the ideas put forward here are not particularly original—rather, this proposal musters existing ideas and integrates them into a policy approach.

DEVELOP A NEW LEXICON

Professor Michael Vlahos has pointed out that the language we use to describe the new threats actively hinders innovative thought.[6] Our terms draw on negative formulations; they say what the environment is not rather than what it is. These terms include descriptors like unconventional, nonstate, nontraditional, unorthodox, and irregular. We call AQ a "non-state actor"; so is Medecins Sans Frontieres. Guerrilla warfare is unconventional; so is nuclear war. Terminology undoubtedly hampers our ability to think clearly: one reason planners in Iraq may have treated "major combat operations" (Phase 3) as decisive, not realizing that in this case the postconflict phase would actually be critical, is that Phase 3 is decisive by *definition:* its full doctrinal name is "Phase III—*Decisive Operations.*" To think clearly about new threats, we need a new lexicon, based on the actual, observed characteristics of real enemies who:

- Integrate terrorism, subversion, humanitarian work, and insurgency to support propaganda designed to manipulate the perceptions of local and global audiences
- Aggregate the effects of a very large number of grassroots accidental actors, scattered across many countries, into a mass movement greater than the sum of its parts, with dispersed leadership and planning functions that deny us detectable targets
- Exploit the speed and ubiquity of modern communications media to mobilize supporters and sympathizers, at speeds far greater than governments can muster
- Exploit deep-seated belief systems founded in religious, ethnic, tribal, and cultural identities, to create extremely lethal nonrational reactions among social groups
- Exploit safe havens like ungoverned or undergoverned areas (in physical space or cyberspace), ideological, religious, or cultural blind spots, and legal loopholes
- Use high-profile symbolic attacks that provoke nation-states into overreactions that damage their long-term interests
- Mount numerous, cheap, small-scale challenges to exhaust us by provoking expensive containment, prevention, and response efforts in dozens of remote areas

These features of the new environment could generate a lexicon to better describe the threat. Since the new threats are not state based, the basis for our approach should not be international relations (the study of how nation-states interact in elite state-based frameworks) but rather anthropology (the study of social roles, groups, status, institutions, and relations within human population groups, often in nonelite, non-state-based frameworks).

GET THE GRAND STRATEGY RIGHT

If the current conflict environment is based on long-standing trends most of which are outside our control, it follows that it may be a protracted, generational, or multigenerational struggle. This means we need both a "long view"[7] and a "broad view" that considers how best to interweave all strands of national power, including the private sector and the wider community. Thus we need a grand strategy that can be sustained by the American people, successive U.S. administrations, key allies, and partners worldwide. Formulating such a long-term grand strategy would involve four crucial judgments:

- Deciding whether our interests are best served by intervening in, and trying to mitigate the process of political and religious ferment in, the Muslim world, or by seeking instead to contain any spillover of violence or unrest into Western communities. This choice is akin to that between rollback and containment in the Cold War, or between a Germany-first or Japan-first strategy at the ARCADIA conference, and is a key element in framing a long-term response.

- Deciding how to allocate resources among military and nonmilitary elements of national power. As we have seen, our present spending and effort are predominantly military; by contrast, a "global counterinsurgency" approach would suggest that around 80 percent of effort should go toward political, diplomatic, development, intelligence, and informational activity and around 20 percent to military activity. Whether this is appropriate depends on our judgment about intervention versus containment.

- Deciding how much to spend (in resources and lives) on this problem. This will require a risk judgment taking into account the likelihood and consequences of future terrorist attacks. Such a judgment must also consider how much can be spent on security, without imposing an unsustainable cost burden on our societies.

- Deciding how to prioritize effort geographically. As we have seen, at present most effort goes to Iraq, a much smaller portion to Afghanistan, and less again to all other areas. Partly this is because our spending is predominantly military, and because we have chosen to intervene in the heart of the Muslim world. Different choices on the military/nonmilitary and intervention/containment judgments might produce significantly different regional priorities over time.

Clearly, the United States is undergoing a transition to a new administration, and the specifics of any administration's strategy would vary in response to a developing situation. Indeed, such agility is critical. But achieving a sustainable consensus, nationally and internationally, on the four grand judgments listed above would provide a long-term basis for policy across successive administrations.

As discussed in chapter 1, at present the U.S. defense budget accounts for well over half of total global defense spending, while the U.S. Defense Department is about 210 times larger than the U.S. Agency for International Development and the State Department combined. This is not to criticize Defense—armed services are labor- and capital-intensive and are always larger than diplomatic or aid agencies. But considering the importance, in this form of conflict, of development, diplomacy and information (the U.S. Information Agency was abolished in 1999, and the State Department includes its tiny successor bureau), a clear imbalance exists between military and nonmilitary elements of capacity. This distorts policy, and is unusual by global standards—for example, Australia's military is approximately nine times larger than its diplomatic and aid agencies combined: the military arm is larger, but not 210 times larger, than the other elements of national power. To its credit, the Department of Defense recognizes the problems inherent in such an imbalance, and said so in the 2006 *Quadrennial Defense Review*.[8] And the administration has programs in train to increase nonmilitary capacity, such as the recently announced doubling in size of the Foreign Service, the surge in training for Iraq and Afghanistan at the Foreign Service Institute, and the creation of the Civilian Reserve Corps and the Coordinator for Reconstruction and Stabilization.[9] But to succeed over the long haul, we need a sustained commitment to build nonmilitary elements of national power. So-called soft power such as private-sector economic strength, national reputation, and cultural confidence are crucial, since military power alone cannot compensate for their loss and since, as we have seen, there are firm limits to what we can achieve unilaterally through military means alone.

These three conceptual steps will take time (which is, incidentally, a good reason to start on them). In the interim, the following two organizational steps could prepare the way.

A leading role in the "War on Terrorism" to date has fallen to special operations forces (SOF) because of their direct action capabilities against targets in remote or denied areas. Meanwhile, Max Boot[10] has argued that we again need something like the Office of Strategic Services (OSS) of World War II, which included analysis, intelligence, anthropology, special operations, information, psychological operations, and technology capabilities. Adjectives matter: *special* forces versus *strategic* services. The SOF are *special*. They are defined by internal comparison to the rest of the military—SOF undertakes tasks "beyond the capabilities" of general-purpose forces. By contrast, the OSS was *strategic*. It was defined against an external environment, and undertook tasks of strategic importance, rapidly acquiring and divesting capabilities as needed. The SOF are almost entirely military; the OSS was an interagency body with a sizeable civilian component, and almost all its military personnel were emergency war enlistees (talented civilians with strategically relevant skills, enlisted for the duration of the war).[11] The SOF trace their origin to the OSS; yet whereas today's SOF are elite military forces with highly specialized capabilities optimized for seven standard missions,[12] the OSS was a mixed civil-military organization that took whatever mission the environment demanded, building capabilities as needed. Identifying which capabilities are "strategic services" today would be a key step in prioritizing interagency efforts.

The capabilities needed to break the accidental guerrilla cycle include those for dealing with nonelite, grassroots threats: cultural and ethnographic intelligence, social systems analysis, information operations (see below), early-entry or high-threat humanitarian and governance teams, field negotiation and mediation teams, biometric reconnaissance, and a variety of other strategically useful capabilities. The relevance of these capabilities changes over time: some that are strategically relevant now will cease to be, while others will emerge. The key is the creation of an interagency capability to rapidly acquire, apply, and proliferate techniques and technologies in a rapidly changing situation.

DEVELOP A CCAPACITY FOR STRATEGIC INFORMATION WARFARE

Al Qa'ida is highly skilled at exploiting multiple, diverse actions by individuals and groups, framing them in a propaganda narrative to manipulate local and global audiences. This propaganda capability, as we have seen, is central to the takfiri objective of creating and manipulating local allies and portraying itself as *at talia al muqawama*, the vanguard of the resistance. Al Qa'ida maintains a network that collects information about the debate in the West and feeds this, along with an assessment of the effectiveness of AQ's propaganda, to its leaders. *Takfiri* terrorists use physical operations (bombings, insurgent activity, beheadings) as supporting material for an integrated "armed propaganda" campaign. The information side of AQ's operation is primary; the physical is merely the tool to achieve a propaganda result. The Taliban, Groupe Salafiste pour La Prédication et le Combat, and some other AQ-aligned groups, as well as Hizballah, adopt similar approaches, as we have seen. Contrast this with our approach: we typically design physical operations first, then craft supporting information operations to explain or justify our actions. This is the reverse of AQ's approach—for all our professionalism, compared to the enemy's our public information is an afterthought.

In military terms, for AQ the "main effort" is information; for us, information is a "supporting effort." As noted, there are 1.68 million people in the U.S. military, and what they do speaks louder than what our public information professionals (who number in the hundreds) say. Thus, to combat *takfiri* propaganda, we need a capacity for strategic information warfare—an integrating function that draws together all components of what we say, and what we do, to send strategic messages that support our overall policy. At present, the military has well-developed information operations (IO) doctrine, but other agencies do not, and are often rightly wary of military methods. Militarizing IO would be a severe mistake, which would confuse a part (military operations) with the whole (U.S. national strategy) and so undermine our overall policy. Lacking a whole-of-government doctrine, and the capability to fight strategic information warfare, limits our effectiveness and creates "message dissonance," such that different elements of the U.S. government send out different messages or work to differing information agendas. We need an interagency effort, with leadership from the very top in the executive and legislative branches, to create capabilities, organizations, and doctrine for a national-level strategic information campaign. Building such a capability is perhaps the most important of our many capability challenges in this new era of hybrid warfare.

Tentative Conclusions

These notions—a new lexicon, grand strategy, balanced capability, strategic services, and strategic information warfare—are merely speculative ideas that suggest what might emerge from a comprehensive effort to find new paradigms for this new era of conflict, perhaps in the context of an

ARCADIA-like summit conference between allies, or as part of a comprehensive attempt to rethink, and move beyond, the concept of a "War on Terrorism." Different ideas may well emerge from such an effort and, in any case, rapid changes in the environment due to enemy adaptation will demand constant innovation. But it is crystal clear that our traditional paradigms of industrial interstate war, elite-based diplomacy, and state-focused intelligence—the paradigms that were so shaken by 9/11 and the campaigns that followed it—can no longer explain the environment or provide conceptual keys to overcoming today's threats of hybrid warfare and a transnational enemy exploiting local, accidental guerrillas.

The Cold War is a limited analogy for today's conflict: there are many differences between today's threats and those of the Cold War era. Yet in at least one dimension, that of time, the enduring trends that drive the current confrontation may mean that the conflict will indeed resemble the Cold War, which lasted in one form or another for 85 years, from the Russian Revolution in 1917 until the collapse of the Soviet Union in 1992. Many of its consequences—especially the "legacy conflicts" arising from the Soviet-Afghan War—are with us still. Even if this confrontation lasts only half as long as the Cold War, we are at the beginning of a very long road indeed, whether we choose to recognize it or not. The new threats, which invalidate received wisdom on so many issues, may indicate that we are on the brink of a new era of conflict. Finding new, breakthrough ideas to understand and defeat these threats may prove to be the most important challenge we face.

A Note on Sources and Methodology

Identifying and Protecting Sources

I have tried to avoid burdening the general reader with extensive footnotes, which disrupt the flow of narrative for the doubtful benefit (solely to me) of covering my rear and making my sources, biases, and data apparent to fellow professionals. Consequently, I have banished most references, including all those that point solely to sources, into a final notes section. The general reader can thus check my sources if desired, but need not wade through masses of references unless inclined to do so.

Those who do take the trouble to examine the notes in detail will find that I have occasionally quoted from informants (local officials, tribal leaders, or members of local communities) without giving their names, though always giving as much other information as I safely can. This is an unfortunate necessity: these people are still in the field, at risk, and would be under threat if their identities were revealed. I hope that the wide variety of my sources—named and unnamed, written and oral—will encourage readers to accept the general thrust of the evidence, even if the identity of every witness cannot be published.

Research Ethics

Some of my data were gathered through fieldwork with local tribes and communities in Iraq, Afghanistan, Pakistan, Indonesia, and East Timor, before and since 9/11. Research of this type imposes special ethical and moral obligations on researchers, because key informants in war zones are more vulnerable than others, and because there is an unequal power relationship between interviewer and subject, imposing a strict "duty of care." In all cases, respondents were briefed on planned and potential uses for their information. Each agreed to provide information on the basis that his or her identity would be protected (hence the anonymity I have afforded these sources in the notes). In Iraq, informants also understood that their information would be used to help Coalition forces build better relationships with Iraqi tribes and that one side-effect of this might include the killing or capturing of terrorists, insurgents, or tribal fighters working with enemy groups. They also understood that information, not including their identity, might be passed to researchers outside Iraq, transmitted on the internet, or used in subsequent research, but would be used openly, not as part of classified or intelligence reporting. All respondents agreed to provide information on this basis, and I have rigorously adhered to that agreement. Field notes have been "sanitized" and direct quotes minimized to preserve confidentiality. Key informants were offered the opportunity to check and comment on field notes.

The Methodology of Conflict Ethnography

This book's methodology is also perhaps worth describing. We might define this methodology, under the rubric "conflict ethnography," as an attempt to study a conflict in its own ("emic") terms, and to internalize and interpret the physical, human, informational, and ideological setting in which it takes place. Borrowing a phrase from literary criticism, conflict ethnography attempts a "close reading"[1] of the environment, treating it like a text: an attempt to understand in detail the terrain, the key actors in the conflict, the people, their social and cultural institutions, the way they act and think. It attempts what the anthropologist Clifford Geertz called a "thick description,"[2] understanding a war holistically, in its own terms and through the eyes of its actual participants, in their words and in their language. Field methods applied include participant observation, face-to-face interviews, open-ended interaction with key informants, proficiency in local languages, long-term presence on the spot, integration of written sources with personal testimony, and developing well-founded relationships of trust with key informants—along with the fundamental ethical responsibility to protect those informants and advocate for their safety and well-being. The aim is to see beyond surface differences between societies and environments, beyond a "military orientalism"[3] that sees warfare through exotic "eastern" cultural stereotypes, to the deeper social and cultural drivers of conflict, drivers that local participants would understand on their own terms. In more detail, this methodology could be summarized as follows:

1. Conduct the research, as far as possible, using primary sources in the local language
2. Get as close as possible (in time and space) to the actual events, ideally by being present when they unfold but, at the very least, by seeking firsthand descriptions from eyewitnesses

3. Use documentary sources (including operational and intelligence reports, captured documents, quantitative data, maps and surveys, media content analysis, and the work of other researchers) to create a primary analysis of the environment

4. Use this primary analysis to identify a more limited number of "communities" (local areas, population groups, villages, or functional categories) for further detailed personal analysis at the case-study level;

5. Conduct firsthand, on-the-spot field studies (applying an extended residential fieldwork approach wherever possible) of these secondary communities

6. Work from unstructured, face-to-face, open-ended interviews (rather than impersonal questionnaires and surveys) during field work, but integrate this subjective qualitative perspective with quantitative data from the primary analysis

7. Revisit, in an iterative fashion, the results of earlier fieldwork and analysis using follow-up interviews and contextual studies

8. Understand and accept the presence of personal and research bias, but act to compensate for it by using the greatest possible variety of human and documentary sources and by explicitly identifying and examining the sources of bias

9. Treat analogies (with other conflicts, societies, or regions) with extreme skepticism: seek to understand the conflict in its own terms rather than by analogy with some other war

10. Accept the fundamental ethical responsibility to protect the identity, and work to further the well-being, of any key sources and informants, seek their informed consent to research and publication, and advocate for policies that enhance their welfare

This methodology is not the only one that works, nor is it a panacea. Indeed, it has some very significant limitations. For one thing, getting the intensely detailed firsthand data we seek, in an active combat environment, is not for the faint of heart: it can be extremely dangerous and indeed sometimes proves fatal. For another, data corruption—especially in the use of officially reported combat statistics such as body counts and "significant activities" reports can frustrate rigorous statistical analysis, leading to an overemphasis on professional judgment and "blink knowledge"—an instinctive feel for the environment based on long experience—that may have been acquired in radically different conflicts, years before.

There is also a selection bias: for example, as senior counterinsurgency adviser in Iraq, I focused my greatest time and attention on coalition units in the toughest areas, units requiring the most hands-on field assistance but not necessarily providing a representative sample of events across the country. In Afghanistan, I spent much of my time with American special operations forces and provincial reconstruction teams, and had little opportunity to talk to local tribal leaders, except for those willing to work with (or at least talk to) the Coalition.

The risk, stress, and effort inherent in war zone fieldwork also clouds judgment and skews emphasis: researchers tend to place more weight on data we collect with difficulty and danger than on insights gathered in the comfort of a library or archive. This research approach's deep regional or district focus, in common with other case-study based approaches, is also not necessarily transferable. And the fact that local-dialect language skills are unattainable for many researchers tends to privilege the views of male, urbanized, educated, and often English-speaking respondents. Last and most important, emotional factors—sympathy for local informants and leaders, intense concern for the welfare of the civil population, distaste for some political factions, and, over time, intense hatred for an extremely savage enemy—undoubtedly clouded my judgment at times in both Iraq and Afghanistan.

But within these limitations, I believe this methodology is the best we currently have for getting into the true microdetails of war zone social behavior, and thus for understanding a forbiddingly complex, dynamic, difficult, and dangerous environment. I hope the reader will ultimately agree.

Notes

Author's Preface

1. David J. Kilcullen, "Countering Global Insurgency," *Journal of Strategic Studies* 28, 4 (August 2005): 597–617.

2. The first two are hill-tribes of the Afghan-Pakistan border; the Kuchi are cross-border nomads of the same area; the Dulaim and Janabi are major tribal confederations (*qabila*) of Iraq.

3. Though men, women, and children play important roles in warfare as a group endeavor in the tribal and traditional societies I have encountered, the act of fighting itself is an overwhelmingly male pursuit.

4. The term "irregular warfare" originated in the CIA and was later adopted by the Marine Corps. It was a key conceptual component of the 2006 QDR and has since passed into widespread use. Unfortunately, as currently defined, the concept is problematic; I prefer the term "hybrid warfare," for reasons I will explore.

5. One of these thinkers was John A. Nagl, *Learning to Eat Soup with a Knife: Counterinsurgency Lessons from Malaya and Vietnam* (Westport, Conn.: Praeger, 2002).

6. I am indebted for the concept of hybrid warfare to Professor Erin Simpson of Harvard University and the U.S. Marine Corps Command and Staff College, and to Mr Frank Hoffman of the Center for Emerging Threats and Opportunities.

7. See David J. Kilcullen, "Twenty-eight Articles: Fundamentals of Company-Level Counterinsurgency," *Military Review* 86, 3 (May–June 2006): 103–8; "Counter-insurgency Redux," *Survival* 48, 4 (December 2006), 111–30; "Subversion, Counter-subversion, and the Campaign against Terrorism in Europe," *Studies in Conflict and Terrorism* 30, 8 (August 2007): 647–66.

Chapter 1

1. This was the month of the EP3 surveillance plane incident, and U.S.-Korean relations were also at a low point. For a discussion of the China incident, see Congressional Research Service, *China-U.S. Aircraft Collision Incident of April 2001: Assessments and Policy Implications*, October 10, 2001; http://opencrs.cdt.org/document/RL30946.

2. Qiao Liang and Wang Xiangsui, *Unrestricted Warfare* (Beijing: PLA Literature and Arts Publishing House, February 1999).

3. Foreign Broadcast Intercept Service (FBIS), translation of interview, June 28, 1999, www.fbis.gov, document no. OW2807114599.

4. Ibid.

5. I am grateful to Dr Janine Davidson of George Mason University for bringing this key distinction to my attention during collaborative work in 2005–2006.

6. I am indebted to Assistant Professor Erin Simpson of the U.S. Marine Corps Staff College and Harvard University for this terminology. See Erin Simpson, "Thinking about Modern Conflict: Hybrid Wars, Strategy, and War Aims" (paper presented to the annual meeting of the Midwest Political Science Association, Chicago, April 7–11, 2005); www.people.fas.harvard.edu/~esimpson/papers/hybrid.pdf.

7. Loup Francart, *Maitriser la violence: Une option strategique* (Paris: Institut de straté-gie comparée, 1999). For an English translation of some key concepts from this work see Loup Francart (a brigadier general in the French Army) and Jean-Jacques Patry, "Mastering Violence: An Option for Operational Military Strategy," *Naval War College Review* 53, 3 (Summer 2000): 144–84.

8. For an insightful discussion of these issues, see Michael Evans, "From Kadesh to Kandahar: Military Theory and the Future of War," *Naval War College Review* and (summer 2003); http://findarticles.com/p/articles/mi_mo JIW/is_3_56/ai_105210224/print?tag=artBody;col1.

9. See Rupert Smith, *The Utility of Force: The Art of War in the Modern World* (New York: Knopf, 2007).

10. I am indebted to Lieutenant Colonel (retd) Bob Killebrew for this insight and for an understanding of the sophistication and importance of modern gang structures and activities in this context. Killebrew, personal communications, March–June 2008.

11. I am indebted for this formulation to Ambassador Hank Crumpton, formerly U.S. coordinator for counterterrorism, who headed the CIA's intervention in Afghanistan in the immediate aftermath of 9/11.

12. John Lancaster and Kamran Khan, "Musharraf Named in Nuclear Probe: Senior Pakistani Army Officers Were Aware of Technology Transfers, Scientist Says," *Washington Post* Foreign Service, Tuesday, February 3, 2004, A13; www.washingtonpost.com/ac2/wp-dyn/A6884-2004Feb2.

13. See Kishore Mahbubani, *The New Asian Hemisphere: The Irresistible Shift of Global Power to the East* (New York: Public Affairs, 2008).

14. For a detailed discussion of these trends see Peter W. Singer, *Corporate Warriors: The Rise of the Privatized Military Industry*, Cornell Studies in Security Affairs (Ithaca, N.Y.: Cornell University Press, 2003) and Stephen Armstrong, *War Plc: The Rise of the New Corporate Mercenary* (New York: Faber & Faber, 2008).

15. The Truman administration (1945–1952) oversaw the establishment of most American security agencies, including the U.S. Air Force, the RAND Corporation, the CIA, the National Security Agency, National Security Council, National Intelligence Council, National Science Foundation, National Aeronautics and Space Administration, and indeed the Department of Defense itself.

16. Michael Howard, "What's in a Name? How to Fight Terrorism," *Foreign Affairs* (January–February 2002).

17. This somewhat arbitrary timeline begins with the conflicts in Greece, Indonesia, Palestine, and elsewhere that sparked as World War II ended and concludes with the fall of Ian Smith's white minority government to ZANLA/ZIPRA insurgents in Rhodesia in 1982, an event that brought down the final curtain on European empire in Africa.

18. Thomas L. Friedman, *The World Is Flat: A Brief History of the 21st Century* (New York: Farrar, Straus and Giroux, 2005).

19. John Ralston Saul, *Democracy and Globalization* (lecture series at the University of New South Wales, Sydney, January 1999); www.abc.net.au/specials/saul/default.htm.

20. Paul Collier, *The Bottom Billion: Why the Poorest Countries Are Failing and What Can Be Done about It* (New York: Oxford University Press, 2007).

21. Thomas P. M. Barnett, *The Pentagon's New Map* (New York: Putnam, 2004).

22. See bin Laden's statement of September 2007, which railed against a series of globalization-related grievances, discussed at www.dissidentvoice.orgz/2007/09/bin-laden-a-lefty/.

23. See the biography of Carlo Petrini, founder of the slow food movement; www.regione.piemonte.it/lingue/english/pagine/cultura/approfondimenti/16_petrini_eng.pdf.

24. For a listing of antiglobalization protest actions by such groups, see the Actions Against Globalization website archive: www.nadir.org/nadir/initiativ/agp/free/action07.html.

25. Thermobaric munitions combine explosive material and oxidants at the molecular level so that, unlike conventional explosives that rely on atmospheric oxygen to function correctly, they produce a sustained and deeply destructive blast wave even in confined spaces like tunnels, buildings, subways, and streets. Their use in conflicts in Chechnya, Afghanistan, and elsewhere has proven extremely effective, with gruesome results.

26. Akbar S. Ahmed, *Journey into Islam: The Crisis of Globalization* (Washington, D.C.: Brookings Institution Press, 2007).

27. I am indebted for these ideas to discussions at the Allen and Company Sun Valley Conference, Sun Valley, Idaho, July 10, 2008.

28. See Barnett, *Pentagon's New Map.*

29. Paul Collier, *Bottom Billion.*

30. This is a modified form of the official U.S. Defense Department definition of insurgency. See Field Manual (FM) 3-24, *Counterinsurgency* (2006); www.fas.org/irp/doddir/army/fm3-24.pdf.

31. I am indebted for this formulation to Michael Scheuer, "Coalition Warfare, Part II: How Zarqawi Fits into Bin Laden's World Front," *Jamestown Terrorism Focus*, April 29, 2005; www.jamestown.org/news_details.php?news_id=109#.

32. See the official website of the Amman Message: http://ammanmessage.com/index.php?option=com_content&task=view&id=13&Itemid=27.

33. See United Nations Development Program, *Arab Human Development Report Series* (2001, 2002, 2003, 2004, and 2005); www.undp.org/arabstates/ahdr.shtml.

34. See Faisal Devji, *Landscapes of the Jihad: Militancy, Morality, Modernity* (Ithaca, N.Y.: Cornell University Press, 2005), and Akbar Ahmed, *Islam under Siege: Living Dangerously in a Post-honor World* (London: Polity, 2003).

35. See "The Operations Man: Ayman al-Zawahiri," *Estimate*, September 21, 2001, http://www.theestimate.com/public/092101_profile.html.

36. Ayman al-Zawahiri, "Knights under the Prophet's Banner," *Al-Sharq al-Awsat*, December 2, 2001.

37. Ibid.

38. See Abuza, Zachary: *2004 NBR Analysis: Muslims, Politics and Violence in Indonesia: An Emerging Islamist-Jihadist Nexus?* (Seattle: National Bureau of Asian Research, 2004). For a slightly different interpretation, see also *Jema'ah Islamiyah in Southeast Asia: Damaged but Still Dangerous*, ICG Asia Report no. 863 (New York: International Crisis Group, August 26, 2003).

39. Vali S. Nasr, *The Shia Revival: How Conflicts within Islam Will Shape the Future* (New York: Norton, 2006).

40. Patrick Cockburn, *Muqtada: Muqtada al-Sadr, the Shia Revival, and the Struggle for Iraq* (London: Scribner, 2008).

41. See David Horovitz, "Editor's Notes: A Searing Indictment," *Jerusalem Post*, May 4, 2007.

42. Andrew M. Exum, *Hizballah at War: A Military Assessment*, Policy Focus no. 63 (Washington, D.C.: Washington Institute for Near East Policy, December 2006); www.washingtoninstitute.org/pubPDFs/PolicyFocus63.pdf.

43. See Nawaf Obaid, *A Shia Crescent and the Shia Revival: Myths and Realities* (Riyadh: Saudi National Security Assessment Project, September 27, 2006); E:2006_09_27_Iran_Project_Phase_A_Brief.pdf.

44. See, for example, the discussion of the separationist Robert Spencer's views: www.amnation.com/vfr/archives/006854.html.

45. Frederick H. Hartmann, *The Conservation of Enemies: A Study in Enmity* (Westport, Conn.: Greenwood Press, 1982).

46. For a detailed discussion of this tendency, see Mary R. Habeck, *Knowing the Enemy: Jihadist Ideology and the War on Terror* (New Haven, Conn.: Yale University Press, 2006).

47. See David Kilcullen, "Countering Global Insurgency," *Journal of Strategic Studies* 28, 4 (August 2005): 597–617.

48. See Mark Bowden, *Guests of the Ayatollah: The Iran Hostage Crisis: The First Battle in America's War with Militant Islam* (New York: Grove Press, 2007).

49. For a description of these events, see Kermit Roosevelt, *Countercoup: The Struggle for the Control of Iran* (New York: McGraw-Hill, 1979), and Stephen Kinzer, *All the Shah's Men: An American Coup and the Roots of Middle East Terror* (New York: Wiley, 2003).

50. See www.globalsecurity.org/military/world/spending.htm for current figures.

51. I am indebted to Ambassador Henry Crumpton, former coordinator for counter-terrorism, for this insight.

52. Andrew Bacevich, "The Islamic Way of War," *American Conservative*, September 11, 2006; www.amconmag.com/2006/2006_09_11/cover.html.

53. Ibid.

54. See, for example, the website of the Earth Liberation Front: www.earthliberationfront.com/elf_news.htm.

55. Discussion with senior civil service official responsible for finance and budgeting in Iraq, July 2007.

56. National Commission on Terrorist Attacks on the United States, *The 9/11 Commission Final Report* (Washington D.C., U.S. Government, 2004), chap. 5; http://govinfo.library.unt.edu/911/report/911Report_Ch5.htm.

57. Robert Looney, "Economic Costs to the United States Stemming from the 9/11 Attacks," *Strategic Insights* 1, 6 (August 2002); www.ccc.nps.navy.mil/si/aug02/homeland.asp.

58. Congressional Research Service, *The Cost of Iraq, Afghanistan, and Other Global War on Terror Operations since 9/11*, Report to Congress no. RL33110, updated June 23, 2008; www.fas.org/sgp/crs/natsec/RL33110.pdf.

59. Compiled from figures in *The Military Balance 2007* (London: International Institute for Strategic Studies, 2007), 15–50.

60. Compiled from U.S. State Department and U.S. Agency for International Development, *Congressional Budget Justification 2007* (Washington D.C.: State Department, 2006), table 9. http://www.state.gov/s/d/rm/rls/cbj/2007/.

61. Scheuer, "Coalition Warfare."

62. Kilcullen, "Countering Global Insurgency."

63. Usama bin Laden, statement of November 1, 2004.

64. See Lawrence Uzzell, "Could the Beslan Tragedy Have Been Avoided?" [Jamestown Institute] *North Caucasus Weekly*, September 8, 2004; www.jamestown.org/chechnya_weekly/article.php?issue_id=3062.

65. Robert Worth, "Blast Destroys Shrine in Iraq, Setting Off Sectarian Fury," *New York Times*, February 22, 2006.

66. Bernard B. Fall, "The Theory and Practice of Insurgency and Counterinsurgency," *Naval War College Review* 51, 1 (winter 1998): 46–57 (first published April 1965).

67. Sheldon W. Simon, "Philippines Withdraws from Iraq and JI Strikes Again," *Comparative Connections* 6, 3 (October 2004): n.p.; www.ciaonet.org/olj/cpc/cpc_octo4/cpc_octo4f.pdf.

68. Sharon Otterman, "Iraq: Ongoing Attacks," *Council on Foreign Relations Backgrounder*, August 21, 2003; www.cfr.org/publication.html?id=7685.

69. For detailed accounts of these events, see Gary Berntsen, *Jawbreaker: The Attack on bin Laden and Al Qaeda* (New York: Crown, 2005), and Sean Naylor, *Not a Good Day to Die* (New York: Penguin, 2005).

70. See Peter Bergen, "The Long Hunt for Osama," *Atlantic Monthly*, October 2004, vol. 294.

71. National Commission on Terrorist Attacks on the United States, *9/11 Commission Final Report*, chap. 5.

72. Intelligence and Security Committee, *Report into the London Terrorist Attacks on 7 July 2005* (London: HMSO, May 2006).

73. Bruce Hoffman, Washington director, RAND Corporation, personal communication, July 6, 2006.

74. David Kilcullen, "Counterinsurgency Redux," *Survival* 48, 4 (winter 2006–7): 111–30.

75. U.S. Department of State, *Country Reports on Terrorism 2005* (Washington, D.C.: Government Printing Office, 2005), chap. 2; www.state.gov/s/ct/rls/crt/2005/64332. htm.

76. See Joe Felter et al., *Harmony and Disharmony: Exploiting al Qa'ida's Organizational Vulnerabilities* (West Point, N.Y.: Combating Terrorism Center, February 2006); http:// cisac.stanford.edu/publications/harmony_and_disharmony__exploiting_alqaidas_ organizational_vulnerabilities/.

77. See Bernard Lewis, *The Assassins: A Radical Sect within Islam* (New York: Basic Books, 2002).

78. See Nicholas Griffin, *Caucasus: Mountain Men and Holy Wars* (New York: Thomas Dunne Books, 2003).

79. Mullah Powindah, the Mahsud leader, led a guerrilla war against British rule in the Tochi valley over decades in the nineteenth century. The Fakir of Ipi, Mirza Ali Khan, waged guerrilla war against the British throughout the 1930s and 1940s and only reconciled with the state of Pakistan in 1954. Ajab Khan Afridi was responsible for the 1923 kidnapping (and release) of Molly Ellis, daughter of a British officer in the Kohat garrison of the North-West Frontier Province, prompting an enormous manhunt, and hid out in the Hindu Kush for decades; he eventually died in his sleep. The Mad Mullah, Mohammed Abdullah Hassan, led a guerrilla movement against the British in Somaliland between the 1890s and 1920.

80. I am indebted to Lieutenant Colonel Chris Cavoli for the terms "repetitive raiding" and "persistent presence"; see my Kunar valley case study in chapter 2 for more detail.

Chapter 2

1. This eyewitness account of the Uruzgan ambush is drawn from an extended interview on September 27, 2006, with a U.S. Special Forces staff sergeant who was a member of an intelligence detachment accompanying this patrol, and a U.S. State Department official who served in the nearby Tarin Kowt Provincial Reconstruction Team.

2. *Degtyaryova-Shpagina Krupnokaliberny*, "Degtyarev-Shpagin Large Calibre."

3. See Michael Futch, "Special Forces Soldiers Honored," *The Fayetteville Observer*, February 22, 2007, http://www.fayobserver.com/article?id=255341.

4. Uruzgan interview, September 27, 2006.

5. In funding terms, counting FY08 supplemental requests, operations in Iraq have cost the United States approximately $608.3 billion since early 2003, whereas the war in Afghanistan since late 2001 has cost about $162.6 billion, or about 26.7 percent of the cost of Iraq. (Congressional Research Service Report for Congress, *The Cost of Iraq, Afghanistan, and Other Global War on Terror Operations Since 9/11*, updated April 11, 2008, CRS, Washington, D.C., pp. 10ff). In terms of force levels, the United States currently has 160,000 troops in Iraq and 32,000 (about 20 percent of U.S. forces in Iraq) in Afghanistan, with additional NATO and non-NATO troops providing for a total of about 47,000 (about 29.3 percent of the Iraq total) in the International Security Assistance Force for Afghanistan. Iraq has a population of 29.3 million and an area of 438,000 km^2; it has a somewhat smaller population than and is about two-thirds the size of Afghanistan, which has a population of 31.9 million and an area of 647,000 km^2.

6. Congressional Research Service, *The Cost of Iraq, Afghanistan, and Other Global War on Terror Operations Since 9/11*, Report for Congress (Washington, D.C.: Government Printing Office, updated April 11, 2008), 10–12.

7. Ann Scott Tyson, "Gates Criticizes NATO Countries on Afghanistan," *Washington Post*, December 12, 2007, www.washingtonpost.com.

8. Olaf Caroe, *The Pathans 550 B.C.–1957 A.D.* (London: St. Martin's Press, 1958), 396.

9. LTC Chris Cavoli, personal communication via e-mail, July 31, 2008.

10. For example, a Pew Global Attitudes Project poll in mid-2005 found that "not surprisingly, virtually all Americans (83 percent) approve of the U.S.-led military campaign against the Taliban and al Qaeda in Afghanistan. Support is nearly as high in Great Britain, where 73 percent approve and 18 percent disapprove. Larger minorities in France, Germany, and especially Italy dissent from this view, but majorities in all three nations agree with their American and British counterparts"; http://pewglobal.org/reports/display.php?PageID=453). Approval for the Afghanistan war has since trended sharply down in Europe and moderately down in the United States but is still (as of mid-2008) much higher than for Iraq.

11. Ibid., and see also CNN News polls: www.cnn.com/2007/POLITICS/03/18/poll.wars/index.html.

12. For a detailed discussion of these issues, see World Bank, *Service Delivery and Governance at the Sub-national Level in Afghanistan* (July 2007); http://siteresources.worldbank.org/SOUTHASIAEXT/Resources/Publications/448813–1185293547967/4024814–1185293572457/report.pdf.

13. Transparency International, *Corruption Perceptions Index 2007*; www.transparency.org/policy_research/surveys_indices/cpi/2007.

14. Discussions with allied intelligence personnel in Kabul, June 26, 2006, and October 22, 2006, and with Afghan elders, Kabul, October 25, 2006, and Kunar valley, March 12, 2008.

15. See Long War Journal, "Afghanistan: Graphing the Violence," April 5, 2008; www.longwarjournal.org/archives/2008/04/afghanistan_graphing.php.

16. See CNN, "NATO: Taliban Mastermind Killed in Afghanistan," May 13, 2007; http://edition.cnn.com/2007/WORLD/asiapcf/05/13/afghan.dadullah/index.html.

17. Compiled from field reporting data (e-mails and personal communications from colleagues in the field), United Nations threat statistics, and media reporting and confirmed as "in the ballpark" by the (unclassified) judgments of intelligence community colleagues with access to more detailed data.

18. Antonio Giustozzi, *Koran, Kalashnikov and Laptop: The Neo-Taliban Insurgency in Afghanistan* (New York: Columbia University Press, 2008), 33.

19. Based on discussions with officials of the NDS (Afghan Intelligence Service), U.S. and NATO military, United Nations mission in Afghanistan, and GOA officials in Kabul, Asadabad, Bagram, Kandahar, and Khost between May 23, 2006, and March 18, 2008.

20. Interview with the governor of Kandahar Province, Kandahar airfield, March 15, 2008.

21. Group interview with Mullah Salam and 11 district elders of Musa Qaleh district, Helmand Province, Kabul, March 13, 2008.

22. William Maley, *Rescuing Afghanistan* (Sydney: University of New South Wales Press, 2006), 34–35.

23. William Maley, personal communication, Coolum Australia, August 11, 2007.

24. Maley, *Rescuing Afghanistan*, 35.

25. See Lester W. Grau, "Something Old, Something New: Guerrillas, Terrorists and Intelligence Analysis," *Military Review* (July–August 2004): 42–49; http://fmso.leavenworth.army.mil/documents/old-new.pdf.

26. For a comprehensive study of Taliban recruitment see Giustozzi, *Koran, Kalashnikov and Laptop*, chaps. 2 and 3.

27. See Ali Ahmad Jalali and Lester W. Grau, *The Other Side of the Mountain: Mujahideen Tactics in the Soviet-Afghan War* (Quantico, Va.: United States Marine Corps Studies and Analysis Division, 1995), 11.

28. This communist-originated term refers to "propaganda of the deed the use both of spectacular or inspirational violence (such as public beatings, killings, arson attacks, destruction of symbolic targets) for political effect and of intimidatory violence (assassinations, executions, and kidnapping)—or the threat of such violence—in order to reinforce propaganda messages or make a political point.

29. Interviews conducted in the field in Kabul in May 2006, October 2006, and March 2008, and in Afghan provincial capitals in May 2006 and March 2008.

30. ABC Newspoll, 2006; http://abcnews.go.com/Politics/PollVault/Story?id=2702516&page=1.

31. For a detailed discussion of Taliban propaganda, see Thomas H. Johnson, "The Taliban Iinsurgency and an Analysis of Shabnamah (night letters)," in *Small Wars and Insurgencies* 18, 3 (September 2007): 317–44.

32. For a discussion of this approach as a classic guerrilla strategy, see Fall, "Theory and Practice."

33. Ibid.

34. I am grateful to Dr. Gordon H. McCormick of the U.S. Naval Postgraduate School, Monterey, for this insight. McCormick, personal communication via e-mail, September 2006.

35. I am indebted for this insight into the information/firepower asymmetry between insurgents and counterinsurgents to Dr. Gordon H. McCormick, Professor and Chair of the Department of Defense Analysis, Graduate School of Operational and Information Sciences at the U.S. Naval Postgraduate School, Monterey, California.

36. For example, representatives from the Senlis Council (an NGO that has argued for legalization of the Afghan poppy trade) and Dr. Julian Lewis, MP, Conservative Party Shadow Defence Minister in the U.K. Parliament, raised this argument with me at the International Institute for Strategic Studies symposium. "A Cohesive Strategy for the Future of Afghanistan Reconciling Counter-Insurgency, Counter-Narcotics and Reconstruction, London, February 14, 2007.

37. United Nations Office on Drugs and Crime, *Illicit Drug Trends in Afghanistan*, report issued June 20, 2008, http://www.unodc.org/documents/regional/central-asia/Illicit%20Drug%20Trends%20Report_Afg%2013%20June%202008.pdf.

38. Ibid.

39. Giustozzi, *Koran, Kalashnikov and Laptop*, 86.

40. Interviews with USAID and U.S. Embassy field counternarcotics program and Poppy Eradication Program officers, Kabul and Kandahar, October 22–27, 2006.

41. Interviews with AID and counternarcotics officials, Kabul, March 2008.

42. Ibid.

43. See www.senliscouncil.net/.

44. See also 2005 opinion polling data showing that only 6 percent of Afghans polled believe it is legally and morally legitimate, and 21 percent believe it is acceptable only if there is no other way to make a living; *Afghanistan Watch Exclusive: Interview with Craig Charney on Afghan Public Opinion* (December 22, 2005); www.charneyresearch.com/2005Dec22_afghaniWatchInterview.htm.

45. Government Accountability Office, *Afghanistan Drug Control: Despite Improved Efforts, Deteriorating Security Threatens Success of U.S. Goals*, Report to Congressional Committees, GAO-07–78 (Washington, D.C.: Government Printing Office, November 2006).

46. Conversation with Afghan governors and military and police officials, Kandahar, March 15, 2008.

47. Giustozzi, *Koran, Kalashnikov and Laptop*.

48. Discussion with tribal elders, Kabul, March 13, 2008, mirroring several earlier conversations with local people in East Timor, Iraq, Pakistan, and Bougainville.

49. See, for example, the comments by the Afghan governor quoted in the epigraph to this chapter.

50. See David Galula, *Counterinsurgency Warfare, Theory and Practice* (London: Pall Mall Press, 1964), 75–76.

51. For a detailed description of this phenomenon during the Vietnam War, see Jeffrey Race, *War Comes to Long An: Revolutionary Conflict in a Vietnamese Province* (Berkeley: University of California Press, 1973).

52. See Stathis N. Kalyvas, *The Logic of Violence in Civil War* (Cambridge: Cambridge University Press, 2006), 40.

53. For example, in Kandahar in early summer 2006, I spoke with a senior commander from a Coalition country who explained to me that his strategy was to bring benefits to the local population; as a result they would in theory come to support the Coalition and the government and would then stop supporting the insurgents. By the time I returned to Kandahar in the autumn, however, that commander had left the theater, and Coalition forces had progressively lost control over the province, faced with an enemy who maintained a 24-hour local presence, including effective night-time intimidation of the population—a combination with which the Coalition's strategy of "niceness" simply could not compete.

54. See Karl D. Jackson, *Traditional Authority, Islam and Rebellion: A Study of Indonesian Political Behavior* (Berkeley: University of California Press, 1980); David J. Kilcullen, "The Political Consequences of Military Operations in Indonesia, 1945–99" (Ph.D. diss., University of New South Wales, 2000); Roger D. Petersen, *Resistance and Rebellion: Lessons from Eastern Europe* (New York: Cambridge University Press, 2001); and Kalyvas, *Logic of Violence in Civil War*.

55. Kalyvas, *Logic of Violence in Civil War*, 12 (emphasis added).

56. See, for example, William D. Henderson, *Cohesion, The Human Element in Combat: Leadership and Societal Influence in the Armies of the Soviet Union, the United States, North Vietnam and Israel* (Washington, D.C.: National Defense University Press, 1985).

57. Examples include Operation Medusa in Kandahar Province in September 2006, and Operation el-Hasn in the Tagab valley east of Bagram later the same year. I directly observed planning for Al Hasn and interviewed coalition officers who participated in Medusa. The Tagab valley operation was also described in detail in Darin J. Blatt, Peter G. Fischer, and Scott T. McGleish, "Operation Al Hasn: Planning and Executing a Full-Spectrum Operation in the Afghan Theater Today," *Infantry*, July 1, 2007.

58. This section is largely drawn from my field notes, compiled over the period mid-2005 to mid-2008, drawing on a variety of published and unpublished primary and secondary sources, as well as three periods of fieldwork in Afghanistan in May–June 2006, October–November 2006, and March 2008.

59. Afghanistan Information Management Services; www.aims.org.af/.

60. Wahhabi presence in eastern Afghanistan and northwest Pakistan is not a new phenomenon: it was remarked on by Caroe, *Pathans 550 B.C.–1957 A.D.* (1958), Fredrik Barth *Political Leadership among Swat Pathans* (London: Athlone Presss,1959), and Akbar S. Ahmed, *Resistance and Control in Pakistan*, rev. ed. (New York: Routledge, 2004).

61. For a detailed description of mountain warfare techniques on the Afghan frontier, see Timothy Robert Moreman, *The Army in India and the Development of Frontier Warfare, 1849–1947* (London: Palgrave MacMillan, 1998).

62. Personal communication, during a conference at the Joint Special Operations University, Hurlburt Field, Florida, May 2006.

63. World Bank, *Service Delivery and Governance at the Sub-national Level in Afghanistan.*

64. Thomas H. Johnson, "Afghanistan's Post-Taliban Transition: The State of State-building after War," *Central Asian Survey* 25, 1–2 (March–June 2006): 1–26.

65. See Barnett R. Rubin, *The Fragmentation of Afghanistan: State Formation and Collapse in the International System,* 2nd ed. (New Haven, Conn.: Yale University Press, 2002).

66. See Philip Carl Salzman, *Culture and Conflict in the Middle East* (New York: Humanity Books, 2008).

67. See Ahmed, *Resistance and Control in Pakistan,* for an extended case-study discussion of a famous instance of agnatic rivalry in Waziristan.

68. Ibid., esp. chaps. 2 and 3.

69. The term *kuchi* is generically applied by non-nomadic Pashtuns to pastoral nomads, of whom there are several million in Afghanistan, traditionally inhabiting the Registan desert in southeastern Afghanistan and other low-production zones astride the border regions of Afghanistan and Pakistani Baluchistan. Though ethnically distinct, their mode of life is similar to that of nomadic Baluch in Iranian Baluchistan. I have also observed Kuchi tents and flocks in the semidesert region near the foothills of the Hindu Kush between Jalalabad and Kabul. These tribes have been decimated by war, natural disaster, and the consequent difficulty of moving across frontiers and accessing traditional sources of pasture and water. A severe drought in 1998 caused the displacement of approximately 100,000 *kuchi* from Registan to temporary settlements between the Arghandab and Helmand rivers. About 57,000 were supported by the UN in camps in Maywand and Panjwayi districts of Kandahar Province. See Allen Degen and Noam Wiesbrod, "Can Pastoral Nomads Return to Their Traditional Livelihood of Raising Livestock in the Registan Desert of Southern Afghanistan?" *Nomadic Peoples* 8, 2 (December 2004): 214–29.

70. Lieutenant Colonel Chris Cavoli, personal communication via e-mail, July 31, 2008.

71. Discussion with tribal leaders, Peshawar, June 24, 2006.

72. Discussion with Professor Akbar Ahmed, Washington D.C., March 2006.

73. See Max Gluckman, "Inter-hierarchical Roles: Professional and Party Ethics in Tribal Areas in South and Central Africa," in M. J. Swartz, ed., *Local Level Politics: Social and Cultural Perspectives* (Chicago: Aldine, 1968).

74. Kilcullen, "Political Consequences of Military Operations in Indonesia, 1945–99."

75. See Max Gluckman, *Order and Rebellion in Tribal Africa* (London: Cohen and West, 1963), and "Some Processes of Social Change, Illustrated with Zululand Data," *African Studies* 1 (1942): 243–60.

76. Akbar S. Ahmed, *Resistance and Control in Pakistan*, rev. ed. (London: Routledge, 2004), 144–47.

77. Ahmed, personal communication via e-mail, August 2, 2008.

78. Ahmed, *Resistance and Control in Pakistan*.

79. Field note on conversation with Pakistani journalists and writers, Peshawar, June 24, 2006. *Field Notebook 04/06, Northwest Frontier and Afghanistan*, b30.

80. Ibid.

81. For an alternative analysis of Taliban organizational structure that is somewhat at variance with mine, see Shahid Afsar, Chris Samples, and Thomas Wood, "The Taliban: An Organizational Analysis," *Military Review* (May–June 2008): 58–72.

82. For a detailed description of the flying column technique and its invention by the IRA in the early 1920s, see Tom Barry, *Guerilla Days in Ireland* (Dublin: Anvil Books, 1981).

83. For an excellent and extremely detailed description of Taliban operational methods, recruitment, and organizational development, see the comprehensive study in Giustozzi, *Koran, Kalashnikov and Laptop*.

84. Discussion with tribal affairs officers, Kabul, October 26, 2006.

85. Caroe, *Pathans* 550 B.C.–1957 A.D., 393: "The nearest I can get to it is to liken the Mahsud to a wolf, the Wazir [the other main tribe of Waziristan] to a panther. Both are splendid creatures; the panther is slier, sleeker and has more grace, the wolf-pack is more purposeful, more united and more dangerous."

86. Discussion with tribal leaders, Peshawar, June 24 and 25, 2006.

87. Discussion with Afghan intelligence officials, Kabul, Kandahar, and Asadabad, May 25, 2006, and March 12–16, 2008.

88. Discussion with surrendered Taliban leader and local tribal elders of Musa Qaleh District, Helmand Province, March 12, 2008. Discussion with provincial governor of Kandahar, police officials, Afghan army officers, and local community leaders, Kandahar, March 15, 2008.

89. See Ernesto "Che" Guevara, *On Guerrilla Warfare* (New York: Ocean Press, 2006), and Régis Debray, *Révolution dans la révolution?* (Paris: Editions Maspero, 1972).

90. Julian Schofield, "Why Pakistan Failed: Tribal Focoism in Kashmir" (paper presented at the annual meeting of the American Political Science Association, Philadelphia, August 31, 2006); www.allacademic.com/meta/p153463_index.html.

91. In Pakistan, the Civil Armed Forces (the Pakistan Rangers, Frontier Corps, and Pakistan Coast Guards) are the field organizations of the Ministry of Interior, while the Armed Services belong to the Ministry of Defence.

92. See Lester W. Grau, ed., *The Bear Went over the Mountain: Soviet Combat Tactics in Afghanistan* (Washington, D.C.: National Defense University Press, 1996), 93, 108–9, and 180.

93. Ibid.

94. Dr. Carter Malkasian, personal communication via e-mail, July 30, 2008.

95. LTC Chris Cavoli, personal communication via e-mail, July 31, 2008.

96. Dr. Carter Malkasian, Center for Naval Analyses and Asadabad PRT, personal communication via e-mail, April 27, 2008.

97. Lieutenant Commander Chris Cavoli, personal communication via e-mail, May 1, 2008.

98. Ibid.

99. Field note, March 13, 2008, in *Afghanistan 2008 Fieldnotes* (1), a39–a40, unpublished field notebook entry in the author's possession.

100. Ibid., a40–a41.

101. Interviews with Commander Larry Legree, Washington, D.C., May 1, 2008, and Cavoli, Garmisch, Germany, March 18, 2008; e-mail discussions with Colonel Chip Preysler, Lieutenant Commander Bill Ostlund, and Malkasian, April–May 2008.

102. Cavoli, personal communication via e-mail, May 2008.

103. Lieutenant General Eikenberry, personal communication by e-mail, November 1, 2008.

104. Ibid.

105. Ibid.

106. Ibid.

107. Ibid.

108. Interviews with Legree, Asadabad, March 13, 2008, and Washington, D.C., May 1, 2008.

109. Malkasian, personal communication via e-mail, April 27, 2008.

110. Cavoli, personal communication via e-mail, May 1, 2008.

111. Ibid.

112. In fact, a similar attack to this occurred about 20 miles south of this location on July 13, 2008.

113. Field note, March 13, 2008, in *Afghanistan 2008 Fieldnotes* (1), a41–a45.

114. Legree, interview, Washington D.C., May 1, 2008.

115. See "Operation Mountain Fury by Afghan and Coalition Forces Launched," *Afghan PenLog*, September 17, 2006; http://afghanpenlog-en.blogspot.com/2006/09/operation-mountain-fury-by-afghan.html.

116. See Ely Brown, "Battle in the Mountains, but Using More Than Force: U.S. Forces See Local Solution for Ridding Troubled Area of Afghan Insurgents" *Nightline*, September 11, 2006; http://abcnews.go.com/Nightline/story?id=2422004&page=1.

117. Ibid.

118. Ibid.

119. Cavoli, personal communication via several e-mails, May 2008, and Amber Robinson, "Chosin Soldiers See Improvements on the Ground," *Fort Drum Blizzard Online*, September 28, 2006; www.drum.army.mil/sites/postnews/blizzard/blizzard_archives/news.asp?id=2&issuedate=9–28-2006.

120. Cavoli, personal communication via several e-mails, May 2008.

121. Ibid.

Chapter 3

1. Note on sources: this chapter draws on participant observations and interview notes from my tour in Iraq as senior counterinsurgency advisor to General David Petraeus, which were recorded as a series of narratives, interview and meeting notes, analysis notes, and participant observations in three field note journals between February and August 2007. It also draws on two field note journals compiled during temporary duty assignments to Iraq in 2006. All sources used are unclassified, open source materials. In addition, portions of this chapter first appeared in *Small Wars Journal* (www.smallwars journal.com) in January–August 2007.

2. Though several are forthcoming, notably by Bob Woodward, Linda Robinson, and Thomas E. Ricks.

3. *Counterinsurgency*, United States Army, Field Manual 3-24 / United States Marine Corps, Marine Corps Warfighting Publication 3-33.5 (Chicago: University of Chicago Press, 2006); www.usgcoin.org/library/doctrine/COIN-FM3-24.pdf.

4. For an account of this process by one of its key players, see John A. Nagl, "The Evolution and Importance of Army/Marine Corps Field Manual 3–24, *Counterinsurgency*," foreword to *Counterinsurgency*; www.press.uchicago.edu/Misc/Chicago/841519foreword.html.

5. See *History of the Shrine of Imam Ali Al-Naqi and Imam Hasan Al-Askari, Peace Be upon Them*; www.al-islam.org/shrines/samarra.htm.

6. Jassim M. Hussain, *Occultation of the Twelfth Imam: A Historical Background* (London: Routledge, 1986).

7. See Ellen Knickmeyer and K. I. Ibrahim, "Bombing Shatters Mosque in Iraq: Attack on Shiite Shrine Sets Off Protests, Violence," *Washington Post*, February 23, 2006, A1.

8. Discussions with translator, May 2007, Baghdad, in *Fieldnotes: Iraq 2007 (2)*, unpublished field notebook entry in the author's possession.

9. Conversation with locally employed staff, Baghdad embassy, March 2006, *Fieldnotes 01/2006*

10. Field note, Monday, March 6, 2006, Baghdad, *Fieldnotes 01/2006*.

11. Author's personal review of BUA slides from January–June 2006, on the shared MNF-I hard drive, over several weeks in June 2007.

12. Interview with Colonel A.K.M., counterinsurgency school, Taji, June 18, 2007, *Fieldnotes Iraq 2007 no. 3*, unpublished field notebook entry in the author's possession.

13. Discussions with Tom Warrick, U.S. State Department, Baghdad, March 2–7, 2006, and Washington, D.C., May 2, 2007.

14. See Colin Kahl, Michele Flournoy, and Shawn Brimley, *Shaping the Iraq Inheritance* (Washington, D.C.: Center for a New American Security, 2008), 21.

15. Discussions with Colonel H. R. McMaster, Baghdad, over multiple sessions in March–April 2007.

16. Discussions with special forces officer, Kuwait Embassy Regional Security Initiative meeting, Kuwait, March 10, 2006.

17. In north and central Baghdad.

18. Field note, Baghdad, March 4, 2006, Fieldnotes 01/2006.

19. Kahl et al., *Shaping the Iraq Inheritance*, 14.

20. Ibid.

21. Colonel J. B. Burton, *Dagger Brigade Combat Team and the Battle for North-west Baghdad*, briefing delivered April 7, 2007, document in the author's possession. See also Ghaith Abdul-Ahad, "Meet Abu Abed: The U.S.'s New Ally against al-Qaida," *Guardian*, November 10, 2007, for a description of events in Ameriya during and after this period.

22. Field notes, visit to Ameriya bank, March 29, 2007.

23. Discussion with LTC Dale Kuehl, Ameriya, April 2007 (multiple occasions).

24. Discussion with commanders of Fourth Brigade Combat Team, Twenty-fifth Infantry Division, embedded provincial reconstruction team, and Iraqi government officials, May 5–8, 2007.

25. Conversation with Sunni community leaders, Baghdad, March 2007.

26. I am indebted to Brigadier Justin Kelly of the Australian army for this formulation.

27. I am indebted to Dr. Steve Biddle of the Council on Foreign Relations for this insight.

28. Discussions with detainee operations staff, September 2008.

29. Discussion with Thomas E. Ricks, Washington D.C., September 2008.

30. The White House, *President's Address to the Nation*, January 10, 2007; www.white house.gov/news/releases/2007/01/20070110–7.html.

31. Discussion with political advisers and diplomats, Baghdad, March 4–8, 2006.

32. In discussions during the Joint Strategic Assessment Team process, Baghdad, multiple sessions during March 2007.

33. Personal communication, March 2006.

34. Field notes, March 28, 2007, Fieldnotes, Iraq 2007 (1), a48.

35. Lieutenant General Raymond Odierno, remarks to the Third Infantry Division Senior Leaders Conference, Faw Palace, Camp Victory, Baghdad, April 3, 2007 (my recorded note of the meeting, in *Fieldnote, Iraq 2007 (1), ai*).

36. Field notes, March 23–28, 2007, in Fieldnotes, Iraq 2007 (1), a45.

37. Field note, conversation in Baghdad, March 4, 2006, in Fieldnotes 01/2006.

38. For Dr. Sepp's insights based on his tour, see Kalev I. Sepp, "Best Practices in Counterinsurgency," *Military Review* (May–June 2005), 8, http://usacac.army.mil/CAC/milreview/English/MayJun05/MayJun05/sepp.pdf.

39. Field notes, Karkh District and Haifa Street patrols, multiple occasions during March 2007, Fieldnotes, Iraq 2007 (1).

40. Field note, Ameriya battlefield circulation, March 28, 2007, Fieldnotes, Iraq 2007 (1).

41. Peter R. Mansoor, *Baghdad at Sunrise: A Brigade Commander's War in Iraq*, Yale Military History Series (New Haven, Conn.: Yale University Press, 2008).

42. Field notes, visit to 1/325 Infantry, Kadhimiya, May 16, 2007.

43. Field notes, visit to 1/5 Cavalry in Ameriya, March 28, 2007.

44. http://smallwarsjournal.com/blog/2007/06/hq-mnci-counterinsurgency-guid/.

45. See Ralph Peters, "Dishonest Doctrine," *Armed Forces Journal*, December 2007, http://www.armedforcesjournal.com/2007/12/3144330.

46. None of which are particularly original—all these points are made at various places in David Galula's 1964 classic *Counterinsurgency Warfare: Theory and Practice*.

47. Kahl et al., *Shaping the Iraq Inheritance*, 14.

48. I developed this framework while writing a later (October 2004) version of "Countering Global Insurgency" (see http://smallwarsjournal.com/documents/kilcullen. pdf) and covered some elements of it in the Iraq appendix to that paper. I have since presented this framework in various forums, including the Quadrennial Defense Review, 2004–2005; the Eisenhower National Security Series (lectures), on multiple occasions during lectures at the Naval War College and State Department Foreign Service Institute in 2006; and at the United States Government Counterinsurgency Conference, Washington, D.C., September 28–29, 2006. I also briefed it to the Pentagon's "Plan B" team, November 15, 2006.

49. Zinni, remarks, Brookings Institution National Security Seminar, November 2006 (my recorded notes of the meeting).

50. See *Countering Global Insurgency* (2004), appendix. 1; www.smallwarsjournal.com/ kilcullen.pdf.

51. For an account of Rumsfeld's interactions with the media on this issue, see Thomas E. Ricks, *Fiasco: The American Military Adventure in Iraq* (New York: Penguin Press, 2006), 171.

52. For the classic original account of problem wickedness, see H. Rittel and M. Webber, "Dilemmas in a General Theory of Planning," *Policy Sciences* 4 (Amsterdam: Elsevier, 1973), 155–69.

53. For a detailed discussion of operational design in counterinsurgency see *Counterinsurgency*, esp. chap. 4, "Designing Counterinsurgency Campaigns and Operations"; www.fas.org/irp/doddir/army/fm3-24.pdf.

54. Field notes, operation Arcadia II, north Babil Province, May 8, 2007.

55. Field notes, Baghdad, June 2007.

56. Discussions with command group interpreter, multiple occasions in June 2007.

57. See, for example, Max Gluckmann, "Inter-hierarchical Roles: Professional and Party Ethics in Tribal Areas in South and Central Africa"; www6.ufrgs.br/horizon/files/ antropolitica/gluckman_roles.pdf.

58. For instance, one sheikh in a district near Iskandariya south of Baghdad was a business owner, was a mayor of the local council, was connected by lineage to several other tribal and community leaders in the local area, and sponsored the recruitment of large numbers of tribal police and local security forces, giving him multiple overlapping networks of influence.

59. MNC-I tribal analysis document in my possession.

60. Field note, June 5, 2007, *Fieldnotes, Iraq 2007 (1)*.

61. Conversation with company commander responsible for Sadr al Yusufiya, in the field south of Baghdad, May 22, 2007.

62. Field notes, combat advising in AO Commando, May–June 2007, *Fieldnotes, Iraq 2007 (1)* and *Fieldnotes, Iraq 2007 (2)*.

63. Discussion with officers of 1/5 Cavalry Regiment, and personal participant observation, Ameriya, Baghdad, June 5–6, 2007.

64. Colonel J. B. Burton, commanding Dagger Brigade Combat Team, northwest Baghdad, personal communication during several conversations in Washington D.C., April 2008.

65. Briefing prepared by Lieutenant Dale Kuehl, Commanding Officer First Battalion Fifth U.S. Cavalry, "Ameriya Freedom Fighters: Meeting with Dr. Kilcullen MNF-I Senior Counterinsurgency Advisor," June 2007, copy in the author's possession.

66. Sadr al Yusufiya District, Area of Operations Commando, southwest of Baghdad, field notes, multiple occasions in May and June 2007.

67. Dr. Mary Habeck, interview, May 15, 2008.

68. Lieutenant Colonel L'Etoile, interview, Washington D.C., April 11, 2008.

69. Ibid.

70. Ibid.

71. L'Etoile, "Briefing Notes, Joint Urban Warrior 2008," unclassified briefing in the author's possession.

72. Participant observation, Ameriya District, Baghdad, June 2–30, 2007.

73. Iraqi tribal leader in conversation with U.S. battalion commander, central Baghdad, July 2007.

74. Kuehl, personal communication, Baghdad, June 6, 2007.

75. Former insurgent leader, in conversation, Baghdad, June 2007.

76. MNF-I headquarters, working paper on national reconciliation, in the author's possession.

77. Field note, Baghdad, June 5, 2008, *Fieldnotes, Iraq 2007 (2)*.

78. Discussions with company and platoon commanders, 1/325 Infantry, Kadhimiya district, Baghdad, March 28, and May 16, 2007.

79. Discussion with Colonel H.R. McMaster, Baghdad, multiple occasions in April 2007, Colonel J. B. Burton, Washington D.C., April 10, 2008, L'Etoile, Potomac Maryland, April 11, 2008.

80. Field note, Baghdad, June 5, 2008, *Fieldnotes, Iraq 2007 (2)*.

81. Discussions with Iraqi Ministry of Defense, M5, M3, and M2 staffs, Baghdad, multiple occasions in May–June 2007.

82. I am indebted for this insight to Brigadier Justin Kelly of the Australian army.

83. See, for example, the two contrasting accounts of life in Ramadi in 2006 and 2007, in David J. Morris, "The Big Suck: Notes from the Jarhead Underground," *Virginia*

Quarterly Review 83, 1 (March 2007), 144–69, http://www.vqronline.org/articles/2007/winter/morris-jarhead-underground/ and "Trophy Town: Ramadi Revisited," *Virginia Quarterly Review* 84, 1 (winter 2008): 30–53, http://www.vqronline.org/articles/2008/winter/morris-trophy-town/.

84. Discussion with Major General John Allen, Potomac, Maryland, April 9, 2008.

85. Participant observation; Baghdad, multiple occasions in May and June 2007.

86. Participant observation, Ameriya District, June 2–30, 2007.

87. Participant observation, Baghdad, June 2007.

88. But see Kahl et al., *Shaping the Iraq Inheritance*, for an account that does reflect the importance of the Awakening as a political development.

Chapter 4

1. This account is drawn from my personal field notebooks of September 1999–February 2000; from my field notes taken to support the East Timor case study in my doctoral dissertation, "The Political Consequences of Military Operations in Indonesia, 1945–99" (University of New South Wales, 2000); from my company war diary for Operation Warden (Support Company, Second Battalion, Royal Australian Regiment—the Ready Battalion Group of Third Brigade, Australia's rapid deployment force), and from my previously published accounts "Rethinking the Basis of Infantry Close Combat" *Australian Army Journal* 1, 1 (June 2003): 29–40, and "Timor: Model of a Modern Deployment?," in Peter Dennis and Jeffrey Grey, eds., *Battles Near and Far: A Century of Operational Deployment—Proceedings of the Chief of Army's Military History Conference 2004* (Canberra: Australian War Memorial, 2005).

2. See Don Greenlees and Robert Garran, "Black Hawks Downed," *Australian*, May 23, 2002.

3. The mission verb "capture" implies the requirement to fight against opposition. On receiving our orders around midnight the night before in Townsville, I had rashly questioned the accuracy of this: wouldn't the appropriate verb be "secure," since the Indonesians were technically cooperating with us and had agreed (albeit extremely reluctantly) to the intervention? No, I was told, we needed to be ready to fight if need be, and so the mission verb was "capture."

4. The INTERFET was made up of 9,908 troops from 22 nations, of whom 5,490 were Australian. See Bob Breen, *Mission Accomplished: East Timor* (Sydney: Allen and Unwin, 2000), 5.

5. See Seth G. Jones, Jeremy M. Wilson, Andrew Rathmell, and K. Jack Riley, *Establishing Law and Order after Conflict* (Santa Monica, Calif.: RAND Corporation, 2005).

6. See James Cotton, *East Timor, Australia and Regional Order: Intervention and Its Aftermath in Southeast Asia* (London: Routledge, 2004), 26–28, and Paul Monk, "East Timor: Truth and Consequences," *Quadrant*, January 1, 2000.

7. For the definitive official history of the Borneo Confrontation, see Peter Dennis and Jeffrey Grey, *Emergency and Confrontation: Australian Military Operations in Malaya and Borneo 1950–66* (Sydney: Allen and Unwin, 1996).

8. For the text of this treaty see http://untreaty.un.org/unts/120001_144071/16/9/00013476.pdf.

9. For a detailed breakdown of militia structure and activities, see Kilcullen, "Political Consequences," chap. 4; www.library.unsw.edu.au/~thesis/adt-ADFA/public/adt-ADFA20060323.121124/index.html.

10. Participant observation, Batugade, October 2, 1999.

11. James Dobbins, Seth G. Jones, Keith Crane, and Beth Cole DeGrasse, *The Beginner's Guide to Nation-Building* (Santa Monica, Calif.: RAND Corporation, 2007), 124.

12. Total casualties for INTERFET were remarkably low. Out of 9,908 troops deployed (of whom 5,490 were Australian), total deaths were 4 and injuries/illnesses were 1,080—a total casualty rate of 10.9 percent. See Breen, *Mission Accomplished*, 5.

13. See ibid. for detailed accounts of these incidents.

14. See Kilcullen, "Political Consequences," 123.

15. See http://news.bbc.co.uk/2/hi/americas/2146395.stm for an obituary of this brilliant and cultured man, whose loss was one of the lesser tragedies amid the greater and even more tragic lost opportunity of Iraq in 2003.

16. See Jones et al., *Establishing Law and Order after Conflict*, and Dobbins et al., *Beginner's Guide to Nation-Building*.

17. A typical Timorese mixture of Portuguese and Tetuñ, this meant "Major Kilcullen, frontier region near Balibo" (Portuguese) then "Good friend of the people" in Tetuñ-Praça, the lingua franca of East Timor.

18. For a sanitized discussion of this incident and more broadly of formal and informal power structures among local leadership groups, see Kilcullen, "Political Consequences," 145–50

19. The Timorese concept of "houses of origin" derives from both place and ancestry, so does not directly equate to the standard anthropological concepts of clan or tribe. I use these terms here as a form of shorthand only.

20. Kilcullen, "Political Consequences,"

21. Ibid., 149, 163.

22. James Dunn, *Timor: A People Betrayed* (Sydney: ABC Books, 1996), 304.

23. Abel Guterres, "An East Timor Briefing," in P. Kingsbury and G. Barton, eds., *Difference and Tolerance: Human Rights Issues in Southeast Asia* (Geelong, Australia: Deakin University Press, 1994), 61.

24. See field notes cited in Kilcullen, "Political Consequences," chap. 4.

25. J. G. Taylor, *Indonesia's Forgotten War: The Hidden History of East Timor* (London: Zed Books, 1991), 7–8.

26. J. J. Fox and C. Sather, *Origins, Ancestry and Alliance: Explorations in Austronesian Ethnography* (Canberra: Research School of Pacific and Asian Studies, Australian National University, 1996), 134.

27. Kilcullen, "Political Consequences," 210.

28. Ibid., chap. 4.

29. Near Balibo on November 15, 1999.

30. Participant observation, Balibo, successive Sundays in November 1999.

31. See Australian Defence Force, *Future Warfighting Concept*; www.defence.gov.au/publications/fwc.pdf.

32. See Russell W. Glenn, *Counterinsurgency in a Test Tube: Analyzing the Success of the Regional Assistance Mission to Solomon Islands (RAMSI)* (Santa Monica, Calif.: RAND Corporation, 2007).

33. I am indebted to Professor Erin Simpson of the U.S. Marine Corps Staff College for drawing my attention to this conceptual framework.

34. See Stathis N. Kalyvas, *The Logic of Violence in Civil War* (New York: Cambridge University Press, 2006).

35. There were rumors to this effect in 2002, and later a specific allegation in 2005 that four AQ members had entered East Timorese territory, but these were subsequently discounted. See "Al-Qaeda Slipped into East Timor: Reports," *Sydney Morning Herald*, March 10, 2005; www.smh.com.au/news/Global-Terrorism/AlQaeda-slipped-into-East-Timor-reports/2005/03/10/1110417610691.html.

36. See David J. Kilcullen, "Globalisation and the Development of Indonesian Counterinsurgency Tactics," *Small Wars and Insurgencies* 17, 1 (March 2006): 44–64.

37. See Kilcullen, "Political Consequences," chap. 4.

38. Conversations with fellow language students, staff, and members of the student community (including people of Papuan and Timorese origin), Bandung, Indonesia, multiple occasions in June–August 1993 and March–July 1994.

39. For example, many activists claimed that the denial of education in Tetuñ for East Timorese students was a form of "cultural genocide." In mid-October 1999, I had the opportunity to examine in detail the teaching materials in the almost intact Balibo schoolhouse, and found Tetuñ-language teaching materials for pupils up to late primary school, and both Tetuñ- and Indonesian-language materials for older students—in other words, precisely the same policies applied to Javanese in Java, and to other ethnic groups elsewhere in Indonesia.

40. Discussions with students and staff at Sekolah Staf Angkatan Darat (SESKOAD), the Indonesian Army Command and Staff College, May 2001.

41. Ibid.

42. Kilcullen, "Globalisation and the Development of Indonesian Counterinsurgency Tactics."

43. Ibid.

44. Kilcullen, "Political Consequences," chap. 4.

45. For a particularly energetic version of this assessment, see Clinton Fernandes, *Reluctant Saviour: Australia, Indonesia, and the Independence of East Timor* (Melbourne: Scribe, 2004).

46. For the eventual full report of this commission, established in March 2005, see National Reconciliation Commission, *Overcoming Violence through the Power of Reconciliation: Report of the National Reconciliation Commission* (Bangkok: Secretariat of the Cabinet, May 16, 2006); http://thailand.ahrchk.net/docs/nrc_report_en.pdf.

47. Ibid., 9.

48. Peter Chalk, *The Malay-Muslim Insurgency in Southern Thailand: Understanding the Conflict's Evolving Dynamic*, RAND Counterinsurgency Study, paper 5 (Santa Monica, Calif.: RAND Corporation, 2008), 10.

49. For an insight into this controversy, see Michael Connors, "War on Error and the Southern Fire: How Terrorism Analysts Get It Wrong," *Critical Asian Studies* 38, 1 (March 2006): 151–75.

50. For example, the U.S. ambassador in Bangkok during this period, Ralph "Skip" Boyce, was highly energetic, deeply versed in regional affairs, and extremely capable—but was heavily constrained by security regulations (imposed from Washington) that prevented him from visiting or staying overnight in the South. The Australian ambassador, Bill Patterson, made frequent visits to the area but toward the end of his tour became increasingly constrained by Canberra-imposed security restrictions (interviews with Boyce, Jakarta and Bangkok, January 18–20, 2006; Patterson, Canberra, August 29, 2008).

51. The 2000 census, quoted in the 2008 edition of the *CIA Factbook* (www.cia.gov/library/publications/the-world-factbook/geos/th.html#People) identifies the religious makeup of the Thai population as Buddhist, 94.6 percent; Muslim, 4.6 percent; Christian, 0.7 percent; other, 0.1 percent.

52. Discussion with academics from the National Reconciliation Council, Bangkok, January 22, 2006.

53. Field notes, "Field Visit to Southeast Asia," *Fieldnotes 01/2006*, Bangkok, January 22, 2006, and January 23, 2006.

54. David Galula, *Counterinsurgency Warfare: Theory and Practice* (London: Pall Mall Press, 1964), 14.

55. Quoted in Seth Mydans, "Muslim Insurgency Stokes Fear in Southern Thailand," *International Herald Tribune*, February 25, 2007.

56. Duncan McCargo, *Tearing the Land Apart: Islam and Legitimacy in Southern Thailand* (Ithaca, N.Y.: Cornell University Press, 2008), 158.

57. Ibid., 158–63.

58. See U.S. Department of State, *International Boundary Study No. 57, Malaysia—Thailand Boundary* (Washington, D.C.: Office of the Geographer, Bureau of Intelligence and Research, State Department, November 15, 1965); www.law.fsu.edu/library/collection/LimitsinSeas/IBS057.pdf.

59. For details of some of the more oppressive measures of this period, see International Crisis Group, *Southern Thailand: Insurgency not Jihad*, report no. 98 (Brussels: International Crisis Group, May 18, 2005), 2–5.

60. McCargo, *Tearing the Land Apart*, 3–4.

61. For a detailed, if very Malay-slanted, account of the history of Patani, see Ibrahim Syukri, *History of the Malay Kingdom of Patani*, translated from the Jawi by Conner Bailey and John Miksic (University of Ohio: Swallow Press, 1985) (originally published as *Sejarah Kerajaan Melayu Patani*, 1950).

62. McCargo, *Tearing the Land Apart*, 4 (emphasis added).

63. International Crisis Group, *Southern Thailand*, 2005.

64. McCargo, *Tearing the Land Apart*, 1.

65. Most militants in the south appear to reject the "separatist" tag, arguing that since the authority of the Thai state over Patani is illegitimate, they are not seeking secession but merely the restoration of legitimate independence.

66. International Crisis Group, *Southern Thailand*, 2005.

67. Ibid.

68. Ibid.

69. McCargo, *Tearing the Land Apart*, 16.

70. International Crisis Group, *Southern Thailand*, 2005.

71. Ibid.

72. National Reconciliation Commission, *Overcoming Violence*, 11 (emphasis added).

73. For examples of this analysis, see Andrew Holt, "Thailand's Troubled Border: Islamic Insurgency or Criminal Playground?" *Jamestown Terrorism Monitor* 2, 10 (May 20, 2004): 4–5 Zachary Abuza, "A Conspiracy of Silence: Who Is behind the Escalating Insurgency in Southern Thailand?" *Jamestown Terrorism Monitor* 3, 9 (May 6, 2005), and Rohan Gunaratna and Arabinda Acharya, eds., *Conflict and Terrorism in Southern Thailand* (Singapore: Marshall Cavendish Academic, 2005).

74. *Ustadz* are religious teachers, primarily filling the role of instructors at *pondoh* (Islamic religious schools) and at private Islamic colleges, which teach a combined religious and secular Thai curriculum. The term *ustadz* also covers teachers at *tadika*, weekend Islamic religious classes aimed at students attending regular school.

75. See "Thailand Now Fake Passport Capital for Criminal Underworld, Terrorists," *Irrawaddy*, July 25, 2008.

76. For an account of Hambali's arrest and speculation by the Thai government on his operational role, see AFP news report, "Hambali Planned Action in Thailand before Arrest: Thai PM", August 16, 2003, http://quickstart.clari.net/qs_se/webnews/wed/cu/Qattacks-hambali-thailand.RTS__DaF.html.

77. See CNN, "September 11: The Asian Blueprint," March 11, 2002; http://edition.cnn.com/2002/WORLD/asiapcf/southeast/03/11/gen.phil.terror.blueprint/?related.

78. For an official U.S. government account of Hambali's activities see U.S. Department of Defense, *Summary of Evidence for Combatant Status Review Tribunal—Hambali*,

Riduan bin Isomuddin (Washington, D.C.: Government Printing Office, March 28, 2007); www.defenselink.mil/news/ISN10019.pdf#1.

79. Discussion with Bill Patterson, Australian ambassador to Thailand, Canberra, August 29, 2008.

80. McCargo, *Tearing the Land Apart*, 137.

81. Ibid., 136.

82. Ibid., 134–39.

83. See International Crisis Group, *Recycling Militants in Indonesia: Darul Islam and the Australian Embassy Bombing*, Asia Report no. 92 (Singapore and Brussels: International Crisis Group, February 22, 2005).

84. See Ronald Lukens-Bull, *A Peaceful Jihad: Negotiating Identity and Modernity in Muslim Java* (London: Palgrave Macmillan, 2005).

85. See, for example, the findings in S. Kartodirdjo, *Protest Movements in Rural Java* (Singapore: Oxford University Press, 1973).

86. Kilcullen, "Political Consequences," 59.

87. East Timor, field note T47/AF/1, referenced in Kilcullen, "Political Consequences," 59n.

88. McCargo, *Tearing the Land Apart*, 137.

89. For a discussion of liberation theology and the mainstream Catholic Church's rejection of it, see Christian Smith, *The Emergence of Liberation Theology: Radical Religion and the Social Movement Theory* (Chicago: University of Chicago Press, 1991).

90. Chalk, *Malay-Muslim Insurgency in Southern Thailand*, 13–14.

91. "Thailand: Senior Australian Police Officer outlines Regional Challenge," Radio Australia, September 21, 2007; www.radioaustralia.net.au/programguide/stories/200709/s2038313.htm.

92. Australian Government, Department of Foreign Affairs and Trade, *Technical Assistance and Training: AUSTRAC's Counter Terrorist Financing Work in South East Asia* (Canberra: Australian Government Printing Office, December 7, 2007); www.austrac.gov.au/technical_assistance_and_training.html.

93. See www.usdoj.gov/criminal/opdat/ for details.

94. See the website of the Joint United States Military Advisory Group Thailand: www.jusmagthai.com/.

95. Chalk, *Malay-Muslim Insurgency in Southern Thailand*, 15.

96. Malay Muslim *mufti* in Pattani province, quoted in Chalk, ibid., 16.

97. See for example the detailed particularistic study of *bibiane* elite Pukhtun women in the traditional society of Swat, Pakistan, recounted in Amineh Ahmed Hoti, "Death and Celebration among Muslim Women: A Case Study from Pakistan," *Modern Asian Studies* 39 (2005): 929–80.

98. Participant observation, during travel in the FATA and in Khost and Kunar provinces, Afghanistan, 2006–2008. Fieldnotes, *N. W. Frontier and Afghanistan 2006*, "Traveling into the FATA"; and *Fieldnotes, Afghanistan-Pakistan, Autumn 2006*; and *Afghanistan Fieldnotes 2008 (1)*, "Afghanistan field visit, March 2008."

99. Winston L. Spencer Churchill, *The Story of the Malakand Field Force: An Episode of Frontier War* (London: Thomas Nelson, 1916), 273.

100. Ibid., pp. 231–24, 267–90.

101. Ibid., pp. 269–70.

102. Ibid., 272.

103. See, for example, Declan Walsh, "Demolished by the Pakistan Army: The Frontier Village Punished for Harbouring the Taliban," *Guardian*, May 20, 2008, http://www.guardian.co.uk/world/2008/may/20/pakistan.

104. Imtiaz Ali and Massoud Ansari, "Pakistan Fury as CIA Airstrike on Village Kills 18 in Damadola," *Telegraph*, January 15, 2006, http://www.telegraph.co.uk/news/world news/asia/pakistan/1507895/Pakistan-fury-as-CIA-airstrike-on-village-kills-18.html; see also Bill Roggio, "The Pakistani Frontier" (January 2006), at the website ThreatsWatch: http://threatswatch.org/inbrief/2006/01/the-pakistani-frontier/.

105. Eid ul-Adha (the Festival of Sacrifice; عيد الأضحى 'Id ul-' *Aḍḥā* in Arabic, known as *Loy Akhtar* to local Pashtuns) is a major Islamic festival celebrated worldwide that commemorates, somewhat ironically in this case, Allah's release of Ibrahim (Abraham) from a vow he had made to kill his beloved son (Ishmael in the Islamic teaching, Isaac in Judeo-Christian tradition) as a sign of religious devotion.

106. Craig Whitlock, "The New Al-Qaeda Central: Far from Declining, the Network Has Rebuilt, with Fresh Faces and a Vigorous Media Arm," *Washington Post*, September 9, 2007, 1; www.washingtonpost.com/wp-dyn/content/article/2007/09/08/AR2007090801845_pf.html.

107. Salman Masood and Mohammed Khan, "Pakistan Says It Killed 80 Militants in Attack on Islamic School," *New York Times*, October 31, 2006, http://www.nytimes.com/2006/10/31/world/asia/31pakistan.html.

108. Ibid.

109. Jason Burke, "Al-Qaeda Chief Dies in Missile Air Strike," *Observer*, June 1, 2008; www.guardian.co.uk/world/2008/jun/01/alqaida.pakistan.

110. Interview with member of NAS staff, Peshawar, June 24, 2006, Fieldnotes, N.W. Frontier & Afghanistan 2006, b27.

111. See CNN, "U.S. Suspects Taliban Leader behind Bhutto Plot," December 29, 2007; www.cnn.com/2007/WORLD/asiapcf/12/28/bhutto.dhs.alqaeda/index.html.

112. The Deobandi or Devbandi school of Islam is a Sunni revivalist movement named after the town of Deoband in India's Uttar Pradesh Province, where in 1866 its founders established the Darul Uloom school to propagate its teachings. Deobandi thought follows the Hanafi school of jurisprudence and the Maturidi theology (*aqida*), favors an extremely strict interpretation of *shari'a*, and includes *jihad* as one of its five pillars. Having been founded partly as a reaction against the corrupting effect of British imperialism in colonial India, it has a strongly anticolonial and anti-Western streak. Deobandism has spread to Afghanistan, Pakistan, South Africa, and the United Kingdom, and has links to militant and activist organizations including the Taliban, Tablighi Jamaat, and Hizb-ut Tahrir.

113. Fieldnotes, N. W. Frontier and Afghanistan 2006, "Dinner with FATA Legislators, May 24, 2006," b54–55 (conversation in Pashtu through a U.S. Embassy translator).

114. For accounts of this period see Ahmed Rashid, Taliban: Militant Islam, Oil and Fundamentalism in Central Asia (New Haven, Conn.: Yale University Press, 2001), and Descent into Chaos: The United States and the Failure of Nation-building in Pakistan, Afghanistan and Central Asia (New York: Viking Adult, 2008). See also William Maley, The Afghanistan Wars (Palgrave Macmillan, 2002).

115. For a comprehensive account of successive Pakhtun uprisings and violent episodes of resistance to external rule, see Olaf Caroe, The Pathans 550 B.C.–1957 A.D. (London: St. Martin's Press, 1958).

116. Thomas H. Johnson and M. Chris Mason, "No Sign until the Burst of Fire: Understanding the Pakistan-Afghanistan Frontier," International Security 32, 4 (spring 2008): 67–68.

117. Personal communication, Washington, D.C., July 2008.

118. Lawrence Wright, The Looming Tower: Al Qaeda and the Road to 9/11 (New York: Knopf, 2006), 129–30, 179.

119. For detailed accounts of the history of AQ and of Usama bin Laden, see Peter Bergen, Holy War Inc.: Inside the Secret World of Osama bin Laden (New York: Free Press, 2002), and The Osama bin Laden I Know: An Oral History of al Qa'eda's Leader (New York: Free Press, 2006).

120. See Maley, Afghanistan Wars, and Rashid, Taliban, for details of this growth.

121. Discussions with USAID mission personnel, Islamabad and Peshawar, multiple occasions during June and October 2006.

122. Discussions with Narcotics Affairs Section staff, Islamabad, June 22, 2006, Fieldnotes, N. W. Frontier and Afghanistan 2006, a15.

123. Interview with member of Narcotics Affairs Section staff, Peshawar, June 24, 2006, Fieldnotes, N. W. Frontier and Afghanistan, 2006, b27.

124. Interview with AID mission staff, Islamabad, June 22, 2006. Field notes, N. W. Frontier and Afghanistan 2006, pp. a13–14.

125. See Center for Defense Information, Action Update March 15–28; www.cdi.org/program/document.cfm?DocumentID=2160&from_page=/index.cfm.

126. See Frontline, "The Return of the Taliban," aired on U.S. television October 3, 2006.

127. Rahimullah Yusufzai, "Nek Muhammad: Profile," BBC News, June 18, 2004; news.bbc.co.uk/1/hi/world/south_asia/3819871.stm.

128. Unclassified conversations with intelligence and operations officers in Kabul, Bagram, and Khost, multiple occasions in October–November 2006. Fieldnotes, Afghanistan, Autumn 2006.

129. Discussion with political agent, Khyber Agency, and chief secretary, FATA Secretariat, Peshawar, June 25, 2006.

130. See Akbar Ahmed, Resistance and Control in Pakistan (London: Routledge, 2004), app. A.

131. Discussion with political agent, Khyber Agency.

132. For the purposes of this assessment, the following references describe counter insurgency best practices, as adopted by U.S. and allied forces, and are used as the template against which Pakistani operations are evaluated: Cohen, E., Crane, C., J. Horvath, and J. Nagl, "Principles, Imperatives and Paradoxes of Counterinsurgency," *Military Review* (March–April 2006): 49–53; D. J. Kilcullen "Twenty-eight Articles: Fundamentals of Company-level Counterinsurgency," *Military Review* (May–June 2006): 103–8; J. A. Nagl, *Learning to Eat Soup with a Knife: Counterinsurgency Lessons from Malaya and Vietnam* (New York: Praeger, 2005); K. Sepp, "Best Practices in Counterinsurgency," *Military Review* (May–June 2005): 8–12; *Counterinsurgency*, U.S. Army Field Manual 3-24 (draft), May 2006; U.S. Marine Corps, *Small-unit Leaders' Guide to Counterinsurgency* (draft), June 20, 2006.

133. Briefing provided by director of military operations (DMO), Rawalpindi, June 23, 2006.

134. Ibid., and discussions with Inspector General Frontier Corps (IGFC), Peshawar, June 25, 2006.

135. Briefing provided by DMO.

136. Pakistan's total helicopter fleet is 153, including 22 aircraft used only for training, another 20 reconnaissance helicopters, and 22 attack helicopters, leaving a total of 89 for use throughout the country for all trooplift and support purposes; *The Military Balance 2006* (London: International Institute for Strategic Studies, 2006), 239. Only 19 trooplift aircraft are forward-deployed in the FATA. Given the limited cruising range at altitude of trooplift helicopters, only the 19 that are forward-deployed can be considered to be directly supporting counterinsurgency efforts. Typical helicopter maintenance schedules result in 70–80 percent (i.e., 12–15 airframes) being available at any one time.

137. Briefing provided by DMO and discussions with IGFC.

138. Briefing provided by DMO.

139. Discussions with IGFC.

140. Discussion with Inspector-General of the Frontier Corps, Peshawar, June 2006.

141. *Military Balance 2006*.

142. Briefing provided by DMO.

143. Comments by DMO and Director-General Military Operations (DGMO), Rawalpindi, June 23, 2006.

144. Briefing provided by DMO and discussion with field personnel.

145. Note: provision of attack helicopters (which are kinetic strike assets) does not make up for lack of trooplift. Indeed, given the tendency to kinetic operations already identified, it may exacerbate the problem.

146. The Pakistan army has M113 armored personnel carriers, which, though proof against small-arms fire, are highly vulnerable to rocket propelled grenades, heavy machine guns, and IEDs. The Frontier Corps has a total of 45 UR-416 armored cars (*Military Balance 2006*, 240). The UR-416 is a riot-control vehicle proof against light weap-

ons but lacking in cross-country mobility, and providing virtually no protection against IEDs; British Army, *Army Recognition Journal* (June 2004).

147. Comments by DGMO.

148. Briefing provided by DMO, discussions with IGFC, and discussions with Khyber Rifles escort officer, Khyber Agency, in the field near Peshawar, June 25, 2006.

149. Comments by DGMO.

150. See E. Cohen, C. Crane, J. Horvath, and J. Nagl, "Principles, Imperatives and Paradoxes of Counterinsurgency," *Military Review* (March–April 2006): 49–53; D. J. Kilcullen "Twenty-eight Articles: Fundamentals of Company-level Counterinsurgency," *Military Review* (May–June 2006): 103–8; J. A. Nagl, *Learning to Eat Soup with a Knife: Counterinsurgency Lessons from Malaya and Vietnam* (New York: Praeger, 2005); K. Sepp, "Best Practices in Counterinsurgency," *Military Review* (May–June 2005): 8–12; *Counterinsurgency*, U.S. Army Field Manual 3-24 (draft), May 2006; U.S. Marine Corps, *Small-unit Leaders' Guide to Counterinsurgency* (draft), June 20, 2006, all of which references specify the need to move away from these tactics.

151. As with my Thailand case study, I have not been able to conduct detailed fieldwork with European immigrant communities but have had the opportunity to discuss the issue with Islamic religious leaders, community leaders from immigrant communities, intelligence and law enforcement officials, government ministers, diplomats, and military personnel from several European countries since 9/11. Having lived in Britain in the 1990s and made several trips per year to Britain or other European countries since that time, I have also been able to track some significant changes in the European environment in that time. Still, as with my Thailand case study, in this example I have placed much greater weight on secondary sources and fieldwork by other analysts, and have decided to include Europe because of its importance as a comparative example.

152. For references to the use of European bases in the preparation of the 9/11 attacks see Marc Sageman, *Understanding Terror Networks* (Philadelphia: University of Pennsylvania Press, 2004).

153. Peter R. Neumann, "Europe's Jihadist Dilemma," Survival, 48, 2 (Summer 2006): 74.

154. U.S. Department of State, *Country Reports on Terrorism 2005* (Washington, D.C.: Government Printing Office, 2005), chap. 2; www.state.gov/s/ct/rls/crt/2005/64332.htm.

155. For a discussion of London's role as a center for asylum for political refugees, see Melanie Philips, *Londonistan* (London: Encounter Books, 2006). Philips's characterization of the environment in London's Muslim community must be regarded with a high degree of caution; nevertheless, the facts she cites have not been substantially disputed—though their interpretation has been questioned.

156. Sageman, *Understanding Terror Networks*.

157. "Mutual Incomprehension, Mutual Outrage," *Economist*, February 9, 2006; www.economist.com/world/displaystory.cfm?story_id=5494646.

158. Neumann, "Europe's Jihadist Dilemma," 71.

159. See "Terrorist Safe Havens," chap. 3 of U.S. Department of State, *Country Reports on Terrorism 2005*; www.state.gov/s/ct/rls/crt/2005/64333.htm.

160. Bruce Hoffman, Washington director, RAND Corporation, personal communication, July 2006.

161. Kilcullen, "Counterinsurgency *Redux.*"

162. U.S. Department of State, *Country Reports on Terrorism 2005*, chap. 2; www.state.gov/s/ct/rls/crt/2005/64332.htm.

163. Ibid.

164. See William Rosenau, *Subversion and Insurgency*, RAND Occasional Paper No. 172, Corporation, http://www.rand.org/pubs/occasional_papers/OP172/.

165. Joel Kotek, "Youth Organizations as a Battlefield in the Cold War," *Intelligence and National Security* 18, 2 (June 2003): 168–91.

166. See Neumann, "Europe's Jihadist Dilemma," 76–78, for details of insurgent support networks identified in Europe.

167. For a detailed discussion of al Qai'da–linked foreign fighter networks and their regenerative capability, see Andrew Phillips, "Subverting the Anarchic Society: Religious Radicalism, Transnational Insurgency, and the Transformation of International Orders" (paper presented at the Second Oceanic Conference on International Studies, University of Melbourne, July 5–7, 2006).

168. See U.S. Department of State, *Country Reports on Terrorism 2005*, chap. 3.

169. See the website www.islamicawakening.com/ as an example of this viewpoint.

170. Jørgen Nielsen, director, Danish Institute, Damascus, personal communication, July 2006.

171. See Mark Steyn, *America Alone* (New York: Regnery, 2006), for a detailed version of this argument.

172. Jytte Klausen, "Counterterrorism and the Integration of Islam in Europe," in *Foreign Policy Research Institute E-Notes* 7, 7 (July 2006); www.fpri.org/ww/0707.200607.klausen.integrationislameurope.html.

173. Klausen, "Counterterrorism and the Integration of Islam in Europe."

174. Olivier Roy, *Globalized Islam: The Search for a New Ummah* (New York: Columbia University Press, 2004), 33–36.

175. Quintan Wiktorowicz, "Anatomy of the Salafi Movement," *Studies in Conflict and Terrorism* 29 (2006): 207–8.

176. Kilcullen, "Political Consequences," chap. 5.

177. International Crisis Group, "Indonesia Backgrounder: Why Salafism and Terrorism Mostly Don't Mix," Asia Report no. 83 (Brussels: International Crisis Group, September 13, 2004); www.crisisgroup.org/home/index.cfm?id=2967&l=1.

178. International Crisis Group, "Saudi Arabia Backgrounder: Who Are the Islamists?" Middle East Report 31 (Brussels: International Crisis Group, September 21, 2004); www.crisisgroup.org/home/index.cfm?id=3021&l=1.

179. François Burgat, *The Islamic Movement in North Africa*, trans. William Dowell, Middle East Monograph Series, Center for Middle Eastern Studies (Austin: University of Texas Press, 1997).

180. Interview with confidential source, Baghdad, February 2006.

181. Algemene Inlichtingen-en Veiligheidsdienst, *Annual Report 2003* (The Hague: Algemene Inlichtingen-en Veiligheidsdienst, 2003); www.aivd.nl.

182. Wiktorowicz, "Anatomy of the Salafi Movement," 208.

183. Sageman, *Understanding Terror Networks*.

184. See M. Fortes and E. E. Evans-Pritchard, eds., *African Political Systems* (London: Oxford University Press, 1940), for a series of studies of this phenomenon, among others, in the context of detribalization in Africa.

185. Kilcullen, "Political Consequences," chaps. 1, 5.

186. See M. Gluckman and E. Colson, *Seven Tribes of British Central Africa* (Manchester: Manchester University Press, 1959), and Max Gluckman, *Custom and Conflict in Africa* (London: Blackwell, 1970).

187. See Karl D. Jackson, "Urbanization and the Rise of Patron-Client Relations," in K. D. Jackson and L. Pye, eds., *Political Power and Communications in Indonesia* (Berkeley: University of California Press, 1970), and Karl Jackson, *Traditional Authority, Islam and Rebellion: A Study of Indonesian Political Behaviour* (Berkeley: University of California Press, 1980). See also Kilcullen, "Political Consequences," chaps. 2 and 4.

188. See Roy, *Globalized Islam*, chaps. 1 and 2.

189. Fernando Reinares, professor and chair of political science, King Juan Carlos University, Madrid, personal communication, July 2006.

190. See United Kingdom, *Security Service Act, 1989* (London: HMSO, 1989–), art. 1(2); www.opsi.gov.uk/ACTS/acts1989/Ukpga_19890005_en_2.htm#mdiv1.

191. Rosenau, *Subversion and Insurgency*, 2.

192. Bruce Hoffman, *Islam and the West: Searching for Common Ground—The Terrorist Threat and the Counter-Terrorism Effort*, RAND Testimony Series CT-263 (Santa Monica: RAND Corporation, 2006), 15.

193. Quoted in Rosenau, *Subversion and Insurgency*, 1.

194. Kilcullen, "Political Consequences."

195. Rosenau, *Subversion and Insurgency*, 8.

196. See United Kingdom, *Security Service Act, 1989*, art. 1(2).

197. U.S. Department of Defense, *Glossary*, Joint Chiefs of Staff Publication 1–02 (Washington, D.C.: Government Printing Office, n.d.).

198. Philip Selznick, *The Organizational Weapon: A Study of Bolshevik Strategy and Tactics* (Glencoe, Ill.: Free Press, 1952), 2.

199. U.S. Department of the Army, Headquarters, *Human Factors Considerations of Undergrounds in Insurgencies*, pamphlet no. 550-104 (Department of the Army, Washington D.C.: September 1966), 28–29.

200. Ibid.

201. Richard Bach Jensen, "Daggers, Rifles and Dynamite: Anarchist Terrorism in Nineteenth-Century Europe," *Terrorism and Political Violence* 16, 1 (spring 2004): 116–53.

202. For examples of this phenomenon in American and British intelligence, see David Martin's study of CIA counterintelligence chief James Jesus Angleton, *Wilderness of Mirrors* (New York: Ballantine Books, 1981), and Peter Wright, *Spycatcher: The Candid Autobiography of a Senior Intelligence Officer* (New York: Viking Books, 1987), which—albeit unwittingly—portrays in detail the extremely damaging effects on MI5 of Wright's counterpenetration operation against then MI5 director Sir Roger Hollis.

203. See David Kilcullen, "Globalisation and the Development of Indonesian Counterinsurgency Tactics," *Small Wars and Insurgencies* 17, 1 (March 2006): 44–64.

204. Bradley Bamford, "The Role and Effectiveness of Intelligence in Northern Ireland," *Intelligence and National Security* 20, 4 (December 2005): 600.

205. Ernesto Guevara, *Guerrilla Warfare* (1960) (Lincoln: University of Nebraska Press, 1998), particularly chap. 1.

206. Carlos Marighella, *Minimanual of the Urban Guerrilla*; www.marxists.org/archive/marighella-carlos/1969/06/minimanual-urban-guerrilla/index.htm.

207. See the 1970 manifesto *Build Up the Red Army!* http://home.att.net/ rw.rynerson/rafgrund.htm.

208. Justus Reid Weiner, "The Use of Palestinian Children in the Al-Aqsa Intifada," in *Jerusalem Letter/Viewpoints*; Jerusalem Center for Public Affairs, www.jcpa.org/jl/vp441.htm.

209. Kalev Sepp, "Best Practices in Counterinsurgency," *Military Review* (May–June 2005): 8–12.

210. Kilcullen, "Twenty-eight Articles."

211. See Selznick, *Organizational Weapon*.

212. For more on the operational concept of leaderless resistance, see Louis Beam, "Leaderless Resistance"; http://home.ddc.net/ygg/ot/ot-04.htm.

213. Mehmood Naqshbandi, *Islam and Muslims in Britain* (London: Metropolitan Police, New Scotland Yard, 2006), 28.

214. Direction de la Surveillance du Territoire, *Processes d'Enrolement des Jeunes Musulmans dans le Jihad* (Paris: Direction de la Surveillance du Territoire, 2003).

215. Algemene Inlichtingen-en Veiligheidsdienst, *Recruitment for the Jihad in the Netherlands: from Incident to Trend* (The Hague: Algemene Inlichtingen-en Veiligheidsdienst, 2002).

216. Michael Taarnby, *Recruitment of Islamist Terrorists in Europe: Trends and Perspectives*, Research Report funded by the Danish Ministry of Justice (Aarhus: Centre for Cultural Research, University of Aarhus, January 2005).

217. House of Commons, *Report of the Official Account of the Bombings in London on 7 July 2005* (London: The Stationery Office, May 2006).

218. "Video of 7 July Bomber Released," *BBC News*, July 6, 2006; http://news.bbc.co.uk/1/hi/uk/5154714.stm.

219. Sheikh Musa Abubakar Admani, personal communication, London, July 2006.

220. "An Underclass Rebellion," *Economist*, November 14, 2005.

221. Ibid.

222. Dr. Garbi Schmidt, National Danish Institute of Social Research, Copenhagen, personal communication, July 2006.

223. "Mutual Incomprehension, Mutual Outrage," *Economist*, February 9, 2006.

224. Personal communication, confidential source, quoting a British assessment.

225. Roy, *Globalized Islam*, 49.

226. Confidential source, personal communication, quoting a British assessment, July 2006.

227. See "Islamist Extremism in Europe," testimony of Daniel Fried, Assistant Secretary of State for European Affairs, before the Senate Foreign Relations Committee Subcommittee on European Affairs, April 5, 2006.

228. See "PC Sentenced for Leaking information," *BBC News*, October 4, 2004; http://news.bbc.co.uk/1/hi/uk/3713816.stm, and "Translator Jailed for Leaking AIVD Files"; www.expatica.com/source/site_article.asp?subchannel_id=1&story_id=26165&name=Translator%20jailed%20for%20leaking%20AIVD%20files.

229. "Al Qaida 'Trying to Infiltrate MI5'"; http://news.excite.co.uk/uk/9234.

230. See U.S. Department of State, *Country Reports on Terrorism 2005*, chap. 5; www.state.gov/s/ct/rls/crt/2005/64342.htm.

231. James Bakker, "Radical Islam in the Netherlands," *Jamestown Terrorism Monitor 3*, 1, (January 13, 2005).

232. Roy, *Globalized Islam*, 41.

233. Hizb-ut Tahrir, *The Method to Re-establish the Khilafah* (London: Al-Khilafah, 2000), 1.

234. Ibid., 105–6.

235. Vladimir Ilich Lenin, "What Is to Be Done?" *Lenin: Collected Works* (Moscow: Foreign Languages, 1961), 5:347–530.

236. Robert G. Spulak, Jr., and Jessica Glicken Turnley, *Theoretical Perspectives of Terrorist Enemies as Networks*, Joint Special Operations University report 05–3 (Hurlburt Field, Fla.: Joint Special Operations University, 2005).

237. See particularly Joseph D. Celeski, *Operationalizing Counterinsurgency*, Joint Special Operations University report 05–3 (Hurlburt Field, Fla.: Joint Special Operations University, 2005).

238. I am indebted to Richard Higgins for these categories, which are based on work conducted by Joseph Celeski.

239. Neumann, "Europe's Jihadist Problem," 79.

240. See John Lewis Gaddis, *The Cold War: A New History* (London: Penguin, 2005), 98.

241. See Lawrence Freedman, "The Transatlantic Agenda: Vision and Countervision," *Survival* 47, 4 (winter 2005–2006): 24, for a description of the process of cultural competition as a factor in the collapse of Communism in Europe.

242. Jensen, "Daggers, Rifles and Dynamite."

243. Ibid.

244. U.S. Institute of Peace, *Report on Wilton Park Conference: Towards a Community-based Approach to Counter-Terrorism* (Washington, D.C.: U.S. Institute of Peace, March 22, 2006); www.usip.org.

Chapter 5

1. Jeffrey Race, *War Comes to Long An: Revolutionary Conflict in a Vietnamese Province* (Berkeley: University of California Press, 1972).

2. For a discussion of force ratios in counterinsurgency and nation-building, see Seth G. Jones, Jeremy M. Wilson, Andrew Rathmell, and K. Jack Riley, *Establishing Law and Order after Conflict* (Santa Monica, Calif.: RAND Corporation, 2005).

3. Conversation with Iraq desk officer, National Security Council, Washington, D.C., September 22, 2008.

4. Jean-Marie Colombani, "Nous sommes tous Américains," *Le Monde*, September 12, 2001, translated in *World Press Review* 48, 11 (November 2001); www.worldpress.org/1101we_are_all_americans.htm.

5. Discussions with counterterrorism official, Paris, December 10, 2006.

6. Discussions conducted during the Center for a New American Security Solarium II project, Washington, D.C., August–October 2007.

7. Ron Suskind, *The One Percent Doctrine: Deep Inside America's Pursuit of Its Enemies Since 9/11* (New York: Simon and Shuster, 2006).

8. Barton Gellman, "The Shadow War, in a Surprising New Light," *Washington Post*, June 20, 2006, C01.

9. For a detailed discussion of this phenomenon and its role in terrorist strategy, see Bruce Hoffman, *Inside Terrorism*, 2nd ed. (New York: Columbia University Press, 2006), especially chaps. 2 and 7.

10. National Security Council, *National Security Strategy of the United States of America* (Washington, D.C.: National Security Council, June 1, 2002); www.whitehouse.gov/nsc/nssall.html.

11. Charles P. Pierce, "The Cynic and Senator Obama," *Esquire*, June 4, 2008.

12. Matt Bai, "Kerry's Undeclared War," *New York Times Magazine*, October 10, 2004.

13. Personal observation, Multi-National Force–Iraq Coalition Conference, Tampa, Florida, April 28, 2007, and Afghanistan/International Security Assistance Force Regional Command South Conference, Ottawa, February 12, 2007. The one significant exception to this pattern has been General David Petraeus's Joint Strategic Assessment Team of March–April 2007, which sought and received detailed input from a range of Coalition partners and civilian agencies. Not coincidentally, this effort produced the most effective and comprehensive campaign plan yet seen in the "War on Terrorism."

14. See M. Matloff and E. M. Snell, *Strategic Planning for Coalition Warfare, 1941–42* (Washington, D.C.: Office of the Chief of Military History, Department of the Army, 1953–59), chap. 5.

15. Ibid., chap. 6.

16. For the full text of the *Declaration by the United Nations* (January 1, 1942), see www .ibiblio.org/pha/policy/1942/420101a.html.

17. For details of the strategy, see the website of the British Government in the United States: http://ukinusa.fco.gov.uk/resources/en/pdf/counter-terrorism-strategy.

18. Discussions with Cabinet Office official and officials of the Foreign Office, Secret Intelligence Service, and Security Service, London, July 2006.

19. See Michael Scheuer, *Imperial Hubris: Why the West Is Losing the War on Terror* (Washington, D.C.: Potomac Books, 2007).

20. Andrew J. Bacevich, "The Petraeus Doctrine," *Atlantic Monthly*, October 2008.

21. Colin L. Powell, "U.S. Forces: Challenges Ahead," *Foreign Affairs* (winter 1992–93); www.foreignaffairs.org/19921201faessay5851/colin-l-powell/u-s-forces-challenges-ahead.html.

22. See, for example, Charles Krauthammer, "What Happened to the Powell Doctrine?" *Jewish World Review*, April 27, 2001, http://www.jewishworldreview.com/cols/krauthammer042701.asp.

23. John Hillen, "Superpowers Don't Do Windows," *Orbis* 41, 2 (spring 1997): 241–58.

24. John A. English, "Great War 1914–18: The 'Riddle of the Trenches,'" *Canadian Defence Quarterly* 15, 2 (autumn 1985): 41–47.

25. See J. F. C. Fuller, *Tanks in the Great War 1914–1918* (1920) (Nashville Tenn.: Battery Press, 2003).

26. General Oskar Hutier, commander of the German Tenth Army on the Eastern Front in World War I, devised such successful infiltration tactics that the French subsequently referred to such tactics as "Hutier tactics."

27. For a discussion of this dynamic in Clemenceau's case, see Eliot A. Cohen, *Supreme Command: Soldiers, Statesmen and Leadership in Wartime* (New York: Anchor Press, 2003).

28. Quoted in Alfred Vagts, *A History of Militarism* (Glencoe: Free Press, 1967), 15.

29. I am grateful to Dr. Janine Davidson of George Mason University for this insight.

Conclusion

1. An earlier version of portions of this chapter appeared in U.S. *State Department eJournal USA*, May 2007; http://usinfo.state.gov/journals/itps/0507/ijpe/kilcullen.htm.

2. See Rupert Smith, *The Utility of Force: The Art of War in the Modern World* (New York: Knopf, 2007), especially 3–28 and 269–335.

3. See Gerald K. Haines and Robert E. Leggett, *Watching the Bear: Essays on CIA's Analysis of the Soviet Union* (Langley, Va., Central Intelligence Agency, Center for the Study of Intelligence, 2003), especially chaps. 6 and 7.

4. See Kevin M. Woods et al., *Iraqi Perspectives Project: A View of Operation Iraqi Freedom from Saddam's Senior Leadership* (Norfolk, Va., Joint Forces Command, Joint Center for Operational Analysis, 2006), 92.

5. See David Kilcullen, "Countering Global Insurgency," *Small Wars Journal* (November 2004); www.smallwarsjournal.com/documents/kilcullen.pdf; Williamson Murray, ed., *Strategic Challenges for Counterinsurgency and the Global War on Terrorism* (Carlisle, Penn.: Strategic Studies Institute, 2006) and Bruce Hoffman, "From War on Terror to Global Counterinsurgency," *Current History* 105, 693 (December 2006): 423–29.

6. Professor Michael Vlahos, Johns Hopkins University Applied Physics Laboratory, personal communication, Baltimore, December 2006.

7. I am indebted to Mr. Steve Eames for this conceptual formulation.

8. U.S. Department of Defense, *Quadrennial Defense Review Report* (Washington, D.C.: Government Printing Office, February 2, 2006), 83–91.

9. See "Secretary Launches Civilian Response Corps" and "Relevant and Timely," *State*, (September 2008): 5, 14.

10. See Max Boot, Congressional Testimony before the House Armed Services Committee, June 29, 2006; www.globalsecurity.org/military/library/congress/2006_hr/060629-boot.pdf.

11. See Central Intelligence Agency, *The Office of Strategic Services: America's First Intelligence Agency*; www.cia.gov/cia/publications/oss/index.htm.

12. The seven standard SOF missions are direct action, special reconnaissance, unconventio nal warfare, foreign internal defense, counterterrorism, psychological operations, and civil affairs.

A Note on Sources and Methodology

1. In using this term I refer less to the "decontextualized" style of the American New Critics, who popularized the term "close reading," and more to the approach of analyzing a given text in depth, in its social, political, biographical, and economic context, that infuses much of the best of biblical textual criticism and was first (and perhaps best) expressed by F. R. Leavis in *New Bearings in English Poetry: A Study of the Contemporary Situation* (London: Chatto & Windus, 1932). Conflict ethnography, then, treats a conflict as a living "text," which requires close reading and contextual analysis in its own terms, as well as evaluation in the "etic" perspective of the external observer.

2. Clifford Geertz, "Thick Description: Toward an Interpretive Theory of Culture," in *The Interpretation of Cultures: Selected Essays* (New York: Basic Books, 1973).

3. I am indebted for this notion to Dr. Patrick Porter of King's College London, whose forthcoming work *Military Orientalism: Eastern War Through Western Eyes* (London: Hurst Publishers, 2008) discusses the problems of this attitude in detail.

Index